Economics for an Information Age

Economics for an Information Age examines the central role of information within economics and society. The neoclassical economic model, taught as 'mainstream economics' in universities around the world, relies on a mathematical model of 'resource allocation' in which private advantage gives rise to public advantage in the shape of an optimal allocation of resources. However, this model assumes 'perfect information'. In the present 'information age' such an assumption is even farther from the reality than it was in the past. People disseminate and manipulate information to further their interests.

This book explains economic behaviour in terms of a theory of 'money-bargaining' and political and intellectual 'support-bargaining', in which the dissemination of information plays a central role. It uses this lens to explain how information is created, manipulated, disseminated, organised, understood, interpreted, used, bought and sold.

This book will be of interest to mainstream and heterodox economists alike, as well as historians of economic thought, and anyone who seeks to better understand the impact of the information age on economic behaviour.

Patrick Spread received his first degree from Oxford University and a PhD from the London Business School, UK. On leaving Oxford he worked for a few years in London, then undertook various long-term assignments overseas, firstly in the Pacific and subsequently in Asia and Africa. He has written seven books on support-bargaining and money-bargaining, and several journal articles.

Routledge Frontiers of Political Economy

Class and Property in Marx's Economic Thought
Exploring the Basis for Capitalism
Jørgen Sandemose

Economics, Ethics and Power
From Behavioural Rules to Global Structures
Hasse Ekstedt

Supranational Political Economy
The Globalisation of the State–Market Relationship
Guido Montani

Free Cash, Capital Accumulation and Inequality
Craig Allan Medlen

The Continuing Imperialism of Free Trade
Developments, Trends and the Role of Supranational Agents
Edited by Jo Grady and Chris Grocott

The Problem of Political Trust
A Conceptual Reformulation
Grant Duncan

Ethics and Economic Theory
Khalid Mir

Economics for an Information Age
Money-Bargaining, Support-Bargaining and the Information Interface
Patrick Spread

For more information about this series, please visit: www.routledge.com/books/series/SE0345

Economics for an Information Age

Money-Bargaining, Support-Bargaining and the Information Interface

Patrick Spread

Routledge
Taylor & Francis Group
LONDON AND NEW YORK

First published 2019 by Routledge

2 Park Square, Milton Park, Abingdon, Oxfordshire OX14 4RN
52 Vanderbilt Avenue, New York, NY 10017

Routledge is an imprint of the Taylor & Francis Group, an informa business

First issued in paperback 2020

British Library Cataloguing-in-Publication Data
A catalogue record for this book is available from the British Library

Library of Congress Cataloging-in-Publication Data
Names: Spread, Patrick, 1944- author.
Title: Economics for an information age : money-bargaining, support-bargaining and the information interface / Patrick Spread.
Description: Abingdon, Oxon ; New York, NY : Routledge, 2019. | Series: Routledge frontiers of political economy ; 249 | Includes index.
Identifiers: LCCN 2018027458 (print) | LCCN 2018029131 (ebook) | ISBN 9780429437014 (Ebook) | ISBN 9780429792694 (Pdf) | ISBN 9780429792687 (Epub) | ISBN 9780429792670 (Mobi) | ISBN 9781138611283 (hardback)
Subjects: LCSH: Knowledge economy. | Information theory in economics.
Classification: LCC HC79.I55 (ebook) | LCC HC79.I55 S68 2019 (print) | DDC 330—dc23
LC record available at https://lccn.loc.gov/2018027458

ISBN: 978-1-138-61128-3 (hbk)
ISBN: 978-0-367-66508-1 (pbk)

Typeset in Bembo
by Swales & Willis Ltd, Exeter, Devon, UK

To my wife, Evelyn

Contents

But men may construe things after their fashion,
Clean from the purpose of the things themselves.
Cicero in *Julius Caesar*, William Shakespeare

Introduction

It is a well-recognised psychological trait in humans that, when asked a particular question, they often provide an answer to a different question to which it is easier to respond.[1] The trait is apparent in the work of neoclassical economists. Instead of answering the question that everyone wants to know the answer to – how does economic exchange work? – they have chosen to answer a different question: what does a system look like in which individual self-interest leads to communal advantage with an optimal distribution of resources? The answer to their preferred question is the neoclassical economic model.

The question of the relationship between self-interest and communal interest was foremost in Adam Smith's mind when he wrote *The Wealth of Nations*, though he found himself obliged to acknowledge that the self-interest of some individuals was likely to be detrimental to society.[2] In the late nineteenth century Léon Walras and other economists used Smith's work selectively to create a mathematical model that showed how the exercise of individual self-interest would lead to social advantage.[3] The mathematical approach caught on. It seemed to give economic theory a rigour and validity comparable to that of physics, as well as giving the portrayal of 'markets' moral elevation. The status of the model was reaffirmed in 1932 when Lionel Robbins defined economics as, 'the science which studies human behaviour as a relationship between ends and scarce means which have alternative uses'.[4] That concept has constituted the mainstream of economic theory and teaching ever since. The mathematical content of economics courses has increased over the years.

The idealism expressed through the mathematical formulation comes at heavy cost in realism. The use of mathematics has necessitated various assumptions that are not compatible with observation of economic transactions. To minimise the impact of human volition it has been necessary to assume that humans always act rationally. Human behaviour becomes regular and predictable so that it can be captured, like the relationships of physics between material things, in mathematical formulations. It is necessary also to assume that all the information relevant to a particular transaction is freely available to all involved, so that all can exercise their reason without any inhibitions arising from lack of information, or uncertainties about the accuracy of the information they have. These necessary assumptions mean that the mathematical model cannot be expected to accord with empirical observation. While the mathematics apparently draws economic theory closer to the physics model, the assumptions necessary to the mathematics mean that neoclassical economists must abandon the requirements for empirical consistency that are the bedrock of natural science. Neoclassical economists claim instead that the mathematical model is 'near enough to be useful' – a claim that is strongly disputed by others.

Copious efforts are made by mainstream economists to make the model more realistic, or at least add codicils to it that take account of its unrealism. It might even be said that mainstream economic theory is concerned with reconciliation of observations of actual economic processes with the mathematical model. For the most part, there is extreme reluctance to recognise that the model is so unrealistic as to be untenable. George Stigler, who first drew attention to the inadequacies of the model in relation to information, argued that the information issues constituted modification to the model without requiring rejection of it.[5] That has been the pattern in most subsequent treatments of information issues. The mathematical model seems just too much fun, at least for mathematicians. It also sustains and justifies the individual interest, and individual freedom, in societies concerned with encroachment of 'collectivist' or group ideals. Its role as a 'frame of reference' means that it is too precious to abandon.

It is also important to professional group interests. The Robbins definition has become strongly entrenched in the institutions that teach economic theory. A successful career in economics for the most part means teaching neoclassical theory and advancing understanding of economic issues by reference to the neoclassical model. Appointments and acceptances for publication tend to come more readily to those loyal to the neoclassical model than to those who contest its status.[6] Because the professional consequences of rejecting the basic model are so severe, the mainstream theory group is tolerant of heretical expression, so long as it is accompanied by protestations of loyalty to the basic model.

The concerns over information within mainstream economics and the professional interests that impede the emergence of alternatives are apparent in the work of Joseph Stiglitz. Stiglitz recognises that the problems of information are so great as to invalidate the basic model. He does not, however, propose any alternative. For Stiglitz, it is just not worth trying to change the paradigm entirely, because the incumbent authorities are so resistant to radical change. He prefers instead to maintain the mathematical model as the basis of understanding, whilst modifying only that part of it concerned with information.[7] That the modification concerning information invalidates the whole model is just something he is prepared to live with, and the profession as a whole must live with. Loyalty to the model, which is at the same time loyalty to the academic theory group which sustains it, is maintained against all the evidence. Stiglitz's work on asymmetric information is considered further in Chapter 4.

This loyalty to model and the institutional arrangements that sustain it is apparent in comments of Paul Krugman, another economist who, like Stiglitz, has been accorded the highest accolade of his profession, a Nobel Memorial Prize. In a talk to the European Association for Evolutionary Political Economy, Krugman makes clear his affiliations. He writes, 'Personally, I consider myself a proud neoclassicist', and characterises himself as 'basically a maximization-and-equilibrium kind of guy'. He writes also:

> Most economists who try to apply evolutionary concepts start from some deep dissatisfaction with economics as it is. I won't say that I am entirely happy with the state of economics. But let us be honest: I have done very well within the world of conventional economics. I have pushed the envelope, but not broken it, and have received very widespread acceptance for my ideas. What this means is that I may have more sympathy for standard economics than most of you. My criticisms are those of someone who loves the field and has seen that affection repaid.[8]

Krugman is well-known to a wide public as a columnist for the *New York Times*. In an article following the financial crash of 2008, Krugman asked in his title: 'How did economists get it so wrong?'[9] The answer is apparent from the earlier talk: economists put group loyalty before empirical evidence. They choose to remain members of an academically dominant theory group, with all the career advantages that that entails, rather than develop a theory of economics that accords with the evidence of economic practice. Krugman approves the 'simplification' justification for neoclassical economics, referring to the work of Milton Friedman, 'who asserted as early as 1953 that neoclassical economics works well enough as a description of the way the economy actually functions to be "both extremely fruitful and deserving of much confidence"'.[10]

Stiglitz and Krugman follow the precept of markets: provide what people want. But they violate older academic precepts, and even common social precepts, regarding information. There exists a culture amongst thoughtful people, inculcated in all the best schoolrooms, that insists on the overriding importance of 'truth'. In particular: don't utter what you know to be false. In terms of theory-making, the pursuit of truth means provision of theory that provides explanations consistent with what is observed and experienced in the functioning of society.

Stiglitz is surely right in his condemnation of the neoclassical paradigm on grounds of its treatment of information. Information is not just a 'constraint' on an otherwise satisfactory model. Nor is it just a matter of 'asymmetries' of information. The treatment of information in the neoclassical model involves a total misconception of the way economies function. Information is the immediate matter of our attention and must consequently be understood more as a starting point than a constraint on some other system. People operate on the basis of information. They disseminate information conducive to their advantage. They talk up their products and services to make them attractive to buyers. They search for information that is necessary to or even just desirable for the transactions they contemplate. Lacking crucial information, they will not go ahead. Economic exchange is fundamentally concerned with the dissemination and acquisition of information with which agents of a money-bargaining system can conclude transactions advantageous to their interests. An information interface is created for the conduct of economic exchange. Without a decent theory of information, this whole dimension of economic transactions is lost, and it is impossible to understand how an economy functions.

This book introduces a theory of information. Its origins lie in concerns over the treatment of information in economic theory and it remains concerned with economic theory. But information has much wider importance. People are deceived in all walks of life. Politics is notorious for deception. So the development of a theory of information necessarily means leaving the bounds of economic transactions, economic theory and even the bounds of 'political-economy', the frame of reference in which the debate over economics was largely conducted in the nineteenth century and early twentieth century, before the narrowing of economic theory to mathematical modelling. Information is what our minds deal with. We can work only with information. It comes between us and any external reality that exists independently of human minds. Our 'world', social and material, is built up from the information we assimilate. What we refer to as 'observation and experience' is information derived from observation and experience. To explain the role of information in the economic sphere requires a comprehensive explanation of the role of information across the whole range of human experience and thought. The theory presented here takes into account the particular treatment of information not just of economists, but also natural scientists, sociologists, psychologists, philosophers and cartographers. It also covers the way ordinary people deal with difficulties over information.

A theory of information is perhaps of particular importance in the present age, frequently referred to as an 'information age'. We have unprecedented access to immense volumes of information rapidly and cheaply through the information technology of computers, tablets and smartphones. Even these bounteous sources have only recently supplemented older electronic media, such as television and radio, that provided levels of information that were remarkable by historical standards. The still older print media of newspapers, magazines and books remain major sources of information. The printing press was identified in *The Evolution of Economies* as a technology that formed the basis for one of the major company formats of the industrial revolution. The commercial viability of large-scale printing and publishing using steam-powered printing presses made possible the dissemination of the large amounts of information required for an industrial revolution.[11] In the present information age global companies – Google, Apple, Facebook, Alibaba, Tencent, Microsoft – have emerged within a few decades based on electronic information technology. We have access to astonishing volumes of information. But we have very little theory by which to understand its role and impact.

The reason why no theory of information has been developed is that it is necessary first to establish that societies function as a process of support-bargaining and money-bargaining. Only with that theory is it possible to explain how information is used in societies. The dynamics of information are an essential part of the dynamics of support-bargaining and money-bargaining. Economists could make assumptions about information to suit the sort of theory they wanted to promulgate because there was no strong established theory of information. It is conceivable that if the functioning of an economy had been explained much earlier in terms of money-bargaining, instead of in a mathematical model, issues surrounding information would have been recognised, and a theory of information developed. Given that politics also runs on information, such a theory might have given rise to a theory of politics as a support-bargaining process. But economics took a wrong turn, so problems of information have not been properly addressed.[12] This book is concerned with the way an information interface is created and used in support-bargaining and money-bargaining systems.

The idea of support-bargaining and money-bargaining accounts for social processes in terms of exchange based on situation-related interest. It answers a question, 'How do societies function?', with money-bargaining most concerned with the question posed at the beginning of this Introduction, 'How does economic exchange work?' 'Support' and 'money' constitute bargaining counters, each best adapted to certain types of exchange. The bargaining processes are conducted on the basis of information. The processes involve propagation of information on the basis of which transactions can be identified and concluded. Chapter 1 reviews the accounts of information provided in a neoclassical economic context, and introduces the idea of money-bargaining to resolve the difficulties. The chapter also gives a summary account of broader approaches to information and knowledge, including the idea of 'social construction' of reality. Chapter 2 explains these broader approaches in terms of support-bargaining and money-bargaining.[13] References are given throughout to earlier coverage of subjects that are given limited attention in this book. The References section of this book lists all the material published on support-bargaining and money-bargaining, all of it referenced at some point in the book. The content of earlier books is summarised briefly in the last section of this Introduction.

The idea of support-bargaining includes an idea of 'intellectual support-bargaining'. In this process 'theory groups' are formed, the 'schools' of the various academic disciplines. Theory formation in the different disciplines is thus incorporated in the theory of support-bargaining and money-bargaining. Stiglitz and Krugman are loyal to their theory group. This gives the theory of support-bargaining and money-bargaining the role of 'parent' in relation to other theories of the functioning of societies. Theory making becomes part of the functioning of society, rather than a matter of independent observation. Theory makers are then active participants in social and political processes, rather than external commentators. The theory of support-bargaining and money-bargaining is not so much an interdisciplinary theory as a theory that encompasses other disciplines. It provides, as it were, a wide-frame picture of a society, in which narrow-frame theories can be identified.

This identification of other theories makes it possible to recognise their functions, their strengths and their weaknesses. Much of the weakness arises simply from the failure to recognise the intellectual support-bargaining process by which they are formed. Theory-making is as much driven by personal and group interest as by the desire for realistic theory, or the pursuit of truth. But the weakness arises also from associated deficiencies in understanding of the role of information. Failure to recognise the intellectual support-bargaining process, and failure to recognise the function of information within the intellectual support-bargaining process, combine to produce theories that cannot explain the phenomena they are supposed to account for. Economic, sociological, philosophical and psychological theories all suffer from deficiencies of this kind.

The parent theory provided here approaches the various disciplines through work that has originated current controversies, or is representative of important factions in current controversies. Work of this character provides the best opportunity for a parent theory to demonstrate its capacity to clarify and explain. The 'information interface' is conceived as incorporating all information, so its scope is vast. The 'information interfaces' associated with each separate discipline are similarly extensive. Comprehensive coverage is not possible; rather the intention is to show how the parent theory can explain the essential questions arising in each sphere. The exposition attempts to cover the issues that ought to be covered in such a context, resisting the inherent instinct of intellectual support-bargaining to select what suits the purpose and avoid the awkward. But it would erode the theory if it were claimed that the exposition is entirely free from the impulses it identifies.

Guide to the chapters

The wide scope of this book, arising from the ubiquity of information, has been touched on above. It may be helpful for readers to have some initial account of the organisation of the book for passage through the different fields of interest. Given the scope of the information issues, and the narrow scope of most institutional theory groups, it is recognised that some readers will be inclined to read selectively. The chapters are not, however, written to stand alone.

Chapter 1, 'Information and interests', provides a summary overview of established approaches to information. The 'economics of information' tries to resolve issues arising from the neoclassical model regarding the treatment of information. The idea of money-bargaining provides an alternative account of information as central to a money-bargaining process. In a broader context, religious faith has historically been the background to most enquiry into truth, including most prominently the 'big question' of what exists independently of human minds. Natural scientists have provided an alternative 'window on the world' with notions of truth based on evidence. Neoclassical economics models itself on physical science, at least with regard to mathematical foundations. The idea of 'social construction' of reality has become prominent in sociological and philosophical approaches to questions of 'truth' and 'reality'. The pursuit of truth is complicated by the pursuit of interests other than the interest in truth.

Chapter 2, 'Support-bargaining and the information interface', explains in terms of support-bargaining some of the difficulties of established information theory identified in Chapter 1, serving at the same time as an introduction to the idea of support-bargaining. In the context of support-bargaining, the 'big question' fragments into many small questions regarding the accuracy or truth of information relevant to the many minor transactions of a support-bargaining and money-bargaining system. The central interest in whatever there may be of external reality is displaced by the pursuit of many interests through the social bargaining system. 'Intellectual support-bargaining' advances interests through assembly of support for theoretical formulations, such as neoclassical economic theory. Support-bargaining constitutes a process of 'social construction'. What is constructed is an information interface in which support-bargaining and money-bargaining are carried on.

Chapter 3, 'Creation and manipulation of the information interface', explains how an information interface is created through the process of support-bargaining and money-bargaining. Concepts of 'situation' and 'frames of reference' are established as a means of focusing perception and interpretation for the advance of interests. Linguistic codification and attribution of motivations are important in the manipulation of information. Interests may include an interest in the pursuit of truth, but agents often seek support through the advance of non-truth interests. The creation of the information interface is strongly influenced by unconscious psychological drives.

Chapter 4, 'Economics and the information interface', explains the use and role of information in economic transactions, contrasting the understanding of neoclassical economic theory with that of money-bargaining. The neoclassical frame of reference derives from Adam Smith's description of economic transactions. Neoclassical economics adopts mathematical codification, on the grounds that it is more precise and rigorous than linguistic codification. However, the assumptions necessary to mathematical codification mean that the neoclassical model must abandon aspirations to empirical realism. The assumption that all necessary information is available to agents of the neoclassical system is essential to mathematical formulation, but it involves exclusion of great swathes of economic activity. The inconsistencies involved with mathematical codification are apparent in George Akerlof's treatment of 'quality' and 'asymmetric information'. The function of an information interface is described in relation to the activities of consumers, companies and governments in a money-bargaining system.

Chapter 5, 'Economics and behavioural economics', deals with the psychological approach to economic choice associated with Daniel Kahneman and Amos Tversky. Their analysis of choice is contrasted with that of support-bargaining and money-bargaining. It is suggested that they make a mistake similar to that of neoclassical economists in basing their analysis of human behaviour on mathematical probability theory. Humans instinctively make decisions by reference to their situations. The 'micro-psychological' traits described by Kahneman in *Thinking, Fast and Slow*, are identified with 'macro-psychological' traits, such as situation-related interests, identified in the theory of support-bargaining and money-bargaining.[14]

Chapter 6, 'The information interface and reality', discusses the relationship of the information interface to any possible reality beyond our minds. This is the traditional 'big question' of philosophical speculation. Alvin Goldman's account of knowledge in a social context, contrasting with the individualist epistemological tradition, is assessed in the context of the idea of support-bargaining. John Searle's assumption of 'collective intentionality' is considered also in the new context. The manipulation of cartographic information provides an illuminating parallel to the treatment of other types of information and their relationship to reality.

Chapter 7, 'Media theory and the information interface', considers the media theory of the 'Toronto School', focusing on the ideas of Harold Innis and Marshall McLuhan. As the essential academic 'media theory' of an age so extensively provided with information it shows remarkable limitations. The focus on the effects of technology is a consequence of the lack of any understanding of the role of information. Technology codifies and transmits information to the information interface. The make-up of the information interface determines the distribution of support in societies. The impact of 'electric' technology derives from its presentation of testimonial information in the form of perceptual information, rather than any mysterious properties of the technology.

Chapter 8, 'Media, governance and the information interface', applies the idea of the information interface to the political sphere. Media organisations, constituted as companies, the specialised agencies of money-bargaining systems, disseminate the information that is essential to popular participation in government. In large part, they create the information interface which determines the distribution of support in a society and determines the decisions that are taken. Information is manipulated in accordance with the money-bargaining and support-bargaining interests of the controllers of the media.

The Conclusion rounds up major elements of the economics of an information age. Some weaknesses of established psychological theory are identified by reference to the distinctive psychology of support-bargaining and money-bargaining. The Conclusion affirms also some far-reaching implications of the concept of an information interface.

Summary of content of previous books on support-bargaining and money-bargaining

This is my seventh book on support-bargaining and money-bargaining. The theory remains relatively unknown, so it may be useful for readers of the present volume to have a brief account of the earlier books.

A Theory of Support and Money Bargaining (1984)[15]

This presents the theory of support-bargaining and money-bargaining in the early stages of its development. It covers extensively academic work that has a bearing on the theory. It introduces many of the main components of support-bargaining and money-bargaining, such as the formation of groups through support-bargaining, choice by reference to situation, the significance of bargaining sets and bargaining position, and the bargaining strength of organisations in both political and economic spheres. It links social and political support-bargaining to the formation of ideas and a process of 'fact-formation'.

Getting It Right: Economics and the Security of Support (2004)[16]

This presents the objections to the neoclassical model and seeks to establish money-bargaining as a more realistic theory of economic exchange. It develops the idea of situation as the basis of consumer choice. People buy what fits their situation. It identifies companies as the specialist money-bargaining agencies of money-bargaining systems. It also develops the idea of support-bargaining in its political context and extends it to intellectual support-bargaining. The role of information in support-bargaining and money-bargaining systems is described, including propensities to manipulate information.

Support-Bargaining: The Mechanics of Democracy Revealed (2008)[17]

This elaborates on and refines ideas introduced in *Getting It Right*. It spells out in detail how informal and formal support-bargaining functions, and how a support convention is established. It also goes into detail on the formation of theories through intellectual support-bargaining, and how frames of reference are developed and used. Theory formation is conceived as an essential part of the support-bargaining process, and hence an essential part of the mechanics of democracy. Theory making assembles support that can be deployed for political purposes. Economic theory is understood as a creation of intellectual support-bargaining, playing its role in the advancement of interests in support-bargaining societies. There is extensive coverage of the function of companies as agents of money-bargaining systems, the viability condition, their locational formats and their role in foreign trade. The book includes also an account of the historic emergence of a support-bargaining society in Britain.

Support-Bargaining: The Mechanics of Democracy Revealed provides the basic account of support-bargaining and money-bargaining.

Support-Bargaining, Economics and Society: A Social Species (2013)[18]

This book establishes a 'backward' link of support-bargaining to Darwin's theory of natural selection. It is suggested that Darwin underestimated the importance of the human instinct for self-preservation, with an excessive emphasis on human aggression. Concern for self-preservation gives rise to a sense of insecurity and a search for reassuring support. 'Altruism' is part of social support-bargaining. Darwin was himself plainly aware of the importance of group action and the deficiencies of his own account of this aspect of natural selection. Darwin's account of natural selection has divided social scientists into those who recognise in society the Darwinian traits of aggression and competition and those who reject the Darwinian understanding, seeing rather the cooperative and sociable instincts of humans. 'Social Darwinism' is analysed in terms of intellectual support-bargaining. The book traces the implications of the modified understanding of natural selection for the understanding of social and economic processes. Cultural evolution is explained as a process of support-bargaining. Money and money-bargaining are outcomes of cultural evolution. 'Money' is conceived as a creation of support-bargaining and money-bargaining shares much of the dynamic of support-bargaining. It is suggested also that our sense of symmetry, regarded as important to natural selection, is important also in economic choice and the behaviour of businessmen.

The Evolution of Economies: Money-Bargaining, Economic Change and Industrial Revolution (2016)[19]

The process of support-bargaining and money-bargaining involves situation-related selection, so that there is an inherent evolutionary dynamic. The book contrasts the evolution portrayed in terms of support-bargaining and money-bargaining with existing formulations of evolutionary economic theory, based largely on analogies to Darwinian natural selection. A central chapter identifies the company formats crucial to the evolution of the British economy in the period of the industrial revolution. Further chapters deal with the evolution of ideas regarding 'free trade' and monetary management in the context of the economic changes of the industrial revolution. A final chapter forms the precursor to the present book, dealing with information and the evolution of communications.

Aspects of Support-Bargaining and Money-Bargaining (2015)[20]

This is a selection of eight articles, six of which were previously published in academic journals. It includes two articles previously published in the

Cambridge Journal of Economics on situation-related selection and the nature of companies. These constitute important components of the theory of support-bargaining and money-bargaining. An article on 'Asymmetric information', first published in the *Real World Economics Review* (*RWER*), focuses on the efforts of economists to modify the neoclassical paradigm to accommodate information issues. 'Science and support', also first published in the *RWER*, follows the contention between neoclassical and heterodox economists in terms of a 'struggle for mastery in economics'. The two articles published for the first time concern the characteristics of groups and Karl Mannheim's conjectures on the possibility of a science of politics. The Introduction provides an account of the origin and development of the idea of support-bargaining and money-bargaining.

Notes

1 Kahneman, Daniel, 2012, *Thinking, Fast and Slow*, London: Penguin, Chapter 9, 'Answering an easier question'. First published in 2011 by Allen Lane.
2 Smith, Adam, 2009, *An Inquiry into the Nature and Causes of the Wealth of Nations*, Project Gutenberg E-book, Adobe Digital Editions. First published 1776. Smith's account of monetary exchange is considered further in Chapter 4.
3 Walras, Léon, 1954, *Elements of Pure Economics: or, The Theory of Social Wealth*, Translated by William Jaffé, London: Allen and Unwin. First published 1874.
4 Robbins, Lionel, 1932, *An Essay on the Nature and Significance of Economic Science*, London: Macmillan, p. 15.
5 Stigler, George J., 1971, 'The economics of information', in Lamberton, Don M. (ed.), 1971, *Economics of Information and Knowledge*, London: Penguin, p. 61. Original emphasis. First published 1961, *Journal of Political Economy*, Vol. 69, No. 3, pp. 213–25.
6 For an account of such professional experience, see Earl, Peter E., 2002, *Information, Opportunism and Economic Coordination*, Cheltenham: Edward Elgar, Introduction.
7 Stiglitz, Joseph, 2002, 'Information and the change in the paradigm in economics', *American Economic Review*, Vol. 92, No. 3, p. 486. See also Chapter 4.
8 Krugman, Paul, 1996, 'What economists can learn from evolutionary theorists', talk given to the European Association for Evolutionary Political Economy, November, available at: http://web.mit.edu/krugman/www/evolute.html. Accessed 16 May 2017.
9 Krugman, Paul, 2009, 'How did economists get it so wrong?', *New York Times*, 2 September.
10 Krugman, 2009. Quotation: Friedman, Milton, 1953, 'The methodology of positive economics', in Friedman, Milton, 1953, *Essays in Positive Economics*, Chicago: University of Chicago Press.
11 Spread, Patrick, 2016a, *The Evolution of Economies: Money-Bargaining, Economic Change and Industrial Revolution*, Abingdon: Routledge, pp. 294–8.
12 Bruni, Luigino and Sugden, Robert, 2007, 'The road not taken: how psychology was removed from economics, and how it might be brought back', *Economic Journal*, Vol. 117, No. 516, pp. 146–73.
13 See also Spread, 2016a. Chapter 1 provides a 'catch up' on the theory of support-bargaining and money-bargaining.
14 Kahneman, 2012.
15 Spread, Patrick, 1984a, *A Theory of Support and Money Bargaining*, London: Macmillan.

16 Spread, Patrick, 2004, *Getting It Right: Economics and the Security of Support*, Sussex: Book Guild.
17 Spread, Patrick, 2008, *Support-Bargaining: The Mechanics of Democracy Revealed*, Sussex: Book Guild.
18 Spread, Patrick, 2013, *Support-Bargaining, Economics and Society: A Social Species*, Abingdon: Routledge.
19 Spread, 2016a.
20 Spread, Patrick, 2015b, *Aspects of Support-Bargaining and Money-Bargaining*, E-Book, World Economics Association.

1 Information and interests

This chapter provides a summary and critical account of the historical debates over the nature of information and knowledge, as background to the explanations based on support-bargaining and money-bargaining, and the use of the information interface, that are developed in following chapters. It provides also an account of the more recent treatment of information in the context of the neoclassical economic model. As intimated in the Introduction, the problems with information encountered in common economic transactions are difficult to reconcile with a mathematical model. The critique of the economics of information serves as an introduction to various aspects of money-bargaining. Support-bargaining and money-bargaining are closely interlinked, so that an account of one necessarily makes reference to the other.

The historical debates have been largely concerned with what lies beyond our minds and how we access it, rather than the everyday usage of information and knowledge. The 'big question' has dominated the field: what knowledge do we have of an external world? how do we obtain it? how do we know it is true? For most of human intellectual history the 'big question' was debated in the context of religious belief. The answer was assumed to be a matter of 'absolute truth' – a truth entirely independent of human minds, but made accessible to human minds by divine concession. Information and knowledge depended on unlocking the codes by which denizens of a supernatural world communicated with the human world.

In the modern era the natural sciences have seemed to give the best 'window on the world', if not answers to the 'big question'. The natural sciences – physics, chemistry, biology and their many associated investigations – have seemed, at least until quite recently, to provide genuinely direct access to the material substance of the world around us. In many respects, and for many people, they have taken over the role of religious doctrine in identifying the nature of the world we live in. The displacement is all the smoother in that the natural sciences generally share the idea of an absolute truth available to humanity through diligent research. The consistency of the laws of natural science with common experience, and the remarkable products that derive from natural scientific knowledge, seem to confirm that we do indeed have direct knowledge of reality. Such an idea has been shaken in the past century by developments in the fields of relativity theory and quantum mechanics. Our access to information about the external world seems less than absolute; even the external reality itself may not be absolute. But natural science remains the most dependable means of extracting information and knowledge from the phenomena of what is still taken to be an external world.

The high status achieved by the natural sciences with regard to identification of true information about the world derives mainly from its adoption of a process of systematic testing introduced formally in England through the foundation of the Royal Society in 1660 for the specific purpose of advancing experimental study of natural phenomena. Evidence provided from experiments was regarded as critical to the acceptance or rejection of the hypotheses the experiments were designed to test. Theory had to be consistent with observations and records of what actually happened in defined circumstances. The key to truth was evidence, and the sort of evidence that everyone could share.

Natural science in its earlier forms and ecclesiastical approaches broadly share an understanding of truth as absolute and potentially accessible. They are, however, sharply distinguished by their concepts of evidence. Something like modern forms of legal evidence were emerging in the fifteenth and sixteenth centuries in Britain, roughly in the period when ideas of scientific evidence took shape, though it is also argued they were not established even by the mid-eighteenth century.[1] The adoption of evidence as the determinant of truth flew in the face of prior religious understanding. Mediaeval 'trial by ordeal' assumed the direct engagement of God in determination of guilt or innocence. A certain procedure was reckoned to give God the opportunity to signify guilt or innocence. The major break of Christians from the Roman Catholic Church was marked by difference over the understanding of the eucharist. Roman Catholics held it as an article of faith that the bread and wine of the eucharist were transubstantiated into the body and blood of Christ by the invocations of a priest. Protestants denied that such a change took place. The only evidence was that of sensory perception. If Catholics could not accept that what looked, tasted and felt like bread was bread, then there was no evidence to determine the issue one way or the other. The truths of faith were not truths that could be revealed by evidence of the sort generated by common perception, nor even by evidence of a more scientific kind, if it had been possible to conceive such an approach. Even today, when there is overwhelming evidence for an evolutionary origin of the human species, many people adhere to the explanation of their faith. Identification of true information through the assembly of evidence by empirical tests remains the cornerstone of natural science.

The empirical tests used by natural scientists involve not only the systematic collection of evidence, but replication of the evidence by different agents. There has to be corroboration of evidence, as with legal evidence, by a second agent and preferably more. Evidence that cannot be replicated is likely to be rejected. The reproduction of scientific evidence implies that it must be possible to replicate the phenomena under investigation, which means they must have some degree of stability, and it must be possible to isolate the phenomena under investigation from other factors that might influence outcomes. Some natural scientific phenomena, for example factors affecting climate change, are unstable and difficult to isolate. Consequently evidence assembled for climate change has been extensively disputed. Scientific method is considered further in Chapters 2 and 6, the former in the context of Bruno Latour and Steve Woolgar's account of 'social construction' and the latter in the context of Alvin Goldman's treatment of scientific realism and veritistic analysis.

The requirement for stability in the phenomena under investigation creates difficulties for the extraction of true information relating to phenomena that do not have such qualities. The social sciences are concerned with phenomena involving human volition, rather than the inanimate phenomena which are typically the subjects of natural scientific enquiry. Replication of phenomena involving many humans, each with their own inclinations, is difficult to achieve. Not only are the phenomena at issue exercising their own volition, but the social scientists themselves have their own volition that is likely to affect their approach to the subject phenomena. Natural scientists can easily be conceived as detached and disinterested investigators of truth, since the behaviour of their inanimate phenomena will be of no personal concern to them. Social scientists may claim the same status, but those who find their results inconvenient are likely to argue that the research was affected by the preferences of the researchers. Social scientists nevertheless recognise the importance of evidence derived by scientific method and adopt such modified forms of scientific method as are feasible with the phenomena they deal with.

Neoclassical economic theory and information

The success of natural scientists in the nineteenth century across Europe and the prestige of its practitioners set students of human society wondering whether a similar approach might yield comparable rewards in their field. The economic theory that developed in the late nineteenth century, commonly referred to as neoclassical economic theory, was conceived on the model of the natural sciences, in particular physics. The aim was to develop a theory of economic transactions that would have status comparable with that of physical science. The concern of economics with physical things like bricks and chairs suggested that the analogy with physics might not be misplaced. Economists could assume, like physicists, that what they were dealing with had an existence independent of any human perception. It was, however, necessary to adopt the practices of physics on a highly selective basis. Mathematics could be used in a theory about 'things', just as it was in physical enquiry, and neoclassical economists adopted a mathematical approach. For many years into the twentieth century debate was maintained over the concepts of economic theory, but in the latter half of the twentieth century the mathematical aspects of the model gained ascendancy. The Robbins concept of economics, mentioned in the Introduction, as a study of resource allocation, became dominant. It came to be accepted in economics faculties of universities that mathematics was the essential means by which the microeconomic mechanisms of exchange, and hence the mechanisms of economic systems, would be revealed. It became the 'mainstream' theory of economics, dominating the institutionalised teaching of economics. To a considerable degree, 'economics' became and remains 'neoclassical economics'. Modifications and alternatives have been proposed, including the present idea of money-bargaining, but none has eroded significantly the dominance of neoclassical theory groups.[2] The global financial crisis starting in 2007 intensified debate over the deficiencies of neoclassical theory.

Mathematics imposed certain requirements on the phenomena it dealt with. These requirements could only be met through assumptions. Economics was concerned not only with 'things' but with human beings. The incidence of human volition was potentially a major stumbling block for a mathematical model. Its difficulties were minimised through an assumption that humans would always act rationally in pursuit of objectives defined in the model. Further necessary assumptions included homogeneity of products, many buyers and sellers, consumer choice based on marginal utility, firms equating marginal revenues to marginal costs, an absence of a spatial dimension and a severely truncated time dimension.[3] While the use of mathematics took neoclassical theory closer to physics, the necessary assumptions for the application of mathematics removed it far from the empirical concerns that are the bedrock of natural scientific enquiry. Neoclassical economists presented mathematics as in itself sufficient guarantee of the truth of its conclusions. Physicists had shown that the universe behaved in accordance with mathematical models, so it was thought reasonable to contend that human exchange could likewise be represented mathematically.

For those not entirely convinced by the mathematical argument, the fall-back was to excuse the lack of scientific rigour on the grounds that the mathematical approach provided at least a useful simplification of economic exchange. Useful lessons could be learnt from the mathematical model regarding the dynamics of monetary exchange. It constituted a useful frame of reference. Observations could be extensively 'interpreted' by reference to the economic model, in the way that adherents of religious faiths interpreted their observations in accordance with their faith.

The lack of empirical concern in economic theory was noted by William Beveridge, author of the 'Beveridge Report' of 1942 that formed the foundation of the National Health Service in Britain. Beveridge devoted his farewell address in 1937 to the London School of Economics and Political Science, after 18 years as its director, to a plea for greater concern for 'observation' in the social sciences and less preoccupation with theoretical speculation.[4] The social sciences should be scientific in their approach, concerned with facts, rather than tolerate so much abstraction. He made the point most strongly by reference to John Maynard Keynes' famous book, *A General Theory of Employment, Interest and Money*, then of recent appearance.[5] Beveridge notes that Einstein's formulation of relativity theory started and finished with observed facts, but Keynes' general theory is quite different:

> Mr Keynes starts, not from any fact, but from the definition of a concept, of what he (Mr Keynes) means when he says 'involuntary unemployment'. He proceeds to a fresh series of concepts and of their definitions. In a large proportion of these definitions, words are used in senses different from those of most other economists and of Mr Keynes himself six years ago. Mr Keynes does not return to facts for verification.[6]

Beveridge then concludes:

> The distinguishing mark of economic science, as illustrated by this debate, is that it is a science in which verification of generalisations by reference to facts is neglected as irrelevant.[7]

In effect, economics neglects the empirical discipline and requirements for evidence that are an essential part of natural science. It is based on mathematically generated concepts of economic behaviour held to operate without necessary reference to empirical observation.

Beveridge remarked also on another characteristic of neoclassical theory apparent from Keynes' *General Theory*. While the neoclassical model is principally modelled on the natural scientific model of physics, it retains characteristics of older forms of enquiry. It shares with religious faith, natural science and common understanding the idea of an absolute knowledge of an external world. There is no question but that potatoes, carts, shoes and bricks exist independently of any human perception of them. Such understanding, being an element of 'common knowledge', is attractive. It gives the neoclassical model a claim to 'realism' and even 'common sense'. But it brings also with that absolute understanding associated ideas, derived from religious faith, of texts as the basis of understanding and an acceptance that theory can properly be sustained by a theory group committed to it. It gives neoclassical theory a quasi-religious character. Without empirical confirmation of theory, it is possible to fall back on faith or group solidarity. Neoclassical enquiry may then be confined to the study of texts, or mathematics in lieu of written texts, in the isolation of universities, without regard to what goes on outside. Beveridge identifies an archaic character in economic theory when he remarks of anyone who read *The General Theory*:

> I do not see how they can avoid the conclusion that economics is not a science concerned with phenomena, but a survival of mediaeval logic, and that economists are people who earn their livings by taking in one another's definitions for mangling.[8]

That, of course, has not been the judgement of posterity on *The General Theory*. It has been elevated to something like the status of sacred text in the mainstream economic theory group. It takes the place of 'facts' in an intellectual environment in which people do not have the same confidence in access to 'facts' as was possible for Beveridge. But Beveridge could formulate a programme of communal welfare services in Britain because he was free from the constraints imposed by the neoclassical economic model. Keynes' General Theory is questioned in the context of the idea of an evolving money-bargaining system in *The Evolution of Economies*.[9]

Economics of information

It was seen in the Introduction that economists have not been entirely indifferent to the shortcomings of the neoclassical model. Its inadequate understanding of information has in particular been the subject of extensive debate and supplementation. The neoclassical model makes the assumption that the rational people engaged in economic transactions have all the information necessary to the rational conclusion of a transaction. Other assumptions of the model mean that these rational people need very little information. But any mental step outside the model into a realistic environment shows that the assumption is clearly misplaced. In 1961 George Stigler published an article on 'The economics of information', drawing attention to the naivety of the assumptions regarding information in the neoclassical model and their manifest inaccuracy. Stigler writes:

> One should hardly have to tell academicians that information is a valuable resource; knowledge *is* power. And yet it occupies a slum dwelling in the town of economics. Mostly it is ignored; the best technology is assumed to be known; the relationship of commodities to consumer preferences is a datum. And one of the information-producing industries, advertising, is treated with a hostility that economists normally reserve for tariffs and monopolists.[10]

Lack of information and costs of searching were chiefly apparent in price dispersion – the lack of a single 'market price' resulting from an interaction of supply and demand. Stigler provides a mathematical analysis of a search process to identify the lowest price of a product. He provides also a mathematical analysis of advertising, conceived as the main means by which search costs are reduced and information is disseminated to consumers. The article initiated an enduring debate over the role of information in relation to the neoclassical model.

George Akerlof and Robert Shiller in their 2015 book *Phishing for Phools* echo and amplify Stigler's argument regarding the complications of information. They provide an extensive account of the systematic use of information to make people believe what the providers of the information want them to believe. They recognise that such practice calls into question the integrity of the neoclassical economic model: 'modern economics inherently fails to grapple with deception and trickery'. They recognise that deception is 'inherent in the workings of competitive markets'.[11] They do not, however, see any necessity to abandon the neoclassical market model. They savour its identification of a 'Pareto optimal' allocation of resources. They endorse Adam Smith's idea of an 'invisible hand'. They remark, 'Adam Smith wrote that, with free markets, as if "by an invisible hand . . . [each person] *pursuing his own interest*" also promotes the general good'.[12] All they advocate is the modification of the understanding of the neoclassical model such that the 'Pareto optimality' is recognised as being an optimal allocation based on consumer tastes arising from the manipulation of information.[13] It is, in effect, an optimal allocation for fools.

The problems with the neoclassical model are ignored rather than resolved. With products understood in terms of manipulated tastes, the homogeneity of products that is essential to the mathematical model is lost. Everyone is buying a different product, shaped in their own minds. It becomes impossible to conceive and draw the supply and demand schedules which are fundamental to the model. Rational people are all the same in their rationality, but fools are all different in their foolishness. Every transaction is unique. This is why information is so important in money-bargaining.

A similar selective perception is apparent in the appeal to Adam Smith's 'invisible hand'. As bishops know the Bible, Akerlof and Shiller will know *The Wealth of Nations*, and will know that the 'invisible hand' is not part of Smith's analysis of markets. It is used in the context of investors' preference for their own domestic industry over foreign industry. In the quotation from Akerlof and Shiller above, Smith is not writing about 'free markets', but about 'preferring the support of domestic to that of foreign industry'.[14] The support of Smith is enlisted through inaccurate representation of Smith's account of the 'invisible hand'. It is fooling people into support for neoclassical theory. The idea of an 'invisible hand' is considered further in Chapter 4. But, to anticipate, an 'invisible hand' that favours domestic investment over foreign investment is not an agent of optimal allocation of resources.

Akerlof and Shiller provide an admirable range of illustrations of the provision of false and misleading information, but they give no indication of how economic transactions might be conducted without information or, given the need for information, the form it might take to allay their concerns over manipulation. Their contrast is with the 'perfect information' assumed in the economic model. They would presumably not claim their own exposition to be a model of the provision of information free of all influences of marketing. They make plain that manipulation of information is reprehensible, but offer no alternative theory of information that might suggest a way out of the dilemma of manipulated information. It is just a question of 'look out!' Their account of information is simply layered over the neoclassical account of market exchange, without regard for incompatibility.

Debate over information issues that followed Stigler's 1961 article was particularly prominent in the context of issues arising from an article by Ronald Coase on 'The nature of the firm'.[15] The article was published in 1937 but became prominent only in the latter part of the twentieth century. Coase argued that the depiction of 'the firm' in neoclassical theory as a matter of equating marginal revenue to marginal cost was unrealistic and incompatible with what could be readily observed regarding the role and functions of firms. Coase attributed the existence of firms to the incidence of 'transaction costs', and chief amongst the transaction costs was the acquisition of information. The idea of transaction costs was developed in the context of other ideas concerning industrial organisation and management, such as 'bounded rationality', contracting and 'opportunism'. In all these information, and the acquisition of information, was recognised as a major factor.[16]

In a 1994 article titled 'Information, knowledge, vision and theories of the firm', Martin Fransman argued that most of the functions attributed to companies could be understood as related to problems of information acquisition and information processing. He opens with the commitment for his article: 'The first purpose is to demonstrate that many of the best-known approaches to the firm in economics have in common a starting-point which sees the firm as a response to information related problems'.[17] In Fransman's article information is about 'states of the world' and consequences of natural or social events.[18] This, together with the assumption of asymmetric information, is the basis for well-known concepts of the firm:

- If information were perfectly available, as is conceived in the neoclassical model, none of the organisation of companies would be needed. As it is, information provides the impulse to form teams for the conduct of business, the defining impulse behind the formation of companies, according to Armen Alchian and Harold Demsetz.[19]
- The conclusion of contracts requires acquisition of extensive information, so that Michael Jensen and William Meckling's concept of a company as a 'nexus of contracts' is dependent on information.[20]
- Contracts are the means by which transactions are accomplished, so that acquisition of information is an essential element in the transaction costs identified by Coase as the basis of companies.[21]
- If information could be processed perfectly, an implicit assumption of perfect competition, Herbert Simon's concept of bounded rationality would not be a relevant consideration. So the exercise of bounded rationality in companies originates in problems of information.[22]
- If information were perfect, there would be no scope for opportunism – in Oliver Williamson's definition, 'self-interest-seeking with guile', but perhaps more easily understood as manipulation of information for the advance of interest.[23]
- The use of routines, the essential feature of companies, as described by Richard Nelson and Sidney Winter, is dictated by considerations of bounded rationality, and hence is also a means of coping with information.[24]

Thus all the major accounts of the functions of companies are rooted in requirements for information.[25]

Ian Molho, in a 2001 book titled *The Economics of Information: Lying and Cheating in Markets and Organisations*, summarises the position in terms of the resolution of issues of coordination and motivation either through 'markets' or 'hierarchies'.[26] Information is needed in both markets and hierarchies. Contracts could resolve the motivational problems were it not for the 'lying and cheating' that is 'opportunism'. Information also implies the necessity for 'bounded rationality'. Information is so abundant and so important that it overloads human mental capacities, causing people to act with 'bounded rationality'. Information costs are the transaction costs that are the reason for the formation of companies, and impose other costs that affect economic organisation and behaviour. In spite of this impact of information on a central feature of economic exchange, the functioning of companies, Molho remains an adherent of the neoclassical model. He affirms: 'One of the outstanding intellectual achievements of traditional economic theory has been to show that under certain conditions the outcome of such a system is Pareto efficient'.[27]

Simon's idea of 'bounded rationality' features prominently in these explanations for the existence of companies.[28] 'Bounded rationality' rests principally on the recognition that human minds have cognitive limits that restrict the amount of information they can deal with. That recognition leads immediately to the question of how information is filtered or selected for the exercise of reason.

Simon contends that people in administrative organisations form rough and simple models of the situation confronting them and then adopt what he calls 'satisficing', a mixture of being 'satisfactory' and 'sufficient', to make a decision. 'Satisficing' is the behavioural alternative to 'maximising'.[29] According to Simon, 'Economic man purports to deal with the "real world" in all its complexity', whereas an administrator deals only with a simplified version of the real world.[30] With that simplified version, reason can be applied.

The idea of 'bounded rationality' is thus contrasted with a neoclassical idea of 'unbounded rationality', in which economic man deals rationally with all the information of the real world. But the neoclassical model is itself a simplified model of the real world. It is bounded by assumptions specifically aimed at reducing the information content to what can be dealt with rationally. The model is designed for the exercise of reason. The agents of the neoclassical model must maximise their incomes, their utility and their profit and are conceived as doing so by the exercise of reason. Simon's 'bounded rationality' is necessary to circumstances of unbounded information. But the rationality of the neoclassical model is bounded – by the assumptions that are fundamental to the model. The reasoning process is the same in the administrative context as it is in the neoclassical model. The difference lies in the volumes of information that have to be dealt with.

In a later book, *Reason in Human Affairs*, Simon contends that 'emotions' focus the mind on what is important and permit the exercise of rationality within the bounds of the focus. He remarks, 'A very strong case can be made . . . that focusing attention is one of the principal functions of the process we call emotions'.[31]

Emotions can certainly give a strong focus for human attention. But emotions are more likely to make people accept unreflectingly the information they receive when it accords with the lead of their emotions. Emotions in general understanding are more likely to override reason than provide a basis for the exercise of reason. Furthermore, minds need to focus on issues that don't arouse any considerable degree of emotion. 'Cognition' is directed by something other than emotion. Cognitive processes enable us to distinguish between true and false information, or at least attempt the distinction, so a theory of cognitive processes must reflect such capacity.

The theory of support-bargaining and money-bargaining suggests that individuals focus on what is important by reference to their situation.[32] This basic idea is apparent in Simon's idea of formation of a simple model of the situation in an administrative context on the basis of which something like reason can be exercised. In support-bargaining and money-bargaining, however, the idea of situation is something more various and more fundamental to human psychology. It is not confined to administrative procedures. Rather, it plays a dominant role in human thought and action, including collective assessments. It comprises information not as model of some actual situation but as the whole extent of human grasp. The concept of situation ranges from the simplest physical understanding to the highest abstraction. It is a response to the same psychological requirement for reference that is apparent in the use of 'frames of reference' in a theoretical context. It dictates perception and interpretation of what is perceived. When what is perceived can be interpreted in accordance with a situation concept, there arises the sense of understanding. Concepts of individual and group situation are part of a person's identity. The fundamental nature of situation-reference is apparent in instinctive human reactions to threatening situations. Defensive reactions are clearly conducive to survival of the species. But the importance of situation as reference is apparent in the most commonplace situations, including those of consumer choice. The idea of situation reference has also fundamental importance in support-bargaining and money-bargaining as the basis of its evolutionary dynamic and the contrast with the 'equilibrium' concept of neoclassical economic theory.[33] The identification of interests in relation to situation is considered further in the following chapter. The particular use of situation as reference in consumer choice is detailed in Chapter 4.

The idea of a 'model of situation' and a 'framework' as part of the phenomenon of 'understanding' is apparent in Friedrich Hayek's account of human psychology. He writes,

> explanation consists in the formation in the brain of a 'model' of the complex events to be explained, a model the parts of which are defined by their position in a more comprehensive structure of relationships which constitute the semi-permanent framework from which the representations of individual events receive their meaning.[34]

To understand information it is necessary to establish a frame of reference that gives information a context and significance, such as it has in common experience. That is why, as noted in the Introduction, no strong theory of information is possible without the theory of support-bargaining and money-bargaining.

The individual concept of situation is influenced by group associations. Support-bargaining will cause individuals to adopt an understanding of individual situation compatible with what the group has determined to be appropriate, albeit that in certain circumstances an individual will resist the influence of the group. Support-bargaining within administrative organisations will produce outcomes that might be understood as 'satisficing'. There is agreement that the chosen option is acceptable, even if none of those concerned regard it as the best.[35] The 'fitting to situation' process is more an exercise of the human sense of symmetry than of reason. The sense of symmetry, not rationality, is the essential cognitive capacity.[36] The sense of symmetry is inseparable from the sense of understanding. The identification of interests in relation to situation is considered further in the following chapter. 'Bounded rationality' is discussed further in Chapter 5.

Molho identifies 'signalling' as a major aspect of the handling of information.[37] The idea of 'signalling' derives from Michael Spence, who suggested, principally in the context of educational attainments, that applicants for a post could 'signal' to those offering the post the qualities that suited them to it.[38] Spence creates a mathematical model of signalling with relatively confining variables and assumptions and evaluates it by reference to achievement of equilibrium, concluding that there is no determinate equilibrium. He notes that his model assumes relative infrequency of signallers in the market, and consequently the model probably does not have general application.

More simply, 'signalling' in the employment market can be understood as information provided by applicants to potential employers signalling that they have the necessary capacity for the employment. In general, 'signalling' is the provision of information, wittingly or unwittingly, by an informed person to a lesser informed person. In common parlance, 'signalling' is communication. The idea of 'signalling' is prominent in the economics of information, earning its originator a Nobel Memorial Prize. Molho provides an illustration of the effects of signalling, though blunting its impact with the acknowledgement that, 'it is not (and is not meant to be) realistic as a model of the labour market'. While the economics of information is an attempt to make mainstream economic theory more realistic, its starting point means that it tends to take frequent advantage of the dispensation from reality inherent in the neoclassical economic model.

Both Fransman and Molho emphasise 'asymmetric' information as a crucial aspect of information with regard to impact on industrial organisation. Some of those engaged in economic transactions, including the negotiation of contracts, know more than others. They have information relevant to a transaction that can be withheld from others. The significance of asymmetric information was identified in a famous article of 1970 by George Akerlof titled, 'The market for "lemons": quality uncertainty and the market mechanism'.[39] While Stigler, in his article 'The economics of information', drew attention to the difficulties of specifying 'quality',[40] Akerlof showed in a mathematical model the potential impact on markets of 'quality' with a mathematical codification. Akerlof's article established 'asymmetric information' as central to the debate over the role of information. Akerlof's article is considered in detail in Chapter 4. Molho provides some criticism of Akerlof's account, and provides an alternative model of the consequences of asymmetric information, though he remarks, 'The model is highly stylized and not intended to be realistic'.[41] In that, he follows Akerlof. Joseph Stiglitz has taken up the challenges of asymmetric information and its effects. His work on the subject is also considered in Chapter 4.

While Stigler's 1961 article extended enquiry into the use of information in economic transactions and its compatibility with the neoclassical model, an earlier article by George Richardson provided an objection to the model that was recognised as profoundly destructive. Richardson argued that the perfect competition of the neoclassical model was not theoretically conducive to the emergence of equilibrium because producers would not be able to coordinate their investment. Producers would not have information about each other's investment plans and so the optimal level of investment for any product would not be realised. Under perfect competition, with the same unit costs at all levels of production, producers would not be able to distinguish their own output from that of others, so the optimal level of investment would be very unlikely to emerge. Even if unit costs fell with rising levels of production, producers would not know the investment intentions of others, and no optimal level of investment would be achieved.[42] As Nicolai Foss and Brian Loasby put it:

> Richardson demonstrates in a long-run Walrasian setting that general equilibrium cannot be a configuration that a perfectly competitive economy could be expected to approach. Producers are unable to coordinate their investment decisions because they lack the necessary knowledge of other producers' plans.[43]

Richardson's argument has not been refuted.

Money-bargaining, information and the model

These problems of information, whether identified by Richardson, Stigler, Akerlof and Shiller, Fransman or Molho, or the many others who have contributed, suggest that the neoclassical model is wrong to the extent of falsified. Louis Phlips makes it plain. He notes that the economics of imperfect information is an integral part of the theory of industrial organisation, and concludes:

> Rather than trying to save the concept of a perfectly competitive market and the 'law of supply and demand' which is supposed to clear this market, a lot of energy is saved if one simply admits that this law is inadequate.[44]

But while there is much affirmation of the importance and difficulties of information, the writers on the subject are generally reluctant to draw the obvious conclusion regarding the status of the neoclassical model.

The reluctance of economists to follow the evidence is apparent in a comment of Mark Casson: 'Critics of economic theory often find it difficult to understand how economics manages to survive what they perceive to be their devastating criticisms'.[45] Don Lamberton, in his second collection of articles on information theory, titles his Introduction 'Threatened wreckage or new paradigm?'.[46] There is apparently no option to stay with the neoclassical paradigm. Casson suggests that one reason for the survival of the neoclassical model is that no alternative has been provided. He does not ask himself what brings about the survival of a theory – whether it is the accuracy of the theory or something else. He seems to accept that the evidence is against neoclassical theory. The idea of intellectual support-bargaining suggests that survival of a theory depends on the maintenance of support for a theory. The reason for the survival of neoclassical theory is then the support of a dominant theory group. Whatever the evidence, the theory group supports the neoclassical model, in furtherance of other interests, so the theory survives. But this does not entirely discount Casson's first reason, the absence of an alternative. The existence of theory groups is a matter of intellectual security. The group needs some theory around which it can assemble support. It will assemble around false theory if there is nothing better on offer. An alternative will provide an alternative focus for the assembly of support and potentially make possible the reassignment of support to a better theory.

So whatever the defects of its theory, the dominant theory group will maintain its support until something better turns up. It may not be sufficient just to provide a better theory in terms of consistency with information derived from empirical observation. The neoclassical theory group has hidden attractions. The neoclassical model is defended as best it can be in the notion that it was not set up to be empirically inviolable. The assumptions necessary to the application of mathematics preclude empirical confirmation, and the assumption concerning information is just one amongst the several that make the model possible in mathematical terms. The model was set up for the exercise of mathematics, and is claimed to be 'useful' as a basis for understanding the dynamics of economic transactions. The model is 'useful' rather than accurate. It was suggested in the Introduction that its usefulness extends beyond 'useful' in understanding economic transactions to 'useful' in sustaining a dominant theory group and the principle of individual freedom. An alternative theory, however accurate, must somehow win over the support deriving from these other attractions.

Covert interests, or 'side-interests', are a common feature of support-bargaining. Academic pursuit of truth is easily diverted by the covert pursuit of non-truth interests. Simon contends that an organisation is never deciding what it purports to be deciding. A committee debating a new curriculum for students is actually debating the implications of the new curriculum for faculty positions.[47] While the overt subject of debate is the content of a new curriculum to meet the interests of students, the covert interests of the debaters lie in the implications for faculty posts arising from changes to the curriculum. The negotiations may be delicate. No economics curriculum committee would be likely to agree a curriculum based on money-bargaining simply because it provides an accurate account of monetary exchange. The pure pursuit of truth is probably beyond the virtue of humans. Our psychology has evolved to protect our interests rather than pursue truth. Such mixed motives are apparent in virtually all spheres of support-bargaining, including boardrooms and strategy committees, parish councils and city assemblies, national cabinets and parliamentary committees.

The difficulties over information, and asymmetric information in particular, noted by the above writers all appear as difficulties by reference to the neoclassical economic model. The model is so mathematically confined and so empirically indifferent that it inevitably throws up 'difficulties' in relation to observations of actual economic activity. The difficulties must remain difficulties while the would-be resolvers have nowhere else to go – no alternative frame of reference that will allow them to assimilate their observations without stress, without regarding them as 'difficulties'. Even the modifiers of the neoclassical model are trapped in its bubble. They see ordinary phenomena as anomalous, as requiring explanation, because their understanding is dominated by the content of the neoclassical frame of reference.

They do nevertheless unwittingly adopt an alternative – that of the common frame of reference. The 'difficulties' associated with information are difficulties because the neoclassical frame of reference conflicts with information derived from observation and interpreted in a common frame of reference. In the common frame, people understand that you can't believe everything you are told; people will exercise the utmost guile in advancing their interests; people will not necessarily act rationally; communication is commonplace; people see without difficulty that some people know more than others. Such phenomena are not anomalous to the common frame of reference. That is why people are sometimes bemused by the predilection of economists for awarding themselves prizes for complicating the obvious. Yet this alternative of the common theory is not an avowable option for professional theory makers specifically committed to enquiry beyond the common understanding.

The theory of support-bargaining and money-bargaining also identifies the industrial organisation, which is so strong a focus of attention for neoclassical writers on the economics of information, as a matter of bargaining advantage. Organisations in general are used for the development of strong bargaining positions. They focus a group to a purpose and introduce money-budgets to take advantage of the motivations of money-bargaining. In a money-bargaining system, organisations in the form of companies are specialist money-bargaining agencies, with the strongest bargaining positions. Companies are formed to meet as a minimum a viability condition that 'revenues exceed costs', or 'sales × price > unit costs × production'. Companies adopt technologies which will enable them to meet the viability condition. The viability condition makes prominent the importance of the relationship between unit costs of production and the level of production.[48] The importance of 'sales' to viability causes companies to disseminate information that presents their products and services to potential buyers as best fitting to their situations. Companies and the viability condition are considered further in Chapter 4.

This understanding of companies means that 'markets' and 'hierarchies' are not different systems of resource allocation, but are both matters of money-bargaining. Hierarchies are artificial bargaining structures designed so that those at higher levels have stronger bargaining positions relative to those at lower levels. Those above can then determine to a large extent what work is done by those lower down. It makes it possible to focus the work of all those employed by a company on activities that will ensure the company meets the viability condition. Those joining a company accept the differential bargaining positions in return for the monetary payments and other returns they gain from the company. This role of hierarchies is apparent in all organisations.[49]

'Sales' are the one element of the viability condition that is not in the control of companies. Sales depend on decisions of buyers outside companies. Companies are then obliged to disseminate information to persuade potential buyers to buy their products. Companies compete through provision of a great variety of information posted to the information interface through which potential buyers can see what is fitting to their situations. Rather than just a standard product and a price, the information covers all aspects of transactions. Richardson sees a problem in the coordination of investment for production of homogeneous products. But companies all invest for production of products that are varied in accordance with the situations of potential buyers. By differentiating their output, they give themselves bargaining position, and hence the chance of meeting the viability condition. Nor do they confine themselves to product differentiation. As well as designing products that will appeal to consumers in different situations, they will use technology to produce at low cost; they will locate in certain areas where they see opportunities; they will ensure that their products are available when consumers are likely to buy them; they will ensure that finance is available for buyers; and so on. The investment will not be coordinated between companies, but the rivalry will promote the accommodation of consumer interests. Companies that cannot persuade sufficient numbers of buyers to buy at a price determined by their unit costs will not survive.

There is a great variety of potentially successful formats. As noted above, Stigler cites price dispersion as evidence of imperfect information. But differences in bargaining positions, as well as disparities of information, explain price dispersion. Everyone knows that corner stores are generally more expensive than supermarkets, but still corner stores can sell enough to maintain their viability. They depend on a clientele constrained in their bargaining positions by circumstances of space and time. The supermarket option is not open to them, given that it is some way off and they do not have time to spare.

Fransman and others see information as being about a 'state of the world', implying not only the existence of an external world, but one that it is possible to know about. The support-bargaining and money-bargaining frame conceives information as all that the human mind can countenance. Fransman treats information as fundamental to theories of firms, but it is fundamental to those theories because it is fundamental to everything – to the extent of being all we can deal with. That understanding makes plain the great scope for organisation and manipulation of information for the advance of interest. It makes plain how information is manipulated to form an information interface in which people must of necessity conduct themselves socially, intellectually, politically and monetarily. It makes plain how frames of reference are created in the information interface to influence perception and evaluation in favour of certain interests. In this context, asymmetric information is as much opportunity as problem. It is a fundamental feature of bargaining positions. People actively cultivate information advantages for the strengthening of their bargaining positions. 'Phishing for phools' is the dissemination of information to an information interface to strengthen the bargaining position of the disseminator.

The situation-related understanding of interests in support-bargaining and money-bargaining explains the conduct of 'search' that is so prominent in the economics of information, as presented by Stigler and the information theorists of industrial organisation. Search for useful information is carried out by reference to situation, including notions of space and time. Transactions have to be concluded in dimensions of space and time, so that the use of search will be conducted on a basis of how information already held fits the situation as conceived, and the prospects for improving the fit by further search. Such further search will be conducted within situational constraints, of which time will often be preeminent. The sense of 'fit', or symmetry, is essential to this process. It is a 'jigsaw', rather than the more familiar type of algebraic equations. Our behaviour was honed under the exigencies of natural selection, so we probably search for the best products at the best prices using the same faculties that formerly preserved us from sabre-toothed tigers and suchlike, at least well enough for the survival of the species, and too well for the survival of sabre-toothed tigers.

Fransman notes that Simon's approach to psychology and rationality is individualist, whereas company decisions may be more of a social process, involving discussion and agreement between individuals. Decisions within organisations may then be made socially, 'in the context of the processes of inter-personal dynamics, power relationships, etc., that exist within the organization'.[50] Decisions are made through group support-bargaining, subject to hierarchical distinctions of bargaining positions.[51]

As noted above, Akerlof and Shiller present a varied range of examples of misleading information from different spheres of activity. But they do not deal with misleading information in the academic environment. At a 2017 conference Sheila Dow presented a paper titled, 'How far are economists purveyors of fake news?' She opens her paper with the comment:

> For self-professed experts these are disturbing times. We identify ourselves as developing in order to promote the public good. Yet there has been a widespread rejection of expertise – especially economic expertise – and a flourishing of 'fake news' as an alternative basis for support for particular political positions. Where does this leave us? As experts of course we need to defend our role. As 'seekers after truth' we see ourselves as better able to contribute to policy-making than the purveyors of 'fake news'. It seems so obvious that we should support the role of experts and condemn the rejection of facts as fake news. But clearly there is a common view among much of the citizenry that experts and their presentation of facts do not correspond to lived experience.[52]

The idea of 'fake news' became prominent following the assertions of President Donald Trump regarding the dissemination of 'fake news' in the United States media. When the President of the United States, with his extensive proven support, and the power that goes with it, makes such assertions against the reputable press of his own country, the idea of fake news, or propaganda, or deception, is not just commonplace but resurgent in a new and challenging form. Dow's analysis assesses whether the neoclassical frame of reference used by mainstream economists causes them to purvey what might be regarded as 'fake news'. In the context of intellectual support-bargaining, 'fake news' can be provided unwittingly from a frame of reference that is mistaken. And since frames of reference are formed and used for the advance of interests, the 'fake news' will be of such a kind as to advance the interests of its purveyors. From there it is hardly a step to the semi-witting – to writing what is known to be of doubtful accuracy but advances the writer's cause. From there, many will easily recognise that there is advantage to be gained from outright invention of news.

Knowledge and institutions

The 'quasi-religious' character of neoclassical economic theory referred to above connects the theory with the long historical debate over the nature of information, knowledge and the 'big question' over human understanding of an external world. In historical debate, 'knowledge' was understood in terms of 'justified true belief'. Alvin Goldman, as will be seen in Chapter 6, sets out to defend the idea of knowledge as 'true belief'. Economists retain the idea that information at least is about 'states of the world' – how things are beyond human minds.[53] Kelvin Lancaster makes the point that product differentiation requires not just knowledge about the existential state of a product, as is all that is required in the neoclassical model, but information about its qualities or characteristics.[54] Phlips links the 'state of the world' to mental understanding in three elements of an 'information structure': 'the set of possible states of the world; the set of possible signals, and the probability that a signal is observed given that a state prevails'.[55] 'Information' is conceived as being about something that exists independently of any mental perception of it.

Most writers on the economics of information take a straightforward view of the existence of 'things' as its subject matter, thus largely pre-empting any big existential question. They are nevertheless concerned with 'knowledge', mostly as a store of information, but in some cases involving 'belief'. G. B. Richardson uses the term with strongly personal reference: 'what, in this paper, I shall loosely term "knowledge", is of the form of personal estimates or opinions which may differ and which cannot be shown at the time to be certainly true or false'.[56] Brian Loasby takes the more scientific view that:

> all knowledge should be considered as conjectural, in Karl Popper's (1963) sense of hypotheses which, though apparently corroborated, always remain open to refutation, but that it is nevertheless possible in some circumstances to attain knowledge that is highly reliable.[57]

In the latter part of his 1994 article, starting at Section 4, Fransman contrasts the idea of the firm as response to problems of information with the idea of the firm as a 'repository of knowledge'. He cites Nelson and Winter's concept of companies as 'repositories of productive knowledge'.[58] The knowledge is understood as stored in the 'routines' that are principally designed to enable firms to cope with complexity. Fransman emphasises the distinction between 'information' and 'knowledge', which he sees as crucial to the effective conduct of business – the difficulties of IBM in the 1980s are seen as a consequence of maintaining a belief about the potential of mainframe computers when available information indicated the better prospects of personal computers. He contrasts information and knowledge as follows: 'Information is defined, as above, as data relating to states of the world and the state-contingent consequences that follow from events in the world. Knowledge, on the other hand, is defined as belief'.[59] The 'vision' of Fransman's title is the knowledge or beliefs predominant in a firm regarding the firm's circumstances and future.[60] Processed information is an important input to them, but they are more than processed information. No necessary 'truth' or 'justification' is attached to these beliefs. Mistaken beliefs would not qualify as 'knowledge' in the philosophical understanding of knowledge as 'true belief'. The beliefs held by IBM regarding the potential of mainframe computers would not be classified as knowledge in the philosophical sense. As has been seen (at note 50), Fransman recognises that the management of firms will be conducted on a group basis rather than by an individual, with the 'power' relationships inevitable in groups. The knowledge and beliefs by reference to which firms are managed will be collective knowledge and beliefs.

The idea of knowledge as 'justified true belief' suggests that knowledge is an accumulation of information tried and tested for its veracity in a society, or amongst a particular group taking on responsibility for the evaluation of information. Though the adherents of knowledge of a religious nature would not accept that the endorsement of their information came from any other source but divine, the incidence of such major disparities in the knowledge derived from different divine sources, all recognised as 'justified true belief', suggests that the critical factor is the support accruing around the understanding of knowledge, in both the groups responsible for evaluation of information and the populations relying on them. The identification of what can be regarded as 'knowledge', 'truth' and 'facts' is a matter of intellectual support-bargaining. Such a process applies also to the conception of knowledge adopted by Loasby. Knowledge depends for its acceptance on the support accruing to it as knowledge. Certain procedures can assemble a body of information or knowledge that is consistent, and the accepted consistency can be used to evaluate further information. Support for these procedures and the information or knowledge they produce raises the probability that the information is part of an overall consistent assembly of information, but there will remain the possibility that information is acquired that shows particular information, or even the whole edifice of knowledge, to be mistaken. Knowledge is then, even in the sense of 'true belief', and extending to the sense of 'justified true belief', group bound. Within the IBM management they would regard their assessment of the potential of mainframe computers as both 'true belief' and 'justified true belief', and hence it would be properly designated 'knowledge' within that group. In the context of wider group understanding, the IBM group suffered from mistaken belief, and consequently lacked knowledge.

The idea of 'knowledge' as an accumulation of information associates 'knowledge' with the 'information interface'. Support-bargaining and money-bargaining are carried on in an information interface. It might be said that human interaction has always been maintained in the context of 'knowledge'. Knowledge of deities has always circumscribed the activities of individuals. What anyone believes influences their behaviour. The idea of an 'information interface', however, makes plain that the basis of human behaviour is a generally unreliable agglomeration of information designed not to establish 'truth' but to advance the interests of its creators. While an information interface is conceived mainly as a public information interface, comprising information in many forms, it will include also the information held by every individual, public only to the extent that the information is shared by others. As Richardson's personalised understanding of 'knowledge' suggests, the public information interface will merge with entirely private information interfaces. In accordance with Fransman's account of knowledge in a firm, the directors and personnel of a firm will establish a distinct corporate information interface. This corporate information interface will delineate the firm's situation and form the basis for identification of its interests and appropriate actions. It will be composed of information that is reckoned conducive to the interests of the firm, but also information conducive to the particular interests of the contributors. The prevalent understanding of the situation of the firm will be reached through support-bargaining and perpetually reviewed in the same process. The IBM management drew on fallacious information from the information interface to make their assessment of the prospects for mainframe computers. Loasby touches on this concept of an information interface when he provides as a principle of his enquiry into the use of knowledge in economic systems:

> that all action is decided in the space of representations. These representations include, for example, neural networks formed in the brain by processes which are outside our conscious control, carefully constructed formal models, maps, organisation charts, corporate strategies, conventional wisdom and locally applied rules of thumb. None are direct copies of reality; all truncate complexity and suppress uncertainty.[61]

A similar connection is apparent in Casson's comment that:

> The conventional view of the real economy is highly materialistic, and the legacy of this view is still reflected in the theory of the firm. It emphasises the flow of tangible resources such as physical products, rather than intangible resources such as information.[62]

The theory of support-bargaining and money-bargaining adds that the physical products too are known only by information, so that humans deal only with information.

Responsibility for evaluation of information and the accumulation of knowledge was commonly assigned in most societies to particular people assembled in institutions (in the organisational sense). Such institutions were invariably set up on the premise that truth derived from divine revelation. The Christian church embodied the idea of its adherents that a fundamental truth had been revealed to humanity by supernatural authority, and the enlargement of that truth was necessary to their redemption and salvation. The truth could not be attained independently of commitment to the Christian faith, and could not be pursued outside the institutional boundaries of the faith. It was not recognised that the pursuit of truth was thereby meshed with the interests of the institution responsible for its attainment. The neoclassical theory group has similarly become institutionalised in universities and other institutions of higher education, imposing its theory on scholars as a condition of advancement within the institutions.[63] By this means, what might at best be an interesting mathematical appendix to textbooks on money-bargaining became 'mainstream economics'.

The religious understanding of truth implies also a certain method for the pursuit of truth. It implies the study of texts, the contemplation of their meaning and repeated requests to the deity for further revelation. It does not involve engagement with the society around the investigators. In fact, it seemed that the more the truth-seekers were removed from society around them, the more likely they were to receive revelations of truth. Hence a monastic mode of investigation came to be recognised as the road to enlightenment. The neoclassical model, being purely mathematical, lends itself to that sort of monastic environment. Beveridge's comment quoted above (at note 8) on the nature of economic enquiry reflects this monastic heritage.

Neoclassical economics was not alone in maintaining a monastic approach to truth. The experience and tradition of religious learning has had long-lasting effects on the understanding of truth and the means of approaching truth, sustained even amidst the waning of Christian belief. Philosophers in particular have sustained the pursuit of truth in something like the form understood by Christians, though reason, deduction and logic have replaced the idea of revelation. Epistemology is concerned specifically with the nature of truth and the procedures or practices most likely to reveal it. There is the same understanding of truth as something absolute and something to be pursued as a primary target through rigorous procedures. There is a degree of institutional commitment, in that the epistemological approach is primarily associated with academic philosophers working in university departments of philosophy, though clearly this institutional element does not bound research in the way of a Catholic Church.

The influence of religious enquiry and its preoccupation with texts can be discerned also in the preoccupation of many Western philosophers, in the decades following the Second World War, with language as the key to understanding of the human relationship with the external world. Analytical philosophy involved examination and isolation of the logical structures underlying language. Like their monastic predecessors philosophers pondered the 'meaning' of texts. Rather than developing a theory of information, philosophers conceived language as the immediate subject of their enquiries into the nature of the external world and the human relationship with it. Language, rather than information, was treated as the 'interface' between human minds and external reality. The role of language is considered further in Chapter 3.

Individual knowledge and social construction

The commitment of the neoclassical economic theory group to a mathematical approach necessitated also a concept of individual decision making and action. The actors of the economic model, in so far as they are anything more than disembodied rational automatons, are assumed to be exclusively individual. It is hard to deal with human groups in mathematical terms, and even harder to deal with rational action of human groups. Individuals in religious theory groups seek salvation through their group, or the intermediation of their church. But *homo economicus* is distinctively on his own. There is no concept of 'group' in neoclassical theory.

Neoclassical individualism accorded with a general elevation of individual responsibility in the thinking of Enlightenment philosophers. The concept of human social groups, or human society, has generally been too vague for them to be approached as thinking, acting and aspiring agencies in anything more than rhetorical terms. Groups were seen more as the carriers of the authoritarianism and superstition that were opposed by Enlightenment thinkers. At worst, groups were understood in the organised form of military groups. Epistemology, starting with Descartes, was conceived in terms of an individual pursuit of truth.[64] Knowledge was accumulated by individuals, and individuals necessarily took responsibility for ensuring that their knowledge was true. Knowledge, in the sense of 'true belief', could be obtained through individual perception, memory, reason, testimony and introspection.[65] Groups could not aspire to knowledge. But while groups might not be able to have knowledge themselves, they have been of decisive importance in their endorsement and acceptance of the ideas of individuals. Societies have developed their own answers to the 'big question', in the sense that people have endorsed the views of their intellectual leaders. Religious groups acknowledged their scriptures and the views of writers on their faiths, perpetuating them through institutions. Natural scientists as a community or theory group endorse the findings of individual members through the natural scientific method approved in the community.

Individuals have, however, provided answers to the 'big question' that are notably divergent from the answers endorsed by their societies. Bishop Berkeley was concerned in the eighteenth century that the idea of the existence of material things independent of human minds posed a threat to religion. If material things existed, they might exist independently of the deity. People might put their faith in such material things, rather than in God. The Bishop argued accordingly, to the consternation of most, that there is no good reason to believe in the independent existence of material things.[66] Similarly, Immanuel Kant later questioned the existence of material things: 'Perhaps the central and most controversial thesis of the Critique of Pure Reason is that human beings experience only appearances, not things in themselves'.[67] But while Bishop Berkeley saw the rejection of materialism as likely to foster religious faith, Kant was concerned that the objects of faith might be regarded as no more than appearances. He was at pains to reconcile his philosophical speculation with his religious faith, and the faith of the Königsberg censors. That is perhaps one reason why, 'there is no such thing as the standard interpretation of Kant's transcendental idealism'. He is nevertheless recognised as, 'the central figure in modern philosophy'.[68]

Sociologists have in recent decades emphasised the role of groups or society in the accumulation of knowledge. They argue that knowledge is established through a social process. What an individual holds as knowledge is accumulated by himself or herself, but is a product also of the society in which he or she is involved. There is a social dimension to knowledge. Even 'truth' may be 'socially constructed'. 'Reality', the truth about the world and human society, may be 'socially constructed'.

Sociologists mean something more by 'social construction' than the endorsement of theories developed by individuals, as referred to above. They seem to be answering the 'big question' about the existence of an external reality: it is all 'social construction'; there is nothing else out there. The 'social construction' of 'social reality', the relationships between human beings and the institutions they create for the operation of their societies, seems plausible. One group may be in conflict with another, and each will construct its version of the conflict, and understand it as reality. Institutions such as parliaments and courts of law are established in response to the requirements of their societies and fulfil a function in those societies. Yet some take the idea of 'social construction' as covering also the 'social construction' of material reality. The idea that trees, cliffs, the sea, mountains and all those material things are constructions of 'society' is more contentious. Radical social constructionists claim that reality does not exist at all. The 'evidence' by which ordinary people recognise the existence of material things can be explained away as mere illusion. The evidence, however, remains sufficient to maintain the conviction of ordinary people, of the great majority of the human group, that there is something 'out there' beyond our minds. And if those material things exist beyond our minds, it seems possible also that there is a reality of conflict between human groups that is not entirely captured by the social constructions of the conflict that are effected by those involved or by observers. In the context of conflict, 'getting to the bottom of it' implies pushing beyond the superficial to more fundamental sources of conflict that are present but would not normally be recognised.

Latour and Woolgar argue in *Laboratory Life: The Construction of Scientific Facts* that even natural science involves the social construction of reality. Systematic observation of scientists at work in the physics laboratories of the Salk Institute was held to show that the scientists there were not in fact pursuing science in accordance with the approved 'scientific method', but were engaged in a social process of negotiation to establish what would be accepted as 'facts'.[69] Thus, even in the best laboratories the ideal of scientific method and production of secure evidence is never realised. Scientific research and scientific conclusions are matters of social engagement. Requirements for evidence may, however, be seen as implying recognition that social and personal influences may affect findings. If there were no such influences, exacting standards of evidence would not be required. Latour and Woolgar's account of social construction is discussed in the following chapter.

The sociological arguments regarding 'social construction' have been taken up by philosophers, at least to the extent of recognition that epistemology is not the purely individual matter that had previously been assumed. Alvin Goldman recognised the social content of knowledge in *Knowledge in a Social World*. He follows epistemological tradition in assuming the existence of some independent 'truth'. He also retains much of the traditional individualist approach, merely giving it a social context. Communities influence individuals in their pursuit of truth. He falls short of any distinctly 'group' concept of epistemology. Individuals are still seen as the agents of epistemological endeavour, though they work in a communal context. Goldman is initially committed to the pursuit of 'truth' in the traditional sense of something obtainable if the right procedures are adopted.[70] His approach depends significantly on finesse of linguistic expression, the honing of definitions; if the right form of words can be found, the truth will be snared. His confidence in the hunt identifiably wanes in the course of his book. His work is discussed in the following chapter and more extensively in Chapter 6.

John Searle, in *The Construction of Social Reality*, cuts to the action by insisting that there is something he calls 'collective intentionality', no matter how it comes about. It is 'collective intention', analogous to 'individual intention', that creates the social reality.[71] With 'collective intentionality', groups can pursue, act, conceive, determine over a great range of issues. Searle nevertheless confines his idea of 'social construction' to the construction of social reality, or 'social facts'; material reality, or 'brute facts', remain beyond the scope of social construction. There is an external world that societies cannot construct. Searle's ideas are pursued in the following chapter and in Chapter 6.

Whether in affirmation of an independent social and material reality, or in affirmation of 'social construction', the debates centre on the idea of 'truth': whether it is there; whether it can be attained; how it might be attained; whether it is a matter of individual attainment; or a matter of communal attainment. Truth has a magnetic attraction. The on-off approach to truth seems to derive from the very wide acceptance, including complete popular acceptance, that there exists an external world independent of our minds, whilst the analytical processes adopted and revered in Western societies can confirm no such thing.

Issues of interests

Theory makers largely regard themselves as in pursuit of truth, as opposed to advancing their interests. There is an understanding that 'theory-making' is necessarily concerned with the pursuit of truth, while anything tainted with interest is 'ideology'. The former is the proper pursuit of serious scholars, while the latter is the perfidious concoction of charlatans and politicians. Dow's comment, quoted above (at note 52), confirms the pursuit of truth, at least by conscious intention. Religious truth was pursued with no notion that interests other than that of truth could be at stake; no notion that the institutions concerned could be pursuing their own interests. Natural scientists insist on scientific method to prevent or impede natural scientists from advancing their own interests to the detriment of advances in scientific truth. Epistemologists define their work in terms of the pursuit of truth. Neoclassical economists regard themselves as so confined by the discipline of mathematics as to make them necessarily disinterested and in pursuit solely of the truth. They identify a 'positive' economics which dispassionately describes how things are and a 'normative' economics that suggests how they should be. The dividing line is difficult to define. It is widely held amongst its opponents, particularly those on the left of the political spectrum, that neoclassical theory is an ideology of the right.

While theory makers conceive themselves as above the everyday affrays of society and so devoid of interest, they may recognise that the subjects of their theory-making, ordinary people, pursue interests. People are recognised as pursuing their own advantage or the advantage of their group. Politicians and business people in particular pursue their interests. But while such motivation is recognised, the makers of theory seem generally inclined to minimise the role it plays in their theoretical formulations. There may be concern that providing a theory overtly concerned with the pursuit of interest may encourage and condone the pursuit of interest. Theories tend to be presented rather more as idealised behaviour, albeit susceptible to corruption by the interests of 'bad' people. They become, in effect, means of persuading people to act in certain ways and thereby advance the interests of society, as understood by the theory-makers. This is strongly apparent in religious theory, where the theory is intended to redeem people from the evils into which their interests draw them. Asking people to 'walk in the way of truth' is preferable to asking them to behave themselves for the good of society. The latter request inevitably invites questions about other ways in which the good of society might be understood. The influence of religious modes of thought has perpetuated an idea that theory should take the form of the pursuit of truth, on the tacit understanding that the pursuit of truth is conducive to the good of society. The main Western theory of government presents an idealised form of government under which people are assumed to pursue a 'general good', the good of their society as a whole. Politicians are castigated for acting in pursuit of their own interests, whether career advancement or higher incomes. Providing a theory of social dynamics based on interest has apparently been regarded as likely to promote social acceptance of the pursuit of self-interest.

The insouciance of academic theorists with regard to the pursuit of interest is apparent in the formulation of neoclassical economic theory. 'Rationality' and a mathematical formulation were accepted as sufficient to ensure that the theory was disinterested and dispassionate, with a clear claim to representation of the truth about human conduct. It was concerned with the pursuit of self-interest, but the rational self-interest of *homo economicus* could be seen as neutral in its morality. There could be no moral objection to reasonable behaviour. Yet the theory has plainly advanced the interests of those who favour an individualistic and competitive approach to social engagement. It is widely seen as condoning self-interested behaviour beyond anything that can be seen as rational. It is frequently reviled as a legitimation of 'greed'.

Any theory that impinges on interests, whatever the intent of its formulators, will be taken up or opposed by those whose interests are affected. Support assembles for the advance of interests, and support will assemble for or against theories that have any impact on interests. Even Charles Darwin's theory of natural selection has been adopted for the advance of interests in imperial expansion, economic competition and eugenics.

The insouciance of theorists was shaken when the question of covert pursuit of interest was plainly asserted. All decent people were shocked at the assertion by Karl Marx that economic and social theory was a tool for the advance of the interests of the ruling class. Perhaps much of the shock to decent people lay in the fact that someone should assert something which was already an uneasy suspicion. Marx gave voice to something better left unsaid as far as most people were concerned, especially as the ruling class included religious leaders. He put into theory something that theorists had hitherto tried to exclude. Moreover, Marx's theory explicitly encouraged bad behaviour. The shock of the pursuit of interest in the formulation of theory was compounded by the even more shocking idea that the interest of the industrial proletariat lay in the violent overthrow of the ruling class. Marx's theory marked the introduction of human interest as a central element in the formal understanding of economic and social behaviour.

But it did so whilst remaining still, according to its author, within the traditional concept of theory-making as the pursuit of truth. Marx was insistent that, while existing theory was a conspiracy to protect the interests of the ruling class, his own theory was nothing less than truth. Marx claimed that his 'science' of historical determination proved beyond doubt that his predictions would be realised. Resistance was therefore futile. Marx demanded that he be understood as a theorist of the traditional kind, set apart from the social fray, endowed with the god-like status of observer and disinterested interpreter of social processes. But at the same time he presented himself as champion of the interests of industrial workers and wholly immersed in their struggle. His theory was 'the truth', but, like other theories, it was also going to do good. As with religious theory, Marx's theory implied a commitment to certain actions. Whilst it might be accepted that theory is created by the ruling class to advance its interests, there is plainly need also for modification to encompass the creation of theory by those intent on ruling.

Karl Mannheim recognised as a generalisation that theories were formed in accordance with the interests of their makers. He nevertheless did not deny the magnetism of truth. He favoured the monastic mode of enquiry. Hope for the identification of truth lay in the existence of persons set apart from the interests of society. He suggested that the truth about society might be attained through a 'socially unattached intelligentsia'.[72] As they had done in religious institutions, selected scholars might be set apart from society and charged with the identification of truth about society. It is another expression of the idea of the disinterested onlooker observing, reporting and interpreting the doings of society. The theory itself, coming from a scholar, rather demonstrates the generality of the influence of interest on the making of theory.[73]

The pursuit of interests other than those in truth constitutes the chief impediment to the pursuit of truth. The pursuit of non-truth interests causes people to spread false and misleading information. The accumulation of knowledge is radically complicated by the potential for systematic accumulation of false knowledge designed to advance interests. The best hope for attaining truth must lie in circumstances in which interest is interest in truth, with no non-truth interest involved.

But interest in truth for its own sake seems of no account. Useless truth would not be worth a moment's pursuit. The search for truth carries an implication that knowing the truth is itself a matter of interest. The pursuit of truth necessarily starts from the identification of interest. If we had no interests to advance, we would not know whether to seek the truth regarding the velocity of a bug crossing a minor track in a rural wasteland of the Asian steppe, or to seek the truth regarding the velocity of a vehicle approaching us on a highway which we are about to cross. Pursuit of truth is necessarily selective in accordance with interest. Human pursuit of interest is fundamental to the survival of the species and fundamental to the social behaviour of the species. For all our curiosity, our 'interest' in the sense of attracting our attention, each of us knows only a tiny part of the reality or truth that surrounds us, because only a tiny part impinges on our interests, in the sense of giving us advantage. The idea that truth is important independent of interests arises only because some interests are so obvious as to be scarcely worth identification. If certain plants are poisonous, we need to know about them. If certain actions entail eternal damnation, we need to know them. We instinctively know our basic interests and pursue truth accordingly.

The omission of any process of selection in epistemological enquiry may be another inheritance from monastic modes of enquiry. In that tradition, the scriptures defined the proper objects of enquiry. The pursuit of truth began with the scriptures. If eternal damnation was a real prospect, we needed to know how to avoid it. There was no question of selecting what might be of interest. Hence the later assumption that the subjects of enquiry were not selected but given, and consequently no mechanism of selection had to be identified.

There remains a tendency for academics in general to assume themselves above the social fray, inheritors of the traditional status of ecclesiastical scholars, or adherents of a secular scientific disinterest, able to interpret dispassionately the behaviour of humanity. For the most part, they conceive themselves as onlookers and commentators rather than players. Academic debate is generally couched in the neutral terms of logic and reason. This does not, however, prevent the emergence of particular groups or 'schools' of thought, each very often recognisably associated with interests of 'right' or 'left', individual or group. Each school tends to select what it will debate in accordance with its ideological reference. The schools may clash on ostensibly technical grounds, but the animosities generated are often those of political faction.

The distinction between 'onlookers' and 'players' depends on the understanding of the 'game'. In this loose informal verbal context, the common assumption is that the 'game' is a matter of politics and social advancement, or the pursuit of wealth in business or other employment. In terms of conventional understanding, scholars are onlookers. Their theories, however, assemble support, and support is the vital requirement for advancement of political interest. Those who assemble support, whether churchmen, politicians, trade unionists or academics, are involved in politics. If Mannheim's 'disinterested intelligentsia' assembles support, as it must if it is to sustain itself, then it is part of a political process. Those who create theories necessarily assemble support, and support is the bargaining counter of politics. It is then scarcely any distinguishable step, and perhaps no step at all, to creating theories for the express purpose of assembling support.

The distinction depends also on the understanding of 'interests'. If scholars are engaged in a single-minded search for the truth, and are institutionally insulated in monasteries or universities so as to relieve them of any quotidian interests of politics, business, or daily bread, then it would seem that they have an interest only in the revelation of truth. It may then seem irrelevant, or even insulting, to suggest that they are pursuing personal interests in income, appointments and promotions. But observation and experience of human behaviour in all walks of life suggests that these personal concerns are major determinants of behaviour. Even the scientists studied by Latour and Woolgar at the Salk Institute were pursuing career interests. Even the scholars referred to by Simon in debate over a new curriculum were pursuing career interests. However devoted people may be to the pursuit of truth, they must still acquire the necessities of life. Most will have an interest in something more than the necessities. It was suggested in the Introduction that the mainstream economic theory group is sustained by such group and personal interests.

The importance of information to the pursuit of interest is apparent in the copious information collected and disseminated by media of all kinds. If a solid theory of information were to be developed anywhere, it might be expected to derive from the sphere of social activity specifically concerned with the dissemination of information. An information age needs a theory of information. Yet the absence of any idea of support-bargaining has meant that no strong theory of information has been formed. Media theory consists of little more than the gnomic aphorism of Marshall McLuhan, that 'the medium is the message'. If the function of theory is to explain phenomena of the world, then McLuhan's theory constitutes anti-theory, since it positively reduces our understanding of the nature and effects of information. His theory is considered further in Chapter 8.

Notes

1 Langbein, John H., 1996, 'Historical foundations of the law of evidence: a view from the Ryder sources', *Columbia Law Review*, Vol. 96, No. 5, pp. 1168–1202, p. 1170.

2 The theory of money-bargaining was first set out in Spread, Patrick, 1984a, *A Theory of Support and Money Bargaining*, London: Macmillan. On the dominance of mathematical economics, see Backhouse, Roger E., 1993, *Economists and the Economy: The Evolution of Economic Ideas*, London: Transaction, p. 196. See also Spread, Patrick, 2016a, *The Evolution of Economies: Money-Bargaining, Economic Change and Industrial Revolution*, Abingdon: Routledge, pp. ix, 9–11.

3 On the characteristics of the neoclassical model, see: Spread, Patrick, 2004, *Getting It Right: Economics and the Security of Support*, Sussex: Book Guild, pp. 12–15, 33–4; Spread, Patrick, 2008, *Support-Bargaining: The Mechanics of Democracy Revealed*, Sussex: Book Guild, pp. 71–3, 103–7, 191–205, 242–73, etc.; Spread, Patrick, 2013, *Support-Bargaining, Economics and Society: A Social Species*, Abingdon: Routledge, pp. 170–1, 190–5, 206–8, 232–3, etc.

4 Beveridge, William, 1937, 'The place of the social sciences in human knowledge', *Politica*, Vol. 2, No. 9, September, pp. 459–79; Farewell Address as Director of the London School of Economics and Political Science, 24 June 1937.

5 Keynes, John Maynard, 1961, *The General Theory of Employment, Interest and Money*, London: Macmillan; New York: St. Martin's Press. First published 1936.

6 Beveridge, 1937, p. 464.

7 Beveridge, 1937, p. 465.

8 Beveridge, 1937, pp. 465–6.

9 Spread, 2016a, pp. 220–43.

10 Stigler, George J., 1971, 'The economics of information', in Lamberton, Don M. (ed.), 1971, *Economics of Information and Knowledge*, London: Penguin, p. 61. Original emphasis. First published 1961, *Journal of Political Economy*, Vol. 69, No. 3, pp. 213–25. For further comment on Stigler's article see Spread, 1984a, paras 3.19–44.

11 Akerlof, George and Shiller, Robert, 2015, *Phishing for Phools*, Princeton: Princeton University Press, p. 164.

12 Akerlof and Shiller, 2015, p. 5. Emphasis added by Akerlof and Shiller.

13 Akerlof and Shiller, 2015, p. 6.

14 Smith, Adam, 2009, *An Inquiry into the Nature and Causes of the Wealth of Nations*, Project Gutenberg Ebook, Adobe Digital Editions, p. 325. First published 1776.

15 Coase, Ronald H., 1937, 'The nature of the firm', *Economica*, New Series, Vol. 4., No. 16, pp. 386–405.

16 On Coase's theory, see Spread, Patrick, 2004, *Getting It Right: Economics and the Security of Support*, Sussex: Book Guild, pp. 58–66; see also Spread, Patrick, 2016a, *The Evolution of Economies: Money-Bargaining, Economic Change and Industrial Revolution*, Abingdon: Routledge, pp. 83–5.

17 Fransman, Martin, 1994, 'Information, knowledge, vision and theories of the firm', *Industrial and Corporate Change*, Vol. 3, No. 3, pp. 713–57, esp. p. 713.

18 Fransman, 1994, p. 714.

19 Alchian, Armen A. and Demsetz, Harold, 1972, 'Production, information costs, and economic organization', *The American Economic Review*, Vol. 62, No. 5, pp. 777–95. See Fransman, 1994, pp. 718–19.

20 Jensen, Michael and Meckling, William, 1976, 'Theory of the firm: managerial behaviour, agency costs, and ownership structure', *The Journal of Financial Economics*, Vol. 3, No. 4, pp. 305–60. See Fransman, 1994, pp. 719–20.

21 Coase, 1937. See Fransman, 1994, pp. 720–3.

22 Simon, Herbert A., 1957, *Models of Man: Social and Rational: Mathematical Essays on Rational Human Behavior in a Social Setting*, New York: Wiley; Simon, Herbert A., 1997, *Administrative Behaviour: A Study of Decision-Making Processes in Administrative Organizations*, Fourth Edition, New York: Free Press. First published 1947, New York: Macmillan. See Fransman, 1994, pp. 725–31.

23 Williamson, Oliver E., 1987, *The Economic Institutions of Capitalism*, New York: Free Press, p. 30. See Fransman, 1994, pp. 723–5.

24 Nelson, Richard R. and Winter, Sidney G., 1982, *An Evolutionary Theory of Economic Change*, Cambridge, MA: The Belknap Press. See Fransman, 1994, pp. 735–6.

25 For further discussion of Fransman's article and theories of the firm, see Spread, Patrick, 2016b, 'Companies and markets: economic theories of the firm and a concept of companies as bargaining agencies', *Cambridge Journal of Economics*, Vol. 40, No. 3, pp. 727–53.
26 Molho, Ian, 2001, *The Economics of Information: Lying and Cheating in Markets and Organisations*, Oxford: Blackwell, pp. 6–8.
27 Molho, 2001, p. 5.
28 Simon, 1957. Simon, 1997. For earlier discussion of bounded rationality, see Spread, 1984a, paras 3.94–106.
29 Simon, 1997, p. 119.
30 Simon, 1997, p. 119. See also March, James and Simon, Herbert, 1993, *Organisations*, Oxford: Blackwell Business, p. 190. First published 1958, New York: Wiley.
31 Simon, Herbert A., 1983, *Reason in Human Affairs*, Stanford: Stanford University Press, pp. 20–1.
32 Spread, Patrick, 2011, Situation as determinant of selection and valuation', *Cambridge Journal of Economics*, Vol. 35, No. 2, pp. 335–56. Reprinted in Spread, Patrick, 2015b, *Aspects of Support-Bargaining and Money-Bargaining*, E-Book, World Economics Association.
33 Spread, 2016a, p. ix.
34 Hayek, Friedrich A., 1952, *The Sensory Order, An Enquiry into the Foundations of Theoretical Psychology*, Chicago: University of Chicago Press, p. 179. On the idea of 'frames of reference', see also Sherif, Muzafer, 1936, *The Psychology of Social Norms*, New York: Harper & Brothers; Goffman, Irving, 1974, *Frame Analysis: An Essay on the Organisation of Experience*, Cambridge MA: Harvard University Press; Spread, Patrick, 2008, *Support-Bargaining: The Mechanics of Democracy Revealed*, Sussex: Book Guild, Chapter 11: Frames and echoes.
35 Cf. Simon, 1983, p. 85.
36 On symmetry, see Spread, 2013, Chapter 10: Social Symmetries.
37 Molho, 2001, pp. 61–80.
38 Spence, Michael, 1973, 'Job market signalling', *Quarterly Journal of Economics*, Vol. 87, No. 3, pp. 355–74. For further discussion of Spence's theory see Spread, Patrick, 2015a, 'Asymmetric information, critical information and the information interface', *Real-World Economics Review*, Issue 70, pp. 121–40, ref: pp. 132–3. Reprinted in Spread, 2015b.
39 Akerlof, George A., 1970, 'The market for "lemons": quality uncertainty and the market mechanism', *Quarterly Journal of Economics*, Vol. 84, No. 3, pp. 488–500.
40 Stigler, 1971, p. 79.
41 Molho, 2001, p. 20.
42 Richardson, George B., 1990, *Information and Investment: A Study in the Working of the Competitive Economy*, Second Edition, Oxford: Oxford University Press, pp. 32–5. First published 1960.
43 Foss, Nicolai and Loasby, Brian (eds), 2013, *Economic Organization, Capabilities and Coordination: Essays in Honour of G. B. Richardson*, Abingdon: Routledge, Introduction; electronic resource, Bodleian Library, Oxford.
44 Phlips, Louis, 1988, *The Economics of Imperfect Information*, Cambridge: Cambridge University Press, pp. 4, 6.
45 Casson, Mark, 2000, 'An entrepreneurial theory of the firm', in Foss, Nicolai and Mahuke, Volker (eds), 2000, *Competence, Governance and Entrepreneurship*, Oxford: Oxford University Press, pp. 116–45.
46 Lamberton, Don M. (ed.), 1996, *The Economics of Communication and Information*, Cheltenham: Edward Elgar.

47 Simon, 1983, p. 82.
48 Spread, 2016b pp. 727–53. Reprinted in Spread, 2015b. See also Spread, 2008, Chapter 4: 'Functions and Format'.
49 On hierarchies, see Spread, 2008, pp. 135–40; Spread, 2013, Chapter 3: 'Power and Hierarchy'; Spread, 2016a, p. 29.
50 Fransman, 1994, pp. 730–1.
51 Spread, 2008, pp. 135–40; Spread, 2016b, p. 746.
52 Dow, Sheila, 2017, 'How far are economists purveyors of fake news?', Annual Conference of the Institute for New Economic Thinking, October, available at: www.ineteconomics.org/research/research-papers/how-far-are-economists-purveyors-of-fake-news. Accessed 12 January 2018.
53 See Fransman, 1994, p. 714; Loasby, Brian, 1999, *Knowledge, Institutions and Evolution in Economics*, Abingdon: Routledge, p. 1; Phlips, 1988, p. 2; Molho, 2001, p. 55.
54 Lancaster, Kelvin J., 1981, 'Information and product differentiation', in Galatin, Malcolm and Leiter, Robert D., 1981, *The Economics of Information*, The Hague, London: Martinus Nijhoff Publishing.
55 Phlips, 1988, p. 2.
56 Richardson, George B., 1998, *The Economics of Imperfect Knowledge: Collected Papers of G. B. Richardson*, Cheltenham: Edward Elgar, p. 1.
57 Loasby, 1999, p. 2. Loasby's reference: Popper, Karl, 1963, *Conjectures and Refutations*, London: Routledge and Kegan Paul.
58 Fransman, 1994, p. 737.
59 Fransman, 1994, p. 755.
60 Fransman, 1994, p. 755.
61 Loasby, 1999, p. 10.
62 Casson, 2000, p. 116.
63 See, for example, Earl, Peter E. (ed.), 2002, *Information, Opportunism and Economic Coordination*, Cheltenham: Edward Elgar, Introduction.
64 Goldman, Alvin I., 2003, *Knowledge in a Social World*, Oxford: Clarendon Press, p. 4. See also Goldman, Alvin and Blanchard, Thomas, 2016, 'Social epistemology', in Zalta, Edward N. (ed.), 2016, *The Stanford Encyclopedia of Philosophy*, Summer Edition, Introduction. Available at: http://plato.stanford.edu/archives/sum2016/entries/epistemology-social.
65 Steup, Matthias, 2014, 'Epistemology', in Zalta, Edward N. (ed.), *The Stanford Encyclopedia of Philosophy*, Spring Edition, 4. Sources of Knowledge and Justification. Available at: http://plato.stanford.edu/archives/spr2014/entries/epistemology.
66 Downing, Lisa, 2016, 'George Berkeley', in Zalta, Edward N. (ed.), *The Stanford Encyclopedia of Philosophy*, Summer Edition, 2. Berkeley's critique of materialism in the *Principles* and *Dialogues*. Available at: http://plato.stanford.edu/archives/sum2016/entries/berkeley.
67 Rohlf, Michael, 2016, 'Immanuel Kant', in Zalta, Edward N. (ed.), *The Stanford Encyclopedia of Philosophy*, Spring Edition, 3. Transcendental Idealism. Available at: http://plato.stanford.edu/archives/spr2016/entries/kant.
68 Rohlf, 2016, Introduction.
69 Latour, Bruno and Woolgar, Steve, 1986, *Laboratory Life: The Construction of Scientific Facts*, Princeton: Princeton University Press. First published 1979, Sage Publications. See also Goldman, Alvin, 2010, 'Social epistemology', in Zalta, Edward N. (ed.), *The Stanford Encyclopedia of Philosophy*, Summer Edition, 1. History of Social Epistemology. Available at: http://plato.stanford.edu/archives/sum2010/entries/epistemology-social.
70 Goldman, 2003, pp. 4–5.

71 Searle, John R., 1996, *The Construction of Social Reality*, London: Penguin, p. 23–6.
72 Mannheim, Karl, 1936, *Ideology and Utopia: An Introduction to the Sociology of Knowledge*, trans. Louis Worth and Edward Shils, London: Harcourt, pp. 154–6.
73 For discussion of Mannheim's theory, see Spread, Patrick, 2015d, 'Intellectual support-bargaining and Mannheim's conjectures on a science of politics', in Spread, Patrick, 2016b.

2 Support-bargaining and the information interface

It was seen in the previous chapter that philosophers and sociologists have generally pursued issues concerning information and knowledge in the context of a quest for 'the truth' about an external world, a world beyond human minds. This approach was seen as deriving from ecclesiastical tradition in which truth was very distinctly bound up with the nature of a supernatural being and might be reached through the study of scriptures regarded as deriving from God. Scholars sought the answers to the 'big question' of what lay beyond human experience.

Support-bargaining and money-bargaining are concerned instead with the great range of transactions through which individuals relate to each other and through which societies are governed. The interest lies not in the 'big question' but in the many interests that people pursue both on a day-to-day basis and with broader concern for the conduct of their societies. The day-to-day questions concern interests such as: What is the weather like in London? What time does the bus go to Oxford on a Thursday? Why did the plants die in our neighbour's garden? The interests of broader concern are such as: What are the best economic arrangements to benefit everyone? Should the state provide bus services? The 'big question' is set aside for engagement with many smaller questions, and the question of 'truth' comes down to truths about these many smaller concerns. People pursuing their interests have to work out what they can and cannot believe with regard to the many minor transactions that must be concluded to meet their interests.

The 'big question' loses its prominence. Those who are interested will consider it, but the questions over information and the role of information in society are overwhelmingly those that arise in the conduct of ordinary everyday affairs. The traditional concerns of philosophers and sociologists over information and knowledge scarcely impinge at all on the understanding of information in the context of a support-bargaining and money-bargaining system. Information is used for bargaining and manipulated for bargaining advantage.

The 'big question' becomes peripheral also for a more fundamental reason: in the idea of support-bargaining and money-bargaining we have only information, the stuff our brains deal with, and anything beyond is simply unknowable. Ideas may be formed about the nature of the external world from the experience we have of it. Large and influential, even dominant, groups may be formed on the basis of ideas about the world beyond our minds. But such a world is fundamentally unknowable. We know only the information we assemble and evaluate in our minds. The main reason for maintaining interest in the 'big question' is perhaps no more than that the need for an answer has led to the formation of such large and assertive groups.

The many small questions about 'truth' and 'reality' arise from the transactional view of social intercourse in support-bargaining. People are constantly trying to evaluate the pros and cons of different transactions, and need reliable information to do so. The sweeping role of an information interface can be recognised only in the context of a support-bargaining and money-bargaining system. This is the reason why so little attention has been given to issues of information in the social sciences, and why the attention given has been so deficient in advancing understanding of the role of information. While those concerned with the nature of 'information and knowledge' saw their interests as wholly bound up with salvation in a life after death, it was naturally understood that any useful information and knowledge would relate to this interest. Theory regarding the transactions of the economic sphere developed in a way that set aside any concern with information. Information issues were matters of abstruse philosophy, so their exclusion from economic theory was tolerated. But a transactional view of social intercourse, using both support and money as bargaining counters, reveals the full requirements for information, the sort of information that is required, the scope for manipulation of information, and hence the role of an information interface in societies.

The advance of many interests depends on their being recognised as communal interests. This means assembling communal support in favour of those interests. Support-bargaining is concerned with the assembly of support for interests. This can be a matter of assembly of support for immediate interest, but it involves also the assembly of support for ideas that will facilitate the assembly of support for other interests. If people can be induced to support broad ideas, then they will support many interests associated with those broad ideas. If you can get people to support the idea of the efficacy of 'free markets', then many interests will be advanced under that commitment. If people can be induced to accept the idea that communal services are best provided by communal agencies, then state-run bus services are likely to be accorded support.

The day-to-day interests, like the time of the bus to Oxford, or weather in London, seem simple matters of fact, posing few threats of contention. But they can still be distorted. Someone may give the time of a particular bus service and withhold another, because the former is more profitable to them. Someone may exaggerate the clemency of the weather in London to encourage the enquirer to travel to London. The death of plants in a neighbour's garden may be attributed to malicious actions by another neighbour. The truth, or 'facts', are always likely to be distorted by the desire to advance interests other than the truth. To get at the truth, there is often little option but to accept the information that is best supported. People seek corroborative evidence when in doubt about the truth of what they are told. The critical factor to acceptance of truth is the assembly of support, whether it be the support of a scientific community for scientific facts, or the support of ordinary people regarding the need for a better bus service. The information bound up with these questions and answers, distorted and conflicted because of the interests involved, constitutes the information interface in which support-bargaining and money-bargaining is carried on.

The pursuit of interest is the core motivation in support-bargaining and money-bargaining, with information manipulated for the advance of interest. The concern is then with what information can be accepted and what cannot be accepted; what can and cannot be believed. Those engaged in support-bargaining and money-bargaining have to determine what they will accept as 'true'; what they will accept as 'reality'. They have to identify 'hard facts' from what are presented as 'facts'. They have to distinguish fact from fiction, realism from fantasy, honesty from deception. These issues are considered further in Chapter 6. Scientific method is seen as a procedure adopted by a specific group aimed at eliminating the influence of non-truth interests in the identification of what is true about certain mainly material phenomena. People in general use a makeshift form of scientific method to sift what is most likely true from what is most likely false. They assemble information repetitively from their own observation and experience, and compare information deriving from the observations of different individuals and groups. The aim, as with scientific method in its strict form, is to assemble an information interface in which each element of information is consistent with all other elements.

The importance of support to the advance of interests and even to the definitions of truth that will prevail in a society lies in its importance to every individual. While the pursuit of interest is the core motivation of support-bargaining, the pursuit of support can be regarded as a yet more fundamental motivation, since it is itself an immediate interest, and is also the key to advancement of other interests. Every individual needs the support of associates. Support is essential to the psychological well-being of all individuals and in violent circumstances essential to their physical survival. The need for support stems from a sense of insecurity arising from a human instinct for self-preservation in circumstances that were and are easily understood as threatening. It was suggested in *Support-Bargaining, Economics and Society* that Darwin underestimated the importance of the human instinct for self-preservation and, consequently, was unable to explain the group formation that he clearly understood as vital to human survival.[1] Darwin identified the biological evolution of the human species through the advantages of physical attributes to an aggressive predator, but he overlooked the biological–psychological element in evolution that made it possible for humans to form the groups necessary to survival. The instinct for self-preservation and the associated propensity to seek support are psychological traits, but they no doubt originate from some biological structure of the brain, or some genetic coding, and are consequently fundamentally biological.[2] Support maintains from these origins an association with violence.

Assembly of support consequently influences behaviour. People instinctively defer to high levels of support. People advance their interests through assembly of support.

Our interests derive from our situation or circumstances. Our instincts seem naturally in many cases to take into account our circumstances. Under threat from an approaching vehicle, we jump out of the way. This capacity to assess a situation and act accordingly would have been important to survival of the species. More considered assessment of interest is also based on situation. We buy houses with reference to the size of our family and the available budget. We may also buy with reference to the location of our employment. This situation-related assessment of interest is central to support-bargaining and money-bargaining.[3]

Given this importance of situation, it is clearly important also that we can assess the truth about our situation. We need to judge realistically the velocity of an approaching vehicle. The survival of many groups must in the past have depended often on an accurate understanding of the terrain around them and the location of animal or other threats. Our interests will very commonly involve a contiguous interest in the truth about the matters we have in hand. When foraging for food, we need to know which plants are edible and which are poisonous. Parents teach their children survival skills which are in large part concerned with such truth about the world around them as is relevant to their survival. We need to know also the commonplace truths about products and services we propose to buy, and whether 'a bargain' is really a bargain.

Interest, however, is not necessarily advanced by truth. Interest may bring about distortion even of something so apparently plain as the weather in London. Personal interest can be advanced by manipulation of information and outright falsehood. People seeking jobs, promotion or prestigious appointments may edit the record of their lives to present themselves in such a way as to emphasise their suitability for what is on offer. They will claim a major role in a successful enterprise, when in reality their role may have been minor. They will claim, if they claim any role at all, a minor role in an unsuccessful enterprise when they may have been an essential contributor to its failure. When the need arises, people may spread false accounts of the capacities and integrity of rivals.

Given the importance of groups and group cohesion, human interests may at times be better served by collective illusion, if that helps to maintain the cohesion of the group. In August 2014 large numbers of people in many parts of the world marked the centenary of the outbreak of the First World War. Most of the societies and armies engaged in that conflict, on both sides, maintained their cohesion partly through common adherence to Christianity. The centenary was marked in many countries by ceremonies of Christian faith. Yet large numbers of people in the old heartlands of Christianity question the truth or realism of that faith. It may be no more than texts, statues, structures, icons, paintings, costumes and ritual constituting an information interface that may or may not have a reality behind it. People take it for reality when it may be no more than information interface. On the face of it, the god portrayed in the information interface would not permit the carnage of the Great War. Yet the cohesion of the groups, past and present, seems to require that the nations keep faith with the information interface that sustained the courage and commitment of the combatants.

Natural science and support-bargaining

It was suggested in the previous chapter that the natural sciences have been seen in the modern era as providing the most reliable 'window on the world'. The wonders of natural scientific discovery give the very secure impression that secrets of the 'real world', the world beyond human minds, have been unlocked. The procedures of 'scientific method' seemed to be genuinely effective in providing information independent of human involvement. But as was also seen, Bruno Latour and Steve Woolgar, in their study *Laboratory Life: The Construction of Scientific Facts*, question whether scientists did actually use scientific method to unlock secrets of 'the real world' in the way they claim (Chapter 1, p. 35). The process seemed much more like a 'social construction of facts'. As part of this social construction Latour and Woolgar assess the interests of individual scientists in terms of 'Cycles of Credit'.[4] Much of the assessment is based on the sociological understanding of 'group norms' – behavioural characteristics that are accepted in the group. The 'orthodox' expectation would be that scientists conform to the 'norms' of science, but this is not necessarily what motivates scientists. They ought to follow carefully and with total transparency the procedures that constitute scientific method. But scientists do not act in that way. They have other motivations.

> One way to answer these questions [regarding what motivates scientists] is to postulate norms impressed upon the scientist during his training and silently enforced during his subsequent career . . . however, attempts to derive the existence of norms from the kind of material available to us are prone to major difficulties. In particular, we were unable to identify explicit appeal to the norms of science except in very few instances. Some of these more nearly constituted an appeal to counternorms (Mitroff, 1974): 'everyone pushes ones' own stuff, it's normal – Normal? – I mean human (IV, 57)'.[5]

It becomes clear that a large part of the motivation of the scientists is the same as that which drives most other people – they advance their own careers. An aspect of the 'credit' that is acquired is the credit that goes towards building reputation and hence the prospects for promotion or moving elsewhere to better positions. In terms of support-bargaining, it is the accumulation of support that will bring about the accommodation of interest – that is, career advancement. Appointments committees and recruiters will elevate those who have won their support and who are known to have won support across the communities in which they are required to operate.

It is the strength of this concern for personal advancement that makes necessary the insistence on procedures of scientific method designed implicitly to neutralise the pursuit of private interest. Before principles of scientific method had become established, in the infancy of empirical research, scientists sought to offset the potential distortions of personal interests by social means. The strict world of scientific endeavour may have originated partly in the social world of gentlemanly conduct, at least in Britain. In *A Social History of Truth*, Steven Shapin writes in the Introduction:

> One argument contained here has some chance of being visible as straightforwardly historical. It is a claim about the *origins* of the practice known as English experimental philosophy. I say that this new culture emerged partly through the purposeful relocation of the conventions, codes, and values of gentlemanly conversation into the domain of natural philosophy.

A particular social group in Britain developed a code of behaviour that required its members to be truthful, on pain of expulsion from the group: 'I draw particular attention to the role of truthfulness and mendacity in this culture. The relevant literature indicates a special relationship between the idea of a gentleman and the idea of truth-telling'.[6] Harnessing the need for scientific integrity to the cultural conventions of a social group meant that the scientific interest would potentially be protected by the social practices that sustained the group culture. If a scientist acted improperly, he would be subject to the withdrawal of support by his social group – the same sanction as protected the group culture. Of course, the protection would be no more dependable in the scientific context than it was in the cultural context. But a 'gentleman' had something important to lose if he were caught cheating.

Scientists, like people in other walks of life, have different degrees of personal career ambition. But in certain spheres of natural science, most notably where the boundaries of science are most conspicuously being pushed back, there is intense competition between scientists. The requirement is to be first in the field with new discoveries, whether as a claim to 'immortality', a claim to a prestigious prize, a claim to a potentially lucrative patent or a claim to a coveted position. The rewards are fame, position, income, deference – broadly speaking the pleasures of support and the enjoyment of material advantages that commonly accompany support. The 'second prizes' are notably less attractive than the first prizes. The history of the revelation of the structure of the genome illustrates the competitive nature of scientific research in the 'immortality stakes'.[7] In academia more generally there is a 'dolce vita' for the most prominent in their fields that, for many, is worth the strategic effort in intellectual support-bargaining.[8]

It is not only career interests that are pursued as personal interests in support-bargaining. People have interests in maintaining the support of their family and friends. Historically people in important positions were expected to assist their family and friends to 'preferment'. The 'democratisation' movement of the past century and more has seen advancement by 'merit' as essential to the wider distribution of social advantages, though people are still inclined to help their friends. As well as the returns of friendship, there is less risk in employing friends, greater prospect of loyalty, and potentially greater fun. There tend to form in all walks of life – political parties, national government, local government, the law, the military, business sectors, the media, show-business, academia and so on – circles of people who maintain social contact as well as professional contact with each other and who will do each other favours. In authoritarian systems this readily turns into the system dubbed 'crony capitalism' in which the ruler helps friends and relations to jobs, contracts, licences, concessions, houses, subsidies and other advantages. It is an identifiable technique of rule. In business circles friends at the heights of the hierarchies ensure through executive remuneration committees that the rewards of their exertions are bountiful. Even in an open political support-bargaining system such as is operative in the United Kingdom there are frequent accusations of preference given to insiders. The 'Westminster village', or those inside the 'Westminster bubble', look after friends, family and neighbours. Old school and university pals of the prominent may fare better than equally or even more meritorious strangers. Political, social and intellectual support-bargaining networks intertwine, and intertwine with money-bargaining networks, to shape the evolution of societies. Support-bargaining and money-bargaining are powered by interests and, while the support-bargaining process generates support for designations, both informal and legally formal, of certain spheres as appropriate to political support-bargaining, other spheres as appropriate to social support-bargaining, and other spheres as appropriate to money-bargaining, it is not always feasible to enforce such designations, so that the different modes of bargaining, and the different bargaining counters, become intermixed. Breach of the legal designations involves formal penalties on conviction. The informal designations may involve a degree of tolerance, but those going beyond the tolerance may be subject to social sanctions.

One of the most momentous outcomes of support-bargaining for the advance of interest has been the creation of money and the practice of 'money-bargaining'. Money constitutes a visible, material, precise and divisible bargaining counter, functionally superior in many transactions to 'support'. Being useful, it gets the support of those who use it in a society, and hence its use is sustained. It permits engagement in a money-bargaining process that has a dynamic similar to that of support-bargaining. The role of money is considered further in Chapter 4.

Intellectual support-bargaining

It was noted in the previous chapter that while scholars tend to regard themselves as onlookers rather than players in social affairs, their assembly of support in validation of their theories necessarily means that they have significance for political support-bargaining. Support assembles on the basis of theories, ideas and information. Any agent who contributes to the information interface is necessarily a participant in a support-bargaining process. The 'intellectual' aspect of support-bargaining is specifically concerned with the assembly of support through deployment of information and ideas. As was seen above, if people can be induced to adopt certain ideas, they will be inclined to give their support to measures consistent with those ideas. Hence establishing ideas in a community is a means of advancing interests in the community. These ideas constitute crucial components of the information interface since they are crucial to the assembly of support. In its purest form, 'intellectual support-bargaining' is the process of theory-making in institutions of higher education, though in adulterated forms it pervades support-bargaining. Political support-bargaining depends heavily on support accumulated for ideas through an intellectual support-bargaining process centred around government, in civil services and in the media, as well as drawing on the theories created in universities. The scholars who, on the monastic model, are disinterested onlookers and commentators on the behaviour of humanity, are active participants in the assembly and direction of support through their contributions to the information interface.

The support-bargaining process is basically a matter of implicit or unconscious 'negotiation' between individuals who need support and groups that depend for their influence or authority on maintenance of a cohesive membership. Individuals want support on their terms; groups want the support of individuals on their terms. Support-bargaining brings about the necessary compromise. In a political context the assembly of support becomes more conscious and contrived. In the academic context it is conducted more on the assumption that all those involved are engaged exclusively in a search for 'the truth', or explanations consistent with what is observed. The interest in truth may, however, be substantially diverted by the assembly of support for theories and ideas formulated for the advancement of non-truth interests. This is the counterpart in the academic context of the distortion of simple day-to-day truths, like the weather in London, by incidence of other interests. It is the counterpart too of the preference for friends over the meritorious. 'Truth' is endlessly compromised by interests of self-advancement, friendship and loyalty; compromised too by enmity and grudges; and by pursuit of monetary gain. In the political sphere, truth is notoriously corrupted in the competition for support between political parties.

The conflict of truth with friendship is well illustrated in intellectual support-bargaining by an account of a macroeconomic research group by Paul Romer.[9] Romer was for many years at the centre of economic research as the leading exponent of 'endogenous growth theory'.[10] In 2016 he left academia to become Chief Economist in the World Bank. Moving out of an academic theory group left him free to reflect on his academic experience. His account of the research in growth theory confirms that Joseph Stiglitz and Paul Krugman, as described in the Introduction, are not rare amongst economists in attaching greater importance to group loyalty than to sound theory. Romer records his disillusion with the techniques employed by researchers on Dynamic Stochastic General Equilibrium (DSGE). He describes econometricians feeding what they call 'priors' into their models and treating them as if they were true, so as to get the expected results.[11] Romer designates these priors as 'factors with uncertain truth values' (FWUTVs). In a section headed 'Loyalty can corrode the norms of science', he cites three leading exponents of mathematical macroeconomics as pursuing their own friendships at the expense of the quality of their research. The concern for group cohesion and the maintenance of social support within the group is given precedence over the pursuit of the truth about macroeconomic relationships that is the public purpose of the theory group. In a relatively small group isolated by the esoteric nature of its research the members can determine for themselves what they will proclaim as 'true' and acceptable. Provided they remain cohesive, no one is in a position to contradict them. Only when an ex-member of the group, such as Romer, chooses to remonstrate on the neglect of the avowed purpose of the group and the preferences adopted within the group is it possible for outsiders to see how the group has diverted its attentions from its presumed objectives.

Romer mocks the approach as 'post-real',[12] though the post-real era started at the end of the nineteenth century with the formulation of the neoclassical economic model. It degenerated into analytical fantasy with the formulation of the Arrow-Debreu model in the 1950s, still recognised in the profession as the defining exposition of the neoclassical model.[13] It is 'fake news' generated by economists defending their frame of reference, as described by Sheila Dow, recorded in Chapter 1. Romer notes the confidence, confinement, quasi-religious purpose and indifference to inconvenient evidence of the group, traits which are characteristic of rigid groups. He even uses a military metaphor to affirm their loyalty to one another: 'They shared experience "in the foxhole"'. He records that after criticising a paper by Robert Lucas he was accused by an infuriated supporter of 'killing Bob'.[14]

Romer generalises the malaise of economic theory with the comment that:

> Several economists I know seem to have assimilated a norm that the post-real macroeconomists actively promote – that it is an extremely serious violation of some honor code for anyone to criticize openly a revered authority figure . . . and that neither facts that are false, nor predictions that are wrong, nor models that make no sense matter enough to worry about.[15]

This comment well identifies the consequences of support-bargaining within a cohesive group. It is not just 'several economists', but the whole neoclassical theory group that sustains false theory. Nor is it just a matter of 'some honor code' – career advantage in the institutionalised theory group depends on adherence to the neoclassical model.[16] The theory group has become isolated by its expertise. The members redouble their support for one another to provide security against opponents and shore up their own confidence. The group ignores contrary evidence, so that it is incapable of moving out of the intellectual confines it creates for itself. The sense of 'honor' it creates is that of simple loyalty to the group and its recognised authorities; the principle of the most unintellectual and insecure groups. It assembles support for protection of the group rather than the advance of understanding of economic issues. It distorts the information interface. Shapin's 'gentlemen' were obliged to be truthful, on pain of forfeiting the support of the group, but no such sanctions are felt by neoclassical theorists. The ills of academic economic theory have arisen because the internal support-bargaining of the group has diverted it from its proper purpose.[17] It is the same dynamic as holds together and makes rigid other theory groups, such as religious cults and even revolutionary groups.

That such commitments arise in a group so apparently committed to the investigation of issues of paramount importance to the prosperity of nations is a reflection of the importance of support for human psychological well-being. It is a glue, and sometimes a 'superglue', that can bind people together in pursuit of aims that are regarded with distaste or worse by those outside the group. Such group dynamic goes into the building of the information interface. Theory groups construct their information interface with information conducive to their cause, and exclude information inimical to their interests.

Right and left in intellectual support-bargaining

The conflict between individual and group interest gives support-bargaining systems their basic feature of 'right-wing' groups concerned with individual interests and 'left-wing' groups concerned with the group interest. This feature is most apparent in political support-bargaining. But it is apparent also in intellectual support-bargaining. Academic writers commonly maintain at least nominal neutrality with regard to political affiliation, but it is invariably plain whether their sympathies lie with the right or left of the political spectrum.

The affiliation of theory-makers to right or left factions is of differing strength. Some are wholeheartedly and exclusively committed to the right or the left, and wholly acknowledge their affiliation. Some maintain a commitment to right or left but prefer that it should not be overt or acknowledged in their scholarly output; it is left to others to make the assignment. In most it is more a matter of emphasis – they recognise the interests of both right and left but veer more to one side than the other. The affiliation may be apparent in little more than the subjects chosen to talk or write about. Those tending to the right prefer to provide information about individual rights and freedoms, self-reliance, the benefits of free enterprise, the 'fairness' of reward for hard work and the desirability of limiting the role of the state. Those tending to the left emphasise the importance of communal rights, the 'fairness' of social equality and equitable distribution of income, the importance of social justice, the necessity for compassion and the 'greed' that motivates capitalism. Affiliates of both persuasions feed information in accordance with their views into the information interface.

The sympathies of many agents, perhaps most agents, with both right and left are a reflection of the central importance of each to the other. As conceived in support-bargaining, support is a fundamental psychological requirement of individuals. Individuals adjust their opinions and actions to get it. On the other hand, groups need the talents and energy of particular individuals to advance the group interest, so members of groups adjust the demands they make on the individuals they seek to secure in the group – the group interest is conceded to individual interest. There are 'support-bargains' to be struck, but they normally take place in an overarching context of mutual accommodation of interests and shared interest in what can be done cooperatively.

Ambivalence of affiliation is to some extent inherent in the dynamic of support-bargaining. Those favouring the 'individualist' side must nevertheless assemble a group of 'individualists' to support the individualist cause. Compromises have to be reached on individualist positions to keep the individualist group together. Those favouring the group interest find that they nevertheless need the services of individuals with certain capacities to assemble the group and coordinate its commitments. Compromises have to be made with the interests of individual leaders on the left. Conflicts over individual leaders are more apparent in the British Labour Party, committed to communal dominance, than in the Conservative Party, where individual leadership is more consistent with the Party's ideals.

The contributions of theory-makers to the information interface have the effect of assembling support for or against right or left, and for or against the many other interests that are present in human societies. Support is the determinant of action, both informally and in the formal support-bargaining systems through which 'democratic' societies are governed. Under a 'support convention' violence is ruled out, so it is through the information interface that factions gain ascendancy and the actions they favour are implemented.[18] What is done changes situations. New interests will emerge from the changed situations, and support will be sought for the new interests. Thus societies will evolve under the impulses of their support-bargaining.

These right–left affiliations are apparent in the work of the philosophers and sociologists on epistemology and the sociology of knowledge. As was suggested in the previous chapter, the philosophical epistemologists work in something like the old ecclesiastical tradition, searching for a truth which is open to human attainment. The tradition was individualist; the quest for truth could only be an individualist enterprise. Then sociologists insisted that knowledge was a social matter. Social groups created knowledge and even reality itself. The philosophers saw at least something in it and turned their attention to what they called 'social epistemology'. Much of the argument of the sociologists was absorbed into the old epistemological framework, with 'society' searching for truth alongside individuals or, at least, with individuals still searching for truth but influenced by their social connections. But it is apparent that philosophers such as Alvin Goldman are averse to many of the ideas of 'social construction' and 'postmodern' innovation proposed by the sociologists.

Goldman suggests that his opponents suffer from a psychological condition which he calls 'veriphobia':

> Having outlined my veritistic approach to social epistemology, I must hasten to observe that the playing field of social epistemology has been substantially pre-empted by worldviews quite opposed to the veritistic conception. I allude to such views as social constructivism, postmodernism, pragmatism, cultural studies, and critical legal studies . . . they all share a deep scepticism or utter repudiation of truth as a viable criterion for studying epistemic phenomena . . . I think they suffer from an affliction that may be called *veriphobia* . . . they share the idea that the study of social 'knowledge' should be confined to the interpersonal and cultural determination of belief: not true or false belief, just plain belief. When veriphobes talk of knowledge, they do not refer, as I do, to *true* belief, but to something like institutionalized belief.[19]

It is apparent that banners of 'truth' are being unfurled to combat what is characterised as a psychological affliction of an opposing theory group. The conservative 'old school' is confronting the 'progressive' agents of communal innovation. The writer is assembling support for his cause. The 'right' is confronting the 'left'. Goldman comes from an individualist perspective, accommodating what he recognises as 'social' knowledge, but reluctant to concede much to the group conception of knowledge. Social constructivists assert that groups determine what is. The negotiation of the individual–group balance of power is part of the philosophical and sociological debate.

Goldman condemns the postmodernists as 'veriphobes', but his real objection is that they are socialists, or perhaps even further to the left. Such thoughts are not prominent, but that may be only because philosophical theory groups generally withhold support from those who openly introduce factional politics into intellectual debate. Goldman remarks simply that, 'Most postmodernists, moreover, are activists whose theory is motivated by interest in social change'.[20] Postmodernists seek to undermine convention, foster intellectual confusion and, amidst the confusion, overturn the established political order.

Neoclassical economists claim a different 'truth', but with scarcely less political import. Neoclassical theory claims the disinterested status of natural science. It deals with human beings only as rational agents. Their rationality is expressed largely in mathematical terms, with an assumption that mathematics cannot be partisan. Economists are 'onlookers' rather than 'players' with direct access to truth defined in mathematical terms. It is demonstrated mathematically that the unfettered initiative of individual agents, acting rationally within defined assumptions, leads to an optimal allocation of resources, and consequently is of the greatest benefit to society as a whole. But the approach merely excludes the propensity of humans to seek support and form groups. Hence all the group interest and group dynamic is missing from economic theory. It is only rational within the bounds set by assumptions. It would not be rational to ignore the group if the predictable consequence were annihilation. Without a group interest and group dynamic, there is no scope for expression of 'leftist' interests. The 'right' commands the field. Neoclassical economic theory has sustained conservative views of the importance of individual freedom and free enterprise.

Businessmen may privately question whether such a curious model really does reflect the nature of their activities, but the benefit to them from the accumulation of support around economic theory is so great that they are not inclined to vent criticism of it too forcefully.[21] Academic institutions are in any case specifically set up to reveal the truth about human society, and staffed with the cleverest people, so it can be difficult to assemble support for criticism of their pronouncements. There is little incentive to try when the pronouncements are so advantageous to interest. Neoclassical theory has established a major frame of reference for the organisation and understanding of economic information in the information interface, and has thereby assembled extensive support for the individualist faction in society. Neoclassical economists are some of the most important players in the support-bargaining process through which 'democratic' societies are governed. Postmodernists are cunning, but not as cunning as economists!

Support-bargaining and 'social construction'

It was seen in the previous chapter that the relevance of the 'big question' was forthrightly challenged by the argument that reality is a matter of 'social construction'. If reality is a 'social construction', then plainly the answer to the 'big question' about the nature of reality beyond what is conceived in human minds is simply that it is anything that society cares to construct. But the advocates of 'social construction' notably fail to provide any account of the process by which 'reality' is constructed. Merely describing it as 'social construction' is not very helpful. Clearly it is not, as the word 'construction' might suggest, a matter of bricks and scaffolding. 'Social construction' is at best a metaphor for something that is not well understood.

It is easily seen that 'social construction' is a process of support-bargaining. Support is assembled around certain ideas, understandings, concepts and propositions which, with support of sufficient volume and intensity, effectively defines what constitutes the reality of that society. The idea of 'social construction' is applied most prominently and perhaps with least controversy to ideas of 'social reality'. It is also applied to ideas of 'material reality', though here opinion is more sharply divided. The 'old school' finds it hard to concede that their 'big question' can be brushed aside by a metaphor. How can tables and chairs, Mount Everest and the White Cliffs of Dover be 'socially constructed', even in a metaphorical sense?

The idea of 'social construction' of reality was advanced most strongly by Latour and Woolgar in their study *Laboratory Life: The Construction of Scientific Facts*. Their account, however, appears to have run into significant difficulties in the intellectual support-bargaining that followed publication. The study is generally referred to as arguing the 'social construction' of scientific theory. The authors specifically refer to a process of 'social construction': 'Instead, we claim that the TRF [Thyrotropin Releasing Factor] *is* a thoroughly social construction'. And again, when noting their late focus on the concerns of individual scientists: 'This may seem odd in an essay avowedly concerned with the *social* construction of facts'.[22] The book certainly seems to be concerned with processes that are clearly not 'technical' in the scientific sense and might reasonably be regarded as 'social'. Yet in their Postscript to the second (1986) edition, Latour and Woolgar disclaim any idea that they provided a theory of the social construction of reality. They claim that their use of the term 'social' in the book is 'ironic'. 'Social construction' is disclaimed on the grounds that the term 'social' no longer has any meaning:

> So what does it mean to talk about 'social' construction? There is no shame in admitting that the term no longer has any meaning. . . . By demonstrating its pervasive applicability, the social study of science has rendered 'social' devoid of any meaning.[23]

The implication is that misuse of the word 'social' in the context of 'social construction' has rendered the term unfit for continued usage. Or it might be said that the metaphor has been found not to illuminate the subject in any useful way. Latour and Woolgar seem to have confused themselves, so it is scarcely surprising if readers are confused.

The idea of support-bargaining restores meaning, and not just metaphorical meaning, by suggesting that the process is a matter of assembling support in communities for the different propositions put forward by members of the communities. Support-bargaining constructs social abstractions of many kinds, including theories, ideas, concepts, facts, truth, reality, morality, beliefs, purposes, institutions and currencies. The abstractions so constructed adapt in accordance with movements in support. Without support they degenerate and disintegrate. Scientists and other theorists engage in a process of 'intellectual support-bargaining' that results in the focusing of support around certain propositions. Theories are established, or facts are established, by the assembly of support around them. Ordinary people engage with ideas, beliefs and moral issues, moulding them into some agreed forms. Latour and Woolgar themselves describe the scientific process as a matter of 'negotiation':

> In Chapter 4, we move from an historical exposition of the construction of a fact to a consideration of the microprocesses of negotiation which take place continually in the laboratory. The construction of facts depends critically on these microprocesses, and yet the retrospective characterisation of scientific activity frequently replaces them with epistemological descriptions of 'thought processes' and 'logical reasoning'.

Based on their observation of scientists in action at the Salk Institute, Latour and Woolgar produce a description of a social bargaining process.

This might have led them to recognise a critical feature of scientific method: it incorporates an implicit theory concerning the assembly of support, and with it an implicit theory of information. Scientific method recognises implicitly that people will advance their interests by assembling support for their hypotheses, and that they may be inclined to assemble support not on the basis of the truth of the hypotheses, but simply because it is advantageous to them, whether psychologically or for careerist reasons, to assemble support. Assembly of support may involve the distortion of information regarding scientific experiments. Scientific method counters these impulses by requiring that it must be possible to replicate the results of scientific experiments. Other scientists must be able to reproduce the results of an initial experimenter. Scientific method is clearly designed to eliminate or at least minimise the effects of the social negotiations identified by Latour and Woolgar. It is designed to minimise the distortions that can potentially arise in identification of consistent truth or reality through the pursuit of social and personal interests in intellectual support-bargaining. Science is committed to assembling support for what is true and realistic, but it can be diverted if the scientists concerned divert to the assembly of support for their own psychological or careerist interests. Romer's account of DSGE research constitutes a vivid account of the kind of 'negotiations' observed by Latour and Woolgar among the scientists at the Salk Institute. The econometricians diverted their attention from the pursuit of truth that was formally their purpose to the advance of their own personal interests. At the Salk Institute, Latour and Woolgar observed distortionary social bargaining, but there remained also a commitment to meet scientific standards of evidence through adherence to scientific method. If the diversionary interests were not present, scientific method would not be necessary.

It is implicitly assumed that, being different individuals, subsequent experimenters will be independent of the first. But this would not necessarily be so. If subsequent experimenters have the same frame of reference as the first, or employ the same paradigm, they might observe with the same bias and reproduce the same false results. The idea of support-bargaining implicit in natural scientific method does not extend to the group influences that are essential to the present idea of support-bargaining. That extension was made by Thomas Kuhn. In his study of scientific revolutions, Kuhn overlaid the idea of group preconception onto scientific method.[24] 'Normal' science is carried on using scientific method; scientific 'revolutions' occur when the scientific group as a whole changes its paradigm and sees things differently. It can be seen that the implicit theory of information incorporated in scientific method is dependent on the idea of support-bargaining, in particular the propensity to seek support. The accumulation of support involves establishing an information interface that will cause people to recognise the truth of the hypotheses under investigation. But information can potentially be manipulated so that support accumulates for results that are false. A scientist can gain support, and with it psychological and institutional advantages, by posting information that implies the truth of a hypothesis, which on the basis of other information can be shown to be false. It was suggested in the Introduction that a full theory of information depends on the prior recognition that societies function as support-bargaining systems.

Support-bargaining confirms the problem of association between testers in scientific method. It also confirms a problem with replicative testing. The highest levels of support naturally go to those scientists who innovate, who break new ground with their experimental results. Those who repeat the experiments can expect much less kudos if they merely confirm what has been found before, and they may even experience loss of support if they do not confirm previous experimental results. If they do not confirm, they imply that the initial experiment was wrongly carried out, or might even have been duplicitous. If the scientists who carried out the initial experiment have important institutional positions, the query over the results may be damaging to the replicative tester. The expectation is that replicative testing will not be a popular activity amongst scientists. Little return, in terms of support, can be expected, and there is the risk of adverse consequences. It has been remarked that, 'Professional egos, the exigencies of career-building and the restricted sizes of grants and budgets all conspire against the rerunning, in universities, of old studies instead of the conducting of new ones'.[25] When replicative testing is carried out, the results can be disconcerting, both as regards the subjects of the tests and the adherence to scrupulous procedure that is also part of scientific method. When Amgen, a Californian drug company, attempted to reproduce the results of 53 cancer research papers they found that only six confirmed the original results. An analysis of 98 psychology papers in 2015 by researchers centred on the University of Virginia satisfactorily replicated only 39 per cent of the original results.[26] Replication is an essential part of scientific method, but the exigencies of the intellectual support-bargaining process mean that it is neglected. Perhaps because of that, the results of experimental tests may not be as reliable as they might be. The knowledge that their results are unlikely to be subjected to any confirmatory testing may incline experimenters to attend more closely to their private interests and less to the validity of the hypotheses they are testing.

Science in university or similar educational research laboratories is now rivalled by research carried on in business organisations or in research laboratories set up with a view to the identification of scientific knowledge that will have business applications. Technology is fundamental to the successful format of companies. Superior technology is one of the principal elements of competitive advantage. Companies develop their own technologies by in-house scientific research or cultivate connections with independent laboratories. The use of scientific method in a laboratory context remains important, but it can be overtaken in importance by the commercial requirement that technology should be functional. Instead of replicative testing of a particular hypothesis, a hypothesis is tested repetitively by the functionality of technology based upon it. Tablets and smartphones derive from scientific research, but their functionality is the best evidence for the validity of the science.

Technology developed in the commercial context has the further requirement that its costs are such as will enable a company using the technology to establish a viable format. The technology has to be adapted to use in a money-bargaining system. The large financial rewards of successful technological innovation offer great incentives for scientists to pursue research into promising hypotheses. In this context, the demands of functionality constrain their scope for distortion of results for personal advantage even more than the demands of a scientific community for scrupulous adherence to scientific method. Intellectual support-bargaining is strongly influenced by the requirements of money-bargaining. Successful researchers will be rewarded with the support of their colleagues and the leaders of the organisation in which they do their research, but an essential part of the return will be monetary. Any pursuit of truth is conditioned by the requirements of company formats. This conditioning applies principally to decisions regarding what will be researched. Research that promises the best monetary returns, rather than research that is recognisable as of most pressing interest for the well-being of mankind, or even of most interest to the researchers, will be pursued. Selection of which truth to pursue is dictated by interest. But within that context, 'the truth' must still be pursued, given that only 'the truth' will ensure functional technology. If there is no consistency of results in the laboratory, there can be no expectations that technology based on the results will perform in a manner that is consistent with expectations.

Collective intentionality and support-bargaining

Latour and Woolgar analyse the social construction of reality in the context of natural scientific procedures. The philosopher John Searle identifies a different and broader mode of construction. 'Collective intentionality' is regarded as counterpart to individual intentionality and just as secure and valid a concept. Searle affirms that, 'An understanding of collective intentionality is essential to understand social facts'.[27] A football team has a collective intentionality that is not reducible to individual intentionality, even though, within the context of the collective intentionality, individuals may exercise individual intentionality, as an offensive lineman has the individual intention to block the defensive end as part of the collective intention of the team to win a match. Searle maintains that, 'Collective intentionality is a biologically primitive phenomenon that cannot be reduced to or eliminated in favour of something else'.[28] Collective intentionality is seen by Searle as the basis of the construction of social reality.

Searle queries how it is that so many philosophers are convinced that collective intentionality must be reducible to individual intentionality. He suggests that the answer to the query is that because all intentionality necessarily exists in the heads of individuals, the form of the intentionality can only have individual reference. He continues, 'So it has seemed that anybody who recognises collective intentionality as a primitive form of mental life must be committed to the idea that there exists some Hegelian world spirit, a collective consciousness, or something equally implausible'.[29] In other words, if there is to be a 'collective intentionality', there must be the collective equivalent of an individual mind to sustain it. Searle argues instead that, although all mental life is inside the individual brain, it does not follow that all mental life must be expressed in the form of a singular noun phrase referencing the individual. 'We intend' is just as intelligible as 'I intend'.[30]

With the idea of support-bargaining, it becomes unnecessary to evoke a 'Hegelian world spirit' or similar collective imagining to establish the idea of collective opinion, collective intentionality and collectively held facts. Support-bargaining predicates that individuals need the support of others as a matter of psychological security, and in violent circumstances as a matter of physical security. Individuals modify their behaviour and opinions to gain the support they need. Hence there emerges a group opinion and approved group modes of behaviour. Groups can form group purposes. Individual inclination fuses with group inclination, or group purpose. As a condition of survival of the species groups of humans were able to form with a group purpose of survival. Alongside the struggle for survival, or in the intermissions between fights for survival, human groups were able to develop other group purposes, apparent in the long social and cultural evolution of human societies. Individuals form groups for security and in the process of group formation they create group intentionality, along with group opinion, group beliefs and group purposes. 'Collective intentionality' is an outcome of support-bargaining.

Searle asserts that collective intentionality is a biologically primitive phenomenon, suggesting that it has something to do with survival. But he earlier praises Darwin for excluding any sense of intentionality in his theory of evolution. Searle writes:

> One of Darwin's greatest achievements was to drive teleology out of the account of the origin of species. On the Darwinian account, evolution occurs by way of blind, brute, natural forces. There is no intrinsic purpose whatever to the origin and survival of biological species.[31]

So 'collective intentionality' has no part in natural selection, and hence is not entirely primitive. Support-bargaining is, however, primitive. While not a part of Darwin's account of natural selection, it constitutes the essential mechanism for group formation, and consequently an essential part of natural selection. It was seen above that Darwin underestimated the importance of the instinct for self-preservation that underlies the pursuit of support. 'Collective intention' is formed through support-bargaining and is a primitive trait, but it can only be understood in this way by the addition of the support-bargaining dynamic to Darwin's theory of evolution. It was noted in *Support-Bargaining, Economics and Society* that if we had antennae on our heads that picked up indications of support, as our eyes respond to light, the importance of support would have been earlier understood and given its proper place in the explanation of human social processes.[32]

'Social construction' of the information interface

The philosophers and sociologists whose work has been described in this and the previous chapter all conceive that what is socially constructed is 'reality'. Some hold that it is just 'social reality' that is constructed, but others hold that the reality of the 'natural' physical world is also constructed. Latour and Woolgar argue that 'facts' are constructed. They write: 'Scientific activity is not "about nature", it is a fierce fight to *construct* reality'.[33] Peter Berger and Thomas Luckman argue that 'human reality' is constructed, being both social reality and an external reality presumed by humans to exist: 'The sociology of knowledge understands human reality as socially constructed reality'.[34]

In the understanding of support-bargaining what is constructed is that great range of theories, ideas, beliefs, morality and so on which people support as essentials of their society and their mental world. All these abstractions are, however, codified and shared in an information interface, so what is constructed is more accurately an information interface. The information interface covers both 'social reality' and 'material reality' without any queries or contrivance. How that information interface relates or does not relate to any external reality that might exist independent of human minds is a separate question. How it is answered can be no more than an addition to the information interface, since human minds cannot countenance anything but information. It can be said with assurance that it will never be possible to discern an external reality independent of the information interface. If we behave as if we know about an external world, it is because we have learnt that an information interface used in a certain way works well enough as proxy for whatever external world there might be. 'Used in a certain way' means that, for the most part, we find adequate safeguards against the distortions and deceptions of the information interface that are inevitable, given the way it is created. It is inconceivable that there could be a simple one-to-one, mirror image, or perfect correspondence relationship of the information interface to any external reality that may exist. The information interface works well enough as a proxy for any external world in the sense that, used in the appropriate way, it provides information that is consistent over a great range of observations and experience in different circumstances and at different times. That 'makeshift scientific method' referred to above gives sufficiently reliable information for the conduct of daily affairs.

Latour and Woolgar emphasise the literary output of the Salk Institute scientists. Early on they introduce the notion of an 'inscription device', which is: 'any item of apparatus or particular configuration of such items which can transform a material substance into a figure or diagram which is directly usable by one of the members of the office space'.[35] They comment later that the justification for introducing the notion of an 'inscription device' was that, 'writing was not so much a method of transferring information as a material operation of creating order'.[36] Writing as both a means of transferring information and ordering information was an essential part of the scientific process. They assert also that, 'they [the scientists] claimed merely to be scientists discovering facts; he [the observer] claimed doggedly that they were writers and readers in the business of being convinced and convincing others'.[37] The implication is that the scientists were creating an information interface ordered according to certain principles for communication and persuasion. They were creating an information interface conducive to the advancement of their interests. They were assembling support for their findings. If they were creating order, it was an order designed to present their findings in a form most likely to elicit the support of others.

The construction of an information interface is apparent also in what Alvin Goldman calls the postmodernist 'obsession with language as the great determiner, the determiner of both knowledge and reality'.[38] Goldman quotes Jacques Derrida, celebrated for his idea of 'deconstruction' and one of the leaders of the 'postmodern' approach, to the effect that, 'The text is all and nothing exists outside of it'.[39] Language is conceived not as expressing understanding of reality but of actually constituting all the reality there is. According to Goldman, postmodernists tend to conflate knowledge, reality and truth, when they should be kept distinct. Goldman insists that knowledge and thought can be regarded as products of language more easily than can reality or truth, though even here the role of language has been 'oversold'.[40] While the concern with language is regarded as beyond 'modern' and characteristic of the 'postmodern', it was also characteristic of early theological scholars, who scoured sacred texts for their truth.

In terms of support-bargaining, language is the codification of thought and ideas, giving them the form of communicable information. Much of the information interface is in the form of language. Language has characteristics that suggest it was formulated for bargaining purposes.[41] It is designed to value and persuade as well as to inform. It has a major role in the creation of the information interface. There are other means of conveying information, for example body-language, pictures, drama, sculpture, mathematics, sound and films, but language, spoken and written, is the major means of codification of information. 'The text' may seem to be 'all', but that is only because it codifies and enables transmission of the information that forms the information interface. Ideas, understandings, concepts, propositions and intentions are codified and transmitted or shared around a group through the information interface.

One reason for concluding that language is formulated for bargaining purposes is that language incorporates many opportunities for the sort of manipulation that is conducive to bargaining advantage. Languages characteristically have many words meaning much the same thing in objective reference but which are understood in use as having pejorative or complimentary implications, encouraging a listener or reader to support or not support the propositions put forward, according to the desires of the speaker or writer. The pursuit of 'meaning' in language by linguistic philosophers constitutes a misunderstanding of the nature and purpose of language. As was noted in the Introduction, a strong theory of information depends on the theory of support-bargaining. Similarly, a theory of language depends on recognition of language as the primary form of codification of information, and hence depends also on recognition of the role of information in support-bargaining. It depends also on recognition of support-bargaining as the basic dynamic of social intercourse.

Language codifies information for transmission, but we receive uncodified information in the form of direct or perceptual information. We receive information by sight, hearing and touch. Such information requires codification before it can be transmitted to others and becomes part of the public information interface. Nevertheless, perceptual information, particularly visual information, is exceptional in the conviction it carries with its recipients. We tend to believe the veracity of 'the evidence of our own eyes' more strongly than testimonial information. Even though we recognise that perceptual information can be distorted by idiosyncrasies of our visual or aural organs, or our sense of touch, still such information is uniquely 'ours', untrammelled by the interests of others, and consequently more trustworthy than the testimonial information that potentially carries the imprint of the interests of others. The major drawback of perceptual information is its restricted range. We can only see what is within eyesight. The greater part of information that is used in support-bargaining and money-bargaining is testimonial information. The distinction between perceptual and testimonial information has been complicated by the advent of technologies that make it possible to present testimonial information in perceptual form. This feature of the communication of information is considered further in Chapter 7 on media theory.

Besides perceptual and testimonial information, the sources of knowledge identified by epistemologists recorded in the previous chapter include 'memory' and 'introspection'. These both imply some internal working of the mind on information for the production of information. Both are generally recognised as highly unreliable with regard to accurate correspondence to reality as commonly understood. Both are regarded as highly susceptible to 'self-deception'. People tend to remember events in ways that advance their own interests. Witnesses in courts of law will 'remember' what suits their interests in the court and, while some evidence may be consciously adjusted for this purpose, in some cases there seems to be genuine recollection, albeit selective recollection, of what is conducive to interest. Nevertheless, memory must play a prominent part in the information we bring to bear on issues confronting us. We recollect our experience, we recollect what we have heard and read, and use that information in the formulation of responses to our further experience.

Similarly, 'introspection' can be self-justifying. Introspection is akin to 'conscience', which in theological understanding constituted the guidance of God. God was thought to bring sinners to repentance and atonement through the promptings of their consciences. In this theological understanding, introspection tells us things we do not want to know. We are deterred from taking certain actions because our consciences tell us they are wrong. But whether self-justificatory or condemnatory, introspection necessarily plays a large part in the information we impart to ourselves and the information we select for codification and transmission. Writers, particularly writers of fiction, have to 'look inside themselves', or review their experience, for what they will codify in language. Theorists debate with themselves or 'mull things over' to arrive at the conclusions they will write down and transmit to others. Introspection is the only means anyone has of access to the content of their own minds. Whatever distortions are involved, whether it is true or false, it contributes to the information interface and the pursuit of interest.

The idea of support-bargaining suggests that our minds normally operate as 'self-protectors' and for the advancement of our interests more pervasively than is suggested even by the self-justifying aspects of memory and introspection. It was argued in *Support-Bargaining, Economics and Society* that the search for support was an integral part of our biological survival. Human beings are frequently focused on their own individual interests; children frequently act selfishly and have to be reminded to 'think of others'. But children also run to their parents for comfort when threatened. Sometimes they have to be told to 'stand on their own two feet'. A sense of personal insecurity causes humans to seek the support of others, which is to engage in support-bargaining, and the process by which groups are formed. Humans have selfish interests, but their selfish interests include the need for support from a group. This pursuit of support is for the most part instinctive and uncontrived. When it appears that someone is contriving to acquire support in social circumstances, the support may be withheld on the grounds that the person is ingratiating and insincere.

Our minds are by implication 'hard-wired' to look after our interests, whether individual or communal. Without any necessary conscious attention, our minds will act on our behalf. We may at times admonish ourselves for acts we have committed 'instinctively' or 'impulsively' which we find to be at odds with our craving for communal support. We may, for example, tell a lie on the spur of the moment to protect ourselves from blame or other retribution. That can be understood as our minds protecting what they conceive to be our interest. Telling a lie is feeding false information into the information interface so that others will evaluate the situation in accordance with our interests. Our minds then join in the communal condemnation of a selfish action. We are contrite. It is suggested that our minds perpetually act in this way. Some minds cause their possessors to do far worse than tell lies. Consciously and unconsciously, the information interface is created and manipulated for the advancement of interest.

Notes

1 Spread, Patrick, 2013, *Support-Bargaining, Economics and Society: A Social Species*, Abingdon: Routledge, Chapter 1: The problem with natural selection.
2 Spread, 2013, p. 113.
3 See Spread, Patrick, 2008, *Support-Bargaining: The Mechanics of Democracy Revealed*, Sussex: Book Guild, pp. 5–6, etc.; see also Spread, Patrick, 2011, 'Situation as determinant of selection and valuation', *Cambridge Journal of Economics*, Vol. 35, No. 2, pp. 335–56.
4 Latour, Bruno and Woolgar, Steve, 1986, *Laboratory Life: The Construction of Scientific Facts*, Princeton: Princeton University Press, Chapter 5: Cycles of Credit. First published 1979, Sage Publications.
5 Latour and Woolgar, 1986, p. 189. Their reference: Mitroff, Ian I., 1974, *The Subjective Side of Science: a Philosophical Inquiry into the Psychology of the Apollo Moon Scientists*, New York: Elsevier, Chapter IV, p. 57.
6 Shapin, Steven, 1994, *A Social History of Truth*, Chicago: University of Chicago Press, pp. xx–xxi.
7 See Watson, James and Jones, Steve, 1999, *The Double Helix: A Personal Account of the Discovery of the Structure of DNA*, Second Revised Edition, London: Penguin.
8 Cf. Ietto-Gillies, Grazia, 2008, 'A XXI-century alternative to XX-century peer review', *Real-World Economics Review*, Issue 45, pp. 10–22, p. 15. Available at: www.paecon.net/PAEReview/issue45/IettoGillies45.pdf.
9 Romer, Paul, 2016, 'The trouble with macroeconomics', lecture, delivered 5 January 2016 as the Commons Memorial Lecture of the Omicron Delta Epsilon Society. Available at: https://paulromer.net/wp-content/uploads/2016/09/WP-Trouble.pdf. Accessed 27 April 2017.
10 Romer's 'endogenous growth theory' treats technological and other innovation as part of the process of macroeconomic growth. The contrast is with the earlier established 'exogenous growth theory' that treats such innovation as external influences or 'shocks' to a system functioning in accordance with the neoclassical economic model. The concept of companies in money-bargaining 'endogenises' technological change by incorporation of technology as an essential factor in the format of companies. See Chapter 4, at note 56.
11 Romer, 2016, pp. 6–7.
12 Romer, 2016, p. 5.
13 For comment on the Arrow-Debreu model, see Spread, 2016a, pp. 49–55.
14 Romer, 2016, pp. 15–17.
15 Romer, 2016, p. 21.
16 Cf. Spread, Patrick, 2016a, *The Evolution of Economies: Money-Bargaining, Economic Change and Industrial Revolution*, Abingdon: Routledge, pp. 102–3.
17 On this subject, see Spread, Patrick, 2012, 'Science and support: the struggle for mastery in economics', *Real-World Economics Review*, Issue no. 59, 12 March, pp. 39–57.
18 On the emergence of the support convention in Britain, see Spread, 2008, pp. 386–90.
19 Goldman, Alvin I., 2003, *Knowledge in a Social World*, Oxford: Clarendon Press, p. 7.
20 Goldman, 2003, p. 19.

21 See Spread, 2008, pp. 350–2.
22 Latour and Woolgar, 1986, pp. 152, 188. Original emphasis.
23 Latour and Woolgar, 1986, p. 281.
24 Kuhn, Thomas S., 1970, *The Structure of Scientific Revolutions*, Chicago: Chicago University Press. First published 1962.
25 *The Economist*, 2016a, 'The scientific method: let's just try that again', 6 February, p. 78.
26 *The Economist*, 2016a, p. 78.
27 Searle, John, 1996, *The Construction of Social Reality*, London: Penguin, p. 24.
28 Searle, 1996, p. 24.
29 Searle, 1996, p. 25.
30 Searle, 1996, pp. 25–6.
31 Searle, 1996, p. 16.
32 Spread, 2013, p. 113.
33 Latour and Woolgar, 1986, p. 243. Original emphasis.
34 Berger, Peter and Luckman, Thomas, 1991, *The Social Construction of Reality*, London: Penguin, pp. 210–11. First published 1966.
35 Latour and Woolgar, 1986, p. 51.
36 Latour and Woolgar, 1986, p. 245.
37 Latour and Woolgar, 1986, p. 88.
38 Goldman, 2003, p. 17.
39 Goldman, 2003, p. 17. Reference is to Derrida, Jacques, 1976, *Of Grammatology*, translated by G. Spivak, Baltimore: Johns Hopkins University Press, p. 158.
40 Goldman, 2003, pp. 17–18.
41 On language and support-bargaining, see Spread, 2013, pp. 171–8, 214–15.

3 Creation and manipulation of the information interface

It was suggested in the previous chapter that the process of 'social construction' is a process of support-bargaining, and that rather than constructing 'reality' we construct an information interface. Support-bargaining involves the pursuit of interests, and accordingly the information interface is constructed in the pursuit of interest. Whether it has connections with any 'truth' or 'reality', social or material, is a separate question. Being concerned with interest, the construction of the information interface is necessarily forward looking, rather than strictly confined to what is actually present. It involves construction of concepts of present situation, but that is done with an eye to their effect in advancing interest in the future. Concepts of present situation necessarily involve concepts of the past, both immediate and with all degrees of remoteness, selected and interpreted in accordance with their perceived relevance to the advance of current interest. The whole information interface is actively shaped for the purpose of influencing the evolution of societies. We do not 'say it as it is'; we say it with a view to the assembly of support for how we want it to be. This chapter considers some of the methods employed by agents of bargaining systems to ensure that the information interface is conducive to their interests.

First of all, people need to establish an information interface that causes others to recognise their interests as prominent and important. This involves also ensuring that the others are not distracted by competing interests. Interests depend on situations, so in order to get a set of interests recognised it is necessary to establish that the particular situation that generates the interest is widely recognised as the actual situation in which the society finds itself. People living in rural areas often want recognition of their need for improved bus services, and will seek to establish the want of adequate transport as an essential feature of the rural situation, affecting the lives and work opportunities of the whole community. People with an interest in improved welfare payments will seek to establish the reality of poverty across their society and the real hardships endured in situations of poverty. Business people wanting to move goods around the country, or wanting to provide their services around the country, will point to deficiencies in the existing transport provisions as justifying increased investment in infrastructure and services.

In these cases, interests depend on physical circumstances. To some extent, people know the physical situations by direct perceptual observation. People know about bus services and transport infrastructure, and the circumstances of their poverty, by observing what is around them. At a local level, remedial action may be taken on the basis of direct observation of situations. But the generality of these situations can only be known through testimonial information. Studies and reports on transport systems and poverty are conducted to establish the general circumstances prevailing on these matters. Getting something done through a political system normally means establishing an understanding of a general situation that makes clear the need for remedial action. Support has to be assembled around an understanding of the situation that has relevance for many people.

Recognition of interests can be directed with the broadest generality through the establishment of situations in abstract or theoretical terms. A 'frame of reference' established in an information interface directs people where to look and how to interpret their experience and encounters. People with an interest in the alleviation of poverty will find it useful to direct the attention of others to the actual physical deprivation around the country. But they may assemble a wider range of support by promoting the adoption of a socialist frame of reference that sees poverty and the inequalities of society as of prime and universal importance. If people can be persuaded to adopt that frame, they will automatically pick out what accords with the frame of reference. They will see and understand in the same way as the formulators of the frame.

Frames of reference function as they do because people discern patterns or symmetry. People 'understand' when they recognise that phenomena are falling into a distinct pattern. A frame of reference is constituted of information organised or arranged into a pattern that is readily comprehended. Pattern recognition is an established trait of human psychology.[1] The patterns or symmetries also suggest the possibility of 'fitting in' other observations. We recognise other phenomena as fitting the preconceived patterns, and assimilate them easily as 'understood'. What does not fit the pattern is likely to be ignored or rejected as irrelevant. Frames of reference constitute arrangements of information into patterns that are readily assimilated, but they do not necessarily portray accurately the patterns of human behaviour. They are used to steer human behaviour into conformity with their patterns.

With this organisation of information by reference to frame, it is clearly important for any group seeking to gain acceptance for its interests to ensure that many people share its frame of reference. The first step in the manipulation of information is to ensure that other people will be in a position to identify and accept, to see as relevant to them, the information pertaining to the interest it is desired to advance. So the first step is establishment of the appropriate frame of reference across society. Selections and omissions will be made with reference to the frame. The establishment of the favoured frame will help also to crowd out understanding of rival interests. Rival frames can be challenged as incomplete, distorted or fictitious.[2]

The frame of reference is most commonly understood in terms of theoretical constructions. Socialism, communism, neoclassical economic theory, environmentalism, feminism, nationalism, social constructivism, postmodernism all provide frames of reference through which social and political situations can be understood and information about them organised. In the arts, comparable 'movements' or 'schools' establish frames of reference. The 'romantic' movement called attention to the nobility of certain human sentiments and the emotionally elevating impact of natural phenomena. The 'impressionist' movement cultivated sensitivity to light, seeking to convey in paint the effects of light on water, snow, trees, flowers and other surfaces. The 'cubists' chose to focus on the geometric symmetries of people and nature. Each movement adopted a frame of reference by which visual information could be organised on canvas to convey an understanding of perceptual experience. The frames depend for their creation and maintenance on their use by individuals committed to them and forming groups defined by the frames. The group forms around the frame that is created through group formation. People are invited to adopt the frame and see the world as it is experienced by the creators of the frame.

It was suggested in *Support-Bargaining, Economics and Society* that there is also a 'common theory' which provides an understanding and organising capacity for ordinary people of the phenomena they encounter in their everyday lives.[3] In conventional terms the word 'theory' is generally understood as something more sophisticated; as an abstract distillation or reflection of the truth about the world. It is something constructed by specialist theory-makers in institutions set up for the formulation of theory. The archetype is the scientific theory that identifies universal truths about the physical world. But the idea of support-bargaining incorporates the idea of intellectual support-bargaining through which theories are created. Theories are adopted and established because support is accumulated around them. Support is assembled through observation, experience, argument and experiment. Through this process, at least through observation, experience and argument, a common theory is developed by which ordinary people understand the world. 'Experiment' is unsystematic. It is confined to doing something, or experiencing something, and finding that it works out as expected, or fails to do so. It is the 'makeshift scientific method' described in the previous chapter. The common understanding helps sustain the cohesion of the group; it allows people to live with one another and communicate coherently. The more esoteric type of theory can commonly be traced to issues identified in the common theory, or latent in common theory, so that 'high theory' is a more systematic and sometimes systematically experimental development of common theory.

Thus, while many people will use frames of reference such as socialism or economic theory as their references for the understanding of society and the organisation of information about society, others of perhaps lesser sophistication will employ the 'ready-made' and 'universal' cabinet of common theory. Common theory brings together common observation, common experience, common understanding and common sense. Quite a number of people would probably be happy to acknowledge that they approach life with this sort of reference. Because it is widely shared, it gives societies a cohesion that the more sophisticated theories generally can give only to much smaller groups. It was seen in the previous chapter that conservative philosophers tend to be at odds with postmodernists. Much of the information interface, what might be called the 'common information interface', derives from common theory. People communicate and understand one another on the basis of the common conceptions incorporated in the common information interface. A 'common sense philosophy' was developed in the late eighteenth and early nineteenth century by Scottish philosophers. It was, however, formulated to counter the arguments of 'high philosophy', writers such as John Locke and David Hume, rather than as an independent philosophy. In the understanding of the time, it would not have been sensible to suggest that the common people formulated anything like a theory. The notion of intellectual support-bargaining is necessary to that idea.

In sociological terms, 'norms' govern social behaviour. 'Norms' constitute commonly accepted modes of behaviour, indicating the way people are expected to conduct themselves. They may be regarded as part of common theory. There is, however, no satisfactory and generally recognised mechanism in sociology by which 'norms' are adopted and enforced in society. Support-bargaining provides a very specific mechanism by which certain modes of behaviour and opinion are adopted and sustained. To transgress against the common theory is to incur withdrawal of communal support, and that is something people avoid unless they can readily turn to some other sub-group of society for the support they require. Peter Blau notes the importance of 'social approval' in the conduct of social relations, and its influence on human behaviour. It has a role in some ways similar to that of support in the idea of support-bargaining. But Blau gives social approval a rather restricted application, so that it does not perform the very wide social, political and intellectual functions of support in support-bargaining.[4]

It will be apparent from earlier remarks on the importance of situation as the determinant of interest, and the parallel role of a frame of reference in identifying interest, that situation-related interest is central to the idea of support-bargaining.[5] Groups form most readily on the basis of shared situations because shared situations imply shared interests. 'Situation' is generally understood in physical terms, such as a home, a physical location or physical circumstances. But a reference situation may also be something more abstract, such as a job, or a national economic situation. In some contexts, situation is 'circumstances', implying perhaps a less specific and less physical reference. The 'situation' in theoretical form is the 'frame of reference'. The 'frame of reference' is to intellectual support-bargaining what the 'situation' is to social and political support-bargaining. 'Preconceptions' constitute for the most part a less ordered and less precisely specified assembly of factors that perform much of the role of a frame of reference. A sharply defined frame of reference, such as the neoclassical economic model, may nevertheless be referred to as a 'preconception', commonly with connotations of bias or misconception.

A 'theory' is conventionally understood as something that is true independently of the humans that espouse it. It is objective truth in the old ecclesiastical sense; or in a natural scientific sense. 'Theories' that are more manifestly the product of special interests are regarded as 'ideologies', with a necessary pejorative sense. They intrude interest into what should be a disinterested search for truth. Support-bargaining suggests that all theory is shaped to advance interests. Theory-formation is a process of intellectual support-bargaining. Support is assembled around certain theoretical propositions which the members of the formative group see as 'right' or 'valid', but which rest on the interest of the group in the particular issues covered by the theory and the interest of the group in advancing the issues in certain directions. The group is creating a frame of reference in the information interface that will cause others to recognise their interests and influence them to advance those interests. The imputation of the status 'ideology' to the theories of other groups is merely a means of eroding support from those theories and assembling support for the supposedly pure theoretical formulations of the imputing group.

It was seen in Chapter 1 that Karl Marx introduced 'interest' as a driving force behind the formation of theory. His own theory was recognised as driven by interest and categorised as 'ideology', with the implication that it was not to be taken seriously by serious social scientists. Its historical derivation was seen as mere window-dressing, to give the appearance of natural science and hence appropriate the status of natural science to the theory. Marx was clearly trying to establish an alternative frame of reference in the information interface, one that would cause people to see the world as he saw it, and act as he recommended. His new frame of reference was intended also to drive out all other frames, so that his own would so dominate the perceptions of people, and their actions, that it would be realised in practice in the world at large. He positively advocated the use of violence to drive out alternative frames of reference and the groups that propagated them. His theory was to be advanced by violence – by killing, incarcerating or intimidating into silence those who opposed it. In the heartlands of industrial capitalism Marx's theory found only limited support. But those committed to violent revolution in Tsarist Russia found it a useful focus for the assembly of intellectual support for their actions. Marx's frame of reference, adapted to the requirements of a society of peasant farmers, was adopted by Bolshevik revolutionaries and established as the intellectual basis of the Soviet Union. As Marx advocated, all other frames of reference were driven out. Marxism alone was permitted to direct the perceptions, thoughts and actions of the Soviet people. An information interface was established that excluded all information other than that which was compatible with the Marxist frame of reference. The information interface so constructed proved so inadequate an account of the realities of social and economic life that the regime foundered. The People's Republic of China had a similar experience. In China the information interface remains tightly constrained by a Marxist frame of reference, but not to the total exclusion of all other reference. Sufficient information is in circulation to make possible rapid improvements in socio-economic conditions. These improvements form some bulwark against the assembly of unmanageable levels of support against the regime.

The German word 'weltanschauung' or 'worldview' expresses the idea of a very wide-ranging, capacious and comprehensive frame of reference, spanning distance and time. A 'worldview' is mainly an imputation of philosophers, rather than a reference consciously identified and used by people. It is also largely an imputation to an intellectual type of person, speculating on high theory, engaged in intellectual support-bargaining, rather than to ordinary types concerned with more down-to-earth and local issues. It tends also to be applied retrospectively, when present frames of reference make possible identification of different characteristics in the frames used in the past. Intellectuals are seen as holding a certain 'worldview' unconsciously, which then helps to explain their thoughts, what they will agree to, what they will not agree to, and perhaps what they cannot even contemplate. Intellectuals orient their thinking in accordance with an unconscious 'worldview'. A 'zeitgeist', or 'spirit of the age', is more specifically a temporal reference, though it has similar implications of unconscious influence. Thinking people are imbued with the spirit of their age and their thoughts reflect the influence.

The idea of 'capacity' forms part of 'situation' in the understanding of support-bargaining. Capacity is a measure of what people can offer in return for accommodation of their situation-related interests. In the case of individuals, capacity is primarily the skills, innate or acquired, that are potentially of interest or use to other agents of a bargaining system. In violent times the capacity for violence is important. When the species was struggling for survival, capacity for violence must have been the critical capacity. The survival of particular sub-groups, including nation states, has ever since depended to a significant degree on capacity for violence. Under a support convention, normally operating within the human and territorial boundaries of a nation state, the capacity for violence is no longer of such primary importance. A support convention recognises the potential for violence in everyone, but is instituted with the express purpose of eliminating the necessity to confirm that capacity. Other qualities are valued in people, as contributing to the advance of group interests. In a money-bargaining system capacities for work and skills related to productive processes are naturally valued. 'Capacity' is used familiarly in the context of the 'productive capacity' of a company, particularly in connection with capital equipment, or even more generally in reference to the ability of a company to undertake certain tasks. 'Capacity' in support-bargaining and money-bargaining has the function of 'capital' in economic theory, though it is conceived as a much broader function, incorporating an idea of 'human capital' as well as physical capital. 'Budget capacity' is also important in support-bargaining and money-bargaining.[6] Certain capacities for expenditure are necessary in all agents before they can expect to gain accommodation of their interests through a money-bargaining system. All adult individuals and organisations engage in money-bargaining and their budgetary situation is an important element in their capacity to engage.[7]

Thus the understanding of situation covers both the idea of a situation that is in some ways deficient, giving rise to interests in improvement, and the idea of certain capacities that permit an agent to make returns to others in exchange for accommodation of interest. It covers situations that imply both potential acquisitions and potential disbursements. The word 'situation' is mostly used in the context of support-bargaining and money-bargaining, as a matter of convenience, to refer to situation in the former sense, as determinant of potential acquisitions or requirements. 'Capacity' refers to that distinct element of situation concerned with disbursements.

There is a certain dependency of interest not just on situation in the former sense but also on capacity. People are inclined to create situations that value their capacities. Violent people flourish in violent circumstances, and may foment violence for the opportunities it is likely to bring them. People with a talent for mathematics will advocate a mathematical form of economic theory, where their capacity is most likely to be rewarded. The 'capacity' element of situation has this implication of interest, but it is an indirect mechanism, operating through creation of a new situation. If we have certain tools, we look for situations in which their use will be rewarded, but also try to create situations in which their use will be rewarded. The advance of interest permeates all aspects of bargaining systems. It nevertheless remains useful to distinguish one element of situation as determinant of interest and another element as determinant of potential disbursements.

Situation-related interest gives societies their evolutionary dynamic. People create understandings of their situation and identify the measures necessary to improve it, or protect it. They form an information interface based on their understanding of situation and formulate plans for change. The actions they take change the situation, intentionally in accordance with their plans, but sometimes in ways that are unintended. A new situation is then created, forming the basis of a new assessment of interest and new plans for improvement. Thus societies and economies evolve from situation to situation. The basis for assessment of interest is the understanding of situation established in an information interface, so that the information interface, as distinct from the reality itself, if there is a 'reality itself', is the basis for the evolutionary process.

The frame idea is perhaps best known, at least in a natural scientific context, as the idea of a paradigm. In this form it is now closely associated with Thomas Kuhn's contention that paradigm change is the essential feature of scientific revolutions. According to Kuhn, 'normal science' proceeds on the basis of experimental testing of hypotheses in accordance with a particular understanding of science in the scientific community. Scientists observe certain phenomena and interpret their significance in terms of the communal understanding – normally the paradigm in which they have been taught. Within that paradigm, certain anomalies are encountered which cannot be explained. This anomaly builds up until someone suggests a new way of interpreting observations. The new paradigm makes it possible to explain the old anomalies coherently, and a scientific revolution takes place. Such abstractions as 'force' and 'motion' come to be understood differently as the paradigm changes. As Kuhn acknowledges, the paradigm idea originates in the social sciences. The support-bargaining process makes plain the mechanism of paradigm change. As in the social sciences, scientific theories are formed through intellectual support-bargaining. The processes observed by Bruno Latour and Steve Woolgar, described in the previous chapter, show scientists 'negotiating' their theory. A group working within a particular paradigm will encounter anomalies and the validity of the paradigm will be questioned, most typically by younger scientists eager to make their mark. Max Plank caught the frustration of youth with the immovable convictions of earlier generations when he observed that 'Science advances one funeral at a time'. Someone like Albert Einstein suggests a new paradigm and the younger members of the scientific group support the new concept. A new era of normal science is set in train.[8]

The process testifies to the importance of the information interface. The reality does not change. The way it is observed and interpreted changes. The information interface changes because the organisation of information is changed, so that old information is interpreted differently, and new information is added to the information interface. The scope for change in the way information is organised is perhaps greater in the social and political spheres, where the vagaries of human motivation are prominent, and interests are much more pressing and conflicting. The competition to create frames of reference favourable to group interest is a fundamental part of the construction of the information interface; or rather, shared situation gives rise to the creation of a frame of reference as an integral part of the process of group formation for the advance of shared interest. That is the start of the manipulation of information.

Groups will disseminate information conducive to understanding of their situation and the advance of their interests. They will also want to limit the circulation of other information, or even ensure that it is withheld entirely. Groups will, as a means of securing support to themselves, want to disseminate information that is likely to erode the support of rival groups.

A public information interface in a support-bargaining society is thus composed of information that groups want disseminated for advancement of their interests, and information that is disseminated against the interests of rival groups. Advocates and opponents will select and distribute information according to their established frames of reference.

Political support-bargaining is centrally concerned with the dissemination of information that will attract or repel support. Political parties want information provided to the general public that will either directly advance their own interests or detract from the interests of rival parties. They will also want certain information withheld altogether from circulation outside the party. When in government, parties will have even larger volumes of information to manage for their advantage and protection, and for the advantage and protection of the nation. Information collection agencies, some concerned with the collection of information that other groups go to extreme lengths to withhold, will provide information on which a government can base its understanding of situation and hence its interests. This includes information related to areas where conflict is most prominent, such as military and diplomatic affairs, corruption, drug trading and the activities of terrorists. The whole business of government is conducted on the basis of information, all of it in some degree manipulated for the advance of interest or for the debasement of the interest of rival groups. What is available in the public domain is only a part of the total information impinging on government and the rivalry of political parties.

The frames of reference prominent in the political context are those associated with what has been described as the fundamental division in support-bargaining societies, that between individual and group interests, or the right and the left. For the individualist cause, in money-bargaining, as was seen previously, a highly stylised mathematical framework has become established, ostensibly aligning individual interest with communal interest. The assumptions on which the frame is based are recognised as unrealistic. Neoclassical economists spend much time and effort adjusting the model to reconcile its shortcomings with observed reality. But it is still retained as a frame of reference, largely, it must be concluded, because it serves the individualist cause too well to be abandoned. 'Near enough' is good enough when so fundamental an interest as that of individuals is at stake. For the group interest, a theoretical frame of reference was developed in Europe out of the very real hardships associated with industrial revolution in the nineteenth century, drawing on prevalent religious ideas of compassion, neighbourly support and concern for the underdog. The frame is transparently concerned with the advance of partisan interest rather than advancing any more universal social truth, and is consequently reckoned 'ideological'. It is retained not so much for its value as social scientific theory as for its value in advancing a group interest that many recognise as their interest against the threatening advance of individualist interests.

In the twentieth century rigid or non-negotiable frames of reference relating to both individualist and group interest flourished. On the right, fascism drew on theories associated with the philosopher Friedrich Nietzsche regarding an *Übermensch*, an 'overman' or 'superman', whilst on the left Karl Marx provided a frame of reference conducive to violent revolution of an industrial proletariat. The non-negotiable frames are necessarily incompatible with a support-bargaining process. Their objectives are held to be of such high ethical value as to justify violence. They require not just the support of their adherents for the ethical and moral principles, but also the violence that underlies their support. The support convention is rejected. Regimes based on them came into headlong violent conflict, with the support-bargaining societies caught up in the violence.

Information in the public domain is largely transmitted through commercial media organisations, so that such information is subject to further manipulation for the advancement of media interests. This aspect of the information interface is considered further in Chapter 8.

The above account of frames of reference and their function in selection and interpretation of phenomena is the selection and interpretation of support-bargaining and money-bargaining. As a frame of reference support-bargaining and money-bargaining provides an overarching or 'parental' view of other frames of reference. Uniquely amongst frames of reference, it makes apparent the role of information in the conduct of political, social and economic affairs. It shows how information is organised and manipulated for the advance of interest. It identifies the dynamic of intellectual support-bargaining through which frames of reference are developed in theory groups. They emerge not as dispassionate and disinterested accounts of the functioning of a society, but as group assemblies designed to attract support for ideas that will advance the interests of the group. They focus attention on phenomena and ensure their interpretation in such a way as will assemble support for the causes espoused by their creators.

This function of the theory of support-bargaining as a 'frame of frames' gives the theory a depth of focus that is lacking in other theories. Each 'discipline' tends to be concerned with a relatively narrow range of phenomena, and involves an assumption that it is representative of 'truth' in some fundamental sense. To deal with different phenomena, social scientists turn to different theories. Phenomena are brought into focus separately in the different disciplines. Significant inconsistencies between disciplines are accepted. Support-bargaining provides an account of both foreground issues and the background of beliefs, attitudes, theories and ideas that affect the decisions of the foreground. The connections between the two provide explanations that the subordinate disciplines cannot provide on their own. The information interface, covering the whole of human thought and activity, is an important explanatory factor arising from this fusion of frames.

Words and figures of speech

Adopting a frame of reference means learning a vocabulary and phrases that express the content of the frame. Members of the group committing to the frame will use the same vocabulary and turns of phrase. Adherents of the right wing or 'capitalist' frame use words and phrases such as 'free markets', 'individual freedom', 'enterprise', 'innovation', 'reward for hard work', 'self-reliance', 'excellence', 'competition' and so on. Adherents of the left wing or 'socialist' frame use words and phrases such as, 'communal responsibility', 'communal values', 'social justice', 'equality', 'equal opportunity', 'compassion', 'the working man', 'the people', 'exploitation', and so on. Adherents of right and left also have vocabularies to describe their opponents. The right wing abuses the left as 'dependent', 'scrounging', 'work-shy', 'parasitic', 'covetous', 'envious', 'statist'. The left abuses the right as 'selfish', 'heartless', 'grasping', avaricious', 'greedy', 'oppressive', 'unscrupulous', 'exploitative'. The words and phrases encapsulate the ideas that are systematically developed in the literature of right and left relating to each frame of reference. Such words and phrases are used because they are seen as likely to attract support to the causes of the groups using them, or alienate support from rival factions. Words and phrases with favourable or unfavourable associations or connotations are a preferred means of manipulating the information interface to advantage. So much of the information interface is necessarily constituted by language that it becomes of prime importance to ensure that language favourable to the favoured frame is embedded in the minds of people. People learn the vocabulary and derive the assurance of collective opinion from using it. It constitutes their 'deep thinking'. The vocabulary of faith dominated the thought of earlier periods. Right and left each have a vocabulary to advance their interests and devalue the interests of others.

The affiliations of words can effectively foreclose an issue. A news magazine, conscious of its wordplay, comments in the context of informal business enterprise, 'Plucky entrepreneurs who operate beyond the grasp of venal bureaucrats should surely be celebrated'.[9] The sentence is all but tautologous, or self-confirmatory. We support the 'plucky' and oppose the 'grasping and venal', especially when they are 'bureaucrats'. There is no chance of opposing the sentiment and maintaining popularity with the writer or speaker of such words. It is a matter of 'good' against 'bad'. But 'Entrepreneurs who evade taxation should surely be celebrated', is a decidedly contentious statement. The circularity is similar to that of the circularity arising from the definition of phenomena by reference to preconceptions, including the preconceptions arising from the use of distinct theoretical frames of reference.[10] The chosen words convey the preconceptions of what is to be viewed with favour, and supported, and what is to be viewed with disapproval, and rejected. The sentence then confirms what is preconceived in the word selection.

While the division between right and left no doubt goes back beyond recorded history, the formal engagement of ordinary people in the governance of Western societies goes back little more than a century. Engagement in debates centred on an information interface depends substantially on the ability to understand and organise information. Literacy, the ability to read and write, and not just speak, a language is fundamental. Education, involving training in the organisation and analysis of information, is almost essential. While people were largely illiterate and uneducated, it was possible for leaders of those societies, including leading churchmen, to govern with minimal reference to the interests of ordinary people. The threat of armed force was generally enough to keep the peace. With education and literacy, ordinary people gain the basic capacities for evaluation of information, the identification of their interests, and their expression. They have the vocabularies of their favoured frames and can use them to advance their interests. In the broadest terms they would already understand the conflict between individual and community, but with education and literacy they became equipped to participate more fully in the ongoing debates relating to governance.

Education brings about the construction of a more complex information interface, and an interface more concerned with ideas, for the most part caught in frames of reference. Support-bargaining is then less dependent on personalities, 'warlords', tribal chiefs and established institutions and more a matter of support for ideas regarding the actual circumstances of a society and how they might be improved. It enhances the potential of support to move from traditional loyalties to new groups that are responding to the perceived shortcomings of a society. A degree of flexibility in the movement of support is essential to the functioning of a full support-bargaining society.[11] Of course, even with education, the old loyalties, and new personalities, still exert their attractions. Education does not produce a society of informed judicious citizens, but does move a society on from the most rudimentary group loyalties.

The neoclassical economic model has been adopted as an essential frame of reference for the assembly of support on the right in Western society. It constitutes 'the market model', regarded by some as the foundation of Western prosperity and by others as the origin of its social injustices. The model has been developed, especially in the last half century, largely in mathematical terms, so that innumerate people and people not educated in the intricacies of the model can play little part in how it is evaluated and used. Having reference mainly to the mathematics, a large technical vocabulary has been developed by neoclassical economists that reinforces their support for the model and protects it against, as they would see it, ill-informed queries of the uninitiated and innumerate. 'Optimal allocation of resources', 'opportunity cost', 'economic rent', 'division of labour', 'total factor productivity', 'external economies', 'efficient allocation of resources', 'marginal cost', 'comparative advantage', 'market failure' all convey to members of the theory group respected essentials of the model and recognised successes of the group in reconciling its anomalies. Deployment of the vocabulary often carries users safely around awkward issues. The vocabulary of the model confirms its insights for its members and discourages any intrusion of the uninitiated.

Outside the theory group confidence in the model is certainly not so great. But still many are inclined to assume that if scholars selected by intellect and assembled in institutions specifically established for the cultivation of theories about society hold the model to be useful, then there must be something in it. They accept an information interface on the basis of its provenance rather than an informed conviction that it is right, in the sense of accurately explaining the dynamic of an economy. Acceptance is the easier if they find themselves attracted to the individualist side of the central contention.

The information interface is created as part of the efforts of agents in a support-bargaining system to assemble support. The greater part of the information interface is, as was seen in the previous chapter, codified in written language. The creation of the information interface is almost synonymous with the use of language, so it would be surprising if language itself were not influenced by the requirements of assembling support through the information interface. It was suggested in the previous chapter that language has been developed as a tool of support-bargaining. Groups create language as a necessary part of communication, and since they want to communicate in such a way as to gain support, or impede the assembly of support by others, language has developed to function in this way. Linguistic analysis assumes that the purpose of language is to convey meaning in an objective sense, but the purpose of language is to codify and transmit information in such a way as to assemble support for outcomes desired by its users. Words have connotations of approval and disapproval in the groups that use them. As was seen above, vocabularies have been developed by right and left that are laden with approval or disapproval.

The vocabularies of all languages permit their users to communicate approval or disapproval of some circumstance or event along with the simple communication of the circumstance or event. In fact, it is hard to describe an event or situation in any detail without revealing whether it is approved or disapproved of. Word selection communicates to an interlocutor whether he or she is expected to approve or disapprove of the matter communicated. Aspects of the matter will be selected for communication, but even when the same aspect is selected, the choice of words will reveal whether the desired reaction is approval or disapproval. Someone referred to as 'well-rounded' may be the same size as someone referred to as 'obese', but the former implies a degree of approval, or at least acceptance, while the latter implies disapproval. A 'slim' person may be the same as a 'skinny' person, but the former word denotes approval, while the latter is not just disapproving but disparaging. The capacity of words to convey valuations in this way facilitates the assembly of support. It gives people clues as to what they should assent to if they want to remain in the same group as the communicator; that is, if they want to maintain social intercourse.

'Well-rounded' may be used in conversation with a tone that implies tolerance of something that might not be entirely approved of. It is a kindly way, a way that sustains support, of saying that someone is obese. Euphemism of this kind is used to retain support when matters have to be related that potentially involve withdrawal of support. A 'lovable rogue' may be a vicious criminal to others, but his friends and relations may prefer not to refer to him in a way that implies withdrawal of support. Figures of speech in general are used to manipulate the information interface so that it generates support for those providing the information. Simile and metaphor are used to provide favourable or unfavourable associations for some action or proposal. When Norman Baker resigned from his post as minister for crime prevention in the UK Home Office in November 2014 he described working with the Home Secretary, Theresa May, as 'like walking through mud'. The purposeful stride of an enlightened Liberal Democrat in a coalition government was obstructed by a Conservative Home Secretary 'mired' in the old ways of thinking. It is clear who merits support. The competition of an economic system is sometimes likened to the competition of sport, so that economic competition seems as innocuous as athletics or cricket. The best man wins, and the implication is that there can be nothing wrong with that. George Orwell eroded support for the extreme left with an extended metaphor about an 'animal farm'. The transfer of words from one sphere to another to apply the valuations of one sphere to the other has some of the character of metaphor or simile. The 'scrounger' of political benefits is, or is like, the ordinary social scrounger.

John Searle in *The Construction of Social Reality* illustrates the persuasive potential of language in the context of taking a beer in a Paris restaurant:

> Notice, furthermore, that though my description was intended to be as neutral as possible, the vocabulary automatically introduces normative criteria of assessment. Waiters can be competent or incompetent, honest or dishonest, rude or polite. Beer can be sour, flat, tasty, too warm, or simply delicious. Restaurants can be elegant, ugly, refined, vulgar, or out of fashion, and so on with the chairs and tables, the money, and the French phrases.[12]

Whatever the physical reality, words can be used to express valuations in a bargaining process, and hence to give bargaining position. People will not pay for a 'flat' beer, but a beer that is 'simply delicious' will coax coins from pockets. And never mind the actual state of the beer.

The vocabulary of a language, as well as assigning approval or disapproval, provides a means of organising thoughts. Thoughts can be assigned to categories represented by words. Similarly, the grammar of language provides a means of organising thoughts. Actions and events can be categorised by the selection of appropriate grammatical forms. The simplest and most common organisational mode is that of agent and action; noun and verb: 'The man fed the dog'; 'The people demand their rights'. This mode is the easiest to use and the easiest to understand. For this reason, thoughts are frequently adjusted to take advantage of this most communicative mode of expression.

Thus observations of the consequences of events involving inanimate things are often reclassified to give them the form of agent and action. Something inanimate is personified so that it can act as a human might act. Personification is much used by poets and imaginative writers who depend for readers on the mellifluous nature of their language. 'Sunsets run', 'storms rage', 'brooks babble' and 'death exults' all across English literature. Personification is also commonly used for the communication of complex factual ideas. In *Support-Bargaining, Economics and Society* it was noted that Darwin's theory of evolution is much more simply and accessibly expressed in the sentence 'Nature selects her survivors' than in the sentence, 'Survival under natural selection depends on the presence of variations suited to the environment in which the organism is situated'.[13] Critics of Richard Dawkins' book *The Selfish Gene* note that the whole theory is based on the personification of genes.[14] Deities can be seen as personifications of natural causes.

The conviction carried by personification because of its conformity to the patterns of grammar can lead to unconscious and often misleading use of personification. Alvin Goldman argues that his version of the 'correspondence' theory of truth is given support by the use of the word 'truth' in the sense of faithful – a 'true friend' or 'true to one's word'. 'True' expresses a relationship of faithfulness or fidelity between a person and another object. The correspondence theory of truth is seen by Goldman as putting a description of reality into a similar relationship of faithfulness to reality itself. 'Thus, the basic intuition of the correspondence approach, that (descriptive) truth involves a relation to reality is correct.'[15] Goldman describes as an important feature of the correspondence theory:

> the claim that truth requires *'truth makers'*: worldly entities of some sort that *make* propositions or other truth bearers true . . . The standard candidate for truth makers are facts, and the usual form of the correspondence theory says that there is a distinct fact for each true proposition or sentence. 'Caesar crossed the Rubicon' is made true by the fact that Caesar crossed the Rubicon.[16]

The proponents of correspondence theory in this form personify the reality or 'facts' as 'truth makers' that can 'make' propositions true. 'Worldly entities of some sort' are given human powers of 'making'. Turning 'facts' or 'entities' into 'truth makers' does not make them any more suitable as real correspondents of statements of truth. Personification is not veritistically productive, since on the basis of common theory it discernibly misrepresents the reality. It may, however, be effective in assembling support and advancing interest. Goldman notes certain difficulties with the idea of 'truth makers' in correspondence theory, but concludes that the idea itself is sound: 'The crucial thing to retain is the commitment to truth makers, an element that deflationism and other rival theories either reject or ignore'.[17]

Goldman personifies unconsciously again when he asserts as a fourth condition of the achievement of veritistically good results that 'the asserted premises jointly provide strong support for the conclusion'. In this case it is so widely assumed in logic that premises lead to conclusions with objective force, without any necessity for human judgement, that the suggestion of personification may seem superfluous or even wholly redundant. It is widely accepted in logic that premises can 'imply' conclusions, so premises 'supporting' conclusions seems only a minor step further. But people give support for conclusions on the basis of premises. The personification makes it seem independent of human judgement, and hence fixes it more securely in the information interface. There is no option to say 'but I don't support it', if it is the premises that support the conclusion.

This point is the stronger in conjunction with Goldman's footnote on the fourth condition. He notes that almost all arguments of the type under discussion involve the omission of certain premises that are tacitly presupposed. The fourth condition then is reformulated as, 'the asserted premises *in conjunction with tacit premises justifiably believed by the speaker* jointly provide strong support for the conclusion'. It is not just the stated premises that are claimed to 'strongly support' the conclusion. On their own, they do not do so. It is necessary that the human beings involved bring to the debate a number of other premises which are commonly accepted in order to provide support for the conclusion. The stated premises are thus even less appropriate as agents of the 'support' they are supposed to provide. Again, personification leads its users to skate over important aspects of an analysis.

Acceptance that premises behave in this human way, as agents of support, has arguably blinded scientists and philosophers of all kinds to the empirical observation that what is accepted as fact depends on accumulation of support for a fact being a fact. Personification of premises has helped to remove logic clear of human judgement or human commitment; and concurrently there has been a failure to recognise the necessity for and significance of support and the intellectual support-bargaining process by which it is assembled. If people support conclusions on the basis of their recognition of the validity of the premises, it is a matter of human judgement, and thus a little less secure than the idea that premises alone support the conclusions. The information interface is made to look sturdier than it is. Again, the use of personification passes unnoticed, partly because it is so easy to express understanding in language with sentences constructed on the basis of agent and action. Language can be used to codify and communicate ideas in ways that give the ideas more substance than may be appropriate. The distinction between support given by premises and support given by people who hold premises is not a contrived or pedantic interpretation of logical practice in accordance with preconceived theory. Designating the premises as giving support sidesteps a major element of the dynamic of the creation of ideas and connections between them. Loose language, occasioned by the structure of language, has sustained misunderstanding of the nature of human knowledge. It is not absolute and objective, but the creation of human minds, and created for the advance of interest.

As has been seen, language constitutes the chief means of codification of the information that forms the information interface and it provides the basis for support-bargaining and money-bargaining. One implication of this is that it will be difficult to carry on a support-bargaining process amongst people who do not share a language. Britain opted in a referendum in June 2016 to leave the European Union. The major issues apparently prompting the rejection of the Union were high levels of immigration and a sense of loss of control over the affairs of the nation. But the lack of communication between the leaders of the Union and British people, arising from the lack of a common language, the lack of a common information interface in which to conduct a support-bargaining process, probably contributed to the sense of alienation in Britain. The constitutional structure of the European Union limits the engagement of people in the governance of the Union, giving rise to ideas of a 'democratic deficit' in governance. But the constitution is perhaps no more than recognition of the difficulties of operating a full support-bargaining system in the absence of a common and accessible information interface. The operation of a 'support convention', which in the understanding of support-bargaining is the defining feature of 'democracy', is only possible when those involved communicate freely for the assembly of support across the society.[18] The difficulties of communication must at least have contributed to the British conclusion that the support convention in the European context did not work for them.

Frames and language provide the means of organising information. Latour and Woolgar emphasise their observation of scientists organising the information about their activities and observations.[19] In terms of support-bargaining, the propensity to organise and the need for organisation arise because human beings have a sense of symmetry. Humans need to identify the way the world 'fits together'. They recognise how an observation 'fits' into a frame of reference. They recognise how an 'impressionist' frame enables them to see and understand certain aspects of the reality they experience. Humans recognise and understand through patterns involving multiple observations and accumulations of knowledge, rather than deriving knowledge through discrete observations and the logical relationship of each discrete observation to another. The latter is the form of understanding prominent in academia. But humans in general look for consistency of pattern and will conclude they have understood something if it is consistent with all their other observations and knowledge.

In neoclassical economics mathematics is used to codify ideas regarding monetary transactions, ostensibly portraying transactions without the connotations of language. It is claimed that this relieves neoclassical economics of the linguistic obscurity and tendentiousness that impede clear exposition in other social sciences. But just as the structure of language influences the portrayal of ideas in linguistic codes, so also mathematics imposes demands on economic theory. The concepts of the neoclassical economic frame of reference are selected by reference to the requirements of mathematics. What cannot be formulated mathematically is regarded as irrelevant. 'Products' have to be homogeneous since only then can they be aggregated as 'supply' and 'demand'. People have to be rational so that they always make what are quantifiably the best decisions. Information has to be 'perfect', because only then can a mathematical model be formulated. The marginal concept of neoclassical theory is perfectly suited to the use of calculus. The mathematical codification of neoclassical economic theory is considered further in the following chapter.

Mathematics has to be used in a social scientific context to illuminate concepts established independently of the requirements of mathematics as a system of coding. Mathematics is a tool for use in attaining certain ends, not an end in itself. The idea of support-bargaining and money-bargaining involves symmetry as the psychological process by which humans make their choices. The mathematics of symmetry is then in principle the appropriate mathematics for the analysis of consumer selection and other aspects of economic transactions. It is, unfortunately, recognised as very difficult, but that cannot be allowed to preclude its use when appropriate to conceptual circumstances. To date, we have suffered from conceptual over-simplification of economic relationships for mathematical convenience.

Imputation of motivation

Common theory provides a frame for assessing and if necessary censuring the behaviour of people. In general, common theory, as might be expected, tends to require behaviour that is advantageous to the community rather than to the individual. People are required to act unselfishly, to show concern for others, to contribute rather than extract. Certain motives win approval under the common theory, while certain other motives are condemned.

Hence it is possible to assemble support for a person or group, or alienate support away from a person or group, by attributing motives to them that are commonly favoured or not favoured. This constitutes one of the main means of manipulating the information interface. Because no one can know the motives of others with any certainty, it is easy to attribute good or bad motives to people with little risk of being proved wrong. The vocabularies of approval and disapproval noted above are in many cases concerned with motivations.

In social support-bargaining people may affirm that someone is behaving selfishly in order to deny them support for their behaviour. Someone who takes more than a fair share of space in an office, or who persistently takes more than a fair share of communal food, is likely to be condemned as selfish. Someone who persistently advertises their achievements, or denigrates colleagues to their own advantage, is likely to be condemned as ambitious and suffer withdrawal of support. Motives that give rise to behaviour that is contrary to the interests of the group are likely to be condemned, and such motives may be attributed to people by those who wish to impede their advance.

Altruistic motivation is, on the other hand, likely to be praised. The perpetrator of altruistic actions is likely to receive communal support. It is, above all, the communally approved motivation. People are encouraged to act altruistically for the good of the group, the society. Compassion, an emotion strongly associated with altruism, also receives communal support. People giving to beggars on the street or funding charities for succour of the poor and unfortunate can expect to receive the approval of their society. Such virtuous motivation can be imputed to people in the information interface to promote their advance.

The idea of support-bargaining suggests that while it may be expedient for societies to praise altruistic behaviour in their community, the underlying motivation for altruism is the need for support that is essential to the psychological well-being of the individual. 'Altruistic behaviour' exists only in the context of social control and order. The psychological truth is that altruistic acts are performed for acquisition of something that is in varying degrees essential to the individual.[20]

The group or communal approach to social relations, the 'left' in political terms, sees the motivations of many individuals engaging in money-bargaining as 'selfish'. Instead of working for communal advantage, they advance their own interests, with little concern for others. Societies have nevertheless opted to tolerate such selfish behaviour, recognising that it advances the material prosperity of communities. Companies provide what people need and want, and provide remunerative employment in doing so. Economists since Adam Smith have emphasised the beneficial social consequences of individual enterprise. The neoclassical model purports to demonstrate mathematically the infallible connection between individual self-interest and social advantage.

Societies tolerate more generally the pursuit of individual interest if it is reckoned that the selfish behaviour will make sufficient returns to society. A 'bargain' is made between individual and group. Leaders can indulge all their selfish interests, including interests in social ascendancy, if they can make returns to the society in the form of its ascendancy over other societies, or expanding wealth, or providing peace and stability. Leaders emerge at all levels of society and are permitted to indulge their personal desire for authority so long as they lead their followers roughly in a direction they are prepared to take.

Because certain motives are communally approved under common theory and certain other motivations draw disapproval, there is always an inclination for people to proclaim the former type of motivation even if they act under the latter type. Politicians invariably proclaim to be motivated by a desire to advance the interests of their community, even if their actions suggest a prominent concern for advancement of their own interests. Communally approved motivations, normally relating to the advance of communal interests, are in general advanced as motivations. The communal sense of what is 'virtuous' is commonly a part of proclaimed motivations. People want to help the disadvantaged, help the poor, provide care to the elderly and infirm, or house the homeless. These admirable motivations assemble support, and very often finance, for the proclaimed objectives. Because they are effective in that way, they may also be used to create what is no more than a public information interface facilitating the clandestine advance of personal or even specifically anti-social interests. There are avowed motivations, such as will attract communal approval, and unavowed motivations, that will usually be those that would be expected to give rise to withdrawal of support.

Charitable organisations, openly motivated by a desire to advance communal causes, may harness the motivations of money-bargaining to their causes by contracting companies to raise money on their behalf in exchange for a percentage of the revenues. Such companies, given their concerns over the viability condition, will have less moral inhibition with regard to the methods they use to extract money from people sensible of charitable obligations. The financial motivations of a business organisation are quietly used to support the noisily virtuous motivation of a charity.

Charity prominently advances communal or group interests and consequently has affinities with theories of the left concerned with the advance of group interests. Some charitable organisations assume, as part of their commitment to charitable assistance to the poor and disadvantaged, a commitment to advancement of political parties and groups advocating socialist policies. Those making charitable donations will not necessarily intend to support the associated political commitments. A charitable motivation is not necessarily a political motivation.

The global financial crisis starting in 2007 owed much to the concealment of disapproved motivations beneath claims of approved motivations. Officials of Fannie Mae, a government-sponsored agency for the issue of mortgage-backed securities, convinced the President and many influential interest groups that it had found a new way by which poor people could become homeowners. Subprime mortgages were issued and consolidated into securities on a grand scale. Those sceptical of the innovation were sidelined as lacking in compassionate commitment to promote the well-being of the poor. Approved motivations were noisily used to assemble support for activities involving clandestine motivations that would certainly have brought to an end the whole operation had they been known. Officials of Fannie Mae were later found to have been cooking the books to ensure that they profited from the financial bonuses triggered by achievement of revenue targets.[21] The information interface will feature prominently the 'good' motivations, since they are the proclaimed motivations and the motivations that attract support, but people may be acting on 'bad' motivations.

Even at the grandest theoretical level judgement may be clouded by regard for approved motivations. Charles Darwin attached little importance to self-preservation as motivation, mainly because of the influence of Thomas Malthus, but perhaps partly because it was not a communally approved motivation. Darwin was reluctant to accept that people might be motivated by self-preservation as strongly as they were motivated by the desire to fulfil their obligations in defence of their group. As a consequence, he missed the trigger to support-seeking and the formation of groups, leaving a large gap in his theory of natural selection.[22]

Motivation and 'truth'

Amongst approved motivations, the pursuit of 'truth' is one of the most common and most celebrated. If people are pursuing the truth, then plainly it is to be assumed they are without bias and self-interest. There is one unique truth, and most people will agree that by and large it is better that we know it. But being so attractive, the pursuit of truth provides admirable cover for the pursuit of self-interest. Virtually everyone is part of a religious culture, and finds it widely acknowledged that 'the truth', as far as their society is concerned, lies in some transcendental or supernatural belief. But it is apparent that the pursuit of that particular form of truth has led to the advance of personal, social, institutional and political interests. Many popes and cardinals of the Catholic Church led lives of remarkable personal indulgence. Protestant bishops in Northern Europe enjoyed privilege and power which they used for personal as well as communal advantage. Academia was for centuries infused with the notion that 'truth' was a revelation of faith, and stamped on any suggestions to the contrary. The requirement that dons at Oxford University should have taken holy orders was removed only in 1871. Academics secured their positions in institutions of learning by securing the support of those in authority, most of whom owed their authority to religious affiliations.

There remains in academia a prominent commitment to the pursuit of 'truth', even though the nature of the 'truth' sought has changed over the years. Less prominent is the pursuit of personal career interests. Peter Earl comments:

> Career pressures along with self-image and lifestyle aspirations may shape the kinds of work that gets done. Without an academic position it is hard to do any research in economics, but it may be hard to obtain such a job if one turns out work that is judged unfavourably by mainstream thinkers on appointments committees (for example, mathematical, equilibrium-oriented economists may tend to dismiss behavioural economics as mere 'economic poetry').[23]

The pursuit of truth has to be adapted to the feasibility of such pursuit within the established institutionalised support-bargaining networks of academia. The most common adaptation is acceptance of the prevailing view about what constitutes truth, so that pursuit of a personal career is consistent with pursuit of what is taken to be the truth within the relevant group. As was seen in the Introduction, Joseph Stiglitz and Paul Krugman followed this course, even though both appear to have been aware that they were not pursuing 'truth' even as they understood it.

Goldman's pursuit of truth is motivated, as he would himself claim, by a desire to identify the true and separate it from the false. But as was suggested in the previous chapter, his pursuit of truth involves at the same time the pursuit of interests of a conservative social nature. In the name of his version of truth he approves the exclusion of someone who takes a different view. He attributes to Richard Rorty the theory, in brief formulation, that, 'truth is what peers let you say'. Rorty argued that consensus is important, implying the importance of the group in intellectual forums. It hints also at the role of support-bargaining in defining what is understood as truth. Rorty left Princeton for the University of Virginia. Goldman remarks in a footnote, 'Rorty's move from the philosophy department at Princeton University to the English department at the University of Virginia undoubtedly put him in a milieu more receptive to his theories'. If it is not possible to adapt to the local conception of truth, it may be necessary to move to another locality. Goldman holds that the pursuit of truth should not be motivated by anything other than a desire for truth. That is the motivation he claims for himself. Rorty is condemned as motivated by a desire for the acclaim of his peers, the acclaim of a group, rather than pursuing the truth. So Goldman does not regret the departure of Rorty for Virginia. Yet Goldman frequently cites the opinions of his peers in support of his arguments, without recognising it as anything other than the common practice of his peer group. In effect, he attends to what his peer group will let him say. He is assembling support for his ideas in an intellectual support-bargaining process. Thus, 'most philosophers agree that SS-knowledge ['superstrong knowledge'] is largely unattainable'; 'it is widely accepted that S-knowledge is feasible for external, or moderately transcendent, states of affairs';[24] 'the track record of nonscience is surely not superior to that of science'; 'there is little doubt that people who deploy appropriate scientific methods have vastly better track records of belief';[25] 'How can CSS [Comparative scientific superiority] seriously be doubted?';[26] 'No single view has received a clear majority'.[27] Goldman even appeals for agreement that the idea that agreement is of fundamental importance is an illusion: 'the notion that agreement is the fundamental aim or guide in matters intellectual is surely an illusion'.[28] The ultimate authority is the peer group. That is how 'social knowledge' impinges on individual knowledge.

Paul Romer's account of the trouble with macroeconomic theory, discussed in the previous chapter, is a further exemplar of the theme, involving the departure of Romer himself from the theory group that he criticises for setting personal interests above the truth. Confusion of the pursuit of 'truth' with the pursuit of group support is integral to intellectual support-bargaining. Whatever the underlying motivation, theory-formation can always be glossed as the pursuit of truth.

Claims to the pursuit of truth may also be used to mask motivations of a more political and practical kind. They may be used, for example, to stigmatise certain social groups as undeserving of assistance, or particular races and cultures as inferior. They may be used to erode support from particular institutions. The obverse of this is that societies, including some academic groups, may neglect the pursuit of truth for fear that its outcomes will give rise to hostile reactions from particular communities or institutions. Societies may choose to suspend the pursuit of truth, at the behest of influential interest groups, when it involves threats to social cohesion, or to significant interest groups. Social cohesion may be better served on occasions by ignoring awkward truths or suspending investigation of 'sensitive' issues.

Motivations of left and right

Political parties in a political support-bargaining system constitute specialist support-bargaining agencies. They are set up to assemble support in sufficient volume to give them a majority in a legislature and hence to govern a country. Information is necessarily manipulated to this end. The motivation 'to raise support', pure and simple, is not approved in common theory. It suggests ingratiation and hypocrisy rather than the frankness that is approved in common theory. Politicians consequently avoid references to this fundamental necessity of their adopted profession. Instead, they emphasise motivations consistent with ideas embedded in common theory.

Amongst the foremost of the virtues recognised in common theory are compassion and altruism; the desire to help others and serve the community. These motivations are embedded in the socialist frame of reference. They commit a party to pursue in particular the interests of the poorest and most vulnerable. The vocabulary of the frame, as described above, centres on the virtues of communal care. Thus a left-wing party seeks to assemble support not by pronouncing its commitment to the pursuit of support, but by asserting a motivation that is most likely to assemble support.

The virtues of compassion, sharing, generosity and altruism, so strongly supported amongst ordinary people, do not transfer in the same form to the assembly of support by political parties operating in a political support-bargaining system. In their 'genuine' form they involve personal commitment, even personal sacrifice. In the political context they do not have this implication. The compassion of governments is expressed through expenditures on education, health, social welfare, social housing, pensions and so on. The programmes are funded by impositions on other sections of the community, so that a political party might be said to reap the benefits of compassionate motivation without the sacrifices involved in 'genuine' acts of compassion. Private compassion has different implications to public compassion. The right challenges the motivation of the left by demanding that their personal morality accord with their espoused political morality. If their compassionate policies are genuinely heartfelt, politicians of the left should share more freely the great wealth that some of them possess. If equality is of such importance, they should use the same state facilities as are provided for ordinary people.

The left is centrally concerned with the interests of the group, as opposed to those of the individual. The Labour Party in the United Kingdom was specifically established to advance the interests of working people. So their proclaimed motivations accord with motivations widely approved in the community. The right is more supportive of the individual side of support-bargaining. It is inclined to cultivate motivations associated with self-reliance, innovation and action, such as are displayed in business enterprise. The eradication of poverty, important as it is, is better done through the creation of jobs, through the creation of companies, using motivations of self-reliance and self-advancement, rather than through the exercise of compassion. More people are saved from poverty by getting a job than are saved by compassion. Such people are, furthermore, saved from what is to some the ignominy of dependence on charity. People support the motivations related to individual initiative, but probably not to the same instinctive extent as they value human sympathy and compassion. In historical terms, business innovations have reduced poverty far more than any exercise of charity, and have at the same time made possible the survival of many more people.

In the circumstances, the right cannot afford to ignore entirely the popular support for group-oriented motivations of compassion and altruism as the means of relieving hardship. Right-wing parties have a second string to their bow in the recognition that such motivations can only be exercised if there are funds available to do so. The growth of money-bargaining generates growth in revenues to governments which can be expended on social services. The growth of business is not the alternative to compassionate expenditures, but an essential precondition. The right claims the same compassionate and communal motivations as the left, but claims to pursue them in a more effective, if more roundabout, way. It remains easier for most people to support simple notions of compassion than a 'system' that provides better outcomes. In most cultures, earning is worthy but does not have the same communal approbation as giving. The biggest earners in capitalist societies commonly replenish their social support by big giving.

Support-bargaining is motivated by a primal concern for self-preservation, expressed in a perennial need for support. It has been found possible to base whole political systems on a 'support convention', whereby support substitutes for violence in the establishment and conduct of national governments. The benefits of such a system, to anyone with the least sense of self-preservation and love of peace, are immense. One penalty, however, is that some everyday 'genuine' person-to-person honesty and communal frankness becomes lost in the systematic pursuit of support. Even the expression of support itself is deprived of its humanity. In the political context, popular support is for the most part expressed by a cross on a ballot paper. The primacy of this form of support, the element of hypocrisy that it inevitably introduces, and the loss of common humanity it entails, are amongst the headaches that induce dreams of an alternative society.

Much of the information interface is created by the imputation of motivations to individuals, groups and organisations engaged in support-bargaining and money-bargaining. It is nigh impossible to identify with certainty the motivations by which these agencies act. Proclaimed motivations are perhaps rarely the true motivations, and perhaps never the full motivations. The mixed motivations of Herbert Simon's academic curriculum committee, referred to in Chapter 1, are part of a much broader phenomenon. Unconscious motivations, driven by instincts for the assembly of support, or other psychological impulses, are likely to be as important as the motivations acknowledged. It is as a consequence of this elusiveness of motivation that there is such scope for imputation of motivations in the information interface.

Psychology, support-bargaining and the information interface

Psychologists have failed to recognise how the instinct for self-preservation is expressed in the search for support, and the consequences of this in group formation and the dynamic of support-bargaining. The psychological concern with self-preservation has been confined largely to its role in ensuring individual survival and propagation of the species. Group formation is recognised, but not understood. Abraham Maslow, a leading motivational psychologist, suggested in his 1954 book *Motivation and Personality* that psychologists and people in general neglect the instinct for 'herding': 'And we have largely forgotten our deep animal tendencies to herd, to flock, to join, to belong'.[29] The observation comes in the context of Maslow's identification of the human need for 'love and affection'. It illustrates a major gap in psychological theory, still not filled: there is no clear understanding of the mechanism by which groups form. It is easy to forget such psychological propensity when there is no frame of reference that draws attention to it. The theory of support-bargaining is precisely concerned with the mechanism that causes humans to herd, or form groups.

The lack of recognition of the importance of the instinct for self-preservation in providing the impulse to assembly of support, even by the specialist social scientists in whose domain it lies, tends to confirm what has nevertheless been a prominent contention of psychologists since the work of Carl Jung and Sigmund Freud: that the greater part of what we think and do is unconscious, or thought and done without awareness of what we are thinking and doing. This implies that the information interface is constructed largely on the basis of unconscious drives. Since they are unconscious, it is necessarily difficult to identify what they are. Nevertheless, the emanations of them in the information interface give numerous clues as to what they are and why we have them. The psychology of support-seeking itself is deduced as the 'best explanation', the most consistent explanation, of observed patterns of behaviour.

Psychologists recognise self-preservation as an important driver of human behaviour in the context of survival and propagation – in the context of natural selection. It is, however, a characteristic that is generally disapproved of in societies when there is any threat to their existence. Societies promote bravery and self-sacrifice in defence of the community, and frown upon any inclinations to run away. Darwin characterises self-preservation as the motivation that causes a man to shrink from his duty to save a stranger from drowning when in a position to do so.[30] So it is a 'bad' trait. Societies expend much effort in establishing an information interface that condemns the instinct for self-preservation as unmanly and detrimental to the communal interest. People who are concerned with their own self-preservation are 'cowards', and should know that their society disapproves of them. There may consequently be some reluctance to support any theory that rests on the importance of self-preservation, since any such theory may be seen not simply as resting on its importance, but positively endorsing self-preservation as a driver of action. Because it assembles support for recognition of the importance of self-preservation in human action, it may be construed as assembling support for indulgence in self-preservation. As in the religious context, acceptance of the theory may be taken as implying the necessity of certain behaviour. If interest drives theory making, as is understood in support-bargaining, then theory will necessarily imply actions. Psychologists concern themselves with the working of individual minds, but this includes the relationships between individual minds, so there seems no explanation on that score for their failure to identify the consequences of the instinct for self-preservation on group formation and the process of support-bargaining. It seems possible that they, like Darwin, instinctively avoided propositions that would elevate self-preservation to such a prominent position as driver of human behaviour. Better that 'love and affection' should give rise to 'herding' and belonging, as in Maslow's account, rather than that so contemptible an instinct as self-preservation should generate such an outcome. It is perhaps another instance in which the avoidance of truth has been found desirable in the interests of social cohesion to achieve a social objective.

Some of the phenomena associated with self-preservation are given attention through a focus on 'fear', the psychological alert that registers when our self-preservation is threatened. The reaction to 'fear' is often mellifluously summarised as 'fight or flight'. It gives rise to action that seems most likely to ensure our preservation, whether it is running away from trouble or fighting whatever or whoever is threatening. It is predicated on a very immediate threat coming, as it were, out of the blue, and a reflex action to deal with it. However, the more fundamental reaction to fear and the desire for self-preservation is the formation of alliances with others through the assembly of support. It cannot be the reaction to the 'out-of-the-blue' encounter, but familiarity with just such encounters is likely to give rise to considerations of how they can best be dealt with, in recognition of the risks of further such encounters. The focus on the alert rather than the underlying concern for self-preservation has meant that the strategic reaction to insecurity – the seeking for support – has been overlooked. The options should at least be summarised, rather less mellifluously, as 'fight, flight or form an alliance'.

Psychology and motivation

Motivations originate in psychological predispositions. Motivations might be regarded as the identifiable emanations of psychological dispositions, or the more immediate instigators of behaviour arising from psychological states. Motivation generally implies a movement towards some aim or objective, while a psychological state implies an inner drive. While motivation is generally regarded as being at least in some degree a matter of choice, a psychological drive is more likely to be understood as irresistible. Motivation may be overt or hidden, conscious or unconscious. But psychology is almost always understood as operative through the unconscious mind. Our motivations develop, and may develop into conscious motivations, through the unconscious influence of our psychology.

The instinct for self-preservation, on which the idea of support-bargaining rests, exemplifies this fine distinction between motivation and psychological impulse. Soldiers in action must retain a conscious concern for their self-preservation. They must take cover when bullets are flying around or bombs are falling. People in the ordinary course of their lives must consciously take care of themselves, for example when crossing roads. Self-preservation is in some circumstances a conscious motivation. But, at the same time, it is an unconscious and ingrained psychological drive. We have the reactions of the jungle when caught unawares by something that our minds detect as a threat. We may shy away instinctively from behaviour of others that we find threatening. Our minds tend automatically to remove us from threats to our lives and limbs, and even from mental discomfort. We can consciously seek to preserve ourselves, but we also have extensive automatic propensities to behave in ways that will protect us. The former may be classified as motivation, while the latter is more recognisably 'psychological', even if it is also a hidden and unconscious motivation. It is much stronger than the instinct for aggression. No commander ever had to exhort his troops to run away.

The psychology of situation

Most of the time our minds carry us along in accordance with our interests. Human survival seems to have involved evolution of a capacity for reflexive self-preservation and protection or advancement of interest. This capacity seems to include a sense of the situation by reference to which we must act. Survival in a world of tribal violence would necessitate understanding of situation in terms of relative strengths of the various forces and the nature of the terrain over which combat might take place. We have, it seems, an instinctive sense of situation, and the instinctive sense also to recognise the interests that arise from identification of the situation. It was noted in *Support-Bargaining, Economics and Society*, and recalled above, that it is difficult to describe a situation without revealing whether it is approved or disapproved, and hence revealing what interests are involved.[31] It was suggested that the nature of language gives descriptions this tendentious character, but it is also the case that our concepts of situation are formed with an instinctive sense that involves the identification of interest. Language codifies and communicates inclinations or understandings that are contained in the ideas. The information interface thus incorporates designations of situations shaped to a large extent instinctively by those whose interests lie in such designations of situation.

What is true of the identification of 'situations' applies also to the theoretical counterpart, the propensity to create the frames of reference that govern the more abstract elements of the information interface. We instinctively create theories that are conducive to our interests. It seems to scholars that the theories they are creating are the products of their conscious analytical minds but, in terms of the present theory, they are as much products of unconscious interest expressed in frames of reference. The distinction made by economists between 'positive', or descriptive, accounts of economic activity and 'normative', or prescriptive, forms is intended to separate the 'science' from any interest-led prescriptions for social policy. But, as they are forced to admit, it is not possible to make the distinction with any assurance.[32] Descriptions tend automatically to imply prescriptions. The 'positive' account of the behaviour of individuals and the resulting optimal allocation of resources has inescapable 'normative' implications. Situations and frames of reference imply interests and are conceived for the advance of interests.

Unconscious expression in the information interface

Interest may be more directly advanced through the dissemination of information to the information interface. Our instinctive private inclinations may conflict with what we anticipate our community will expect of us – an aspect of the most fundamental argument of support-bargaining, that between individual and group. We can take a 'public viewpoint'; we can adjust our behaviour as if someone, or 'society', were looking over our shoulder. But on occasions we may find our personal interests of such pressing importance that we ignore communal obligations. We may, as suggested in the previous chapter, tell lies to protect ourselves. The knowledge that we are acting contrary to the interests of the community may cause us to regret the lies. The consciousness that we risk losing the support of the group that is so necessary to us will intensify the alarm at having lied. Telling a lie means, moreover, that we have to be careful to follow the adopted story line of the lie, which is one amongst many that might be adopted, rather than the unique story line of the truth. There is a good prospect of being caught out by the group and punished by withdrawal of support, expressed in mild or strong manner. We may seek reconciliation with the group. We may abandon selfish behaviour to secure the support of those around us. While we are aware of having lied and feel the guilt of it, we are not normally aware of any distinct mechanism involving the requirement for support that underlies our behaviour. We instinctively pursue individual interest in provision of certain false information, but then recognise transgression against the group, and against our own concern for support from the group, and seek reconciliation. We exercise both selfish individual instinct and an instinct, perhaps more tinged with calculation, for the interests of the group. Our individual interest is inextricably tied in with the interests of the group.

Unconscious impulses to certain behaviour are commonly understood as occurring when the conscious mind is at rest, or not engaged in any specific task. Random impulses and inclinations deriving from the unconscious mind give us the traits and foibles that constitute our 'personality' or 'character'. However, the most telling expressions of our unconscious, particularly with regard to the creation of an information interface, may occur when our attention is concentrated on some particular matter. When we concentrate on something to the point of absorption, we lose the conscious, self-aware, deliberative mode of action and permit the play of the unconscious or subconscious mind around the subject of our concentration. Businessmen concentrate on the investment and organisation necessary to business success, and their subconscious minds may direct them in accordance with their purpose. People play computer games with great absorption and it seems likely that their subconscious minds direct their reactions to events on the screen as much as any conscious determination. Musicians similarly become absorbed in their performances, and incorporate emanations of emotion and sentiment deriving from their subconscious reactions to the music. Writers may similarly experience 'the book writing itself', suggesting that their subconscious mind takes over and develops the storyline or the line of thought. The subconscious mind may follow a sense of symmetry or pattern to pursue what is already committed to. The idea of a 'muse', traditionally portrayed as an angelic figure whispering in the ear of a writer or painter, personifies this sense of the subconscious mind determining what is done when a mind is concentrated on a certain subject. What we can concentrate on – music, business, sport, writing – determines largely what we can do over a sustained period, even over a lifetime, suggesting that we can do only what our subconscious minds will work on. We are most 'ourselves', most confined to our own inner selves, when we are concentrating on something that absorbs our minds.

The situation concepts and frames of reference which form the foci of an information interface seem to be constructed largely under the influence of unconscious psychological propensities to assemble support and advance interest. Individual and collective psychological states play out through support-bargaining to establish certain physical, temporal and human features as accounts of situation, albeit rivalrous and often conflicting. The assessments and the interests identified in relation to them constitute the information interface of that society. It determines how the society identifies its interests and the actions it takes. Psychology directly shapes the information interface across the minds of all those involved. We emit, as much from our subconscious as from our conscious thought, what seems advantageous to us and likely to attract support. While much of the information interface is taken up with minor situations and information relating to everyday matters of social goodwill and shopping, there are also issues of broader communal concern, expressed particularly in the political sphere of support-bargaining. Even in peaceful times, security remains a preoccupation. If there is no immediate danger, there may be something shaping up to become so. The instinct for self-preservation is so strong that violence is always a matter of concern, whether conscious or unconscious, and whether deriving from people, animals or objects. Support-bargaining flourishes in such circumstances, and throws up an information interface that assembles support to deal with whatever threats emerge.

Imputation of psychological drives

As was seen above, motives, good or bad, are commonly imputed to those engaged in support-bargaining in order to assist or impede their assembly of support. Psychological drives are similarly imputed. Agents of support-bargaining can be flattered or damaged by the imputation of psychological drives; their assembly of support can be facilitated or impeded by such imputation. This kind of imputation is used much more to discredit people than to give them credit. Psychological drives seem to be generally more shameful than flattering; concerned with the darker depths of the human psyche. People can be made to look unreliable or even deranged, and hence unworthy of support. A person may be described as 'obsessed' with money, status, power, revenge, class, the poor and so on to deprive that person of support in the community for the causes espoused. The implication is of irrational concern with a particular approach to an issue. In Britain Liberal Democrats characterised the Tory Chancellor of the Exchequer, their partner in the coalition government, as 'obsessed' with the budget deficit at their Party Conference in 2014. Even in intellectual support-bargaining, imputation of psychological disposition is used to discredit opponents. As was seen in the previous chapter, Goldman describes opponents of his veritistic approach to truth as 'veriphobes', and postmodernists as 'obsessed' with language.

One of the stranger imputations of psychological drive was the imputation by Boris Johnson, when Mayor of London, that the Kenyan ancestry of Barak

Obama, the President of the United States, made him ill-disposed towards Britain. Johnson was campaigning for Britain to vote 'leave' in a referendum on British membership of the European Union. President Obama, on a visit to Britain in April 2016, undermined the campaign by asserting that a new trade treaty between the United States and a Britain outside the European Union could take five to ten years to negotiate. Britain would be 'at the back of the queue' for a trade deal. It is hardly conceivable that Obama would be aware of such a motivation, and unlikely that it is even an unconscious part of his psychological disposition. His statements seemed designed to support the British government position on membership of the Union. Johnson seems to have imputed a highly unflattering motivation or psychological disposition of post-colonial vengeance to President Obama in order to deter any support he might attract to the faction in Britain that favoured remaining in the European Union. Perhaps even stranger was the appointment of Johnson, three months later, as Foreign Secretary.

The imputation of psychological dispositions often implies that people are of such a mental state as makes them unsuitable for the normal processes of support-bargaining, whether social, political or intellectual. Irresistible urges characteristic of paranoia, arrogance or a domineering disposition imply that the sufferer is a threat to the good sense and compromise that is essential to a support-bargaining system. Donald Trump, in the campaign for the presidency of the United States in 2016, was stigmatised as having a 'narcissistic personality' and other psychological traits that made him unsuitable for the job. He nevertheless won the presidency. Self-assertion at least seems to be a psychological trait advantageous to political leaders in the eyes of their supporters. It would certainly seem unwise to entrust negotiations to those who are too self-effacing and too much given to compromise. Assignment of such characteristics to anyone aspiring to political leadership is likely to erode support from that person and stall their progress. The vocabulary for such characteristics tends more to the colloquial than the psychological: 'weak', 'spineless', 'a pushover'.

The complex functioning of psychological dispositions in human societies may thus be whittled down in the cut-and-thrust of support-bargaining to rather crude imputations of mental weakness or derangement. For those using this method of discredit, it has the advantage of being difficult to refute. Psychological disposition is inherently difficult to identify precisely and beyond doubt. Psychology is even less contestable than motivation. Victims may disclaim 'obsession' or 'fixation', but disclaimers may carry no weight when victims are necessarily unconscious of their unfortunate psychology.

Support-bargaining and the unconscious psychological processes related to it have gone unrecognised by psychologists. The distinction between unconscious and conscious behaviour, or between intuitive and considered behaviour, is nevertheless a major focus of attention in psychology. Support-bargaining and the formation of an information interface identifies the mechanism by which psychological impulses, and attributions of psychological impulse, affect social and political evolution. Daniel Kahneman analyses the distinction between impulse and analysis in the form of 'System 1' and 'System 2' behaviour in his book *Thinking, Fast and Slow*, discussed in Chapter 5.

Notes

1 See, for example, Jain, Anil and Duin, Robert, 2004, 'Pattern recognition', in Gregory, Richard L. (ed.), *The Oxford Companion to the Mind*, Second Edition, Oxford: Oxford University Press.
2 See also Spread, Patrick, 2008, *Support-Bargaining: The Mechanics of Democracy Revealed*, Sussex: Book Guild, Chapter 11: Frames and echoes.
3 Spread, Patrick, 2013, *Support-Bargaining, Economics and Society: A Social Species*, Abingdon: Routledge, Chapter 8: Common theory and personification. See also Spread, Patrick, 2012, 'Science and support: the struggle for mastery in economics', *Real-World Economics Review*, Issue No. 59, pp. 39–57, March.
4 Blau, Peter, 1964, *Exchange and Power in Social Life*, New York: Wiley. For comment on sociological norms and Blau's 'social approval' see Spread, 1984a, *A Theory of Support and Money Bargaining*, London: Macmillan, paras 4.26–31; see also, Spread, Patrick, 1984b, 'Blau's exchange theory, support and the macrostructure', *British Journal of Sociology*, Vol. 35, No. 2, pp. 157–73; reprinted in Spread, Patrick, 2015b, *Aspects of Support-Bargaining and Money-Bargaining*, E-Book, World Economics Association.
5 See Spread, Patrick, 2013, *Support-Bargaining, Economics and Society*, Abingdon: Routledge, pp. 31–4; Spread, 2008, pp. 11–33, etc.; Spread, Patrick, 2011, 'Situation as determinant of selection and valuation', *Cambridge Journal of Economics*, Vol. 35, No. 2, pp. 335–56; reprinted in Spread, 2015b.
6 On capacity, see Spread, Patrick, 2004, *Getting it Right: Economics and the Security of Support*, Sussex: Book Guild, pp. 48–9; see also Spread, 2008, pp. 75–7, 85–93; see also Spread, Patrick, 2016a, *The Evolution of Economies*, Abingdon: Routledge, pp. 30–1.
7 On budgeting, see Spread, 2004, pp. 35–52.
8 For earlier comment on Kuhn's theory of paradigmatic change, see Spread, 1984a, paras 1.20–22, etc.
9 *The Economist*, 2016b, 'The shadow economy: unregulated, untaxed, unloved', 15 October, p. 57.
10 On definition, see Spread, 2016a, pp. 79–82, etc.
11 On rigid groups in support-bargaining societies, see Spread, Patrick, 2015c, 'The political significance of certain types of group', in Spread, 2015b.
12 Searle, John, 1996, *The Construction of Social Reality*, London: Penguin Books, p. 4.
13 Spread, 2013, p. 177.
14 See for example, Kaye, Howard, 1986, *The Social Meaning of Modern Biology*, New Haven: Yale University Press, p. 137–47; see also Spread, 2013, pp. 188–90.
15 Goldman, Alvin I., 2003, *Knowledge in a Social World*, Oxford: Oxford University Press, pp. 60–1.
16 Goldman, 2003, p. 61.
17 Goldman, 2003, p. 63.
18 On the emergence of the support convention, see Spread, 2008, pp. 386–90.
19 Latour, Bruno and Woolgar, Steve, 1986, *Laboratory Life: The Construction of Scientific Facts*, Princeton: Princeton University Press, pp. 33–9. First published 1979, Sage Publications.
20 See Spread, 2013, pp. 180–90.

21 Morgenson, Gretchen and Rosner, Joshua, 2012, *Reckless Endangerment*, New York: St Martin's Griffin. See also Spread, 2016a, pp. 210–17.
22 See Spread, 2013, Chapter 1: The problem with natural selection, esp. pp 20–4.
23 Earl, Peter, 1995, *Microeconomics for Business and Marketing*, Cheltenham: Edward Elgar, p. 96.
24 Goldman, 2003, pp. 23–4.
25 Goldman, 2003, p. 249.
26 Goldman, 2003, p. 250.
27 Goldman, 2003, p. 253.
28 Goldman, 2003, p. 71.
29 Maslow, Abraham H., 1970, *Motivation and Personality*, Third Edition, New York and London: Harper & Row, p. 20. First published 1954.
30 Darwin, Charles, 2004, *The Descent of Man, and Selection in Relation to Sex*, London: Penguin, p. 134. See also Spread, 2013, pp. 23–4.
31 Spread, 2013, p. 173.
32 See Spread, 2008, pp. 288–90.

4 Economics and the information interface

It was seen in the previous chapter that the prime means of advancing interests in a support-bargaining and money-bargaining system is the establishment in the information interface of a frame of reference that will guide perceptions and interpretations in accordance with the desired interests. This chapter seeks to show the process by which neoclassical economic theory became established as the 'mainstream' frame of reference by which economists would observe and interpret economic exchange. Neoclassical economic theory built on Adam Smith's enquiries into the relationship between individual initiative and communal interest to provide a formal demonstration of the merits of 'free markets'.

It was seen in Chapter 1 that work on the economics of information by mainstream economics has emphasised the importance of 'asymmetric information'. The origin of this idea is an article by George Akerlof ostensibly illustrating problems of quality in the market for used cars. The model implies the most unlikely consequences arising from different quality in used cars. Akerlof's article has been interpreted as providing mainstream economics with an account of information that is acceptable as supplementary to the neoclassical model. This chapter suggests that it is more plainly a demonstration of the failure of the model as a useful reference.

The chapter then describes the theory of support-bargaining and money-bargaining as a frame of reference for the understanding of economic transactions. The theory describes the essential role of information. Information is disseminated by the agents of the bargaining system to form an information interface in which support-bargaining and money-bargaining are conducted. Companies disseminate information to promote the transaction they seek to conclude. Consumers acquire information to assess whether products and services will meet the requirements dictated by their situations. Governments engage as agents of the money-bargaining system, though their engagement is dictated by support-bargaining. Money-bargaining originates in support-bargaining and requires continued government attention if its agents are to engage in transactions with confidence. Government provides also various services pertaining to communal interest, some of them essential to the functioning of money-bargaining.

Neoclassical economic theory as a frame of reference

In the theory of support-bargaining and money-bargaining, the development of theory is a matter of intellectual support-bargaining, by which support is assembled for certain ideas or theories, deriving from the interests of their instigators. The support they assemble is potentially of significance to the political support-bargaining of a nation as a whole. The evolution of theory thus has to be understood in the context of the overall political and social evolution of a society.

No theory has been more influential intellectually and politically in Western societies than Adam Smith's *An Enquiry into the Nature and Causes of the Wealth of Nations*, first published in 1776, commonly referred to as *The Wealth of Nations*. Smith drew together the work of various earlier economic theorists into his own context of moral concern over the economic processes and their effects. His original interest lay in moral philosophy. His earlier book, *The Theory of Moral Sentiments*, argued that moral sensibility arose from the human faculty of sympathy with others. By sympathising, or what we might now call 'empathising', with others, we gain insight into the feelings of others and develop a sense of how we should behave towards others. *The Wealth of Nations* was concerned particularly with the way economic activity affected a society. It was a concern very close to that identified as the foundation of support-bargaining – the conflict between individual interest and the group, or 'society'. It was written at a time of significant economic change in Britain. The great majority of people were still employed in agricultural pursuits, but here and there across the country new technologies were transforming lives. James Watt's improved steam engine went into service in the 1860s. People, and increasing numbers of people, were beginning the long migration from the country to towns, from fields to factories, from subordination to landowners to employment by companies. Just thirteen years after the publication of Smith's *Enquiry*, Europe was convulsed by news of revolution in France.

Smith's theory displaced the prominent idea that economic advantage lay primarily in gaining a larger share of a 'fixed cake' of economic returns. With a fixed cake, one person's benefit is necessarily another's loss. Smith identified the division of labour as the means by which the 'cake' could be expanded to the benefit of all. Through a division of labour it was possible to expand output per head and thus increase the size of the cake. Expanding output per head meant also that it was feasible to increase income per head. The abundance arising from a division of labour spreads opulence across a society:

> It is the great multiplication of the productions of all the different arts, in consequence of the division of labour, which occasions, in a well-governed society, that universal opulence which extends itself to the lowest ranks of the people. Every workman has a great quantity of his own work to dispose of beyond what he himself has occasion for; and every other

> workman being exactly in the same situation, he is enabled to exchange a great quantity of his own good for a great quantity, or, what comes to the same thing, for the price of a great quantity of theirs. He supplies them abundantly with what they have occasion for, and they accommodate him as amply with what he has occasion for, and a general plenty diffuses itself through all the different ranks of society.[1]

The division of labour arises from individual initiative in organising and investing in production. Smith thus suggests that the pursuit of individual interest will be advantageous to society as a whole; that the pursuit of private advantage in competitive markets will advance the general prosperity of society.

These circumstances of general prosperity arise, however, only in 'a well-governed society'. They will not come about automatically. When Smith later describes in greater detail the process of monetary exchange it becomes apparent that he does not recognise the exchange process as free from practices that will impede the sort of benign outcome that might otherwise be possible.

Smith designates 'natural prices' as prices which cover the costs necessarily incurred by a business in producing its products.[2] He designates 'market prices' as the prices which arise from excess or deficiency of demand in a market place. Adjustments are made to rents, wages and profits in accordance with market prices, though generally wages and profits bear most of the adjustment.[3] 'Market prices' may be above, below or precisely equal to 'natural prices'. There will be, he argues, a tendency for producers to adjust the quantities they produce to the effective demand, so that prices always tend towards 'natural prices'.[4] Smith notes that it is often possible for businessmen to keep secrets of their trade which enable them to maintain high profits, albeit mostly for short periods. He describes also how grants of monopoly and regulations such as those concerned with apprenticeships can create artificial shortages of supply in relation to effective demand and maintain market prices above natural prices over long periods.[5] Smith notes also that in negotiations over wages, 'masters' are as much disposed to combine in constraint of competition as labourers and, being smaller in number, find it easier to do so, and, being wealthier, can hold out for longer in any dispute. According to Smith, 'Masters are always and everywhere in a sort of tacit, but constant and uniform combination, not to raise the wages of labour above their actual rate'.[6]

Later in the book, at the end of Book I, Smith assesses the relation of the interests of landowners, labour and those who live by profit, the 'master manufacturers', to those of society in general. The interests of the first two, deriving their incomes from rents and wages, are assessed as strictly connected with the interests of society. The interests of the 'third order', however, are assessed as generally different and even opposed to the interests of the public. They try to narrow competition and thereby raise prices above their natural level.[7] Any proposal for laws or regulations from this order,

> comes from an order of men whose interest is never exactly the same with that of the public, who have generally an interest to deceive and even to oppress the public, and who accordingly have on many occasions, both deceived and oppressed it.[8]

At natural prices the third order is connected with the interests of the public, but it contrives to constrain competition and raise market prices above their natural level, to the disadvantage of the public. Their proposals, according to Smith, have to be assessed with scrupulous and suspicious attention. Smith's three orders become, in neoclassical theory, the three resources of land, labour and capital. The order of 'those who live by profit', having interests contrary to those of society in general, become the 'capitalists' of Marxist theory.

As the rise of the 'common man' gained momentum in the course of the nineteenth century, the idea that individual self-interest could be justified on the grounds of its social benefit proved irresistible to those wishing to stem the collective tide. Smith's theory was adapted in the late nineteenth century into a 'neoclassical' theory that made 'natural' pricing the normal circumstance of economic transactions. 'Natural prices' became the 'market prices' of a model economy. Any enhanced profitability that could arise from constraint of trade was ruled out by assumptions regarding rational behaviour in a competitive system. If any businessman was making excessive profits, others would enter his trade, and prices would fall back to their 'natural' level, close to the costs incurred in production. Any excess profits arising from secrecy were ruled out by an assumption of perfect information. Various further assumptions were necessary to make possible the desired outcome. In the first place, all producers had to be of such small size that none of them alone influences a 'market price' that is set by the interaction of the demand of all consumers and the supply of all the small producers. For this market-price-setting process to be feasible, all producers in a particular product market have to produce exactly the same product. Nor is it possible to make any distinctions of location, since, if transport costs are incurred, every location involves a different cost and each location would have a different market price. Each producer maximises his profits by expanding production to the point at which marginal revenue, which is the 'market price', is equal to the marginal cost. The mathematics representing the process suggested that a 'market' operating on these principles would move towards an equilibrium with an 'optimal allocation of resources', in the sense established by Vilfredo Pareto, in which no one can be made better off without someone else being made worse off.

As in Smith's theory, the division of labour is the main source of increases in output and the expansion of the 'cake'. Competition ensures that the incomes arising from expansion of output are shared across individuals in accordance with their contributions to production. Everyone is payed what Smith calls a 'natural' price, which becomes payments in accordance with productivity. Even the technological revolutions across industries in the nineteenth century were not sufficiently apparent to the formulators of neoclassical theory to suggest to them that technology was the major factor behind the expansion of output. That was perhaps too inconvenient when interests of such fundamental social and political importance were at stake.

Smith himself recognised the importance of technology, but explained it as a consequence of the division of labour. Labour divided did simple tasks, such as readily lent themselves to mechanisation. Technology was machinery that did the mechanical tasks of human limbs.[9] But even in the pin factory it might have been observed that the division of labour arose because of the demands of a pin-making machine, rather than the other way round. Smith refers to 'the use of the machinery' in pin-making, but suggests immediately, in parenthesis, that the machinery is probably itself also a result of the division of labour.[10]

The immediate basis for this suggestion is Smith's contention that a great part of the machines used in manufacture were originally inventions of common workmen, arising from their familiarity with the tasks they were engaged in. He acknowledges that not all machines originate with the people who perform the tasks it replaces, which is clearly true, but avoids any recognition that not all machines perform tasks that might otherwise be done by humans, which is surely no less true. He insists on explaining more complex technology as originating in the division of labour amongst 'those who are called philosophers and men of speculation'. The advantages of such division of labour are held to be the same as those deriving from the simple division of tasks: 'this subdivision of employment in philosophy, as well as in every other business, improves dexterity, and saves time'.[11] But while concentration of effort on technological issues is undoubtedly necessary to technological innovation, such specialisation is markedly different in kind from the division of labour in the pin factory. In the pin factory a process is broken down into simple repetitive physical tasks. This division of labour raises productivity. It has further cost implications (not mentioned by Smith) in that simple tasks can be performed by unskilled, and hence low-paid, workers. Here the development of physical dexterity and the time savings involved with the elimination of switches from one task to another are important. But technological innovation is a matter of enquiry and exploration, of initiative and highly irregular activity. It requires certain qualities of mind, rather than dexterity and time saving, or the division of an overall process into simple tasks. Nor are productivity gains and cost savings of the type achieved by the division of labour in the pin factory generally of pressing importance. A crucial innovation can bring ample financial compensation, even if the risks of failure are high. The steam engine is an outcome of this enquiry and exploration. It is much more than automation of human capacities. The early technologies of the industrial revolution depended on the transforming effects of heat on various materials, including, in particular, water and iron. Coal was important as the source of heat. Smith identifies the division of labour as the basic explanatory factor in his frame of reference and is at pains to portray machinery, or technology, as a consequence of the division of labour. It is a fatal flaw in his analysis. As Robert Heilbroner remarks:

> Smith was writing in an age of preindustrial capitalism. He seems to have had no real presentiment of the gathering Industrial Revolution, harbingers of which were visible in the great ironworks only a few miles from Edinburgh. He had nothing to say about large scale industrial enterprise.[12]

For all his prowess as observer, assimilator and analyst, Smith missed some crucial developments of his time, perhaps because his human-scale frame of reference did not direct his attention to the industrial-scale enterprise that was emerging. Ascribing a dominant influence to technological innovation would have implied a radically different account of the process of exchange, the growth of industry, its social impact and even the moral status of business practices. Neoclassical economists found the division of labour nicely compatible with the mathematical model they wished to construct and, on the authority of Adam Smith, were able to treat technology as no more than incidental to the transactions they chose to model.

The incapacity of the neoclassical frame of reference to accommodate technological innovation in any satisfactory form is related to its simple concept of 'the firm'. The output of 'firms' is represented in the neoclassical model as expanding along a marginal cost curve until its marginal cost is equal to its marginal revenue. The concept is dictated by the requirements of the rest of the model for supply and demand curves to create a market price.[13] Technological changes can only be accommodated in the stylised form of shifts of the curve in its totality to reflect a new relationship between output and marginal costs brought about by new investment. The major changes in products and their costs arising from technological innovation cannot be explained by reference to the neoclassical model. Technology is, in the jargon, 'exogenous' to the neoclassical model. Products in the nineteenth century were increasingly products made possible by technological innovations. Companies gained competitive advantage through technological innovation. The technology incorporated in company formats brought about the industrial revolution in Britain and spread it around the world.[14]

Technology is also difficult to accommodate in the neoclassical model since technology is plainly an outcome of evolutionary processes. An existing process might be recognised as unsatisfactory with regard to its speed of operation, the quality of its output, or its costs. Recognising the defects, technologists would work on remedies and come up with new technology. The mathematics of the neoclassical model suggested a tendency to equilibrium with 'optimal allocation of resources'. Technology did not fit well into this conception. The evolutionary process involved extensive disruption and step change. Whole industries were being transformed by technological innovation, rather than by the 'marginal' processes that were the central concept of the neoclassical model.

The neoclassical model retains Smith's ideal concept of small businesses employing and selling at 'natural prices', transformed into the concept of 'market prices' under extensive assumptions regarding the market participants and conditions. Smith's account has 'natural prices' as sufficient to sustain a business.

He is vague about the precise level of 'natural prices', recognising that profits have to sustain a business in times of temporary disruption and, particularly in agriculture, in the face of vagaries of climate. The 'natural price' is the lowest that can be taken, 'for any considerable time together'.[15] In the neoclassical concept these caveats are missed in the mathematical precision of the model. Firms competing in a neoclassical market have the weakest possible bargaining positions; so weak that even if belief is suspended so far as to permit the possibility of their existence, it cannot be extended to the possibility of their survival. The neoclassical conception of firms is purely a matter of fitting them into the mathematical framework of the model. The connection of neoclassical 'firms' with the companies of the real world is little more than the name. Companies have to distinguish their products from those of other companies, select locations most advantageous for their operations, make technological innovations or form cartels in order to ensure their survival and, beyond that, make their owners comfortable. In some cases, for example that of cartels, their manoeuvres are found so advantageous to them in strengthening their bargaining positions, and so correspondingly disadvantageous to other agents, that governments commonly legislate against them.

Smith's account might conceivably have been developed into a theory something like that of money-bargaining; perhaps a theory of 'competitive exchange'. Smith's account of the activities of 'masters' might have been developed into a theory of companies something like that of money-bargaining, in which companies are understood as the specialised agencies of a money-bargaining system, as referred to in Chapter 1 and described in greater detail below. The emergence of the neoclassical model seems to owe something to a desire to eliminate contention from economic exchange. The preference was for a 'rational' system that implied any contention would be resolved in an orderly manner. 'Bargaining' suggests a rather unseemly process of haggling or wrangling. It may in itself be undesirable, but everyone involved in business at the time Smith wrote would surely have recognised it. 'Money-bargaining' conceives monetary exchange as a bargaining system based on 'money' as a bargaining counter. 'Money' is understood as part of the cultural evolution generated through support-bargaining, performing a function analogous to that of 'support' as the bargaining counter of the support-bargaining system.[16] The value of 'money' is sustained by the support of the group in which it is used. Unseemly wrangling is often part of money-bargaining, just as it is part of support-bargaining. Information disseminated to the information interface can both exacerbate and reduce conflict. Very commonly, to reduce the time and friction of wrangling, consumers are offered products at marked prices which are understood to be fixed.

Advance of the neoclassical model

By the start of the twentieth century the neoclassical or 'marginal' model had become well established.[17] In England its major features had been portrayed by

Alfred Marshall, Professor of Political Economy at Cambridge, in his *Principles of Economics*, published in 1890, which over the next forty years increasingly displaced John Stuart Mill's *Principles of Political Economy*, published in 1848, as the dominant textbook for the teaching of economics. Marshall developed the diagrammatic representation of the neoclassical model that became the standard form of instruction. He nevertheless conceived economics in very broad terms, as concerned with the ordinary business of life, the acquisition of the material requisites of well-being. He recognised, moreover, that economic activities involved both individual and social action, and constituted only a part of a wider range of individual and social action.[18] Economics was still 'political economy', in which society was engaged as well as individuals. Marshall's project involved a second volume that was never produced, even though he lived to 1924. Being a meticulous scholar, he perhaps found that his analytical methods could not do justice to his conception.

At the London School of Economics and Political Science, founded by the socialists Sydney and Beatrice Webb, scholars were mainly concerned with the development of a more historically oriented economics. But even there, marginal economics made its way in the person of Lionel Robbins. In *An Essay on the Nature and Significance of Economic Science* Robbins provided what has become the standard definition of economics, the way economics is understood as a 'mainstream' theory. As quoted in the Introduction: 'Economics is the science which studies human behaviour as a relationship between ends and scarce means which have alternative uses'.[19] The definition opens the way to, even requires, the use of mathematics to evaluate different relationships between resources and their usage. It is concerned with human behaviour, but only as a stylised factor in the allocation of scarce resources. Mathematics permits the identification of an 'optimal' allocation of resources. People acting rationally in pursuit of rational interests in certain defined circumstances will produce such an outcome. The neoclassical information interface is dominated by mathematical formulations and diagrams that ostensibly identify relationships between economic variables experienced in the real world. Analysis is frequently conducted on the basis of movement 'along curves' or in terms of 'shifts of the curve' to left or right. An 'optimal allocation' is identified with the maximum output registered on a curve: the point where a rising curve representing rising output turns into a downward curve representing falling output. The information interface so created is instructive within the confines of the assumptions but diverts the attention of analysts from the real world. It nevertheless has the intended effect of all frames of reference: it steers human understanding and observation in accordance with the patterns of the frame.

The mathematical element in the study of resource allocation was strongly developed in an influential textbook by Paul Samuelson, *Economics: An Introductory Analysis*, first published in 1948. It became the dominant text for the post-War English-speaking world, particularly in the United States. Samuelson made a conscious effort to apply to economics the techniques he had acquired from study with physicists. Samuelson's account of economic processes centred on a theory of constrained optimisation.[20] In the latter half of the twentieth century economists became increasingly focused on an analytical frame of reference, and were increasingly divorced from the realities of everyday life. Roger Backhouse remarks:

> Economics has come to be structured not around a set of real-world problems, but around a set of techniques . . . Much research has been driven by an agenda internal to the discipline, even where this has not helped solve any real-world problems.[21]

The comment identifies the weakness of the neoclassical model as a frame of reference: it is more a frame of self-reference, rather than a frame that provides guidance to what is relevant or valuable in the real world of experience. It guides its adherents towards self-sufficiency within their own theory group. To a large extent, analysis can be conducted without any identification of what is in the real world, using just the notions of 'prices', 'products', 'resources', etc. that are sufficient input for the model. The perceptions of the model are diagrams concerning supply, demand, costs, prices, etc. The frame of reference disposes its users to look inward as if all that is to be resolved can be resolved within the assumptions of the model. Issues can be settled within the theory group to the satisfaction of the theory group without reference to external phenomena.

Such phenomena as it does identify are stamped with its own preconceptions. The terms used suggest it is dealing with aspects of the real world as commonly experienced. But closer consideration of the role they play indicates that they are mathematical ciphers rather than actual phenomena of experience. Emmanuelle Benicourt advises a starter student in economics to be wary of the idea that it is a study of the real world, like physics. The words used may suggest realities, but:

> Although some of the words used in his microeconomics class, like 'goods', 'commodities', 'household', 'firm', 'market', 'price' and 'supply and demand' sound familiar, he rapidly learns that the economics teacher is using them to designate objects that have practically nothing to do with what we usually mean by these words. Instead they refer to fictitious entities, and not approximations of something that really exists.[22]

With such words, such vocabulary, neoclassical economic theory creates its own information interface. It operates within its own assumptions and techniques, with only the most limited relationship to the phenomena with which its words would normally be connected in everyday discourse and providing only the most superficial reference by which to take account of and explain the real world. It appropriates the vocabulary of the common information interface and uses it to refer to its own conceptions, making it appear that they are part of the world of common experience. An artificial information interface is created for mathematical analysis, with scant relevance to its ostensible subjects in the real world.

The neoclassical model makes use of mathematical ciphers, or mathematical codification. It can use words as Benicourt describes because words permit flexibilities in usage that mathematical codification does not permit. It was apparent to all that linguistic codification lacked precision, could be interpreted in different ways, was persuasive in an unscientific manner, and might even be tolerant of possible contradictions. Even at its best, linguistic codification was manipulative – the offending traits were apparent even in the *The Wealth of Nations*. Mathematical codification offered an alternative that promised freedom from such distortions. Mathematical codification, however, brings its own restrictions which are seriously counterproductive for a theory of the functioning of societies. The restrictions amount to manipulation of information as misleading as that involved with the use of linguistic codification.

The precision of mathematics requires precision in the concepts it deals with. This is scarcely a drawback when dealing with the precise material things of the natural sciences. To the extent that economics deals with precise quantities of precise material things, such as shoes, pens and spectacles, mathematical codification seems appropriate. But these objects of economic interest are all modified in accordance with human interests and requirements in a way that the gases, fluids, metals and glass of the physical world are not. Shoes have different sizes and styles; pens can be different colours and sizes; they come with and without clips for the pocket; spectacles have different optical specifications and styles. The precision of mathematics can then be misleading. To do justice to such variety, the range, richness and nuances of language are required. Language can deal with a great range of concepts and their subtle variations that cannot be accommodated in mathematical codification. Mathematical codification in economic theory required adoption of assumptions that *made* the phenomena at issue conform to the requirements of mathematical codification and mathematical analysis.

The use of mathematical codification also isolates neoclassical theory as a 'stand-alone' frame of reference, depriving its practitioners of any opportunity to evaluate their observations by reference to other frames of reference. This referencing of observations to other frames makes it possible to discern what are, on grounds of consistency, more probably accurate understandings of phenomena. All frames of reference are 'self-referencing' in that they draw attention to what is already prefigured in the frame. In *Support-Bargaining: The Mechanics of Democracy Revealed*, this characteristic is considered in terms of an 'echo effect'.[23] But the neoclassical model is nevertheless distinctively confined by the requirement for mathematical codification of phenomena. The phenomena it ostensibly deals with are the common phenomena of everyday experience, but the common frame of reference is codified linguistically, so that its observations are not reckoned determinant within the neoclassical theory group. The understandings of the common frame of economic phenomena are substantially different to those of the neoclassical frame. The neoclassical frame of reference provides a unique frame of reference for its adherents, with the distinctive veracity of mathematics, giving them a right, on their own reckoning, to ignore other frames of reference. But what are observed are distinctive creations of the neoclassical frame. The neoclassical frame excludes many of the crucial phenomena of economic exchange, including the role of information. By design, neoclassical economic theory maintains its own exclusive viewpoint and understanding, associating it with common reality only through the associations of its vocabulary.

The phrase 'optimal allocation of scarce resources', following Robbins' definition of economics, runs as a motif through economic theory. It is ostensibly the merely technical state of Pareto-optimal allocation referred to above. But the vocabulary is persuasive. An 'optimal' allocation of resources inescapably implies 'the best' allocation of resources. You cannot improve on what is 'optimal'. So when an economic system based on free individual enterprise and free markets produces an 'optimal' allocation of resources, it is supposed to be a fact of life that cannot and should not be contested. Established as a frame of reference in the information interface, the model causes people to observe and interpret phenomena in a way that is conducive to the interests of those promoting individual freedom. The model is 'sold' on the basis of this quality of providing an optimal allocation of resources, leaving recipients to make what they will of the word 'optimal'. But the technical specification of 'optimal' makes any particular optimal distribution of resources specific to the existing distribution of income. Because of this, any 'optimal state' cannot be regarded as optimal in any universal sense. And certainly, any technical optimal distribution of resources in any Western nation would not be regarded as optimal in the community at large, given prevalent opinion on the distribution of income. Given the skews of income, many people would not mind too much if people at the lower end of the income distribution scale received a little more and people at the upper end received rather less. Being 'optimal' is not the same as being 'the best' or even being acceptable. The promotion of the model as conducive to optimal allocation is in any case deceptive, since the quality of optimal allocation is attributable only to the most basic formulation of the neoclassical model. Relaxing any assumption involves loss of that quality. And assumptions are necessarily relaxed as soon as attention is turned from the mathematical to the empirical.

The metaphor of an 'invisible hand' has also been extensively used to promote the idea of individual interest being unintentionally the instrument of general social benefit. George Akerlof and Robert Shiller, as recorded in Chapter 1, praise markets as expressions of a beneficial 'invisible hand'. The phrase derives from Smith, but does not form part of his main analysis of exchange. It is used late on, in Book IV, in the context of the preference of private businessmen to invest in their own country rather than overseas, thereby making domestic incomes as high as possible, and thereby supposedly rendering benefit to the whole of society.[24] As has been seen, Smith clearly recognises that the activities of his 'third order' may not accord with any public interest. The idea of the 'invisible hand' has been invaluable in the information interface created by neoclassical economics as a striking encapsulation of the role of individual interests in advancing social benefit. While it originates with the great man himself, it is more an incidental allusion, and not consistent with his analysis of markets. Smith may have been frustrated at his inability to establish that private interest was fully compatible with the public good, but his analysis shows plainly that, whatever compatibility there may be, it is far from complete. Smith may have found it particularly frustrating because the incompatibility has to be attributed to what he sees as the avarice of businessmen; that is to say, immorality. Their behaviour spoils society and spoils Smith's ambitions for his theory. Sheer weight of interest overcame such scruples in neoclassical economics. The harmony of individual interest and public benefit was demonstrated in the neoclassical model and the identification of such harmony was attributed to Smith and his 'invisible hand'. Because the phrase has been so widely used to promote the individual interest, it is understandable that it should also have been used to refute what is supposedly Adam Smith's theory. Even sophisticated analysts set up the 'invisible hand' as a 'straw man' to tear apart. Joseph Stiglitz has no ambitions to tear apart the paradigm, so he acknowledges an 'invisible hand', but describes it as 'palsied'.[25]

Even apart from its absence in Smith's analysis of markets, his 'invisible hand' is dysfunctional as the metaphor for the efficacy of markets that neoclassical economists claim it to be. It causes investors to invest in their domestic economy, rather than investing where productivity is highest. The 'invisible hand' is thus an agent of irrational sentiment and a misallocation of resources. Its superficial accord with their ambitions for their theory has caused neoclassical economists to misrepresent what Smith actually describes as the work of an invisible hand.

The neoclassical frame has certainly been effective in assembling support for the idea that free enterprise in free markets is good for society. But economists can hardly claim its success rests on the truth or realism of its propositions. Its success has perhaps owed more to the fear that if support could not be rallied to the cause of free enterprise the alternative theory of a wholly communal approach to economic affairs might gain sway. The group, sustained by socialist or communist theory, might gain total ascendancy, as it did in the Soviet Union and China, or at least an uncomfortable degree of ascendancy. The Cold War against the totalitarian left that followed the Second World War provided real threats to cement Western intellectual support around a theory that, imperfect as it might be, offered the best chance of protection against an enemy. If communism was the alternative, then neoclassical economic theory had to be 'right'. The hearings in the United States instituted by Senator McCarthy on un-American activities in the early fifties must have convinced many economists that the neoclassical model was sufficiently 'right' to be treated as 'right'. The neoclassical group sustained its position as champion of the individual in intellectual support-bargaining against the spread of communist ideas. Within the 'democratic' societies of the West in the twentieth century support-bargaining regulated a balance between individual and group interests, each side deriving intellectual support from its frame of reference.

Concerns over the philosophical, sociological and above all the scientific status of economic theory have been the focus of debates on economic methodology. The assumption of established methodological analysis is that theorists are seeking 'the truth'. Methodologists investigate whether the methods adopted are likely to achieve or have actually achieved this aim. With the idea of support-bargaining, theory formation is a matter of intellectual support-bargaining. The aim is the advance of interest rather than the exclusive pursuit of truth. It may be advantageous to interest to pursue the truth, but the pursuit of interest may dictate other priorities. Scientific method is used by theory groups in pursuit of truth as a means of minimising the distractions and distortions arising from the pursuit of support. The established methodological approach is thus based on markedly different understanding of the objectives of enquiry and theory formation. Neoclassical economic theory is heavily criticised in methodological analyses for its lack of concern for empirical evidence suggesting that its assumptions and analysis are false. Spiro J. Latsis, a leading methodological analyst, wrote in 1976: 'The crucial question is the following: Is all awkward evidence to be regarded as either unreliable or reconcilable or can it serve a serious critical role?'[26] As was seen in Chapter 1, William Beveridge criticised in 1937 the lack of concern for 'observation' in the context of Keynes' *General Theory*. Neoclassical economists appear to have been little disturbed by such questions. They have assembled enough support, arguably because of the political and institutional interests involved, to thumb their noses at methodological quibbles. For the most part, they have persevered with the neoclassical model on the grounds that it is a 'useful simplification', and better than alternative theoretical offerings in the form of, for example, institutional economics or evolutionary economics based on natural selection. Some, as was seen in the Introduction, frankly acknowledge a preference for the comfort of the theory group. Disdain for evidence is far from exceptional. Interest commonly leads the search for selection and acceptance of evidence, rather than evidence leading opinion. But such disregard is contrary to the principles promoted in academic disciplines connected with the natural sciences. The question of the scientific status of neoclassical economics is largely overtaken in the context of intellectual support-bargaining by the question of the status of scientific method itself, discussed in Chapter 6. The specific judgement on neoclassical theory is that it admirably exemplifies the way the process of intellectual support-bargaining can so advance interests as to produce theories of very wide acceptance and influence which are nevertheless transparently lacking in the realism of evidence-based scientific and social theory.

Akerlof and asymmetric information

In the assessment of the economics of information in Chapter 1 it was noted that an article by George Akerlof on 'asymmetric information' had been a source of much debate over the implications of information for neoclassical economic theory. Akerlof's article illustrates what are, from the viewpoint of support-bargaining and money-bargaining, major deficiencies of neoclassical theory, including its deficient understanding of information. Akerlof's article, 'The market for lemons: quality, uncertainty and the market mechanism', concerns difficulties over quality in the neoclassical concept of a market, illustrated by reference to the market for used cars.[27] It introduces the idea of 'asymmetric information', which has become, as noted in Chapter 1, a prominent part of subsequent analysis of the role of information in economic theory. The central argument of the article is that the absence of information about the quality of a product could result in the complete elimination of all transactions involving the product. Markets could be completely lost because of uncertainties over quality. Akerlof argues that if it were not possible to distinguish between different qualities of used car, all used cars would sell at a price based on average quality. Sellers of high-quality used cars would not then be able to get the proper value for their car. They would withdraw from the market, driven out by sales of lower-quality vehicles whose sellers would receive proper value, or even more. In the extreme, a progression could arise in which the bad drove out the less bad until no market existed at all.[28] This conclusion has been extensively cited in the economic literature on quality and information as a consequence of 'asymmetric information'.

Akerlof supports his contention mathematically, referencing techniques that are probably specialist knowledge even amongst neoclassical economists. The mathematics is accessible only to specialist mathematicians. It uses assumptions that, according to Akerlof, are adopted to maintain 'a proper focus'. Thus: 'Again realism is sacrificed to avoid a diversion from the proper focus'.[29] The conclusion of the mathematical analysis is summed up in textual form as:

> However, with price p, average quality is p/2 and therefore at no price will any trade take place at all: in spite of the fact that *at any given price* between 0 and 3 there are traders of type one who are willing to sell their automobiles at a price which traders of type two are willing to pay.[30]

The rationale for the article initially appears to lie in the problems for neoclassical market theory of 'the existence of goods of many grades'[31] – that is, a concern for realistic representation in theory of what is observed in economic practice. Akerlof discusses also, later in the article, problems of insurance, employment, dishonesty and credit in realistic terms.[32] The implication is that realism is the proper focus. The selection of the market for automobiles to develop his thinking and the mathematical analysis employed is, however, based on 'its concreteness and ease in understanding rather than for its importance or realism'.[33]

Akerlof is ambivalent over the role that realism is to have in his analysis. It is a problem related to the selection of frame of reference, and hence the information that will be taken into account. On the one hand, he is concerned that his article should reflect the understanding of common theory regarding what is real and what actually happens. The problem of quality is readily recognisable in the common theory frame of reference. Everyone knows that it can be difficult to tell the quality of products. The discussion of problems of dishonesty and credit provision in East Asia and India, and the remedies adopted, are very much what would be regarded as realistic, even common sense, expositions. But, on the other hand, Akerlof is a practitioner of neoclassical economics, and his audience is fellow members of the neoclassical theory group. He is concerned with how the observed problems of quality can be reconciled with the neoclassical market model, or at least understood in the context of that model. He recognises that the use of the neoclassical model takes him out of the sphere of realism as understood in common theory. The assumptions adopted for his mathematical analysis are acknowledged to be unrealistic, but they are necessary to the sort of mathematical analysis he wishes to undertake. They are an integral part of the approved methodological procedure of the theory group. He wants to deal with real cars, real buyers, real sellers, but the neoclassical model permits him to deal only with the mathematical ciphers of these things. He does not explain or even question the usefulness of understanding the phenomenon of quality in terms of theory that is avowedly unrealistic. The theory group will approve an understanding based on their frame of reference, and that is sufficient justification.

The absence of any concept of information and an information interface in neoclassical theory means that the transactions of Akerlof's account are based on an understanding of people, automobiles and quality as objectively understood entities. The problem is that his frame of reference deals only with homogeneous products. The only compromise Akerlof makes is to designate 'automobiles' as 'new' or 'used' and 'good' or 'bad'. The frame of reference does not deal with 'luxury automobiles' and 'utilitarian automobiles', 'pickups' and 'limousines'; still less can it deal with all the varieties of 'quality' identifiable in cars. It assumes that all the information required for the transactions envisaged in the model is held. Buyers and sellers operate only by reference to simple products and a 'market price'. They just 'know' by some osmosis that there are 'new' and 'old' automobiles with prices conferred on them by a 'market'. The problem is that the osmosis does not extend to issues of quality. But a transaction depends firstly on a buyer, in a certain situation that implies the need for a car, learning that someone who has a car wants to sell it. A seller of a car will make known his position through the dissemination of information about his car. This will normally be done by parading vehicles on a garage forecourt or placing advertisements in local media. Today, though not at the time of Akerlof's article, the information will most likely be on the internet. Information about the car will be disseminated to potential buyers through the information interface. Initial information about the car – saloon, sports or pickup, maker, model, mileage, age, asking price, condition – will be used by potential buyers to assess whether the car has the basic features that will fit their situation. If it has, the potential buyer will contact the seller.

The problem of choosing between a realistic frame of reference or the neoclassical frame of reference is also a problem of codification. To use the neoclassical frame of reference it is necessary that all the phenomena to be taken into account are susceptible to mathematical codification, or at least can be made so without such distortion of the way they are understood in common theory as to alienate even the neoclassical theory group. The realistic frame of reference, or common theory, involves linguistic codification, with all the range and subtlety of linguistic codification, but also with some lack of precision. The central difficulty for Akerlof is then that his focus of attention, quality, cannot be designated in mathematical terms without severe distortion of the way it is commonly understood. It was seen in Chapter 1 (at note 40) that George Stigler drew particular attention to the difficulties of specifying 'quality'. Akerlof's account makes the 'quality' of a car an objective fact about the car. The average quality of cars is represented in the mathematics by the single variable μ (mu), while x_i is the quality of the i'th automobile, and quality is treated as having a linear relationship to utility.[34] But 'quality' is not of that kind. 'Quality' requires linguistic codification. The quality of a car is a collective term for a range of features selected and appraised by seller and buyer. It covers features such as reliability, mileage, condition of bodywork, condition of interior trim, service record, condition of tyres, and so on. The neoclassical model requires that products are homogenous, so it is difficult to work with the model on products that have many different 'features', many of them identified on the basis of their relevance to particular situations of a buyer or seller. Akerlof sees the 'quality' problem superimposed on a neoclassical market of supply and demand for a homogeneous product, impeding the smooth functioning of that kind of 'market'. While the treatment of 'quality' is conspicuously at odds with common theory, it has not proved unacceptable to the neoclassical theory group. The group has accepted with gratitude what suffices as a way out of their problem with imperfections of information.

The second central problem for Akerlof is that of communication. The quotation above summarising the results of his mathematical analysis, at note 30, suggests a problem of communication rather than a problem of quality. In the neoclassical frame of reference there is no provision for communication, since all the required information is assumed to be held. All agents are presumed to have all the information necessary to the transactions they potentially conclude. So in the neoclassical concept there is no need for communication and no way sellers can tell buyers about the quality of their cars. In a money-bargaining system, sellers will disseminate information regarding themselves and their products to potential buyers. Sellers of cars will provide information that positively promotes sales. Buyers will assess whether, on the information provided, the vehicle will meet their situation-related requirements.

A buyer may accept the information provided by the seller. He or she, however, is likely to confirm by inspection and a test drive that the vehicle is in something like the 'good condition' claimed by the seller. A buyer may enlist the services of experts to inspect a car and confirm that it has no evident defects. The agents of a money-bargaining system positively engage in the bargaining process through an information interface. They assemble information codified both linguistically and in figures. The agents of the neoclassical model can only respond rationally to price signals – they are confined to mathematical codifications. Provision and evaluation of information is an integral part of trade, not an awkward adjunct to a system confined to mathematical codifications.

Automobiles and other material products, the common phenomena of economic contemplation, offer extensive perceptual information. The special conviction attaching to such perception is no doubt one of the reasons why the assumption of 'perfect information' has been tolerated in much economic analysis. It assumes away all opportunities for persuasion and haggling. The complexity of cars as compared with, say, buttons or beef, makes these opportunities particularly important, meaning also that the information interface is of particular importance in transactions involving automobiles. It is not possible to change at sight the basic physical state of a car, but it is easy to manipulate information about it. A seller can persuade a buyer that a particular car is the most fitting to his or her circumstances. The sellers of cars with qualities that best meet the requirements of buyers will probably get better prices for them than those selling less suitable cars. If there are traders of type one who are willing to sell their automobiles at a price which traders of type two are willing to pay then communication between the two types will ensure that transactions are completed. The concept of an information interface incorporates quality issues, alongside the general provision of situation-related 'features', in the overall understanding of the process of money-bargaining. Akerlof, using the neoclassical model as frame of reference, is obliged to ignore the realism that presents itself to him through common theory. Realism is sacrificed for neoclassical presuppositions and mathematical codification.

The nature of perceptual information gives assurance of the existence of a physical vehicle, something 'real'; but having regard to the philosophical context, it is not necessary that it should be so. Testimonial information does not convey the same assurance. Perceptual information derives from the perceiver's experience and, if it is in error, the error is that of the perceiver. Testimonial information is the judgement of someone else, and inherently vulnerable to the manipulation of that someone else to advance their interests. Testimonial information from a seller will present the car to a buyer in the form that the seller would like the buyer to conceive it. What the 'reality' or 'truth' is behind such a description is something for the buyer to elucidate through the assembly of consistent information for himself.

Akerlof draws parallels between the mathematical analysis provided in the context of the automobile market with the uncertainties encountered in health insurance, employment of minorities and credit provision, or where there is dishonesty in transactions. In health insurance and credit provision, however, the analogy is incomplete. There is asymmetry of information, but it is the buyers who have information that is lacking to the sellers, and needed by the sellers. In these cases there is a positive inclination to conceal information, whereas the sellers of good quality used cars will be wishing to confide information about their cars to potential buyers. The problem is not just a problem of communication, as with the sellers of quality used cars, but a reluctance to concede information that is inimical to the interests of those that hold it. Dishonesty, or the manipulation of information, is, as has been seen, an inherent part of transactions conducted through an information interface.

Towards the end of his article Akerlof notes that various means have been developed, including guarantees, licencing, brand names and certification, to offset the effects of uncertainty over quality.[35] While inspection and testing can reveal much about the quality of a car, there may still be faults that are not apparent. In the case of Akerlof's mathematical exposition, the market potentially dries up because sellers cannot get a fair price for their vehicles. The more likely cause of the demise of a market is perhaps the withdrawal of buyers because they cannot trust the sellers who hold the vital information. This is apparent in the realistic part of Akerlof's exposition. Sellers consequently find it advantageous to the conclusion of a sale to provide some 'feature' that assures the buyer that the product will wholly conform to the description provided. A guarantee protects a buyer against anything going wrong, whether deriving from a fault known to the seller, or from some hidden fault. A guarantee protects a buyer against deficiencies of the information interface through which the purchase is made. A buyer will find a car on offer with a guarantee more attractive than one without, unless other features make the car without the guarantee more fitting to the buyer's situation. It may also relieve the buyer of any necessity to spend money on extensive testing.

Guarantees are provided by sellers to buyers. The problem with the used car market, as described by Akerlof, is that sellers cannot make known the quality of their cars to buyers, and so get a reasonable price for them. If they cannot communicate the quality of their cars, it seems they will also not be able to communicate an offer of a guarantee. So a guarantee to buyers is not at first sight relevant to their predicament. However, provision of a guarantee implies that sellers can communicate with buyers. It implies a real world of communication; a frame of reference in which communication is taken for granted. The provision is codified in linguistic terms. Once it is accepted that sellers can communicate with buyers, the transaction is understood outside the neoclassical framework, and a seller can inform potential buyers about the quality of his car and justify a higher price. He can also give a guarantee to further enhance the attractiveness of what he is offering. The provision of the guarantee is 'exogenous' to the neoclassical model. There is no risk of the market dying away. The remedy for the prospect identified in Akerlof's mathematical analysis is communication, involving linguistic codification and an information interface.

Guarantees are useful only in so far as they are honoured by their providers. They are based on testimonial information that carries lesser conviction than perceptual information. They are necessarily backed up with provisions for enforcement through courts of law. They may even by superseded by regulatory provisions in law that require sellers to fulfil certain obligations to their buyers. They form part of the extensive regulation that is necessary to the secure expansion of a money-bargaining system. In developed economies, the provision of guarantees and a range of other consumer rights are well established in law and regulations. A regulatory information interface like that which governs the sale of beer to an American in a Paris café is necessary to money-bargaining transactions in general.

Akerlof's article has been widely cited by those using the neoclassical model as frame of reference. For them it provides a treatment of 'quality' issues that, while it highlights a major weakness of the model, gives some defence against attacks on the model on grounds of its difficulties in accommodating issues of quality, or more generally in accommodating issues of information. 'Asymmetric information' is an apparently sophisticated, guilefully technocratic, response – enough to fend off most attacks. It even seems to provide reassurance that the problem is recognised and dealt with. The acceptance amongst neoclassical economists seems conditioned partly by the mere fact of mathematical exposition. There is some tendency amongst neoclassical economists to regard mathematical analysis as definitive, whatever the assumptions and simplifications required to make feasible the application of mathematics. Mathematics, for neoclassical economists, resolves ambiguities, though for others it merely dodges conceptual weaknesses. At worst, it can be little better than a smokescreen to cover incapacities of the model. Within his theory group, Akerlof's article was received with great acclaim, expressed most prominently in the award of a Nobel Memorial Prize. As was seen in Chapter 1, it has been the inspiration for extensive work on the economics of information. To those with a wider frame of reference, or to those making reference to common theory, it will be difficult to see why it is considered helpful to 'resolve' the quality issue on the basis of theory that is so transparently unreal, with a concept of 'quality' that is highly artificial. In the money-bargaining frame of reference Akerlof's exposition is plainly awry; a sticking plaster for a corpse. If it demonstrates anything useful, it is only that the frame of reference is misleading rather than illuminating.

These circumstances are not obscure or difficult to understand. Akerlof clearly recognises the effects of uncertainty and deception in the real world. He explicitly chooses to use the neoclassical model as his frame of reference, at the expense of the realism provided by common theory. He opts for this approach not because it is truthful, or right, or realistic, but apparently because he wishes to impress the theory group. With their support his interest will advance. This is the preference referred to in the Introduction that underlies the failure of mainstream economists to present a realistic theory of economic processes – the preference for community over truth, for support over accurate representation. It is a failure of the theory group to establish empirical integrity as the essential group interest.

Stiglitz and the neoclassical frame of reference

Joseph Stiglitz took up the idea of asymmetric information mainly in relation to those circumstances in which buyers hold information that is of crucial importance to sellers, but which they are reluctant to impart to sellers. Health insurance and credit provision are prominent in his exposition.[36] The provider of health insurance needs to know the state of health of the buyer. The provider of credit needs to know the capacity and disposition of the borrower to repay. In money-bargaining, as in common theory, what is called a situation of 'asymmetric information' is the unsophisticated circumstances in which information relevant to a potential transaction is inaccessible, usually because an agent has an interest in withholding it. In Akerlof's account of asymmetry in car sales, critical information is inaccessible because there is no provision in a neoclassical market for communications between seller and buyer.

In the cases of health insurance and credit provision, the transactions are based almost entirely on testimonial information. There is little perceptual information to go on, as there is with automobiles. The potential provider must obtain critical information from a client, who may well be reluctant to release it. In transactions of this kind, there is a real possibility of transactions being almost entirely curtailed by uncertainties of the sellers over the risks they are taking on. Extensive regulation has been adopted to make such sales possible at a level of risk acceptable to providers. In effect, clients have to guarantee to providers that they have provided honest and complete information by signing an application form. The transaction can be declared void if it later transpires that critical information has been withheld. Sales of these services depend on the existence of legislation that protects providers from potential misrepresentation of their circumstances by clients. The provider is guaranteed against deficiencies of the information interface.

Regulations constitute in part a 'vote of no confidence' in the information interface as constructed by private money-bargaining agents. Because of the way it is constructed, the information it contains is potentially misleading, may be false, and will often be incomplete. Regulations, including guarantees, diminish the risks to those involved. Regulations recognise also that an information interface can be incomplete, both as a consequence of the withholding of relevant information and as a consequence of information simply not being available. They require the inclusion of certain 'features' in transactions, with the transactions potentially void if the required features are not present. The use of regulation removes important impediments to the conclusion of transactions, and hence promotes the expansion of money-bargaining systems. In the case of money-bargaining, the support-bargaining system provides a mechanism through which money-bargaining can be regulated. There is, however, no system for the regulation of support-bargaining except the support-bargaining system itself.

For Stiglitz, an important protection against the consequences of asymmetric information is provided by 'screening', in which, for example, a provider observes the behaviour of an applicant for health insurance to see whether it is consistent with the information provided by the applicant about his or her health. If an applicant is observed to run up several flights of stairs, then it can be taken that they are in reasonable health.[37] Perceptual information, slight as it is in the example given, is taken to be trustworthy information relating to a service transaction that is otherwise almost entirely a matter of testimonial information. 'Screening' means observing what people do as a guide to their capacities and circumstances. It is, in effect, a means of identifying their situation on the basis of their actions. Interests and actions are, in the understanding of support-bargaining and money-bargaining, related to situations, so that it is on occasion possible to work backwards from expressions of interest or from actions to the underlying situation. In the case of the client for health insurance, significant information is obtained about the client's health situation from observation of behaviour.

Stiglitz suggests that some markets, such as traditional commodity markets, are not so dependent on information, and consequently the idea of asymmetric information is much less relevant.[38] But in support-bargaining and money-bargaining the terms of transactions depend on bargaining position, and the assembly of information is important to the identification of relative bargaining positions, and hence the negotiation of advantageous terms for a transaction.[39] While Stiglitz does not see problems of asymmetric information as universal, he nevertheless argues that they are of sufficient importance as to necessitate a change in paradigm for economics.[40]

But it is more modification than change. Stiglitz himself acknowledges that he takes economic theory beyond the existing paradigm only to the extent of challenging the assumption of perfect competition. All other assumptions of the neoclassical paradigm are retained, on the grounds that it is so difficult to get a hearing for new ideas that it is not worth the effort.[41] It might be argued that he invalidates the neoclassical paradigm without putting anything in its place. He speculates 'beyond the limits of information economics' as to what a more fundamental change of paradigm might involve:

> Finally, I have become convinced that the dynamics of change may not be well described by equilibrium models that have long been at the center of economic analysis . . . Dynamics may be better described by evolutionary processes and models, than by equilibrium processes. And while it may be difficult to describe fully these evolutionary processes, this much is already clear: there is no reason to believe that they are, in any general sense, 'optimal'.[42]

Stiglitz recognises that what he observes of the role of information and other phenomena associated with economic exchange is incompatible with the established mainstream theory. The assumption of perfect information in neoclassical theory means that the theory is blind to information issues. Contrivances such as 'asymmetric information' and 'screening' are introduced to effect some reconciliation of the observed phenomena with the paradigm, though the incompatibility remains.[43] Stiglitz faces the same dilemma as Akerlof – whether to be realistic or stick with the neoclassical paradigm. Akerlof opts for the paradigm. Stiglitz also sticks with the paradigm, but modifies it with neoclassical sophistication to suggest it might accommodate the anomalies he observes.

As a matter of individual interest, Stiglitz may be right in recognising, such are the difficulties of promoting new ideas, that it may not be worth the effort. But the theoretical frames are used in the formulation of political programmes of action and affect the lives of many people. It is important that the prescriptions derived from them achieve the designated purposes. Unrealistic theory is likely to generate unhelpful and even damaging prescriptions. Those employed in public institutions to formulate theories regarding the nature of society take on a communal responsibility – that is, continued support from their community is contingent on their willingness to pursue theories that are as consistent as they can make them with the reality of common experience.

Even at the level of individual interest, conservation of effort is not necessarily the best course. People of a certain psychological disposition and subject to certain influences cannot do other than pursue theory that is consistent with a wide range of observation and experience. Constant 'alerts' to anomaly require resolution. There must be consistency. The sense of symmetry must be satisfied.

These traits are in principle generally approved and supported in Western societies. It implies acceptance of innovation and change; an 'open mind'. Great men who have successfully challenged the prevailing orthodoxies – Copernicus, Galileo, Newton, Darwin, Einstein – are held up as models for intellectual enquiry. But when actually encountered, new ideas are more likely to be regarded as disruptive. They disrupt settled theory groups. They deny the support that members are accustomed to receive for their pronouncements on theory. In the institutionalised theory groups, they disrupt established career progressions. Scholars accustomed to respect and admiration are suddenly downgraded. The weight of support arising from these considerations, and the conviction that derives from extensive support, mean that new ideas tend to be rejected, deflected, deferred or ignored. It is more comfortable being wrong with the group than right in isolation. This reaction means that there are high costs involved in promotion of radical new ideas. For the proponents of new ideas there is also the awkward truth that not all new ideas are right.

Money-bargaining and the information interface

In the theory of support-bargaining and money-bargaining 'money' is a creation of support-bargaining. The value of something designated as 'money' is sustained by the support of all members of a particular society for the designation of money as representing value.[44] The convention is maintained because all find it useful. 'Support' is a psychological benefit, and consequently imprecise and often uncertain in value. It is associated with violence, so that withdrawal of support can have major implications for personal security. But it may also be treated as of little account. The support of an ordinary individual, with little capacity for violence, and even less inclination, may be regarded in the common course of life as of no significance. Even where violence is not a prospect, the support of someone with few intellectual or social qualities may be of little account. 'Money', however, is precise and of dependable interest. Where a transaction needs these qualities, money is a useful bargaining counter. Exchanges involving material things, such as food and clothing, can be expeditiously concluded with a counter such as money that offers precise measure and is universally accepted within its supporting society. Provision of services can be given a degree of precision by reference to the time taken to provide them. With 'money' as a bargaining counter, an alternative or supplement to 'support' as a bargaining counter, 'money-bargaining' shares much of the dynamic of 'support-bargaining'. We can bargain with money because we learn early in life to bargain over support.[45]

Support-bargaining is manifestly intensive in the use of information. Once a support convention is adopted, people have to argue and persuade to assemble support for their interests, rather than rattle sabres. The parallel with support-bargaining makes plain the importance of information in money-bargaining. Just as they do in support-bargaining, agents engaged in money-bargaining argue and persuade so that people part with their money in payment for products. Using 'support-bargaining and money-bargaining' as the frame of reference draws attention to the important role of information when bargaining with both 'support' and 'money', and hence to the role of the information interface.

The apparently lesser prominence of information in economic transactions arises because economic transactions deal mostly with material things. They are not understood in terms of information, but more in terms of 'just knowing' they are present. People just know that material things like tables or shoes exist where they are apprehended to exist. There is no need in the ordinary course of events to consider how we know of their existence. The neoclassical assumption of 'perfect information' has been tolerated so much in the neoclassical theory group partly because it is to some degree in accord with this commonplace knowledge of material things. With the introduction of issues of information, it is apparent that we 'know' of these material things through perceptual information, as opposed to testimonial information. As was seen in Chapter 2, perceptual information carries particular conviction. Perceptual information conveys that direct sense of the existence of material things.

But apart from this perceptual aspect, there are other factors that make plain the importance of information to material exchange. Economic transactions are not undertaken simply on the basis of 'a table' or 'a pair of shoes'. They are undertaken on the basis of the features of these things: the size of the table, its wood, its design; or the size of shoes, their material, their colour, their suitability for walking, or for running. Both a table and a pair of shoes are likely to be needed in specific locations at specific times. Kelvin Lancaster, as noted in Chapter 1 (at note 54), drew attention to the requirement for information when a product was recognised as involving something more than mere existence, and was not of the uniform type required by the neoclassical model. The features of products make them fitting or unfitting to the situations of consumers. When 'products' are known only through testimonial information, information requirements are much more apparent. Buying over the internet involves buying on the basis of information about products, although for the most part there is previous experience of perceptual encounter with the products of interest. Acquisition of complex products, such as machinery or computers, involves assembly by buyers of extensive testimonial information to assess the fit of product to circumstances. Exchange involving 'services' is even more readily seen as being dependent on information. A service is itself defined by information about it. Buying insurance on a house, for example, involves assembly and evaluation of information regarding the risks covered and those that are excluded. There is no perceptual information that can give the particular assurance that derives from that type of information.

Microeconomics and macroeconomics

Money-bargaining is both microeconomic theory and macroeconomic theory, or rather money-bargaining makes no distinction between ideas about the observable functioning of an economy in totality and ideas about the dynamics of particular transactions. Particular transactions are collectively the whole. The extensive government engagement in money-bargaining is part of the money-bargaining system, though government engagement is largely dictated by support-bargaining. It is not possible to disentangle a money-bargaining system from support-bargaining.

Neoclassical microeconomic theory is sharply distinct from macroeconomic theory, even to the extent that macroeconomic theory is incompatible with microeconomic theory. This has been an enduring concern of neoclassical economists. The most apparent incompatibility is the engagement of government in macroeconomic processes, whereas neoclassical economics is concerned entirely with individual exchange, or at least the exchanges of individual rational ciphers. Economic activity also takes place in space and time, so that the neoclassical freedom from space and time is incompatible with macroeconomic theory. Macroeconomists must also engage with and evaluate a great variety of information about economies. In macroeconomics, required information has to be specified, assembled and evaluated, so the understanding of information in macroeconomics is incompatible with that of neoclassical microeconomics.

Neoclassical economists have made extensive efforts to reconcile their microeconomic theory with that of macroeconomics, but with little success.[46] An underlying and insuperable incompatibility is the preoccupation of neoclassical theory with equilibrium, whilst economies clearly evolve through technological and other changes. Neoclassical economists continue to pursue research into macroeconomic equilibrium, but with predictably little consequence. Paul Romer's article on 'The trouble with macroeconomics', discussed in Chapter 2, criticised the academic research on 'Dynamic Stochastic General Equilibrium' (DSGE). Greg Mankiw, a prominent American economist, identifies the split between academic macroeconomic research and more practical engagement in macroeconomic management. Academic research has little influence on practical economic management:

> The sad truth is that the macroeconomic research of the past three decades has had only minor impact on the practical analysis of monetary or fiscal policy. The explanation is not that economists in the policy arena are ignorant of recent developments . . . The fact that modern macroeconomic research is not widely used in practical policymaking is prima facie evidence that it is of little use for this purpose.[47]

Research into the tendency to equilibrium, that on the basis of neoclassical microeconomic theory should emerge in macroeconomies, is pursued largely in isolation from the actual management of economies. It may be that the emphasis on agreement in a theory group at the expense of pursuit of sound economic research identified by Romer arose from frustration that the particular research in which the group was engaged was getting nowhere.

While macroeconomic research based on neoclassical understanding of equilibrium may not have had much influence on macroeconomic management, the concepts of neoclassical theory remain potent influences on those engaged in macroeconomic management. The neglect of government interventions that should have been made in the run-up to the global financial crisis that emerged in 2008 have been widely attributed to excessive faith in the self-equilibrating properties of private markets.

The existence of this absurd inconsistency between microeconomic and macroeconomic theory can be related back to the questions identified in the Introduction. The neoclassical model responds to the question: What does a system look like in which individual self-interest leads to communal advantage with an optimal distribution of resources? The neoclassical economic model is the answer to that question. But practical economic management needs an answer to the more obvious question: How does economic exchange work?

The theory of money-bargaining responds to the latter question. Macroeconomic theory was also developed, separately from neoclassical theory, as an answer to the same question, at least as a necessary prelude to its more pressing question: How do we muster resources for the defeat of Nazi Germany? The predicament of the alliance against Nazi Germany necessitated a practical understanding of how economies functioned. There was consequently intensification of the development of national accounts to provide a basis for the practical identification and allocation of resources, public and private, for the pursuit of victory. Since that time economic management has been centred on national accounts, giving it the context of space and time necessary to the accounts. It is because money-bargaining and macroeconomic theory are responses to the same practical concerns that they are largely compatible, the differences being easily attributable to neoclassical concepts learnt by all economists consciously and unconsciously imported into their macroeconomic thinking.

Consumers and the information interface

Smith identifies landowners receiving rents, workers receiving wages and those who live by profit as the 'three great, original and constituent orders, from whose revenue that of every other order is ultimately derived'.[48] He regards the interests of the 'first order' as inseparable from the general interest of society, with the reservation only that they may not have even a tolerable knowledge of their own interests.[49] Smith has a sympathetic tolerance of the intellectual shortcomings of the landed gentry. The interests of the second order, those who live by wages, is also strictly linked to the general interest of society. The problems, for Smith, arise with the third order, those who live by profits, since as has been seen, their interests do not coincide with those of the society in general. The three orders, with their revenues, have interests also as consumers. For Smith, 'Consumption is the sole end and purpose of all production'.[50]

Landowners, wage-workers and businessmen are governed by the requirements of consumers. As in Smith's understanding, consumers in a money-bargaining system are the prime determiners of what is provided through a money-bargaining system. Their behaviour illustrates the importance of information, since in the theory of money-bargaining (as in support-bargaining) selection is situation-related. What people want and will pay for is what will fit with their current situation, either as remedy for its defects or as improving its existing state. What they require before they buy is information to assure them that what they buy will fit their situation. If their car needs a new wheel, they need to know that the new wheel will fit the make and model of the car they own. Just 'a wheel' will not do. All acquisitions need to 'fit' an existing situation in one way or another. The psychology, or perceptual process, is the same as that of the theoretical frame of reference.

The details of the process are described in *Support-Bargaining: The Mechanics of Democracy Revealed*, and further developed in an article, 'Situation as determinant of selection and valuation', in terms of the formation of 'bargaining sets' by consumers.[51] The sets comprise products or the suppliers of products whose specifications fit the requirements of the consumer's situation. A consumer forms a bargaining set on the basis of what will fit a current situation, or what will improve a current situation. They are information interfaces created by consumers through which decisions can be made on acquisitions. Buying a sofa, for example, will involve the establishment of requirements based on the number of people in the household or commonly visiting, the existence of other seating, the size of the room in which the sofa is to be placed, the style of furniture already in the room, and the sum of money which can be expended on the sofa. It is perhaps necessary also that the sofa should be available at a shop near to home, so that it can be seen and sat on before purchase – such perceptual information can be decisive. Credit arrangements may be necessary to accommodate budgetary capacity. The sofa may also have to be available within a certain period – if, for example, friends are visiting it may have to be in place before the visit. It may be necessary to establish also just what 'our sort of people' are buying in the way of sofas. Products are acquired for social support as well as immediate individual gratification. The consumer situation imposes certain requirements for 'features' built in to the sofa or associated with the transaction, implying a certain set of possible sources and models of sofa, which constitute the consumer's bargaining set. The bargaining set includes certain sofas and suppliers, but rules out others.

The formation of the bargaining set may give the consumer an easy choice. Just one sofa from one supplier may fit the situation. But the consumer bargaining set may also be very large and selection may be difficult. The set can be whittled down by imposing a more stringent account of situation. If sofas are on 'special offer', the budgetary position may be reassessed and the money available for the sofa reduced, thus eliminating more expensive sofas from the bargaining set and reducing the bargaining set. The savings on the sofa may be reassigned to other acquisitions. It may be determined that a larger sofa than originally contemplated could be accommodated, with the advantage of giving more seating options for guests. The bargaining set changes with the reassessment of situation. Through this process a selection is made.

The understanding of 'products' in this process is markedly different from the homogeneous products of neoclassical theory. They are designed and built with a variety of 'features' to fit different consumer situations. The terms of the transaction are also designed to fit different consumer situations. Some suppliers will offer 'next-day delivery'. Some will offer deferred terms and zero interest. Some will provide 'free' cushions. Some will offer 'amazing reductions'.

The bargaining set constructed by the consumer is entirely composed of information. Some of it will be perceptual information. Shops will be seen;

sofas will be seen and checked for colour, comfort, pattern and texture. But much of it will be testimonial information. Information about quality and durability will be largely the testimony of the manufacturer and supplier; delivery will be commitments by the supplier. In constructing the bargaining set the consumer constructs an information interface through which he or she makes the selection. The information is assessed in minds whose survival depended, and still depends, on the ability to made decisions on the basis of how available options fit to situation.

The selection process may be done with the consumer largely unaware of the sort of calculations that are being made. We instinctively select by reference to situation. In terms of intellectual understanding, the selection can be conceived as made on a 'best fit' basis from a wide bargaining set, or it can be conceived as a whittling down process, whereby situation is reassessed and reassessed, with tightening definition, until just one option remains. Either way, the consumer reaches a focus on one sofa or one product that seems best to answer to the situation.

There is, of course, plenty of room for error. The sofa, when it arrives, may have to be placed somewhere else because it does not fit in the space originally envisaged for it. The patterns of its materials may clash with those of curtains or carpets. People have different skills in selection, and different tastes or tolerances with regard to aesthetic coordination. Some people buy with little prior assessment and make the best of whatever they end up with. A consumer may become more aware of the factors involved in the selection process, and attend more carefully to them, if there are important incompatibilities within the constructed information interface or bargaining set. An otherwise perfect sofa may only be available on two months delivery. If the 'automatic' selection process is baulked by such incompatibilities, more focused attention is brought to bear, and buyers suffer the stresses of conscious choice.

Companies and the information interface

This consumer selection process implies that the success of companies depends on establishing themselves and their products in the bargaining sets of a sufficient number of consumers, and being the final choice of a sufficient number of consumers for their expenditures. A company must ensure that its products have the specifications, including price specifications, that will fit consumer situations, including their budget situations. And they must fit sufficiently well and in sufficient numbers as to gain for a company the revenues that will cover its costs. And before the questions of 'fit' arise, a company must ensure that consumers know about its products and services. Consumers can only buy what they know about. A company must ensure that consumers know about its products and try to convince them that they are better than anything on offer from rival companies. The claim to be 'better' means in this context 'better fitting to the situations of consumers'. Companies will generally try to substantiate their claims by ensuring that their products actually are better than their rivals, by building into them all the attractive features they can arrive at. But they are likely to make the claim whether or not it is strictly true. Companies have a clear interest in differentiating their products and services from those of others, rather than producing the homogeneous products of neoclassical theory. Companies need to communicate a wide range of factual and persuasive information to consumers. They need to create an information interface that will cause consumers to select their products. Companies can at their discretion omit any information that is not conducive to purchase of their products.

In order to target their information effectively on potential buyers, companies may assemble information about citizens who are in the sort of situation that will incline them to purchase of a company's goods or services. Elderly people have certain needs related to health and mobility, so companies producing products designed to protect health and mobility will be assembling information concerning the numbers of elderly in a community, their locations, their health status and the state of their budgets. Companies may be understood as forming 'vendor sets', comprising those consumers whose situations suggest propensity to buy a company's products.[52] Commercial websites of many kinds collect data on the social circumstances of their customers and sell it on to other companies wishing to direct information to people likely to buy their products. What Stiglitz calls 'screening' is used – people's situations can be deduced from what they purchase. If someone buys a zimmer frame, they are probably old and infirm, and might be interested in other products that assist with age and infirmity.

This is the specialist money-bargaining function of companies. Consumers are intimately engaged in support-bargaining, alongside their money-bargaining, and often in preference to it. Wage- and salary-earners similarly have to find some compromise between their obligations as people, to family and friends, and their function as money-bargaining agents. But companies are established and run as money-bargaining agencies, designed to produce monetary profits for their owners. They assemble inputs of labour and materials to make distinctive products, or provide distinctive services, that give them a strong money-bargaining position. It was argued in *The Evolution of Economies* that the industrial revolution marked the passing of economic, social and political ascendancy from landowners to companies, since companies became the primary agents of money-bargaining, and people became dependent on employment with companies, rather than with landowners.[53]

The essential function of companies is captured in the idea of the viability condition, mentioned in Chapter 1. To survive, a company must ensure that its revenues are greater than its costs. This is the condition, 'sales × price > unit cost × production'. The four components of the viability condition are interrelated. Sales depend on price; price depends on unit cost; unit cost depends on the level of production; the level of production has to be synchronised with the sales that can be achieved at the price implied by the unit costs incurred at that level of production.[54] To achieve the necessary revenues, a company must establish itself in consumer bargaining sets and make sales to the necessary value. The relationship between unit cost and level of production is often a matter of scale of production. In a craftsman's workshop, unit costs will be substantially different making, say, ten chairs per week compared with one chair per week. At the industrial level, the relationship is commonly determined by the technology used. This viability condition, with its interrelated components, sums up the basic understanding of companies as money-bargaining agencies.

Economies of scale, associated with technology, are commonly of major importance in meeting the viability condition. In the neoclassical model they are supplementary and anomalous. No 'optimal allocation of resources' is achieved if there are economics of scale.[55] Plainly, a company with economies of scale will be able to offer goods at a lower price than those without, and will develop a dominant market position. The mechanism for the formation of a neoclassical 'market price' will be lost, and with it any 'optimal allocation'. The viability condition establishes economies of scale as a critical but commonplace factor that is, in neoclassical theory, an awkward intrusion. The viability condition is consistent with the empirical evidence. The idea of companies employing technology to meet a viability condition gives technology the 'endogenous' function seen by Paul Romer as essential, as discussed in Chapter 2, as opposed to the 'exogenous' status it has in neoclassical economic theory.[56]

The viability condition focuses attention on unit cost as the basic determinant of price and hence an important factor in sales. Adam Smith, and neoclassical economists, emphasise the importance of productivity as a means of raising aggregate production. The difference makes plain significant aspects of the two theories. The former is immediately concerned with corporate viability, while the latter is immediately concerned with maximisation of production. In the context of money-bargaining, productivity improvements are desirable because they bring about reductions in unit costs. In the neoclassical context, improvements in productivity arising from the division of labour are desirable because they raise the aggregate level of production. The former is concerned with viability in a process of monetary exchange, with differentiated products, while the latter is concerned with maximising output of homogeneous products from given resources. The viability condition is again consistent with the evidence. Companies are concerned primarily with profitability rather than maximisation of their output.

The idea of 'improving productivity' may be preferred also because it is more likely to be given support. It suggests universal benefit. Maximising production implies the biggest 'cake' and hence a better chance for all of more cake. Linguistic associations make 'improvements' preferable to 'reductions'. The latter will immediately suggest to employees of a company that their jobs are at risk. The threat perceived in words may be more important than their strict meaning.

Companies assemble a wide range of inputs to produce goods and services for sale. They buy inputs by reference to their situation, in the same way as consumers. They create large volumes of information specifying their requirements in order to ensure 'best fit' to their situation. Some acquisitions will be straightforward. Routine supplies of raw materials will be required for a production process. But other requirements will involve extensive deliberation over the situation of the company and the conditions it can expect to encounter in the future. Decisions on acquisition of property, plant and machinery will be reached after careful consideration of a company's current capacity and requirements for the future, including the new technologies that are likely to dominate their future trade. Such investment decisions are part of the evolution of companies and constituents of macroeconomic evolution. They require large volumes of information and human capacities to evaluate it.

Company formats for the provision of information

One of the first concerns of a company trying to establish a viable format is to make its products or services known to potential buyers. The task is eased by the need of potential buyers to assemble information about the availability of products that will fit their situations. The requirements for information for money-bargaining are themselves met through money-bargaining. Advertising companies format for the provision of information on behalf of other companies to potential buyers. Companies also format for the provision of information that buyers want and will pay for. New digital technologies have disrupted established formats in recent decades, with the two elements of format increasingly melded together to produce what might be regarded as a composite third format. Information that people want attracts readers; the costs of provision are met by the dissemination of information on behalf of others.

The dual interest in the propagation of information – some people want certain information disseminated, and others want certain information – gives rise to the dualism of formats. The scope for such formats also arises from the special character of information. It is not a 'commodity' in the neoclassical sense. The mathematical codification of the neoclassical economic model requires that commodities should be homogeneous. Information is distinctively a 'commodity' of a bargaining system. It is as far from 'homogeneity' as it is possible to get. It has to carry 'features' relevant to the interests of its disseminators or relevant to the circumstances of potential recipients. It has to show how products and services 'fit' into the bargaining sets of potential buyers. Information constitutes an extreme of product differentiation, to the extent that it cannot be understood in a neoclassical frame of reference. Information cannot be codified and aggregated mathematically. Potatoes do not have features that dispose their growers both to press them upon other people and at the same time sell them to other people.

Advertising agencies are commissioned by providers of consumer goods and services to disseminate information in persuasive forms to potential buyers. These agencies develop expertise in the presentation of information in forms designed to appeal to and influence potential buyers, and in the placement of such information where potential buyers will encounter it. Older forms of placement include newspapers, magazines and billboards. Cinema, radio and television advertising added to the options in the twentieth century. Late in the twentieth century the internet was developed as a channel for advertising, growing rapidly in importance in the twenty-first century. Advertising agencies use all these channels to propagate information on behalf of other companies.

The channels are attractive to advertisers because the basis of the formats of the companies providing them is the propagation of information that people need and want. Much of it is provided either as outright entertainment or with a strong element of entertainment. Large numbers of people accessing the information mean that the companies providing it can offer attractive rates to advertisers, measured in terms of 'cost per reader' or 'cost per viewer', for the dissemination of the information they want others to have. The formats of companies producing newspapers and magazines rested primarily on the provision of information required by potential readers, for which the readers were prepared to pay. The provision of information on behalf of other companies was, for most of them, regarded as a secondary source of revenue, though it was often essential to their viability.

Technological innovation has changed the scope for company formats for the provision of information. Large volumes of information wanted by readers and viewers can be distributed at very low cost over the internet. Viable formats can be established through provision of this information without charge, while charging advertisers for access to the large numbers of readers/viewers. Large volumes of free information have become available over the internet, with the providing companies deriving their revenues from advertising agencies.

The free information includes large amounts of political, social and business information. It also includes information on demand, and information generated by users themselves, whose provision is made possible by digital technology. Google provides information in response to internet 'search' requests. Its dominance of the 'search' function on the internet brings it advertising revenues that put it amongst the largest companies in the world. Facebook circulates information provided by its users on personal and social affairs, but the advertising that accompanies such information brings in revenues that put it also amongst the largest companies in the world. These developments have made it difficult for companies using traditional newspaper formats to sell information at viable prices. In some cases they have adopted the composite formats of internet providers by distributing their newspapers free of charge and deriving revenues from advertising. Some have moved online, though many of these have found it difficult to get viewers to pay viable prices for the online versions of their newspapers. Companies providing television services have long provided information and entertainment free to viewers with costs covered by revenues from advertising agencies. People know them as providers of information and entertainment, but their viability as companies depends substantially on advertising revenues.

The social media have exploited a further source of revenues. They collect large volumes of data about people's preferences and circumstances. Since interests are situation-related, they are assembling information about people's probable interests, and hence about what they are likely to buy. As was seen above, information assembled by social media companies can be sold on to companies seeking to identify vendor sets comprised of people whose situations will dispose them to become customers.

Technological innovation has dominated the evolution of corporate formats for the provision of information. It has made the present age an 'information age'. It lay also behind the historical evolution of industry and society. Newspapers and magazines were able to achieve the circulations necessary to viable format initially through the introduction of the printing press in the fifteenth century. The invention of the steam printing press in the early nineteenth century increased production rates and reduced unit costs, enabling companies to establish viable formats to meet the increased requirements for information associated with the industrial revolution. The rotary printing press, introduced in the 1840s, further increased the potential for high levels of production at low unit cost, at just the time when the format of railway companies using high-pressure steam engines made it possible to distribute newspapers around a country in sufficient volume to realise the production potential of the rotary press. Further advances in the technology of printing, and expansion of rail networks, made possible the very large circulations of daily newspapers in many countries in the twentieth century. New formats based on new technology in one line of business gave rise to opportunities for new formats with other new technology in other businesses.

Advertising is commonly associated with the dissemination of information about goods and services with a view to sales in a money-bargaining system. But support-bargaining agencies, including in particular political parties, must also disseminate copious information about their programmes, people and policies in a form that will attract support. Much of the free information provided by media is concerned with politics. Such is the popularity amongst readers, listeners and viewers of political information that prominent political leaders normally have little difficulty in gaining access to media for the presentation of party policies. Nevertheless, political advertising is used to purvey political messages untrammelled by the editorial exigencies of media organisations or the interventions of their interviewers. Some of the advertising and marketing companies that provide information about products and services on behalf of money-bargaining agencies offer similar services to support-bargaining agencies. Advertising and public relations companies help political parties to get their 'message' across to potential supporters.

The role of the media in the provision of information and the creation of the information interface on which support-bargaining depends means they have a major role in determining the distribution of support. Hence they have a major role in government. Though contrary to democratic principle, money-bargaining agencies have a major role in political support-bargaining. Their role is considered further in Chapter 8.

The psychology of support-bargaining is apparent in the forms taken by advertising. Because people select by reference to situation, advertisers draw attention to the desirable 'lifestyles' of those who buy their products. The stylish household buys the car, the vacuum cleaner, the oven. Products may be sold with a 'homely' touch, as originating in the recipes of 'Aunt Bessie' or the kitchen innovations of 'Mrs Cooper'. Happy cows on idyllic farms cosseted by bucolic farmers produce the finest dairy produce. Caring domesticity and pastoral bliss are pleasing traditions; stimulating recollection of them in the information interface facilitates the sale of goods. If you do not have the relevant product you may be excluded from a desirable social group or, worse still, you may be depriving your children of the idyllic childhood that is their right. In spite of the regulatory shield, there is still scope for presentational liberties and degrees of deception. The psychological prompting and insinuation of advertising is now increasingly used by official agencies to make people behave in ways conducive to official satisfaction.

The disjunction between the information consumers will attend to, which is often provided without charge, and the information that companies want to disseminate, and will pay to have disseminated, means that the former type of information is constituted as a priority to attract the attention of large numbers of readers or viewers. Accurate, truthful and realistic information does not necessarily gain attention. People respond to the sensational, the strange, the novel. Unscrupulous people made money in the United States presidential election of 2016 by providing sensational but false news about the candidates over social media and through other internet channels. President Trump has subsequently made much of the 'fake news' allegedly disseminated by the United States media, even by the most reputable media organisations.

Communal interest and government

Companies build 'features' into their products and services to meet the situation-related requirements of potential buyers. If the buyers are consumers, the features will be related to individual and family circumstances, since payments will come from individual or family budgets. If the buyers are companies, company circumstances dictate the features, since payments will come from company budgets. In the neoclassical model, consumers and companies, the latter in the form of 'entrepreneurs', are individuals. But in the theory of support-bargaining and money-bargaining group interests have to be considered. Through support-bargaining groups establish group concepts that include group objectives and purposes. In Searle's terms they form 'collective intentions'. Margaret Gilbert identifies the formation of 'plural subjects' that can conceive and act collectively.[57] With that sort of dynamic, groups can develop ideas about communal interests and how they can be fulfilled through a money-bargaining process.

Particular groups within a support-bargaining society will develop ideas regarding their interests and the interests of their society which may become established as 'communal interests' across society, transcending the original group that identifies them. A common communal interest in defence is readily apparent. It seems frequently to have been the interest around which groups or societies have assembled. Nation states mostly have their origins in external threats. But a group support-bargaining process within an established group is apparent in the determination of whether Trident missiles constitute a British communal interest, or whether the communal interest in defence is better served by some other weaponry. Clean air and environmental protection were not recognised as communal interests until the support-bargaining process identified them as such. Through support-bargaining, 'group requirements' for goods and services, with features related to group concepts of situation, are identified for provision by a society.

Without a concept of group interest, the extensive engagement of governments in provision of services in apparent fulfilment of communal interests constitutes an anomaly for neoclassical economics. It has reconciled the anomaly, at least to the satisfaction of the theory group, by identifying qualities in a 'product' that make it a 'public good'. A 'public good' is a good that is non-rivalrous, in the sense that provision of it to one person does not diminish its availability to others, and non-excludable, in the sense that if it is provided at all, it cannot be denied to anyone. 'Defence' is the archetypal 'public good'. The economic concept of the 'public good' thus depends on qualities of the 'good' whereas, in the understanding of support-bargaining and money-bargaining, public provision is dictated by communal identification of communal interest.

Economics designates a 'public good' contrasting with the individual 'goods' commonly understood as allocated through the neoclassical economic model. However, most government provision is of 'services'. But services are conceptually more matters of definition in an information interface than are 'goods', so that the 'non-rivalrous' and 'non-excludability' features of 'public goods' are not so sharply contrasted in the concept of 'public services'. A service can be defined as private or public in accordance with the interests of those involved. Defence against fire used to be organised on the basis of private payments for a private service. It was then recognised as a communal interest, and the service was redefined as a public service. If public provision is to be understood by reference to the qualities of what is provided, then 'public services' would be more appropriate. But with that terminology the distinction between individual services and public services is less apparent. The distinction is what people want it to be; how they define it to be through support-bargaining. That is to say, it is a matter of communal interest.[58]

Even when an interest is identified as a communal interest, it is still necessary, before it can be realised, to establish a budget to pay for it. Companies cannot format to meet communal interests unless the relevant community has established a money budget. Through support-bargaining, societies establish central and local governments with authority to raise revenues and establish budgets through which communal requirements can be met. Governments function as the agents through which social interests can be realised through institutional budgets. Governments can make the necessary provision through their own direct employees, or they can buy services from companies formatted for the provision of services of the kind required. Once there is a budget, the specialist money-bargaining agencies can respond to requirements. In response to group or communal interests, governments provide such services as defence, education, health care, roads and railways, water, sewerage, housing, welfare payments and so on.

The capacity of governments to meet communal interests depends substantially on budget capacity. Budgets of Western governments have greatly increased in size over the past two hundred years, with two world wars in the twentieth century providing major stimuli to increases in government revenues and expenditures. A money-bargaining system comprises a network of transactions feeding money into and out of the budgets of all the agents involved. Governments control budgets of exceptional size, and hence have a prominent role in money-bargaining systems. The expenditures of Western European governments typically amount to between 40 and 50 per cent of GDP.

Though receipts and expenditures are of money, the budgets are controlled through support-bargaining. Control is exercised through provision and use of information. Governments assemble large volumes of information relating to their revenues, service provision, the eligibility of people for communal services and national economic performance, much of it in the form of statistics. The intensity of the information requirements of government engagement mean that those employed by governments include a higher proportion than in private employment of people with the advanced educational attainments that enable them to assemble and analyse large amounts of information.

Governments also respond to communal interest by regulating private money-bargaining. As was seen in Chapter 2 and above, 'money' is a creation of support-bargaining, and hence money-bargaining too is a creation of support-bargaining. Money-bargaining systems remain under the supervision of support-bargaining systems. Money-bargaining systems are regulated in accordance with communal interest. They function under conditions and within limits imposed by support-bargaining.

Support-bargaining and money-bargaining systems run on an information interface, so that the integrity of the information interface is vital to the integrity of transactions. False and misleading information will corrupt transactions. In an unregulated system, buyers could not be reasonably sure they would get what they had paid for; sellers could not be sure they would be paid what their customers had undertaken to pay them. Endless experience of swindling and double-dealing has resulted in the build-up, through the formal support-bargaining system, of a large regulatory information interface, imposing features on transactions that would not be present in a purely private process. It is established with the force of support, with its underlying premise of violence, expressed more moderately in monetary fines or imprisonment. Regulations also impede the emergence of strong bargaining positions through cartel arrangements – what Smith recognised as combination to reduce competition by both 'masters' and labour. They also give effect to notions of morality and ethics developed through social support-bargaining. Regulation has the effect of reducing the risk of losses, disappointment and humiliation through engagement in money-bargaining, and consequently encourages the growth of money-bargaining systems. Without extensive regulation money-bargaining could only be sustained in severely truncated form.

The requirement for regulation is newly apparent in experience with the internet. The internet represents a vast new extension of the information interface. It is highly effective in providing opportunities for companies to inform potential buyers of the goods and services they offer. It gives potential buyers access to information about the goods and services available. But the facility of communication and its impersonality means there is great scope for deception. It is easy for scammers to find victims on the internet. Information is purveyed over the internet designed to persuade those who encounter it to part with money in exchange for what appear to be admirable returns, but which turn out to be nothing. Regulation is an obvious requirement, but the technology of the internet means there are considerable difficulties in formulating and enforcing regulations that sufficiently reduce scamming without substantially reducing also the legitimate use of the internet. The realisation of the full potential of the internet for legitimate trade depends on containment of risk at tolerable levels.

Governments may also protect their societies, or subgroups of their societies, from adverse consequences of the functioning of a money-bargaining system. Companies format to meet the viability condition, and may neglect interests outside the confines in which they operate. Governments commonly legislate to protect the environment against the depredations arising from the operations of companies. A large information interface relating to compulsory features of transactions is established to ensure that money-bargaining is conducted in a manner that meets standards set by society. The rapid growth in money-bargaining over the last two hundred years would not have been possible without the engagement of governments.

The effects of government engagement are apparent in John Searle's account of his visit to a Paris café, referred to in the previous chapter. He goes into the café, orders a beer and drinks it. 'An innocent scene, but its metaphysical complexity is truly staggering, and its complexity would have taken Kant's breath away if he had ever bothered to think about such things'. Amongst other complications:

> the scene as described has a huge, invisible ontology: the waiter did not actually own the beer he gave me, but he is employed by the restaurant, which owned it. The restaurant is required to post a list of the prices of all the *boissons*, and even if I never see such a list, I am required to pay only the listed price. The owner of the restaurant is licensed by the French government to operate it. As such he is subject to a thousand rules and regulations I know nothing about. I am entitled to be there in the first place only because I am a citizen of the United States, the bearer of a valid passport, and I have entered France legally.[59]

For all the metaphysical and ontological mysteries, the point is that buying a beer in a Paris café takes place by reference to an information interface that includes material expressly designed to protect the various interests of those participating immediately in the transaction. The waiter is subject to many regulations concerning his functions and rights as an employee of a licensed restaurant. The price of drinks is available on a list so that innocent tourists do not get swindled; and hence innocent tourists, and everyone else, will more readily drink beer in Paris cafés. Beyond that there is an information interface defining the rights of Americans to travel out of America and their obligations upon entering France. And beyond that, as Searle might have remarked, all concerned are able to read the regulations and notices, to decode the restrictions imposed through the information interface.

Searle might have remarked further that he was able to reach the café from the airport on a road built and owned by the state, with the unmistakable ontological status deriving from perceptual information. The functioning of the café depended on access to it by road. The function of the private money-bargaining network depends on the establishment of an infrastructure for the conveyance of goods and people. If a road is to be open to all, it needs to be constructed on a communal basis, using the communal agency of government. The communal advantages of public provision have given governments a major role around the world in the provision of the infrastructure on which private money-bargaining can be conducted.

The capacity of governments to make these investments for communal interest depends on the budgetary arrangements described above. The revenues for government budgets derive from private money-bargaining systems. Appropriate levels of taxation, and hence appropriate levels of accommodation of communal interests, have been at the centre of the most heated disputes over the last century and more. Those adopting a neoclassical frame of reference ardently oppose levels of government engagement beyond the most basic, whilst those adopting the socialist frame of reference advocate the most extensive government engagement. Understood in the context of support-bargaining and money-bargaining, private enterprise for the fulfilment of individual interest and government engagement for the advance of communal interest seem necessary, complementary, eminently sensible and remarkably effective. Private money-bargaining provides a communal or social return in the form of revenues from taxation of private agents to fund the support-bargaining system, which accommodates communal interests, including the communal interest in a strong money-bargaining system. Creation and acceptance of a money-bargaining system seems predicated on both the services and incomes it provides directly and the social returns it generates for communal purposes.

Such communal advantage deriving from the operations of companies goes entirely unremarked in the neoclassical frame of reference. Neoclassical economic theory is concerned with private exchange and the 'optimal allocation of resources' that arises from unfettered private exchange. It cannot claim for economic exchange the merit of permitting the expansion of communal services, since that would imply a role for government, and an acknowledgement that resources could not be allocated optimally on a purely private basis. It would, moreover, acknowledge the importance of 'communal interest', when a prominent purpose of the neoclassical formulation was to advance the individual interest. Around the world, taxation has been extensively used for provision of services that have been recognised as matters of communal interest. Under a neoclassical frame of reference, one of the major advantages of private money-bargaining driven by company formats has to be ignored. Worse, because the neoclassical frame of reference cannot tolerate engagement of the state, such engagement has been stigmatised as an 'evil of socialism', rather than a triumph of the money-bargaining system.

The support-bargaining system invariably makes receipt of many services and payments from government conditional on the fulfilment of certain conditions relating to situation. In Britain, people of a certain age who have made certain payments during their working life receive a full pension. People in certain family circumstances receiving low incomes and residing in a particular location are eligible for government housing in that location. Companies identify what was referred to above as 'vendor sets', comprising those people whose circumstances make them potential buyers of the company's products. Governments assemble large volumes of information regarding people's circumstances to establish what services and payments they are eligible for. People are typically asked to fill in forms when they apply for such services or payments. Those in charge of hospitals and schools must complete forms to receive budgetary entitlements. The completed forms reveal whether or not a person or an institution falls into the set of those eligible for the benefits in question. Eligibility rests on conformity of the information provided with the situations defined in the relevant legislation. Communal interest has also been recognised in expansion of the capacities of people to perform the tasks necessary to productive life and necessary to participation in a support-bargaining system. A support-bargaining system heavily dependent on information requires that the agents of the system have skills in the assembly and manipulation of information. In developed Western nations governments provide free education. States commonly require that children are educated, since in societies so dependent on information lack of access to written information and lack of some capacity to understand and provide information is likely to be severely restricting in adult life. The uneducated find themselves in weak bargaining positions and open to exploitation by the educated. If you cannot read the notices in a café you may forego service to which you are entitled. If you cannot use the internet many opportunities will be lost.

States also promote more advanced forms of education as the basis for contributions to the running of their societies and their productive capacities. Money-bargaining systems depend most fundamentally for their effectiveness and expansion on the capacities of their individual agents, and the basis of those capacities is established in childhood and youth. The technology that is central to the successful format of companies evolves amongst the educated – not just a few notable individuals but in a general wave of educated people working on issues that have the potential to form the basis of viable businesses.

Physical and mental health have also been seen as essential to human capacities for the performance of communal and business tasks. Alongside educational provision, Western states make extensive provision for health services. In Britain the National Health Service provides treatment and preventive health services without charge on demand to all. The education and health services provided by governments on a communal basis ensure that all individuals develop the physical and mental capacities that enable them to participate in support-bargaining and money-bargaining.

It was noted in the previous chapter that these 'capacities' form the equivalent, over a wider range of provision, of the 'capital' that is identified in economic theory as a prerequisite of economic production. 'Human capital' is not regarded in mainstream economic theory as of comparable status to the physical 'capital' that is part of the production process. 'Rational' beings do not need other capacities. This incapacity of theoretical economics to recognise fully the importance of human capacities is reflected in the classification of health and education expenditures by governments in national accounts as 'consumption' rather than 'investment', except where the expenditures meet the criteria for classification as investment in the accepted economic sense. Health and education are consumed like eggs and bacon, rather than constituting capacities for production like plant and machinery.

The neoclassical approach to government took its cue from Adam Smith. He saw government as largely an impediment to the functioning of a successful economy – that is, one which meets the requirements of consumers. Smith wrote at a time when governments responded to the interests of a relatively small group of aristocrats, landowners and wealthy merchants. Governments granted monopolies to favoured persons or groups and permitted systems of apprenticeship that protected trades from competition, raising costs for businesses and prices for consumers. Governments reduced the competition that is generally advantageous in a society.[60] Smith's arguments against government intervention and in favour of competition played an important role in the acceptance of competition in an economy and the repeal of legislation that gave those in favour with governments exceptional opportunities to amass wealth. That acceptance was important to the industrial revolution and the associated growth of material prosperity across Europe and the world.

Smith was not entirely blind to another side of the argument. He recognised, in Book V, requirements for government expenditures for provision of defence, justice, public works, public institutions and the maintenance of the monarch, and the requirement for revenues to meet these expenditures. He recognised that people, left to themselves, will pursue their own interests, often at the expense of others and of their communities. He recognised that some government involvement might be necessary to safeguard interests against such behaviour. But he seemed reluctant to conclude that governments might intervene more positively to protect their citizens, and highly reluctant to conclude that governments might intervene more widely to advance the interests of their citizens. In general, if government was to be engaged, it should be to the minimum possible extent. As Heilbroner remarks, 'To Adam Smith the least government is certainly the best'.[61] Smith's attitude can be related to his underlying philosophical and ethical concern that the exercise of private interest should be seen as conducive to social benefit. Any emphasis on the necessity for government engagement would detract from that basic contention. His work underestimates the necessity for government engagement with an economy to facilitate economic exchange and protect consumers against abuses of bargaining position. He largely overlooks the opportunities for governments to enhance the lives of their people.

The increasing articulation and influence of ordinary people in the life of Western nations and the extensions of the franchise that accompanied the industrial revolution made governments more responsive to wider communal interests. So it was that governments responded, if not with alacrity, at least with some alleviation of the severe hardships imposed on many of those caught up in the industrial revolution. Governments gradually came to accept, through the burgeoning support-bargaining system, that they had a prominent role to play.

Notes

1 Smith, Adam, 1986, *The Wealth of Nations*, Books I–III, London: Penguin Classics, p. 115; Smith, Adam, 2009, *An Inquiry into the Nature and Causes of the Wealth of Nations*, Project Gutenberg E-book, Adobe Digital Editions, p. 11. First published 1776.

2 Smith, 1986, p. 158 (digital pp. 43–4).

3 Smith, 1986, p. 162 (digital p. 46).
4 Smith, 1986, pp. 158–61 (digital pp. 43–5).
5 Smith, 1986, pp. 162–5 (digital pp. 47–9).
6 Smith, 1986, p. 169 (digital p. 51).
7 Smith, 1986, pp. 356–9 (digital pp. 189–91).
8 Smith, 1986, p. 359 (digital p. 191).
9 Smith, 1986, p. 114 (digital p. 10).
10 Smith, 1986, p. 109 (digital p. 6).
11 Smith, 1986, p. 115 (digital pp. 10–11).
12 Heilbroner, Robert L., 2017, 'Adam Smith', *Encyclopaedia Britannica* online, available at: www.britannica.com/biography/Adam-Smith. Accessed 18 May 2017.
13 Hennings, Klaus H., 1986, 'The exchange paradigm and the theory of production and distribution', in Baranzini, Mauro and Scazzieri, Roberto (eds), 1986, *Foundations of Economics: Structures of Enquiry and Economic Theory*, Oxford: Blackwell, pp. 221–43, esp. p. 240; for comment see Spread, Patrick, 2013, *Support-Bargaining, Economics and Society: A Social Species*, Abingdon: Routledge, pp. 248–9, 283 n. 38.
14 Spread, Patrick, 2016a, *The Evolution of Economies: Support-Bargaining, Economic Change and Industrial Revolution*, Abingdon: Routledge, Chapter 5: The evolution of economies.
15 Smith, 1986, p. 164 (digital p. 48).
16 For a comparison of 'support' and 'money' as bargaining counters, see Spread, 2016a, pp. 17–19.
17 Backhouse, Roger E., 2002, *The Penguin History of Economics*, London: Penguin Books, p. 182.
18 Marshall, Alfred, 1920, *Principles of Economics*, Eighth Edition, London: Macmillan. First published 1890.
19 Robbins, Lionel, 1932, *An Essay on the Nature and Significance of Economic Science*, London: Macmillan, p. 15.
20 Backhouse, 2002, p. 239.
21 Backhouse, 2002, pp. 238–9.
22 Benicourt, Emmanuelle, 2004, 'Five pieces of advice for students studying microeconomics', in Fullbrook, Edward, 2004, *A Guide to What's Wrong with Economics*, London: Anthem Press, p. 85.
23 Spread, Patrick, 2008, *Support-Bargaining: The Mechanics of Democracy Revealed*, Sussex: Book Guild, pp. 337–41.
24 Smith, Adam, 2008, *An Inquiry into the Nature and Causes of the Wealth of Nations*, A Selected Edition, Oxford: Oxford World's Classics, pp. 291–2 (digital p. 325). First published 1776.
25 Stiglitz, Joseph E., 1985, 'Information and economic analysis: a perspective', *The Economic Journal*, Vol. 95, Supplement pp. 21–41, esp. p. 26; Stiglitz, Joseph E., 2002, 'Information and the change in the paradigm in economics', *American Economic Review*, Vol. 92, No. 3, pp. 460–501, esp. p. 460.
26 Latsis, Spiros J., 1976b, 'A research programme in economics', in Latsis, Spiros J., 1976a, *Method and Appraisal in Economics*, Cambridge: Cambridge University Press, p. 11.
27 Akerlof, George, 1970, 'The market for lemons: quality, uncertainty and the market mechanism', *Quarterly Journal of Economics*, Vol, 84, No. 3, pp. 488–500.
28 Akerlof, 1970, pp. 489–91.
29 Akerlof, 1970, p. 490–1.

30 Akerlof, 1970, p. 491. Original emphasis.
31 Akerlof, 1970, p. 488.
32 Akerlof, 1970, p. 495–9.
33 Akerlof, 1970, p. 492.
34 Akerlof, 1970, p. 490.
35 Akerlof, 1970, pp. 499–500.
36 Stiglitz, 2002, pp. 469–70.
37 Stiglitz, 2002, pp. 472, 475, etc.
38 Stiglitz, 1985, p. 30; Stiglitz, 2002, p. 488.
39 Spread, 2008, pp. 93–9; Spread, Patrick, 2015a, 'Asymmetric information, critical information and the information interface', *Real World Economics Review*, Issue 70, pp. 121–40, esp. p. 134. Reprinted in Spread, Patrick, 2015b, *Aspects of Support-Bargaining and Money-Bargaining*, E-Book, World Economics Association.
40 Stiglitz, 2002, pp. 460–3.
41 Stiglitz, 2002, p. 486.
42 Stiglitz, 2002, pp. 486–7.
43 For further discussion of asymmetric information, in particular Stiglitz's work, see Spread, 2015a.
44 On 'money' as an outcome of support-bargaining, see Spread, 2016a, pp. 13–19.
45 On money as a bargaining counter, see Spread, 2013, pp. 200–6.
46 For further comment on microeconomic and macroeconomic theory, see Spread, 2016a, Chapter 3: Macroeconomics and money-bargaining; Chapter 7: Support-bargaining, credit and confidence.
47 Mankiw, Greg, 2006, 'The macroeconomist as scientist and engineer', *Journal of Economic Perspectives*, Vol. 20, No. 4, pp. 42–3. Quoted by Syll, Lars Pålsson, 2016, 'Paul Romer's assault on "post-real" macroeconomics', *Real-World Economics Review*, Issue 76, September, pp. 43–54, esp. p. 49, available at: www.paecon.net/PAEReview/issue76/Syll76.pdf.
48 Smith, 1986, p. 356 (digital p. 189).
49 Smith, 1986, p. 357 (digital pp. 189–90).
50 Smith, 2008, p. 376 (digital p. 486).
51 Spread, 2008, pp. 78–87; Spread, Patrick, 2011, 'Situation as determinant of selection and valuation', *Cambridge Journal of Economics*, Vol. 35, No. 2, pp. 335–56. Reprinted in Spread, 2015b.
52 See Spread, 2008, pp. 90–3, 107–13, etc.
53 Spread, 2016a, pp. 153–5.
54 Spread, Patrick, 2016b, 'Companies and markets: economic theories of the firm and a concept of companies as bargaining agencies', *Cambridge Journal of Economics*, Vol. 40, No. 3, pp. 727–53. Reprinted in Spread, 2015b. See also Spread, 2016a, pp. 29–32.
55 Richardson, George B., 1990, *Information and Investment: A Study in the Working of the Competitive Economy*, Second Edition, Oxford: Oxford University Press, pp. 32–3. First published 1960; Rader, Trout, 1970, 'Resource allocation with increasing returns to scale', *The American Economic Review*, Vol. 60, No. 5, pp. 814–25, esp. p. 814; see also Geanakoplos, John, 2004, 'The Arrow-Debreu Model of General Equilibrium', *Cowles Foundation Paper No. 1090*, Cowles Foundation for Research in Economics at Yale University, p. 122.
56 See at note 10 in Chapter 2.
57 Gilbert, Margaret, 1989, *On Social Facts*, Abingdon: Routledge. Discussed further in Chapter 6.

58 On 'public goods', see also Spread, 2016a, pp. 179–80; see also Spread, Patrick, 2004, *Getting It Right: Economics and the Security of Support*, Sussex: BookGuild, pp. 23–6, 93–7, 107.
59 Searle, John R., 1996, *The Construction of Social Reality*, London: Penguin Books, p. 3.
60 Smith, 1986, pp. 164–5 (digital pp. 48–9).
61 Heilbroner, Robert, 2000, *The Worldly Philosophers: The Lives, Theories and Ideas of the Great Economic Thinkers*, London: Penguin, p. 68. First published 1953.

5 Economics and behavioural economics

At the time of its initial formulation in the late nineteenth century neoclassical economists may not have regarded themselves as lacking psychological sophistication. Luigino Bruni and Robert Sugden, in a 2007 article on 'The road not taken', suggest that at its inception neoclassical theory was at the cutting edge of psychology. The idea of diminishing marginal utility was derived from a broader psychological principle that the intensity of a stimulus diminishes with each successive application of the stimulus: 'The law of diminishing marginal utility – that as consumption of any commodity increases, the increment of pleasure produced by a given increment of consumption falls – was seen as a special case of this more general law of psychology'.[1] Bruni and Sugden suggest there was a distinct parting of the ways in the early development of neoclassical theory when ideas of rational choice, deriving especially from the work of Vilfredo Pareto, were adopted, rather than a theory based on psychological principles:

> It is a central claim of our article that, before the Paretian turn, neoclassical economics was based on what was then state-of-the-art research on the psychology of sensations . . . Thus, what we see as the 'road not taken' is a potential continuation of nineteenth-century neoclassical economics, leading in the direction of behavioural economics.[2]

Taking the road it took has involved economic theory in a perpetual struggle to reconcile the rationality required for a mathematical approach with the psychology necessary to a realistic approach.

The rational approach required exclusion of most of the characteristics that make humans what they are. It was then inevitably difficult to develop a theory of human behaviour in the economic sphere on the basis of psychological suppositions that excluded any concept of humanity beyond the capacity for reason. But the will of the theory group was that economics should be a mathematical investigation, and with that will, a way was found to make it so. Assumptions were adopted, both explicit and implicit, that facilitated the application of mathematics but took the theory far from the realities of humanity and the realities of monetary exchange. The emerging neoclassical economic theory group assembled enough support to ignore the difficulties and proceed on its chosen mathematical road. Its ascendancy was consolidated through institutionalisation. The mathematical approach grew and strengthened through the twentieth century.[3]

The neoclassical movement chose to ignore psychology, but the choice was perhaps influenced by the weakness of the theories that psychologists were able to offer. It was noted in the previous chapter that psychologists failed to identify the propensity of humans to seek support from their associates, and the means adopted for the acquisition of support. Had 'support-bargaining' been identified, and the situation-related reference of interests that is an important part of it, neoclassical economists might have found it more difficult to ignore human psychology to extent they have.

Psychologists have nevertheless challenged the idea of 'rationality' in neoclassical economic theory as an adequate basis for the understanding of economic exchange. These challenges have emerged broadly in two waves: the idea of 'bounded rationality' introduced by Herbert Simon, discussed in Chapter 1, and the identification of various psychological traits bearing on human choice by Daniel Kahneman and Amos Tversky. Their impact on support for the neoclassical model has been limited. Mainstream economists have found it possible to accept behavioural theory as an interesting adjunct to their theory, without any need to deviate significantly from their chosen road. The weakness of Simon's challenge lies in its continued absorption in the idea of human rationality. The weakness of the challenge of Kahneman and Tversky lies in their focus on transactions that can be seen as a minor part of economic transactions in general. But perhaps more critically, the weakness of the challenges lies in a failure to take proper account of the situation-related determination of interests and an individualist concept of choice that neglects the social influences that arise as a consequence of support-bargaining. The psychologists have not provided any radically different psychological understanding to replace the idea of rational behaviour.

As was seen in Chapter 1, Herbert Simon argued that human rationality was limited by the capacity of the human mind relative to the problems that had to be dealt with. Humans act as rationally as possible in the circumstances, employing what Simon characterises as 'satisficing'.[4] They make choices that are 'satisfactory' or 'sufficient', even if they are not optimal. In an administrative context, people construct a 'model of the situation' which can be used for 'satisficing'. Up to the 1980s 'behavioural theory' centred on the idea of 'bounded rationality'. Peter Earl's collection of articles on *Behavioural Economics* of 1988 is mainly concerned with bounded rationality.[5]

The idea of bounded rationality and the responses to problems arising from bounded rationality were strongly influenced by the thinking associated with computer programming.[6] Herbert Simon's initial interests were in computer science and psychology, particularly in relation to artificial intelligence.[7] His 'mind-centred' approach is reflected in the attribution of 'bounded rationality' to limitations of the human mind with regard to the processing of data. The implication of 'bounded rationality' is that the rationality of the neoclassical model is 'unbounded' or 'pure'. But 'economic man' exercises his rationality in highly confined circumstances. He is provided, through the assumptions of the model, with the goals or objectives in pursuit of which he is to exercise his reason. As Simon pointed out in his later book, *Reason in Human Affairs*, reason is instrumental: 'It can't elect our final goals'.[8] Martin Fransman makes the same point, that to be rational it is necessary to have objectives.[9] Outside the bounds of the model, humans must establish their own goals if they are to exercise reason. It is not mental capacity that bounds rationality but the complex circumstances in which it must be applied.

The conception of bounded rationality in terms of human mental shortcomings distracts attention from the actual psychology of the human mind. Humans have very remarkable capacity for dealing with information which is underrated by a presentation in the negative terms of 'cognitive limitations'. Simon's concept of bounded rationality suggests that actual minds are markedly less bright than the rational beings of the neoclassical model, who perform with such comprehensive rationality. He refers to 'the behavior of human beings who *satisfice* because they have not the wits to *maximise*'.[10] In circumstances defined for the exercise of reason it is possible to apply reason. That is, with an information interface limited to what is required for the exercise of reason, it is possible to exercise reason. But the broad information interface of ordinary life has to be approached differently. A mind has first to determine what is relevant. By retaining the emphasis on rationality and the boundaries imposed by the human mind, Simon neglects and even mistakes the contrast between the neoclassical model and real-world experience. He retains the idea of human rationality as an ideal and hence the idea of the neoclassical model as an ideal. As an ideal, it more easily retains the support of its theory group. 'Bounded rationality' compliments and elevates the idea of rationality, rather than exposing its deficiencies as an account of human behaviour. It defines humans as 'failures in rationality' rather than as 'marvels of perceptual acuity'. It demeans the capacity of the actual human mind. It underestimates the capacity of the actual human mind to deal with information. For these reasons, 'bounded rationality' is an unsatisfactory means of introducing human psychology into mainstream economics. They make it also an unsatisfactory concept by which to introduce information issues. 'Bounded rationality' functions largely as a proxy treatment for information issues in the explanations of industrial organisation noted in Chapter 1. It explains the use of information only as expedients made necessary by human mental deficiencies. The role of information is only properly understood in the context of support-bargaining and money-bargaining.

That humans can cope as they do marks mental capacities not properly recognised in the 'cognitive limitations' of bounded rationality, nor even in the more complex psychology described by Daniel Kahneman in *Thinking, Fast and Slow*, discussed below. Humans recognise or identify information that is relevant to their situation. They select by reference to the circumstances, whether a threat from a wild animal to their survival, or a carpet of a particular shade of green that will fit with the curtains already hanging in the living room at home. What is more, they can take account of their social situation. They will select as relevant what is likely to meet with the approval of those with whom they associate. Concepts of situation and what is 'fitting' will be reached through social support-bargaining. This is a new psychological dimension in the handling of information. As was also noted in Chapter 1, the process of 'fitting to situation' involves exercise of a sense of symmetry rather than rational faculties.

'Fitting to situation' through the exercise of the sense of symmetry is likely to precede the identification of specific goals. People form 'bargaining sets' comprising options of products and suppliers that can meet various situation-related requirements. A car, for example, may have to fit a small garage, carry six persons, and have four-wheel-drive. Such situation-related criteria cut down the possibilities. A single goal will arise when a single criterion for selection stands out, or when it is possible to reduce a bargaining set to a single criterion for selection. The identification of a goal itself is a matter of 'best fit' symmetry. An individual may settle on the goal of 'passing the maths exam' after eliminating other options, and direct all rational capacities to the achievement of that goal. Such a goal is likely to be adopted not just from the individual sense of improvement, but with the recognition also that the adoption of it is likely to be supported within the goal-setter's social group. Other goals may be less readily given social support, and for that reason may not be openly identified by those who adopt them. A person opting to buy a 'Jaguar' car may be reluctant to acknowledge that his goal is to gain the social status that is perceived to arise from ownership of such a racy vehicle. But people may, rightly or wrongly, impute that goal to the buyer. It is a rational choice in the context of that goal. Some goals may be identified only in retrospect, by assuming that the trail of decisions and actions that led to a certain outcome were rational decisions and actions taken to reach that goal. A specific goal may only be the determinant of choice after a prior process of whittling down the options; or may be seen as a specific goal only in retrospect. A choice that is made ex-ante using a sense of symmetry can be interpreted ex-post as an exercise of reason. This process of selection reflects the mixed motivations commonly involved in other decisions, as described in Chapter 3.

The idea of 'bounded rationality' has been highly influential. Because of its implicit homage to rationality it has been easy to recognise it as an adjunct or minor modifier to neoclassical theory, without being a replacement. Its influence extends into the second wave of behavioural theory that began with Kahneman and Tversky's 1979 article titled 'Prospect theory: an analysis of decision under risk', published in *Econometrica*, a leading journal of mathematical economics.[11] The article was reprinted by Earl in his 1988 collection on *Behavioural Economics*, but only, as Earl later wrote, 'with rather mixed feelings'.[12] It came to be so accepted amongst economists as to gain for Kahneman the Nobel Memorial Prize for economics in 2002.[13] At the award ceremony he gave an address that was subsequently published as 'Maps of bounded rationality: psychology for behavioral economics'. Kahneman remarks in the article, 'Theories in behavioural economics have generally retained the basic architecture of the rational model, adding assumptions about cognitive limitations designed to account for specific anomalies'.[14] The connection with rationality is maintained through the concept of bounded rationality. Psychology merely identifies certain traits that indicate the boundaries of rationality. Behavioural theory does little to impose a more realistic psychology on neoclassical economic theory. It does not restore mainstream economics to a right psychological road. It seems to concede too much to rationality and hence promote the continued ascendancy of neoclassical economic theory. The idea of support-bargaining and money-bargaining rests on a very different psychology that is incompatible with neoclassical understanding.

Behavioural psychology and the psychology of support-bargaining

It was noted in Chapter 3 that the manipulation of information used to establish an information interface supportive of certain interests includes imputation of psychological predispositions to agents involved. People may be labelled as 'obsessive', 'arrogant', 'domineering', etc. Psychology shapes the information interface; what people think and believe because of their psychological dispositions determines the information on which they act. The buyer of the Jaguar is perhaps psychologically inclined to dominance and, given the popular concept of a Jaguar, he may believe such a car will help him gain the dominant social status he wants. The name 'Jaguar' associates the car with a predator at the top of the jungle food chain. Psychological traits are the linkage between human interests and reactions on the one hand and the neurological processes of the mind on the other. Psychological traits are the observable consequences of neurological processes. People are generally unaware of the psychological factors that drive them. They follow a sense of symmetry that enables them to relate potential actions or purchases to the situations that their psychology has defined for them.

'Unconscious and 'aware' behaviour was presented in Chapter 3 mainly as expressions of quality of mind or character rather than reactions to specific stimuli. Our minds prompt us unaware to do, read, search, enquire, cajole, dissemble, fight, and so on, and thereby reveal to others our character. An agent is nevertheless reacting to a great range of stimuli, most particularly the stimuli identified as part of the support-bargaining process. Agents react to perceived threats and even just hints of potential withdrawal of support. Agents respond to information potentially affecting individual or group advancement. The unaware functions provide a reflexive shield and at the same time a reflexive uptake of opportunities for advancement within a support-bargaining and money-bargaining system. The rapidity of response is made possible by a sense of symmetry. At least a part of the human mind functions like a 'symmetry computer' that identifies patterns in the environment and keys appropriate responses with great rapidity.[15]

In *Thinking, Fast and Slow*, Kahneman investigates the psychology behind human behaviour in the context of 'System 1' and 'System 2' mental processes.[16] System 1 is conceived in terms of very rapid and instinctive responses to stimuli, involving little or no effort. With System 1 people experience 'cognitive ease', because all is automatic. System 2 takes over when System 1 cannot cope. System 2 is slow and involves effort. It is associated with analytical tasks, such as tasks involving figures. '17 × 23' is a System 2 task; System 1 offers no solution. 'System 1 is impulsive and intuitive; System 2 is capable of reasoning, and it is cautious, but at least for some people it is also lazy'.[17] The idea that 'murderers should be executed' would presumably be regarded as a System 1 reflexive reaction to murder, whilst the abandonment of judicial execution on grounds of lack of proven deterrence, or risk of mistake, or compassion for mental weaknesses, or circumstances of extreme provocation, would presumably be regarded as a System 2 approach, more thoughtful and deliberative than System 1.

The System 1/System 2 conception of human psychology has a long history. Daniel Kahneman and Shane Frederick write:

> The ancient idea that cognitive processes can be partitioned into two main families – traditionally called *intuition* and *reason* – is now widely embraced under the general label of *dual-process* theories . . . Dual-process models come in many flavors, but all distinguish cognitive operations that are quick and associative from others that are slow and rule-governed. We adopt the generic labels *System 1* and *System 2* from Stanovich and West.[18]

Thinking, Fast and Slow adopts the same labels. Kahneman notes that System 1 and System 2 might equally well be referred to as 'automatic' and 'effortful'. The 'system' nomenclature is preferred as shorter. Kahneman notes that although the terms System 1 and System 2 were first used by Stanovich and West, they later preferred the designation Type 1 and Type 2.

System 1 processes described by Kahneman are the sort of 'micro-psychological' traits that are revealed by recording the reactions of volunteers to propositions put to them in laboratories. The volunteers are asked to give immediate reflex responses, so that they are employing System 1 capabilities, with none of the analytical enquiry of System 2. Traits identified by Kahneman include:

- People are influenced by 'anchoring'. The asking price for a house will influence what is offered – a high asking price is likely to get higher offers than if the asking price is low.
- Susceptibility to 'priming', so that when a certain issue is introduced early into an exchange, System 1 focuses on that issue, distracting attention from other issues. An 'anchor' may be interpreted as a 'prime'.[19]

- Susceptibility to 'framing'. In a competition between France and Italy, the statements 'France won' and 'Italy lost' have the same meaning, but the different framing gives rise to different associations and will convey different understandings.
- Readiness of 'association', so that given one piece of information, System 1 will rapidly conjure up associated experience.
- Response to 'availability', so that people respond to what is easily available, or easily comes to mind, without clouding their minds with alternatives.
- Susceptibility to 'repetition', so that repetition of a message is likely to establish the message as true in the minds of recipients.
- The influence of 'cognitive ease' – people put at ease become receptive to information.[20]

The sharp dichotomy of System 1 and System 2, as reflex and analytical responses, or as exercise of intuition and reason, separates psychological impulses from the rationality of mainstream economic theory, giving the former less impact on the latter. It becomes easier to see the psychology as identifying impulsive quirks of behaviour, while mainstream economics is concerned with rational human conduct – the analytical, more public and probably wiser approach with regard to advantageous outcomes. The quirks of behaviour are distinctly irrational, possibly amounting in common assessment to mistakes. What a seller wants for his house is not a necessary indicator of what it is worth. 'France won' and 'Italy lost' are rationally the same. Instead of introducing psychological factors into the understanding of human economic choices, the dichotomy of System 1 and System 2 separates the psychological from the deliberative, even to the extent of suggesting that economics can go its own rational way.

The dichotomy seems influenced by the laboratory context in which hypotheses are tested and by its individualist understanding of psychological influences, the individualist understanding accentuated by the laboratory confine. Moved to the 'macro-psychological' setting of support-bargaining and money-bargaining, it is apparent that the sharp distinction is misleading. While we have 'emergency' circuitry in our brains that enables us to respond to threats, identified further below, we always act for the advance of our interests, whether behaving impulsively or with the use of analytical frames of reference. Our actions are always undertaken with reference to the requirement for support from associates. That same requirement is involved in the formulation of analytical frames of reference and in the choice of which frame of reference to employ in any particular situation. The limitations of psychology with regard to group influences are apparent in Abraham Maslow's comments on the 'herd instinct' referred to in Chapter 3 at note 29.

Three of the reflexive traits identified by Kahneman, the use of 'anchors', the susceptibility to 'primes' and the susceptibility to 'framing', are linked to the much broader concept of situation-related assessment of interests or, in a more theoretical context, the use of abstract frames of reference. It was suggested in Chapter 1 that Simon's 'model of the situation' created in an administrative decision-making context can be seen as related to the much wider-ranging creation and use of situation references in all spheres of human affairs. Similarly, 'anchors', 'primes' and 'frames' are micro-psychological aspects of macro-psychological understanding of situations and frames of reference used in all human affairs. The 'frame' is a matter of presentation, as a picture frame displays a picture to best advantage. But a 'frame of reference' is a more complex and wide-ranging psychological phenomenon. What is, in the micro-psychological context, reflex, laboratory based, relatively simple, individualistic and externally selected, becomes, in the 'macro-psychological' context, complex, both reflex and analytical, self-selected from a multiplicity of phenomena and influenced by relationships of an individual with others, potentially involving group formation. While the repetitive and controlled laboratory testing that establishes Kahneman's psychological traits gives the micro-psychological traits better grounding in science than the macro-psychological traits, mainly based on repetitive observation of common behaviour, yet the laboratory testing of the micro-psychological traits lends support also to the macro-psychological hypotheses, given the connections between them. The element of group influence on macro-psychological understanding is largely beyond the scope of laboratory testing, though individuals will carry into the laboratory the group influences already established in them, and their responses are likely to reflect the group interests.[21] The separation of 'psychological impulses' from the exercise of reason misses the human psychology involved in selection and the advance of human interests. The psychology of selection includes the selection of matters about which it is desirable and feasible to apply reason.

The involvement of the micro-psychological impulses identified by Kahneman with the 'macro-psychological' behaviour of support-bargaining and money-bargaining is apparent in common usage. Kahneman's 'anchors', 'primes' and 'frames' are not just individual quirks of behaviour. They can be seen as applying to circumstances of group engagement in social action. It might be said that Scots were 'primed' to vote for independence in the referendum of 2015 by bringing to their attention the combative historical relationship between Scotland and England; or that they were 'anchored' in that relationship, so that their judgements were consistent with it; or that in the 'frame' of that history, Scots would be inclined to vote for independence. But, equally, such content of the information interface might be regarded as giving Scots an account of the 'situation' that they were in as Scots, or even as giving them that situation as a 'frame of reference'. Such ideas are used almost interchangeably and casually in common intercourse. A 'frame' may be something like a picture frame, but it may also be understood as an abbreviation of 'frame of reference'. It is a form of 'preconception'.

Fusion of instinct and analysis

The lack of distinction in common usage between reflex usage of 'anchors', 'primes' and 'frames' and concepts of situation and frames of reference suggests that System 2 behaviour is as much 'psychological' and non-rational as that of System 1. While the principle that 'murderers should be executed' seems plainly to belong in the System 1 classification, the reconsideration of judicial execution also involves instincts and sympathies. People can be 'primed' to see that there are major risks of irreversible miscarriages of justice in the execution of convicted murderers. People can be 'primed' to understand that certain provocations, for example, a man treating a partner brutally, can give rise to a reaction such as, 'Well, he deserved what he got', and a corresponding unwillingness to punish the murderer. The rationale for dispensing with judicial execution is based on instincts as much as is the reflex, 'murderers should be executed'.

The simple reflex is a matter of individual instinct, universal amongst humans. It seems based in the innate sense of insecurity that is seen as the basis for support-seeking and hence of support-bargaining. It is an instinct that will bring people together in any community in support of its prompting. But those favouring abandonment of judicial execution also seek to enlist wide communal support through 'priming' people to share the context or 'frame' in which they see it. Interest, and in particular communal interest, are involved in both System 1 and System 2 behaviour. The assembly of support is of paramount importance because of the violent associations of support. Support functions psychologically as a proxy for violence. Support is assembled through stimulus of people to recognise their interests through 'anchors', 'primes' and 'frames' or through concepts of situation and frames of reference. It means establishing such references in the information interface through which support-bargaining is conducted.

The fusion of System 1 and System 2 is apparent in the idea of 'intellectual support-bargaining'. Theory is conventionally conceived as being objective and absolute, in the sense of unaffected by dispositions of human minds. This conception lies behind the distinction between System 1 and System 2 behaviour. In the former, people are 'psychological' – they act impulsively and often irrationally, and they make mistakes. But in System 2 they consider carefully and rationally how they should act to obtain their objectives. Such rational deliberations are regarded as having something absolute and unchallengeable in them. But, as was suggested in Chapter 1, our psychology has evolved for the pursuit of interest, not for the pursuit of truth. The formulation of the analytical systems employed in System 2 are the result of long deliberation rather than reflex response, but they are no less concerned with the exercise of instinct for the advance of interest. The idea of 'intellectual support-bargaining' suggests that theory formation is a matter of support-bargaining in which, as in other spheres of support-bargaining, people seek to advance their interests. They create the frames of reference that will govern perception and interpretation of phenomena in accordance with their preferences. 'Psychology' is returned to System 2. Neoclassical economic theory, deity theories, socialist theory, all derive from intellectual support-bargaining and all involve the advance of the interests of their creators. System 2 is no less instinctive that System 1, but the instincts are more subtly advanced and are consequently commonly understood in the information interface as something else. System 2 only seems rational and sharply distinct from System 1 because analysts would like it to be so.

The System 1 and System 2 dichotomy carries the suggestion that System 1 instincts are unconscious or unaware, while System 2 analysis is conducted consciously and with awareness. The reflex instincts of System 1 are necessarily unconscious. They are 'fast' because there is no time for deliberation. But we also exercise our ongoing instincts unaware, even into the formulation of analytical theories that appear to be outcomes of conscious and sophisticated deliberation. We follow our instincts unaware, with ongoing application, so they are inevitably less prominent than those which can be isolated and defined through laboratory research. We can think fast and slow, but our instincts are not only expressed in the lightning reactions of reflex. Nor are our analytical faculties necessarily slow in backing up what our instincts have led us to. Self-justification often comes easily. We can think of reasons, or analytical justifications, for actions driven by immediate instinct.

Self-justification is commonly easier for some than for others. The analytical theories or frames of reference created for the advancement of interests are products of intellectual support-bargaining; they are products of factional interest. Consequently, it very commonly occurs that individuals find their individual interests and instincts are contrary to the analytical frames that are recognised as applicable in their community. Immediate instincts or inclinations may conflict with the analytical frames an individual is accustomed to apply. Much personal perplexity can arise from this circumstance. People raised in a certain faith may find it difficult to accept and apply the teaching of the faith in their own lives. Social customs regarding proper conduct may be difficult to accept. A girl may fancy a man from 'the wrong side of the tracks', or from a lower caste, but the sort of analysis that she and her family apply, in the different social support-bargaining systems, may determine that the man is not to be had. In sexual relations in particular, where instinct is so strong, and social prescriptions may seem remote from instinct, the interplay of instinct and more sober social analysis may be particularly wearing. Yet the sufferers not uncommonly impose on their own offspring the same analysis as being 'for the best', or an indisputable matter of 'our culture'.

System 1 and System 2 behaviours come close in reactions to narrative or storytelling. Narrative combines the analysis of plot and personality with attributed motivations and emotions to provide compelling accounts of what life is and how it should be lived. A narrative constitutes a highly accessible and often very engaging frame of reference. Stories read to children inculcate early understanding of how they should behave in order to become accepted in their societies. People react reflexively to stories, but they also interpret their experience by more deliberate reference to the content of stories. The enjoyment of narrative is effortless, but the use of narrative as reference can be demanding.

Kahneman introduces the idea of 'narrative' in a chapter on 'The illusion of understanding' rather than as an aspect of System 1 or System 2 behaviour.

Narrative does not fit well into the System 1 and System 2 classification. A narrative or story is commonly associated with 'fiction', or invented people and events. It offers freedom to incorporate outright falsehoods in frames of reference intended to influence the conduct of readers, though under the accepted protocols of imaginative literature the 'falsehoods' are entirely acceptable. But narrative may refer also to a technique of presentation. 'Facts' presented in narrative form, as a temporal sequence of related events, are compelling. Journalists refer to their reports, supposedly factual, as 'stories', presumably implying that they are written with a narrative technique that makes them attractive and easy to read. Narrative requires that events unfold with plausible psychological causation, whether presented as fact or fiction. Kahneman presents narrative in the context of Nassim Taleb's account of the 'narrative fallacy' – 'flawed stories of the past shape our views of the world and our expectations of the future'.[22] Narratives, or stories, perform the function of frames of reference in an information interface. They cause people to observe and understand in accordance with the understanding their authors wish to promote. It is the intent of narratives to influence the way people behave. The 'narrative fallacy' is of the same kind as what might be called the 'neoclassical fallacy' regarding the benign influence of markets as represented in the neoclassical model.

Narratives derive potency from their engagement of human emotion in their understanding. People are compelled to sympathise with heroes and heroines and be loyal to the ideals they represent. Biblical narratives provided much of the reference on social conduct for people in Europe for centuries. People's conduct was measured by reference to stories about the behaviour of a 'good Samaritan' and the father of a 'prodigal son'. Children brought up in the faith of their parents absorbed the stories of the Bible as ideals of behaviour. Secular narrative can also have immense impact on behaviour and understanding. The narratives of Walter Scott are recognised as having provided the modern concept of what it is to be Scottish. They are used as references with regard to the ideals and interests of the nation. The film *Braveheart* similarly provided a 'narrative' of Scottish history, attractively embellished, suggesting the 'happy ending' was still to come. Narratives are propelled by words and imputed motivations, the major means by which information is manipulated. The impact of films and other electronic media is discussed in Chapter 7 with reference to Marshall McLuhan's views on the importance of media technology.

All this suggests underlying neurological functions that connect instinct with intellect to advance our interest; and coordinate both instinct and intellect with the behaviour and beliefs of those around us. Our brains also constrain our actions, assimilation and thought to that which they perceive as having some kind of symmetry. We are almost entirely unaware of these functions. They give us behavioural characteristics that dictate our response to ongoing experience. While in matters of intellect or analysis we have a sense of awareness of what we are doing, much as we are aware of a sense of 'free will', the scope of what we are aware of, though it necessarily seems very wide because of our exclusive awareness of it, is probably miniscule in relation to what we do and think unaware. We would probably do very little if we did only what we are aware of. It is probably no more than an instance of the confidence that grows within groups that we suppose we have analytical skills that can be applied independently of our instincts and interests. The philosophers of the Enlightenment expected to lead humanity to a new and rational resolution of its problems, but they were discernibly driven by interest in a different sort of society from the authoritarian and superstitious societies of their time. As was seen near the start of this chapter, neoclassical economists wanted a mathematical form of analysis, and made assumptions that gave them what they wanted. Psychology has not produced a frame of reference strong enough to erode the support of mainstream economists from their model. It has even given psychology a subordinate role to the analytical rationality of neoclassical economics.

Prospect theory and situation reference

The 'second phase' of behavioural theory was inaugurated largely by the 1979 publication of 'Prospect theory' by Kahneman and Tversky. 'Prospects' are akin to 'gambles': 'Decision making under risk can be viewed as a choice between prospects or gambles'.[23] The article presents the results of an investigation into the accuracy of 'expected utility theory'. The theory is that the utilities of outcomes in conditions of uncertainty are given by the outcomes weighted by their probabilities. If a return of say, £100, has a probability of 60 per cent, then the expected utility is £60. Kahneman and Tversky conducted laboratory tests to see whether this theory was borne out by actual behaviour. Their experimental subjects were students and university faculty. Kahneman and Tversky conclude that people diverge systematically in their choices from expected utility theory. The laboratory tests show, for example, that people prefer certain (i.e., definite) outcomes to any risk. They show also that people are more strongly averse to loss of assets than they are attracted to an increment on their existing assets of the same amount.[24] Utility in general is reckoned in terms of gains and losses rather than on aggregate outcomes.[25]

'Prospect theory' is Kahneman and Tversky's alternative account of decision making. It involves adjustment to expected utility theory using two weights: the first an adjustment to the probability of an outcome and the second reflecting the subjective value of an outcome. In both cases the weights are based on the responses of subjects to the laboratory test questions designed to evaluate expected utility theory. Kahneman and Tversky note that, 'These departures from expected utility theory must lead to normatively unacceptable consequences, such as inconsistencies, intransitivities, and violations of dominance'.[26] The alternative system means decision makers will make decisions that are contrary to rules that, on the basis of Kahneman and Tversky's overall understanding of the rules implicit in expected utility theory, they would wish to accept.

Kahneman and Tversky remark that their identification of changes as the carriers of value 'should not be taken to imply that the value of a particular change is independent of initial position'.[27] They note that: 'the difference in value between a gain of 100 and a gain of 200 appears to be greater than the difference between a gain of 1,100 and a gain of 1,200'. They conclude that, 'psychological response is a concave function of the magnitude of physical change'.[28] In other words, the value of change lies in its proportion to the base value. The same psychological trait is involved in the notion of diminishing marginal utility, referred to at the opening of this chapter as a part of the psychology of neoclassical economic theory. Neither Kahneman and Tversky nor neoclassical economists derive from this the general principle that value is dependent on situation – that would have given the work of both crucial macro-psychological significance.[29] It implies a generally non-rational approach to choice and would thus be incompatible with neoclassical economic theory. If Kahneman and Tversky had recognised the general principle it would have put them in direct confrontation with neoclassical theory. If the earlier neoclassical economists had recognised it, economic theory would have taken a form different even from Bruni and Sugden's 'road not taken'. We might have had something like money-bargaining much earlier.

One of the criticisms levelled against Kahneman and Tversky's behavioural theory is that it provides information about human psychology in relation to particular decisions, without providing any overall systemic account of human psychology and human behaviour to challenge the rational-agent model.[30] Prospect theory has serious limitations, both in relation to economic decisions and to decisions in general. Peter Earl's mixed feelings about the article included concern that the choices posed in Kahneman and Tversky's prospect theory are not even the choices faced by gamblers. In some there is a prospect of gains with no prospect of losses; in others there is a prospect of losses but no prospect of gains. Earl notes that the sort of risks investigated by Kahneman and Tversky are far from the risks faced by businessmen in decisions on investments.[31] They are even further removed from the exchanges that are the common events of economic theory. The psychological precepts derived from the encounters investigated by Kahneman and Tversky may be no more than minor quirks of behaviour arising in rather special circumstances.

The analysis of decision making needs the broader scope that comes with the full recognition of situation-related valuation and its implications. It becomes immediately apparent that Kahneman and Tversky's basic frame of reference is inappropriate to analysis of the decisions they are dealing with. Expected utility theory, and the prospect theory that is a modified form of expected utility theory, are not applicable when people are engaged in a process of support-bargaining and money-bargaining. The latter involves identification and assessment of situations by reference to which choices and decisions can be made. As a frame of reference, expected utility theory diverts attention away from the important factors in the decisions at hand. It focuses attention on outcomes identified through the mathematics of probabilities in the narrow context of issues presented in laboratory circumstances, rather than the broader context of situations and the implications of decisions in relation to these situations. Because of that, even with their modifications to expected utility theory, they end up with inescapable anomalies. They are well aware of the limitations of prospect theory: 'Although prospect theory predicts both insurance and gambling for small probabilities, we feel that the present analysis falls far short of a fully adequate account of these complex phenomena'.[32] The weighting of prospect theory seems more an expedient than a genuine solution to the difficulties encountered with expected utility theory.

Kahneman and Tversky judge 'appropriate' human behaviour by reference to mathematical probability theory. But psychologists have not universally approved this approach. It has been argued that probability theory relating to human behaviour has to be adapted to what is observed in human behaviour. Gerd Gigerenzer and his colleagues note that the modern acceptance of probability theory as the determinant of what is appropriate in human decision making is a revival of a view that was in the past overtaken by the idea that probability theory had to be adjusted to observed phenomena. They remark, 'But in the new research program, probability theory has replaced physical reality, and the new illusions are discrepancies between the results of probability theory and human thinking'.[33] They record that psychologists were initially dismayed to discover that people did not act rationally in accordance with the laws of probability; that they violated 'the normative view of probability theory as a mathematical codification of rational belief and action in uncertain situations'.[34] In a later book Gigerenzer notes that in the earlier period probability theory was subordinated to human experience: 'When there was a striking discrepancy between the judgment of reasonable men and what probability theory dictated . . . then the mathematicians went back to the blackboard and changed the equations (Daston 1980)'.[35] There is a close parallel with neoclassical economic theory. Not all economists think it appropriate to evaluate human behaviour by reference to the neoclassical market model; rather, they would insist that the theory must be adapted to observation of human practice – that is, to empirical tests. The idea of situation-related support-bargaining and money-bargaining provides a more consistent explanation of human behaviour than expected utility theory, prospect theory or neoclassical economic theory.

Prospect theory, like neoclassical economic theory, confines decision making within very narrow boundaries. It assumes that problems arise in the form of defined probabilities of defined outcomes, thereby truncating the range of information that has to be taken into account. Neoclassical economic theory, as noted above, truncates the information interface through its assumptions. Moving to the context of support-bargaining and money-bargaining involves great extension of the information interface, and a much greater incidence of information that has to be taken into consideration in decision making. It also requires consideration of the distortions of the information interface that are inseparable from the way it is created.

In *Thinking, Fast and Slow*, Kahneman refers to the divergence of people's decisions from expected utility theory as 'bias'. But his own account of the importance of reference points might have alerted him to the use of an improper reference. Humans make their decisions by reference to their situations. Relative probabilities are of concern in so far as certain situations suggest certain outcomes as more likely than others. Human 'bias' is generally reckoned in relation to other humans. A supporter of one team who criticises a referee's decision may be regarded as 'biased' by supporters of the other team. People hold opinions and have ideas that reflect their interests; such opinions and ideas inevitably differ from those held by others with different interests. We are biased in pursuit of our interest, but not in relation to mathematical probability theory. A referee would not be regarded as biased if he did not allow a goal that was missed which, on the basis of probabilities, should have been scored. Humans behave in one way; mathematical probability functions in another way.

People respond to choices presented to them in terms of probabilities with choices that reflect preoccupation with their situations. One of the psychological quirks identified by Kahneman and Tversky directly suggests this replacement of the probability questions with overbearing questions related to other concerns. In *Thinking, Fast and Slow*, Kahneman records that he and Tversky asked themselves early on how people made judgments about probabilities without knowing what probability was. They concluded that, 'people actually judge something else and believe they have judged probability'.[36] As was seen in the Introduction, when asked one question, people are inclined to answer a different question of their own making. Kahneman terms this psychological trait 'substitution' – the substitution of another question for the question that is asked.[37] He conceives substitution as a matter of 'answering an easier question' – the title of his chapter on the subject. But it may be a matter of answering a question more relevant to the interests of the respondent. Asked to choose on the basis of a defined initial position with different probabilities of outcomes, people will respond by considering the choice in the broader context of the threat to their spouse and family, their budgetary commitments, the possibility of losing something important, like their home or other aspects of their actual situation.[38] The substitution of the question about individual interest and social benefit, referred to in the Introduction, to which neoclassical economic theory is the answer, for the question of general interest concerning how economic exchange functions is clearly related to the interests of economists.

In the context of support-bargaining, it can be seen that people substitute a wholly different concept of the circumstances in which they are operating and, in consequence, a different understanding of the question they are asked. Kahneman and Tversky have people responding to propositions in the laboratory world of mathematical probabilities and something like rational choice, but respondents, even students and university staff, who might be better able to handle probabilities than ordinary people, decide by reference to their situations. In effect, they behave in accordance with the dynamics of a support-bargaining and money-bargaining system. It is 'unaware' behaviour ingrained in them genetically and reinforced by experience. It is the way humans have survived and the way they have built their societies. People respond to the information interface they know, rather than what is imposed on them in the laboratory.

The substitution of concerns related to support-bargaining for choices over defined probabilities is suggested by people's engagement in lotteries. The odds of winning the British national lottery are something like one in fourteen million, which suggests that buying a lottery ticket is a waste of time and money, and buying regularly is a regular waste of time and money. Yet millions buy tickets. The explanation seems to be that the purchase of tickets has a very minor impact on budgetary situations, while the outcome, for a winner, is life-changing. The thinking is situation-related, not probability-related. Because of that, and because lottery machines themselves function in accordance with the laws of probability, promoters of lotteries can make heaps of money.

Kahneman and Tversky touch briefly near the end of their article on the limitation of their study of expected utility theory to defined probabilities, being apparently concerned to give behavioural theory wider application. They are, however, unable to adapt their theory to the wider context in which decisions are normally taken. They suggest simply that, in the absence of defined probabilities, the decision weights of prospect theory could be applied to particular events rather than stated probabilities, though they recognise that the perceived likelihood of an event 'could be subject to major biases'.[39] This seems closer to observed and experienced behaviour than the defined probabilities – people probably do assess the likelihood of a range of outcomes before determining to act on the assumption of the most likely. But they probably do so on the basis of their assessments of situations and the likelihood of situations evolving in certain ways. A human has to assess how likely he is to buy a 'lemon', whether an investment will be profitable, whether it is safe to sign a contract, how he can choose a good member of parliament, what information he should accept, what theories he should follow. The 'major biases' will be those arising from the interests that influence assessment of situation. The widening of scope immediately introduces a great range of considerations that cannot be taken into account under the restrictions of expected utility theory and prospect theory. In other words, the information interface in which decisions have to be taken is greatly extended. Expected utility theory and prospect theory are both, in the context of human choice, rarefied mathematical approaches to decisions that present themselves quite differently in the real world.

The expansion of the relevant information interface is reflected in the idea of a 'relevant base' in Gigerenzer et al. Probabilities are defined in the context of establishment of the 'relevant base'. They argue that the more content adopted as necessary to the definition of the base, the more scope there is for different answers.[40] They conclude that there is, 'no single correct or mechanical solution to this question; it is a matter of informed judgment'.[41] That is to say: a matter of the establishment of concepts of situation through support-bargaining, the identification of desirable evolution of situation and assessment of the likelihood of achieving such evolution, or something close to it.

The 'substitution' phenomenon is connected with the 'attribute substitution' described by Kahneman and Frederick in their 2002 article. Respondents to laboratory psychological tests substitute attributes that more easily come to mind for the attributes specified in questions put to them. One experiment suggests how people interpret questions in terms of support-bargaining rather than in the terms established by the question. Test subjects were given a profile of 'Linda' and asked if she was more likely to be a 'bank teller' or a 'bank teller and a feminist'. The profile of Linda recorded that she was concerned with discrimination, social justice and nuclear armaments. Most respondents concluded that Linda was more likely to be a 'bank teller and a feminist', even though a composite probability cannot be more likely than its constituent parts.[42] Being a bank teller *and* a feminist must be less likely than just being a bank teller. Respondents understood Linda in the context of a support-bargaining process. They recognised that a person of Linda's profile was likely to be engaged in some sort of political activism, and they selected the composite probability because it contains the component relevant to political activism. In a support-bargaining system, the activist is always worth attention as a potential ally or as a threat to existing interests. People are always anticipating threats and looking for alliances. People are always engaged in support-bargaining.

The propensity to respond in a context of support-bargaining and concern for situation has parallels in the context of money-bargaining. Faced with questions about money and the economy, people invariably respond with comments that seem designed to protect their bargaining positions in a support-bargaining and money-bargaining system. If they acknowledge they are prosperous and comfortable, there is a risk that their wages will be reduced, or their taxes will be raised. If they say they are struggling, someone may help them, or at least not penalise them. So the information interface of a modern economy, where it is not filled by vendors broadcasting the irresistible features of their products, tends to be filled with complaints about raw deals. Analysis by independent agents based on established frames of reference is the nearest approach possible to identification of the deals people are actually getting and the ratings that might be attached to them.

People respond to questions, experiments, surveys, etc. with replies that assume they are engaged in a support-bargaining process.[43] The default is always the maintenance of support. They will interpret general questions by reference to their implications for the assembly of support. They will not, except with strategic support-bargaining interest, make comments that are likely to alienate support from them. Responses to 'ultimatum games' and 'dictator games' can be readily understood when it is recognised that respondents assume they are participating in a support-bargaining process. People are confronted with proposals that invite 'rational' responses concerned with maximisation of individual returns, in accordance with the assumptions of neoclassical economic theory, but they assume they are engaged in a support-bargaining process, and probe the scope for acquiring support. They substitute the support-bargaining context for the laboratory context in which the choices are presented. It explains why the responses are so different when participants are informed they are playing the game with a computer, rather than with another person. With the computer, they are clearly not engaged in support-bargaining.[44]

Kahneman and Tversky can be seen as playing 'probability games'. The questions are posed in terms of probabilities. But the respondents assume they are making decisions in a support-bargaining process. The given probabilities are seen in that context, not as the prime basis of decisions. In the 'ultimatum' and 'dictator games', the hypothesis on test is that people behave with rational individual self-interest. The results suggest they respond with something that looks like altruism but is easily understood as support-bargaining. The results cannot be explained in the context of neoclassical economic theory. The 'probability games' take it that people should respond in accordance with expected utility theory. The results are interpreted as demonstrating the 'bias' of human instinct.

The laboratory environment is designed effectively to control the information interface. Respondents are required to make decisions on the basis only of the information provided to them in the laboratory. They are provided with what is in effect 'perfect information' – all the information deemed necessary to a decision, just as in the neoclassical economic model. But respondents do not confine themselves to the information provided. Rather, they respond as if they were operating in the familiar wide information interface. They bring their own information into the laboratory and with it the techniques they have for dealing with information. Choices, selections, decisions in support-bargaining and money-bargaining are made in an information interface. Curtailing or otherwise manipulating the information interface necessarily affects the choices made.

Kahneman and Tversky may have responded to the questions posed by expected utility theory with an analysis driven by their selection of a particular psychological frame of reference. Gigerenzer argues that prospect theory is concerned with a particular form of probability theory, concerned with single events. Tversky and Kahneman 'have neglected conceptual distinctions fundamental to probability and statistics'.[45] He argues in particular that the frequentist conception of probability, dealing with the frequency of occurrence of events, rather than with specific events, is more appropriate. 'Probability theory is about frequencies, not about single events'.[46] When the questions of prospect theory are posed in terms of frequencies, the 'biases' identified disappear. Gigerenzer remarks that nowadays, 'If, in studies of social cognition, researchers find a discrepancy between human judgment and what probability theory seems to dictate, the blame is now put on the human mind, not on the statistical model'.[47] Gigerenzer argues that what Kahneman and Tversky identify as errors in probabilistic reasoning are not violations of probability theory. It can be seen that understanding depends on the frame of reference. One sort of probability theory yields one set of interpretations; another sort of probability theory yields a different set. Support-bargaining yields a third set, arguably more satisfactory with regard to human decision-making.

The use of a particular psychological frame of reference, leading to the identification of bias, constitutes manipulation of the information interface, in the sense that it advances Kahneman and Tversky's interest in showing divergence of human behaviour from expected utility theory. It assumes a particular psychological theory to be the appropriate frame of reference for judgements of human behaviour. It is unconscious manipulation. But much manipulation is of that kind. Along with much other manipulation, it exemplifies the ambiguities involved in a sharp distinction between System 1 and System 2 mental behaviour. If System 1 instinct says expected utility theory is mistaken, then an analytical frame of reference can be employed to confirm the indications of System 1. But another analytical frame can potentially nullify the indications of System 1. System 2 analysis can be used to confirm or negate the indications of System 1. System 1 will influence the choice of System 2. System 2 does not operate independently of the promptings of System 1. People act 'unaware' and also think 'unaware'. Kahneman and Tversky lack a frame of reference that would enable them to identify essential aspects of the phenomena they are studying. Because prospect theory was presented in a journal of mathematical economics, their frame of reference was readily accepted by those who read that journal.

Behavioural theory has been assimilated alongside mainstream economic theory with very little trouble, partly because it has been possible to understand it as introducing merely peripheral changes, relating to a limited range of transactions. Kahneman's comment in his Nobel address, quoted at note 14 above, recognises the minor significance of behavioural theory for mainstream economics. Behavioural theory presents no challenge to the established neoclassical treatment of psychological issues. Neoclassical theorists can accept the psychology of behavioural theory as adjunctive to the dominant assumption of rational behaviour.

But the assimilation may also have been easy because behavioural theory shares some important methodological characteristics with neoclassical theory. It puts its faith in mathematics as designating a kind of ideal human behaviour. Expected utility theory and prospect theory involve radical restriction of the information interface. The 'biases' in human choices identified by reference to expected utility theory are interpreted as indicative of human deficiency. Neoclassical economists similarly elevate mathematically tractable designation of behaviour as the ideal, with artificial constraints on the information interface compatible with the required behaviour. With regard to both expected utility theory and neoclassical economic theory, humans fail the test of theory. Prospect theory weights probabilities and the value of outcomes in an effort to reconcile expected utility theory with observed behaviour, but ends up with unresolved anomalies. In neoclassical theory people fail to act with rational self-interest. Numerous modifications to the model are proposed to reconcile the anomalies, though they constitute only indictments of the basic model as a frame of reference. The modest demands and clear methodological affinities of prospect theory meant that neoclassical economists were able to seal the membership of Kahneman in their theory group with the award in 2002 of their highest accolade. Like George Akerlof with his 'lemons', Kahneman stroked the back of the neoclassical theory group so respectfully that it permitted him to tweak its tail.

Self-preservation and confidence

Two psychological traits identified in *Thinking, Fast and Slow* have special resonance in support-bargaining. First, Kahneman identifies particular human sensitivity to threats, as opposed to benign information.[48] Second, humans are described as suffering from pervasive overconfidence.[49] The sensitivity to threats confirms the fundamental importance in humans of the instinct for self-preservation. As regards confidence, Kahneman attributes the propensity to overconfidence to the sense of cognitive ease that generates intuitions of coherence. Support-bargaining suggests confidence derives mainly from the support of associates.

The psychological experiments show that humans are alerted to threats more rapidly than they are to benign phenomena. Volunteers for laboratory experiments react more quickly to images that involve some kind of threat than to images which would normally be perceived as benign. Even when the exposure is so short that they are unaware of the image shown, respondents react to the threat contained in the image. The neurological mechanism through which this rapid alert is achieved has been traced to the amygdala, which provides a 'threat centre' bypassing the normal perceptual process of the visual cortex. As Kahneman puts it, 'The brains of humans and other animals contain a mechanism that is designed to give priority to bad news'.[50] This sensitivity extends to threatening words and even to the processing of statements or opinions which we disagree with.

One of the most prominent and venerated components of the global information interface is Darwin's theory of natural selection. The theory suggests that humans are engaged in a 'struggle for survival' and that the species has survived because of innate capacity for violence, with pronounced aggressive instincts; instincts that have been seen as exhibited also in economic endeavours, to the approbation of some and the disapprobation of others. In *Support-Bargaining, Economics and Society* it was suggested that Darwin underestimated the importance of self-preservation in human behaviour.[51] Self-preservation is the foundation of support-bargaining theory, since the reaction to any threat to self-preservation is to seek support from others. It is proposed as the basis of the mechanism by which groups are formed. Groups are important because in the first place they are essential to effective violence, and having made it possible for a group to survive, they play a major role in the subsequent cultural evolution of societies.

Kahneman's description of the priority of defences against threat in human psychology provides micro-psychological and neurological research evidence for the primacy of the instinct for self-preservation. Humans have inbuilt alerts to threats to their survival and well-being which operate on neurological circuits that give such threats priority over other experience. Humans are not then primarily aggressive, or even primarily seeking their own advance. Their psychological characteristics make them primarily self-protective.

These psychological defences are activated not only by physical threat, but also by intellectual threat. People resist ideas or opinions that they do not share with their interlocutor.[52] This is an important aspect of the theory formation process identified in intellectual support-bargaining, in which theory groups form to protect and nurture theory that is seen as advancing their interests. The integrity of the theory is inseparable from the integrity of the group. It is consistent with the resistance to new ideas identified by Stiglitz, as noted in the previous chapter. The defence of ideas and theory is associated with the defence of the person and the group.

We have a built-in psychological alert system to make us instantaneously aware of threats. As was seen in Chapter 3, in the context of reactions to the 'fear' alert, the options are captured in the phrase 'fight or flight'. An aggressive nature would imply that we always, or nearly always, fight. But we may determine that flight is the better option. We have some capacity for making very rapid calculations as to whether we should stay and fight, or whether we should run. The calculations will depend on the circumstances; that is, the situation. It will depend on the perceived strength of the threat facing us. It will depend on whether there is somewhere safe to run to. It will also depend on who is standing alongside us, either physically, when the threat is physical, or intellectually, when the threat is intellectual. Withdrawal is more likely to be the chosen option when we are on our own.

In *Thinking, Fast and Slow*, Kahneman emphasises the trait of overconfidence in people, involving high levels of unjustified security over their judgments. The judgements and confidence are based on intuitions of coherence. But Kahneman cites research showing that the intuition of coherence derives from the sense of cognitive ease rather than any objective coherence of observations. 'Cognitive ease and smiling occur together, but do the good feelings actually lead to intuitions of coherence? Yes they do'.[53] Kahneman describes assessments he made with a colleague of the suitability of Israeli soldiers for training as officers. He and his colleague were able to agree easily enough on the relative merits of the soldiers as officers. 'Where our multiple observations of each candidate converged on a coherent story, we were completely confident in our evaluations and felt that what we had seen pointed directly to the future'.[54] Yet the feedback from the subsequent performance of their recommended candidates from the officer training school indicated that, 'our ability to predict performance at the school was negligible'.[55] This result might have damaged confidence in their evaluation techniques, but it had only short-term effects. 'The global evidence of our previous failure should have shaken our confidence in our judgments of the candidates, but it did not'.[56]

Support-bargaining suggests that the sense of cognitive ease, confidence and intuitions of coherence are all bound up with the support-bargaining that brings individuals relief from their sense of personal insecurity. People feel threatened and insecure on their own, so they turn to associates for support. With support obtained through the support-bargaining process, the sense of insecurity is lifted. They feel secure, they feel confident, they feel at ease. Within the group, members support each other, and the confidence of the group grows. Members reassure each other of their talent, virtue, courage and so on. The group will endow itself with all sorts of qualities and rights, including in some cases a right to attack other groups and their territory, or a right to impose their own supposedly elevated social order on others. In a group, 'fight' becomes more likely than 'flight'. The cohesion of a group generates a sense of the coherence of its views. Kahneman and his colleague drew confidence not so much from the coherence of their judgements but from the support which each derived from the other. Even a 'group' of two generated significant confidence in the shared judgements. They knew also that they, if not their judgements, would have the support of the larger institution of which they were a part – the Israeli army – so long as they conformed to group rules. Kahneman records their reaction to the news that their predictions were poor: 'But this was the army. Useful or not, there was a routine to be followed and orders to be obeyed'.[57] So long as they retained the support of the army hierarchy they would be secure in pursuing activities that, on the basis of evidence received, were incoherent. The optimism apparent in planning decisions and in decisions in other institutional environments can similarly be interpreted in terms of the confidence developed in group support-bargaining.[58] It is the same group support as sustains the confidence of neoclassical economists such as Joseph Stiglitz and Paul Krugman in theory that is incoherent. Without a theory of support-bargaining, it is not possible to understand the predicament and behaviour of Kahneman and his colleague. Nor is it possible to understand how humans, fundamentally insecure and acutely sensitive to threats, shut down the amygdala and become aggressive. Individuals become belligerent when they have the confidence in their capacities which comes from membership of a supportive group.

This does not discount the influence of individual psychology on confidence and the balance of instinct between belligerence and self-protection, or fighting and fleeing. Common observation and experience suggests that some individuals have greater innate self-assurance than others. Such qualities are generally welcomed in a group if they are seen as likely to contribute to the advance of group interests. Groups tend to accept the more confident individuals as leaders. The confidence of a leader suffuses confidence through the group. The more confident individuals are probably also the more belligerent.

While the sense of coherence seems to derive mainly from group support, group support itself may be influenced by the coherence of its ideas. Kahneman cites an experiment measuring reaction to the words 'salt', 'deep' and 'foam', which are coherently connected by the word 'sea'. Respondents reacted with signs of pleasure to this triad, but without pleasure when a triad of words was presented which had no coherence. 'The impression of cognitive ease that comes with the presentation of a coherent triad appears to be mildly pleasurable in itself'.[59] A group might confer coherence on observations as a consequence of the cognitive ease of doing so within the group. But a group might also come apart if its members could not establish a satisfactory coherence of observation and understanding. Although Kahneman and his colleague were able to see coherence in their jointly held views, the parent group, the Israeli army, was able to establish that their views were inconsistent with subsequent observation of performance at the officer training school. The strength of cohesion within a group, which is often related closely to the threats it faces, is likely to be significant in assessments of coherence. Rigid groups, prominently involving religious belief, commonly have no difficulty in accepting the coherence of beliefs that seem highly inconsistent with observable realities to those outside the groups. Looser groups, and groups that challenge each other, are more likely to apply shared criteria to establish what is consistent and what is not.

The shared criteria of consistence can be seen as deriving from a sense of symmetry. It was suggested in *Support-Bargaining, Economics and Society* that a shared sense of symmetry is important to the formation of groups.[60] People seeing symmetries in the same way find it easier to support each other in the formation of concepts of situation and hence in the identification of group interests. We understand coherence from certain patterns that we recognise as symmetric. 'Salt', 'deep' and 'foam' come together in the containing notion of 'sea'. Patterns can be identified in the association of poverty with poor education and poor parenting. The sense of symmetry is, however, elusive. We can easily be misled into seeing symmetry where there is none; and we can fail to see symmetry in what can be identified with scientific method as symmetric.[61] The allure of symmetry and its elusiveness makes humans fallible, and makes them cling to their failures. The sense of symmetry gives only a weak basis for the determination of coherence in the sense of consistency.

Support-bargaining involves an inherent tension between the interests of the individual and the interests of the group. In the case described by Kahneman, support for each other's point of view was the easier to achieve because neither would have much individual interest in who was selected for officer training and who was not. In a different context, for example in a boardroom, mutual support and consensus would potentially be much more difficult to achieve, since each individual involved would have some personal stake in the outcome. For a person to rise in a company, it is necessary that their ideas and opinions gain support amongst colleagues.

The creation of social 'norms' can be recognised as involving confluence of group opinion to conclusions that have the confidence of the group, whatever their objective or scientific status. This creation of social 'norms' has been simulated in laboratory tests. The results of such tests can also be interpreted in terms of support-bargaining. In the 1930s, for example, Muzafer Sherif conducted experiments that showed clearly the effects of group association on the responses of volunteers to tests of judgement in individual and group circumstances.[62] Sherif used the phenomenon of 'autokinesis' – a point source of light, if observed intently, will seem to move, even if it is held still. The participants in Sherif's experiments were required to assess individually and together the extent of the movement. What Sherif interpreted as the emergence of social norms is more precisely explained in terms of the desire of each individual for the support of the others, and the modification of opinions in order to acquire support. The group arrives at its own sense of consistency, with no necessary correspondence with the actual behaviour of observed phenomena.

The importance of the concern for self-preservation and the consequent sensitivity to threats is reflected in the constitution of the information interface. It is often remarked that newspapers seem always to headline the worst news they can get hold of, and present it in the most sensational terms. The practice is explained by the ready reaction of humans to threat. The threat contained in a headline triggers alarm, which is likely to trigger purchase of the newspaper in order to establish the precise nature of the threat. As has been seen, the sensitivity to threat involves not just sensitivity to physical threat, but also to social and intellectual threat. Even certain words can trigger instantaneous reaction. Sensational headlines of all kinds implying threat to the interests of people elicit immediate attention and potential purchase of further information. The role of the media in construction of the information interface, and hence in the process of government, is considered in Chapter 8.

The confidence of groups also conditions the information interface. People form into large groups to gain the assurance of the support of many people. The information interface is filled with information created for the advancement of the interests of the large groups. Media organisations, through the newspapers and internet material they publish, necessarily respond to the requirements of large groups of buyers, who are the members of the large groups. The support-bargaining process involves group formation and the development of confidence in large groups, so that the information interface is impregnated with information that reinforces the confidence of members of the large groups.

Behavioural theory in the developing world

The behavioural theory deriving from psychologists has been presented mainly in terms of psychological traits identified through responses to propositions put to volunteer respondents in laboratories. It has consequently been possible for theories of wider scope, including economic theory, to assimilate behavioural theory as adjunctive to existing theory, supplementing but not replacing it.

The World Bank takes this approach in its 2015 Development Report on *Mind, Society and Behaviour.* The various psychological traits identified by Kahneman, Tversky and many other writers on behavioural theory are sifted for their implications for such issues as pay-day lending, energy usage, recycling of waste, school enrolment, accident prevention, immunisation and voting. They write:

> The approach expands the set of tools and strategies for promoting development and combating poverty. The strength of standard economics is that it places human cognition and motivation in a 'black box', intentionally simplifying the 'messy and mysterious internal workings of actors'[63] by using models that often assume that people consider all possible costs and benefits from a self-interested perspective and then make a thoughtful

> and rational decision . . . The new tools based on this full consideration of human factors do not displace existing policy approaches based on affecting self-interested personal incentives; rather, they complement and enhance them.

Behavioural theory is seen as complementary to economic theory, reflecting the limited significance of laboratory-derived behavioural theory on the neoclassical economic model. Rational decision-making is still the dominant assumption regarding conduct in the real world. But behavioural theory has already left the laboratory and been put to use in business. The Bank recognises that much behavioural theory is already established and used in a commercial context, and that its application in the context of economic development has lagged behind its commercial use:

> Engineers, private firms, and marketers of all stripes have long paid attention to how people actually make decisions, to the role that context and social preferences play in our decision making, and to the use of mental shortcuts and mental models to filter and interpret information. The development community is beginning to do the same.[64]

Beyond the confines of theory making, human psychological understanding, as derived from behavioural theory, is put to profitable use in money-bargaining. Theory has to catch up with observed practice. The Bank's understanding of the overall significance of behavioural theory is summed up as follows:

> From the hundreds of empirical papers on human decision making that form the basis of this Report, three principles stand out as providing the direction for new approaches to understanding behaviour and designing and implementing development policy. First, people make most judgments and most choices automatically, not deliberatively: we call this 'thinking automatically'. Second, how people act and think often depends on what others around them do and think: we call this 'thinking socially'. Third, individuals in a given society share a common perspective on making sense of the world around them and understanding themselves: we call this 'thinking with mental models'.[65]

The Bank translates the psychological traits identified by behavioural psychologists into a macroeconomic context, retaining the idea that these features are adjunct to economic theory. But in macroeconomic translation they are part of the much broader functioning of a support-bargaining and money-bargaining system, and incompatible with neoclassical economic theory. System 1 and System 2 behaviours merge in the instinctive pursuit of interest both on a reflexive individual basis and through theory formation in intellectual support-bargaining. Traits that can be seen as minor adjuncts to the microeconomic exchange of neoclassical theory become of much greater significance when translated into a macroeconomic context. 'Thinking automatically', 'thinking socially' and 'thinking with mental models' are part of the process of support-bargaining and money-bargaining, but incompatible with a neoclassical economic frame of reference. It was seen in the previous chapter that the neoclassical economic model is incompatible with macroeconomic theory. In the neoclassical context, the introduction of the psychological traits identified in behavioural theory expand very slightly the information interface the model deals with, but in a macroeconomic context they deal with the much more extensive information interface of macroeconomic theory. The mathematical markets of mainstream economic theory are displaced in the macroeconomic context by support-bargaining and money-bargaining. The psychology becomes quite different to that of neoclassical economic theory and overwhelming in its significance.

Behavioural theory translated into the macroeconomic context is no longer conceivable as an adjunct to neoclassical economic theory, but becomes rather an indictment of it. The 'messy and mysterious internal workings' of a macroeconomy are not apparent from neoclassical theory, but are revealed by the theory of money-bargaining. In particular, the stipulation of an information interface created through dissemination of information and the manipulation of that information goes far in explaining the 'messiness'. It also makes clear that it is only an 'internal working' by reference to the superficiality of neoclassical microeconomic theory; to most it is all too apparent. The concealment of the process, which is more distraction from the process, is far from being a strength of standard economics; it is a critical failing. The economic model focuses attention on certain phenomena, distracting attention from other highly relevant phenomena. The understanding of the information interface is essential to the understanding of how economies function. It might be said that the understanding of the formation of the information interface gives the process coherence and system, making it much less of a 'mess' than it appears to be when viewed from the uncomprehending perspective of conventional economic theory.

'Thinking automatically' is the unconscious and 'unaware' behaviour described in Chapter 3, identified in behavioural theory, at least in relation to reflex instincts, as 'System 1', though with the critical difference that a major component of the 'unaware' mode of behaviour is the instinctive engagement in support-bargaining for the acquisition of support. 'Thinking automatically' involves the instinctive support-bargaining that makes possible the survival of the human species and shapes its cultural evolution. It is also the thinking expressed in our ongoing behaviour and casual choices.

In the support-bargaining context, people necessarily 'think socially'. The idea of support-bargaining provides the social and psychological mechanism by which people in contact with each other come to think in similar ways. 'Support' constitutes a psychological necessity for every individual. People acquire and retain support by adapting their opinions and actions to the established preferences of those around them. Their personal security and confidence depends on acceptance in the social group. The development of common understanding of situation through support-bargaining, as part of the process of group formation, means that 'individuals in a given society share a common perspective'.

Many people also 'think politically', reflecting the operation of a political support-bargaining system. People seek ascendant positions in their societies, locally or nationally, by assembling support for themselves and the interests with which they associate themselves. Allocations of public finance will be determined by the outcomes of political support-bargaining. The World Bank will be familiar with the propensity of its clients to think politically, though they may not regard it as a suitable subject for a development report.

The support-bargaining process includes the defining of situation concepts by which interests and values can be identified. These situation concepts are akin to the 'mental models' identified through behavioural psychology. They form part of the information interface in which support-bargaining and money-bargaining are carried on. As noted in Chapter 1 and above, Herbert Simon introduced the idea of the use of 'models of the situation' as a means of controlling businesses under the constraints of bounded rationality. In the context of support-bargaining and money-bargaining, there are wider concepts of situation-related interests and frames of reference. The idea of support-bargaining makes it possible to examine more closely the dynamics of 'thinking socially' and the formation of mental models.

The conception of mental models used in the World Bank report, deriving from extensive research in the relevant literature, is concerned not so much with physical situations or with theoretical frames of reference as with the common 'understandings' or 'presuppositions' that people have about their societies. They are the 'common theory' of their societies, as described in Chapter 3. They are the small-scope 'primes', 'anchors' and 'frames' identified by Kahneman and discussed above. The models include 'categories, concepts, identities, prototypes, stereotypes, causal narratives, and worldviews'[66] that are shared across societies. They reflect the variety and flexibility referred to above in the use made of 'references'. They are seen as imposing significant constraints on the range of information that can be taken into account. With regard to changes in mental models, the report comments, 'The close relationship between mental models and institutions such as cast and gender roles makes the process of changing mental models difficult'.[67] They are, in effect, as common theory, the outcomes of intellectual support-bargaining amongst ordinary people. Intellectual understanding is inseparable from the groups that form the understanding. Categories, concepts, identities, etc. provide a sense of coherence, form patterns, constitute symmetries, that sustain the cohesion of the groups.

The introduction of behavioural theory undoubtedly strengthens the analysis that the World Bank brings to bear on development issues. The analysis would be further strengthened by dropping the continued commitment to the idea of rational behaviour and other assumptions of the neoclassical model.

The theory of support-bargaining and money-bargaining is potentially a more rewarding frame of reference for steering the development process. It centres on the interdependence of individuals and groups, and the eternal negotiations over the terms of association between individuals and groups. It identifies the ways in which information is organised and disseminated for partisan advantage. It has an inbuilt evolutionary or 'development' dynamic. It is of such scope as to accommodate the different frames of reference of different societies and different groups within societies. In international engagement, the understanding of such frames of reference is of particular importance.

Notes

1 Bruni, Luigino and Sugden, Robert, 2007, 'The road not taken: how psychology was removed from economics, and how it might be brought back', *The Economic Journal*, Vol. 117, No. 516 (January), pp. 146–73, esp. p. 150.
2 Bruni and Sugden, 2007, p. 147.
3 For further comment on Bruni and Sugden's article see Spread, Patrick, 2011, 'Situation as determinant of selection and valuation', *Cambridge Journal of Economics*, Vol. 35, No. 2, pp. 335–56.
4 Simon, Herbert A., 1997, *Administrative Behavior: a Study of Decision-Making Processes in Administrative Organisations*, Fourth Edition, New York: Free Press. First published 1947, New York: Macmillan. See also Simon, Herbert A., 1956, 'Rational choice and the structure of the environment', Psychological Review, Vol. 63, No. 2, pp. 129–38.
5 Earl, Peter, 1988, *Behavioural Economics*, Cheltenham: Edward Elgar.
6 For further discussion of 'bounded rationality', see Spread, Patrick, 1984a, *A Theory of Support and Money Bargaining*, London: Macmillan, paras 1.37, 3.94–106; Spread, Patrick, 2016b, 'Companies and markets: economic theories of the firm and a concept of companies as bargaining agencies', *Cambridge Journal of Economics*, Vol. 40, No. 3, pp. 727–53.
7 Earl, Peter, 1995, *Microeconomics for Business and Marketing*, Cheltenham: Edward Elgar, p. 67.
8 Simon, Herbert A., 1983, *Reason in Human Affairs*, Stanford: Stanford University Press, p. 106.
9 Fransman, M., 1994, 'Information, knowledge, vision and theories of the firm', *Industrial and Corporate Change*, Vol. 3, No. 3, pp. 713–57, esp. p. 727.
10 Simon, 1997, p. 118.
11 Kahneman, Daniel and Tversky, Amos, 1979, 'Prospect theory: an analysis of decision under risk', *Econometrica*, Vol. 47, No. 2, pp. 263–91.
12 Earl, 1995, p. 110.
13 Amos Tversky died in 1996 and Nobel Prizes are not awarded posthumously.
14 Kahneman, Daniel, 2003, 'Maps of bounded rationality: psychology for behavioural economics', *American Economic Review*, Vol. 93, No. 5. p. 1469.
15 Spread, Patrick, 2013, *Support-Bargaining, Economics and Society: A Social Species*, Abingdon: Routledge, p. 245.
16 Kahneman, Daniel, 2012, *Thinking, Fast and Slow*, London: Penguin. First published in 2011 by Allen Lane.
17 Kahneman, 2012, p. 48. See also Kahneman, 2003, p. 1451.
18 Kahneman, Daniel and Frederick, Shane, 2002, 'Representativeness revisited: attribution substitution in intuitive judgement', in Gilovich, Thomas, Griffin, Dale W.

and Kahneman, Daniel (eds), 2002, *Heuristics and Biases: The Psychology of Intuitive Judgement*, Cambridge: Cambridge University Press, pp. 49–81, esp. p. 51. Original emphasis. Kahneman and Frederick's references: Chaiken, Shelly and Trope, Yaacov, 1999, *Dual Process Theories in Social Psychology*, New York: Guilford Press; Hammond, Kenneth R., 1996, *Human Judgment and Social Policy: Irreducible Uncertainty, Inevitable Error, Unavoidable Injustice*, Oxford: Oxford University Press; Sloman, Steven A. 1996, 'The empirical case for two systems of reasoning', *Psychological Bulletin*, Vol. 119, No. 1, pp. 3–22; Sloman, Steven A., 2002, 'Two systems of reasoning', in Gilovich, Griffin and Kahneman, 2002, Chapter 22; Stanovich, Keith E. and West, Richard F., 2002, 'Individual differences in reasoning: implications for the rationality debate?', in Gilovich, Griffin and Kahneman, 2002, Chapter 24.

19 Kahneman, 2012, pp. 122–3.

20 Kahneman, 2012, anchoring, pp. 119–28; priming, pp. 52–8; framing, pp. 88, 363–74; association, pp. 51–2, 62; availability, pp. 129–45; repetition, pp. 62, 67; cognitive ease, pp. 59–70.

21 Cf. the discussion of 'ultimatum' and 'dictator' games in Spread, 2013, pp. 113–16.

22 Kahneman, 2012, p. 200. Kahneman's reference: Taleb, Nassim Nicholas, 2010, *The Black Swan: The Impact of the Highly Improbable*, New York: Random House.

23 Kahneman and Tversky, 1979, p. 263.

24 Kahneman and Tversky, 1979, pp. 273–5, 277–8.

25 Kahneman and Tversky, 1979, p. 276. Their reference: Markovitz, Harry, 1952, 'The utility of wealth', *Journal of Political Economy*, Vol. 60, No. 2, pp. 151–8.

26 Kahneman and Tversky, 1979, p. 277.

27 Kahneman and Tversky, 1979, p. 277.

28 Kahneman and Tversky, 1979, p. 278.

29 Spread, Patrick, 2004, *Getting It Right: Economics and the Security of Support*, Sussex: Book Guild, p. 37.

30 Kahneman, 2003, p. 1449. For a summary of current issues relating to behavioural theory, see Harford, Tim, 2014, 'Behavioural economics and public policy', *Financial Times*, 21 March, with comment from specialists, including Gerd Gigerenzer, David K. Levine and Nick Chater. Their publications include: Gigerenzer, Gerd, 2008, *Rationality for Mortals: How People Cope with Uncertainty*, Oxford, Oxford University Press; Levine, David K., 2012, *Is Behavioral Economics Doomed? The Ordinary Versus the Extraordinary*, Cambridge: Open Book Publishers (electronic resource); Chater, Nick (ed.), 2012, *Judgement and Decision Making*, London: Sage.

31 Earl, 1995, pp. 110–11.

32 Khaneman and Tversky, 1979, p. 286.

33 Gigerenzer, Gerd; Swijtink, Zeno; Porter, Theodore; Daston, Lorraine; Beatty, John and Kruger, Lorenz, 1989, *The Empire of Chance: How Probability Changed Science and Everyday Life*, Cambridge: Cambridge University Press, p. 221.

34 Gigerenzer et al., 1989, p. 226.

35 Gigerenzer, Gerd, 1991, 'How to make cognitive illusions disappear: beyond "heuristics and biases"', *European Review of Social Psychology*, Vol. 2, No. 1, pp. 83–115, quotation p. 109. Gigerenzer's reference: Daston, Lorraine, 1980, 'Probabilistic expectation and rationality in classical probability theory', *Historia Mathematica*, Vol. 7, No. 3, pp. 234–60.

36 Kahneman, 2012, p. 98.

37 Kahneman, 2012, p. 97.

38 Note 24 above is also relevant here.

39 Kahneman and Tversky, 1979, pp. 288–9.

40 Gigerenzer et al., 1989, p. 228.

41 Gigerenzer et al., 1989, pp. 230–1.
42 Kahneman and Frederick, 2002, p. 62. See also Kahneman, 2003, pp. 1460–3.
43 On response to surveys, see Spread, 2013, pp. 100–3.
44 Spread, 2013, pp. 113–16.
45 Gigerenzer, 1991, p. 86.
46 Gigerenzer, 1991, p. 88.
47 Gigerenzer, 1991, p. 109.
48 Kahneman, 2012, pp. 300–2.
49 Kahneman, 2012, pp. 261–4.
50 Kahneman, 2012, p. 301.
51 Spread, 2013, Chapter 1: The problem with natural selection. On the application of principles of natural selection to society, see Chapter 7: Theory making and social Darwinism.
52 Kahneman, 2012, pp. 301–2.
53 Kahneman, 2012, p. 69
54 Kahneman, 2012, p. 210.
55 Kahneman, 2012, p. 211.
56 Kahneman, 2012, p. 211.
57 Kahneman, 2012, p. 211.
58 Kahneman, 2012, pp. 249–51.
59 Kahneman, 2012, p. 69.
60 Spread, 2013, p. 232.
61 Spread, 2013, pp. 234–5, 248–50.
62 Sherif, Muzafer, 1935, 'A study of some social factors in perception', *Archives of Psychology*, Vol. 27, No. 187, pp. 1–60. See also Sherif, Muzafer, 1936, *The Psychology of Social Norms*, New York: Harper & Brothers. For further comment see Spread, Patrick, 1984a, *A Theory of Support and Money Bargaining*, London: Macmillan, paras 4.20–26, 32, 36.
63 World Bank reference: Freese, Jeremy, 2009, 'Preferences', in Hedström, Peter and Bearman, Peter (eds), 2009, *The Oxford Handbook of Analytical Sociology*, Oxford: Oxford University Press, pp. 94–114, esp. p. 98.
64 World Bank, 2014, E-mail communication on *World Development Report 2015*: 4 December.
65 World Bank, 2015, *World Development Report 2015: Mind, Society and Behaviour*, Washington DC: World Bank, p. 3, doi: 10.1596/978-1-4648-0342-0. On the contrast between automatic and deliberative processes, the World Bank cites two specific sources: Kahneman, Daniel, 2003, 'Maps of bounded rationality: psychology for behavioural economics', *American Economic Review*, Vol. 93, No. 5, pp. 1449–75; Evans, Jonathan St B. I., 2008, 'Dual-processing accounts of reasoning, judgment and social cognition', *Annual Review of Psychology*, Vol. 59, pp. 255–78.
66 World Bank, 2015, p. 63.
67 World Bank, 2015, p. 70.

6 The information interface and reality

We assume that in our social life, our trading and in political matters we are always dealing with a real world that exists independently of ourselves, and independently in particular of our thoughts about it. We deal with people as they are, with cars, houses, food and drink which can be seen, touched and smelt. We attend to political policies about roads and bridges, immigrants coming into the country, and the state of hospitals and their staff. We are aware that, through misunderstanding, we can 'get the wrong idea' about what is the real situation, or that we can be deceived by others into adopting wrong ideas, but still we assume that, by and large, we are dealing with the realities of life. We may qualify what we are dealing with through words such as 'seems to be' and 'apparently is', but we are mostly confident that we are penetrating beyond the 'seems' and the 'apparent' to the reality.

The idea of an 'information interface' brings to the forefront of attention these considerations of 'seems' and what is 'apparently' happening. It recognises what is almost too obvious to be frequently remarked: that we are dealing only with information about the outside world, the world beyond our minds. Our minds can only receive and evaluate information. Like computers, we have to have input of a certain kind if our minds are to go to work on it. We can only make decisions when we have information.

It was suggested in Chapter 2 that, rather than 'constructing reality', we construct an information interface. The question then arises as to how the information interface constructed by and for our minds relates to the world beyond, if such a thing exists. Philosophers argue rather grotesquely that we could be just a 'brain in a vat' – a disembodied consciousness suspended in a vat. Any human might comprise just thoughts, and all those thoughts might just be illusory with regard to the reality which they seem to imply or represent. If 'I think', I know only my thoughts. Whatever I may deduce from my thinking, it remains only deduction, nothing more. We have no access to 'absolute reality'. There is no logical reason why what is in our heads should correspond to an external reality. While this logical barrier to direct knowledge of reality is the focus of much philosophical debate, customarily regarded as 'deep thinking', it is no more than a commonplace fact of life. Given the nature of the barrier, it hardly merits the effort expended in devising means of getting round it. That it has gained such prominence is possibly the result of the claims of most of the world's religions to access absolute reality.

The fact that we have no logical reason to believe in the existence of an absolute reality does not mean there is no absolute reality; an absolute reality which may or may not correspond to the ideas about it formed in our minds and hence in the information interface. And if there is a world beyond our minds, there must be a very pragmatic interest in understanding how an information interface relates to it. It is immediately apparent that in many respects what is in our heads is likely to be markedly different from any reality beyond. An information interface is formed through support-bargaining. The paramount driver of support-bargaining is individual and group interest, so that the information interface is suffused with information conducive to the advance of interest. As was seen in Chapter 3, information can be and most commonly is manipulated for the advance of interests. The information interface is comprised of information with purpose rather than just inert observation and disinterested testimonial. Ambitions, desires, hopes and fears are all registered in the information interface, along with whatever there may be of realistic information.

Purpose involves selection. The information interface incorporates only such information as is elicited through support-bargaining and the interests engaged in support-bargaining. The information interface experienced by any particular agent of a bargaining system will incorporate the limited range of information that is relevant to that person's situation and the frames of reference deployed by him or her. Much will be missing, including a potentially substantial range of information that is relevant to the individual's interest but which has not been obtained. The information interface conceived as the sum of what is known incorporates an immense volume of information relevant to the interests of humanity, but there must be also an even greater extent of what might be called 'latent information' that has not been identified.

It is perhaps partly because the pursuit of interest through manipulation of information is so apparent that our society advocates so strongly the pursuit of truth. But it must also be because we have a strong interest in the identification of truth. Truth, or reality, features in the information interface because humans commonly have a pressing interest in discerning the truth, and of acting in accordance with what is possible, given the realities. Our survival as a species must have depended on the establishment of an information interface that enabled us to take into account the physical and social realities that confronted us. Even if it was not an 'absolute reality', it was an 'effective reality'. The experience turned out to be sufficiently in accordance with the conceptions incorporated in the information interface as to permit our survival. Beyond survival, our safety and well-being requires an information interface that allows us to act in such a way that we achieve what we expect to achieve, and do not injure ourselves by actions that are incompatible with reality as we experience it.

If we jump from a high window on the understanding from an information interface that there is no such thing as gravity, then we will suffer for it. An information interface that causes us to act in defiance of common experience of reality is highly detrimental to our interests.

Those parts of the information interface that are derived from perceptual experience tend to be accorded greater confidence with regard to their representation of reality than those parts that are derived from testimony. Material objects which can be seen and touched suggest more strongly an absolute reality than those which we hear about or read about. And when our actions in relation to material objects have consequences consistent with our understanding of the material objects, the absolute nature of the reality seems confirmed. The expected, experienced or effective reality is consistent with what we conceive as absolute reality. Consistency is the vital ingredient. With extensive experience of consistency, we feel justified in presuming that our conceived reality is an absolute reality.

Our interest in truth extends well beyond the simple requirement for accommodating matters of perceptual experience. If a god is going to consign us to eternal torment if we do not follow his instructions during our lifetime, then clearly we need to know about it and act upon the information. If it is a truth, then our interest is very much in knowing the truth. That part of the information interface that deals with such issues is, however, derived from testimony. The prospect of eternal torment was accepted as a fundamental truth in the Christian world for many centuries, and many people acted extensively as if it were true. Yet there was no means of confirming its truth. Those who acted upon that presumed truth seemed to fare no better in this world than those who did not. No empirical confirmation was available or feasible, since the prospective bad outcomes would arise only after death. 'Visions' were seen by some, and 'voices' were heard, suggesting confirmation of the testimonial information by perceptual information, but such individual and isolated experience was accepted only by those who had already credited the testimonial information. The interest in truth easily becomes mixed up with other interests in the construction of an information interface through support-bargaining. The truth status of particular components of the information interface depends on the views expressed in the support-bargaining process.

Even so, the truth status of the law of gravity and the truth status of eternal torment seem to fall into different categories. Even the most ardent of traditional believers would perhaps not have had the same assurance concerning eternal torment as of the workings of gravity. Information derived from perceptual experience seems to outrank testimonial information in truth status. With perceptual knowledge we can presume knowledge of an absolute reality, but with the testimonial knowledge that describes eternal torment, even the designation of a 'conceived reality' seems rather stronger than is warranted. It is, of course, difficult to enter into the minds of people whose society is entirely agreed on the certainty of eternal torment.

Historically it is clear that humans can 'get by' and even flourish with very significant deviations of conceived reality from whatever is beyond our minds. Not all religious faith can provide an accurate conception of reality, so that many people must live with conceptions of reality that are very far from the absolute. As argued previously, the reason for this appears to lie in the importance of group cohesion for survival of the human species.[1] It is more important to sustain group cohesion on some basis than to sustain conceptions of truth that accord with absolute truth, so long as the conceptions of truth are not deviant in areas that are critical to survival, and so long as they do not distract attention from truths that are critical to survival. In some groups, 'true believers' choose to display their faith by exposure to venomous snakes and other risks, trusting that the particular conception of truth embodied in their faith is correct, rather than the conception of truth held by natural science, or in common theory, and that they will come to no harm. Such exposure is sometimes fatal. But, in general, religious practitioners have sufficient respect for science and common theory as to abstain from actions that either or both warn against.

This caution is not confined to religious believers. Alvin Goldman remarks that anti-realist theoreticians still behave as if there is an absolute reality:

> Some of them simply deny the existence of the external world. Their behaviour, however, belies what they write. Why do they bother to write or give lectures at all if they do not believe that other people exist (including their bodies) and can read the (physical) books they publish?[2]

Postmodern sociologists seem to lack conviction over the information they disseminate to the information interface. Inconsistency of the actions of those disseminating information in an information interface with the information they disseminate can call into question the 'good faith' of the information provided. The suspicion is that it is disseminated in pursuit of interest, rather than in pursuit of truth, and moreover disseminated in full consciousness that it is probably not the truth. In the case of the postmodernists, Goldman notes that their interest lies in social change. It is conducive to the interests of postmodernists that they should discount in their theory the realities that are clear to everyone outside their theory group. But their interests in employment and income determine that they do not act in accordance with their theories. If they did, the snake might bite them.

'Actions' suggests an escape from the information interface. 'Thought' and 'action' are commonly distinguished, and since thoughts are conveyed as information, while action seems almost the contrary of thought, and certainly an alternative to thought, it can seem that action escapes from the information interface. The direct association of action with reality derives in large part from the absence of any requirement for linguistic, pictorial or other medium to depict the reality.

But action is experienced and observed through the same mental capacities as are employed in thought. Action is experienced as perceptual sensations. The information derived from action is not codified, but it remains information – the only thing our minds can deal with. Riding a bicycle or boarding a train is not prominently a matter of information, but it is still a perceptual experience, and consequently a feature of the information interface. Actions are, nevertheless, the prominent test-bed of the relationship between an information interface and reality as it is experienced, presumed to be an absolute reality. It is difficult to ride a bicycle that does not exist; though a 'brain in a vat' could do it; or someone dreaming. Riding a bicycle confirms at least that the idea formulated in the information interface regarding the riding of bicycles is consistent with the information derived from actual experience. If someone lands a spacecraft on the moon, then the perceptual information interface arising from the action is shown to be consistent with the information interface constructed to describe the behaviour of the moon in relation to the earth. The information derived from experience of the spacecraft is consistent with the information describing the movement of the moon in relation to the earth. Consistency is again the important factor. Nothing need be affirmed about the absolute nature of the earth, moon or spacecraft and their movements.

The distinction between that part of the information interface that is constructed from perceptual information and that part which is constructed from testimonial information is apparent in John Searle's categorisation of reality into different forms. Searle identifies 'brute facts' and 'social facts'.[3] The brute facts are the natural or physical facts, such as the fact that the sun is 93 million miles from the earth. According to Searle, brute facts exist independently of any human understanding of them. Social facts include 'institutional facts', 'such as the fact that Clinton is president'.[4] Institutional facts depend on humans for their existence. They involve a 'collective intentionality'[5] and 'constitutive rules'. Searle argues that while social facts are socially constructed, they nevertheless depend on brute facts, 'a socially constructed reality presupposes a reality independent of all social constructions, because there has to be something for the construction to be constructed out of'.[6] But the construction does not require an absolute reality. All that is required is perceptual information and the conviction of an external reality that it promotes. Human minds function with information. 'Brute facts' are understandings of the mind derived from perceptual information.

Brute facts and social facts, brute truths and social truths, brute realities and social realities, are useful distinctions. In an information interface they have different implications, because of the different status accorded to them, arising from the different nature of the information relating to them, and because of the different opportunities they offer for amendment and manipulation. But there are many sub-categorisations to both, and even cross-categorisations. Brute facts encompass the sun, trees, hills and rivers. Bridges and roads apparently exist independently of our knowledge of them, but would not be there if we had not thought of them in a social context. Cathedrals similarly are apparently brute facts, but born of social thought. Even the brute fact of the sun being 93 million miles from the earth has admixtures of human social thought in the concept and measurement of distance.

Groups and their reality

It was noted at the start of this chapter that in the ordinary course of our lives we take it for granted that we are dealing with a real external world that corresponds closely to our experience of it. There is, in effect, a communal understanding of the nature of reality that answers well enough the demands of ordinary living. 'Common theory' incorporates ideas about the nature of the world, material things and social phenomena that are adequate for the living of life with advantage and in reasonable security. There is normally no need to differentiate between reality as experienced and reality as it is.

Similar practical adaptation is made in more specialised groups. Each group in society adopts a particular understanding of reality – what it will be and how it can be reached. The understandings adopted are based pragmatically on the purposes or interests of each group. In effect, each group engages in an internal process of intellectual support-bargaining to determine how it will understand 'reality' in the context of the group's interests. The group is then free of any inhibitions arising from concerns over what might really and truly be the absolute reality. They have an idea of reality adequate to their group purposes. Different spheres of activity generate their own understanding of what will be regarded as 'reality' or 'truth', just as they develop their own ideas of good behaviour, manners and morality. These understandings of reality are all in the form of information, though thought of more as 'the way things are'.

Philosophers have been the most active and persistent in probing the nature of the reality in which we apparently find ourselves. Most of them have, however, been severely handicapped by the necessary adoption of a frame of reference that assumed, asserted and insisted on a knowledge of absolute reality in the form of a deity or deities. Western philosophers were inhibited by the social necessity of maintaining a commitment to the 'truth' of Christian belief. This 'truth' was so firmly accepted and institutionalised in Western society that any thought inconsistent with it was firstly difficult to think and secondly likely to be abruptly and sometimes painfully repudiated. The desire to penetrate the mysteries of the gospels was at the same time a desire to understand the absolute, so that the problem of access to an external world might be regarded as created by the very prominent assertion of Christian faith that its followers had direct access to absolute truth.

It was seen in Chapter 1 that Immanuel Kant, still inhibited by Christian commitment, nevertheless held that humans were bound by 'appearances', thus laying the foundations of scepticism about the existence of an external world that has been sustained ever since, at least in philosophical theory groups. Reason and logic were conceived as the means by which problems could be identified, broken down and resolved. Reason and logic have certainly identified and broken down many problems, but they have not necessarily resolved them. On the question of an absolute reality, they seem to have hardened the scepticism. Postmodern philosophers might be regarded as asserting the post-faith truism that we can have no access to absolute reality. If they act inconsistently with their philosophy, it may be that they think and act by reference to the ideas of the particular group they associate with at the moment of thought or action. As philosophers, they think rational thoughts; as ordinary people, they act in accordance with the common theory. The snake bites in common theory, so in a common context, beware of the snake. As regards 'appearances', the suggestion here is that we create and know an information interface, derived from perceptual and testimonial information, all of it manipulated for the advance of interests. We can experience something we interpret as reality through this smoky pane, but we can never access absolute reality.

While philosophers are most at home with abstractions, natural scientists are required to deal very directly with the truth about the real world. They have found it expedient to adopt rigorous procedures for the separation of what can be regarded as true from what must be regarded as false. Given the rigour of their approach, it is perhaps not surprising that they are commonly more disposed than other groups, except perhaps philosophers, to acknowledge that they can never reach 'the truth' or define 'reality' with any assurance. Confronting the confusing behaviour of sub-atomic particles in quantum theory in particular they seem inclined to relinquish any claim to identify an absolute truth. Quantum mechanics is so curious that existence seems to depend on the presence of a knowing agent. The natural scientific approach to the discernment of truth and reality is considered further below.

The law must be more pragmatic. Legal practitioners seek a 'truth' that is adequate to maintain confidence that the legal system dispenses justice by punishing people when they are guilty of breaching the law. They need a 'truth' that is accepted within the community they serve as sufficient to achieve this purpose. Criminal guilt in Britain must be proved 'beyond reasonable doubt'. Laws regarding the admissibility of evidence are established so as to ensure that the best possible approximation to 'truth' is achieved on all occasions, and verdicts based on misconstrual of 'truth' are rare. Issues of logic and contradiction are important. Empirical considerations are also important. If an accused can show that he or she was elsewhere when a crime was committed, it serves as a conclusive defence, since, whatever the attributes of sub-atomic particles, it is a universal truth that the same person cannot be in two places at once.

In commerce, traders establish from experience an understanding of which firms can be trusted to do what they undertake to do. Firms cultivate and protect their reputations, since loss of trust means potential expulsion from the network of trade in which they wish to be engaged. The cultivation of trust is particularly apparent in the financial sector, partly because so much of what is traded depends on testimonial information. Practices, such as signatures and countersignatures, or the use of letters of credit, are established to protect against malpractice. 'Truth' sufficient for purposes of maintaining trade is sustained across a trading community.

Teachers have to resolve the difficulties involved in giving a 'true' mark of their pupils' essays. The profession accepts that, for the most part, discretion lies with the teacher to assess a 'true' mark, with the qualification that the teacher must have gone through a programme of training that establishes in him or her the ability to judge a 'true' mark in accordance with the group judgement of such issues. For important exams, it is possible for those examined, or their parents, to appeal against the marking of a single examiner, so that the specific marking is checked for its consistency with group opinion, as understood by the appeal examiner. The procedure is found adequate in its context.

Ordinary people, using common theory, find it unnecessary to distinguish between reality as experienced and reality as it really is. But they distinguish between truth and the content of the information interface. Most people exercise caution about what they take to be the truth. They evaluate testimony reaching them through the information interface. They consider the interests of the people who provide information, and how it might affect the information provided. They consider the past records of the purveyors of information – who can be trusted and who cannot be trusted. Some newspapers and websites will be trusted; others will not. Sub-groups are formed, such as religious groups, or secular societies such as Freemasons, in which members feel greater confidence in the information provided by other members than in that provided by non-members. While common theory is concerned widely with what is 'obvious' about the nature of the world and society, it incorporates also an awareness of the potential manipulation of information in the support-bargaining processes in which people are necessarily engaged. Everyone recognises the potential in themselves to tell fibs or worse, and attributes the same propensities to others.

Truth and the assembly of support

The social concern for truth was associated above with the common pragmatic interest of humans in knowing the truth. Actions undertaken on the basis of understanding derived from an information interface commonly depend for success on consistency of that understanding with the information derived from experienced reality. It seems that our conceptions of the reality need to be close to the 'absolute reality', or to whatever is beyond our minds, in order for us to survive, avoid injury and prosper. But, given the limits of our minds, we can only know when our conceptions of the reality are not borne out by our experience of reality; or when our conceptions are manifestly inconsistent with our experience. The codified information of the public information interface has to accord with the uncodified information of experience.

This interest in truth for survival's sake, or for the avoidance of injury, or for the advance of prosperity, gives it very prominent approval in human society. 'The pursuit of truth' is almost everywhere reckoned as a noble aim and a communal duty. Children are taught to be truthful and punished when they are not. Being referred to as an 'honest man' is a high compliment. The qualities of honesty and truthfulness elicit high levels of support in a community, and hence everyone has an incentive to be honest and true.

Truth also engenders a sense of security – what Daniel Kahneman would refer to as cognitive ease. Because truth is unique, what is true must be consistent with everything else that is true. What is consistent is most easily agreed amongst people, giving rise to a sense of communal assurance and cognitive ease. Untruths give rise to inconsistency and confusion. The 'oneness' of truth constitutes one of its strongest defences. Societies that abandon the pursuit of truth are condemned to inconsistencies, insecurity and instability. Truthfulness builds support in a society.

Yet while these attributes of truth attract great support in a community, the absence of tests other than those of consistency make it difficult to be sure where truth lies. In the natural sciences the material qualities of many of the phenomena of interest and the perceptual nature of much of the information derived from them make tests of consistency feasible, but information about other phenomena can be tested only on a more 'rough-and-ready' approximation to scientific method, and in many cases can scarcely be tested at all. The way is then open for the assembly of support for ideas and observations that advance non-truth interests. Assembly of support is key to the attainment of social ascendancy, so the non-truth interests advanced tend to be those that will assemble support. Their truth or falsehood, their consistency with other observations, becomes of secondary importance. It was seen in previous chapters, especially Chapter 3, that the construction of the information interface involves the establishment in the information interface of frames of reference by which various agents anticipate that they will cause people to think and act in ways conducive to the interests of the formulators of the frames. What people see as consistent, and hence what they interpret as 'true', is what fits with their preconceptions. This is at the same time what fits with the preconceptions of the groups of which they are members. Groups will form with support focused on a selected frame of reference. Any loose ends of inconsistency can be brushed aside in the euphoria of communal support.

The most strongly defined frames of reference, such as democratic theory, neoclassical economic theory, or socialist theory, are naturally those most widely supported. The theory of support-bargaining and money-bargaining presented here aspires to assemble support for a more truthful theory of how societies and their economies function, in the sense of explanations more consistent with observable and experienced phenomena. It includes as an essential element the idea of an information interface constructed by reference to interest so as to influence the distribution of support and, by influencing the distribution of support, influencing the governance of the society. Neoclassical economic theory and socialist theory have clear partisan purpose. Democratic theory is partisan in the sense that it is opposed to autocracy – a commitment now so broad that it almost ceases to be partisan. But democratic theory nevertheless suffers from acute inconsistencies as an account of how societies are or can be governed.

Religious frames of reference similarly claim to be 'non-partisan'. They make the strongest claims to the identification of 'truth' in the absolute sense. All the major religions claim to reveal truths that are beyond the workings of human minds, or beyond any information interface. Religious frames of reference make intelligible or consistent within their ambit the phenomena that, under guidance of the frame, their adherents will recognise as relevant.

Religious frames of reference have historically been most effective in assembling support. The groups forming and sustaining them have achieved strong bargaining positions in their societies, giving them positions of high authority within nation states. In some cases they have established themselves as rulers of nation states, but their role has more commonly been as teachers of appropriate thought and conduct, alongside and usually in support of secular rulers. The latter most commonly establish their authority by force of arms, sheltering a religious group by the same force so long as the teachings are conducive to their continued rule. The religious group creates and sustains the information interface which dominates the thoughts and actions of the people of their society.

This function of religious groups as arbiters of right thinking and right conduct in autocratic societies can be seen in the work of Peter Berger and Thomas Luckman. They argue that certain individuals or groups of individuals can serve as 'definers of reality' in a 'socially constructed universe'.[7] Such groups come to be acknowledged in their societies as having jurisdiction over the 'ultimate definitions of reality'.[8] These groups 'legitimate' social actions: 'One does certain things not because they *work* but because they *are right* – right, that is, in terms of the ultimate definitions of reality promulgated by the universal experts'.[9] The definitions may be accepted in society as a matter of assimilation of group understanding, especially through childhood instruction. The role of group support is apparent: 'highly abstract symbolizations (that is, theories greatly removed from the concrete experience of everyday life) are validated by social rather than empirical support'.[10] Or a group may be so allied with the authorities of its society as to have its definitions established by force. An authoritarian state will coerce its people into conformity. What Berger and Luckman call a 'pseudo-pragmatism' is operative, because the theories *work* 'in the sense that they become standard, taken-for-granted knowledge in the society in question'.[11] Berger and Luckman describe Brahman theory, and specifically the caste system of social differentiation, as the basis of social order in India: 'The Brahmans, *qua* experts in ultimate reality, succeeded to an astounding degree in impressing their definitions of reality upon society at large'.[12] Berger and Luckman make their case in terms of definitions of 'reality', but it might equally be said that such groups are defining 'truth'. Such groups themselves commonly make claims to have acquired 'truth', and a 'reality' beyond what they regard as the superficial reality of common theory. This definition of 'reality' and 'truth' depends on the same assembly of support as the localised group process of definition according to group purpose, as for example in a legal system, described above, but aggregated in this case to the purpose of social dominance and encompassing almost an entire national group. A significant difference, however, is the strong admixture of violence and intimation to offset any lack of volunteered support.

Berger and Luckman would be amongst the critics Goldman has in mind when he notes that one of the criticisms of his 'veritistic social epistemology' is that 'appeals to truth are merely instruments of domination or repression, and should be replaced by practices with progressive social value'.[13] Social ascendance requires that a society be imbued with the frame of reference, the understanding of truth, of the ascendant group. Appeals to 'truth' may be more in the nature of appeals for support for the advance of non-truth interests. Michel Foucault similarly argued that human sciences are concerned with social domination. The psychotherapies and medical procedures associated with prison regimes in particular have functioned as instruments of power and subordination.[14] Foucault's treatment elevates this use of knowledge for the acquisition of power into a general indictment of Western society. The idea that appeals to truth and the formulation of theories by which truth can be grasped constitute strategies for the achievement of social ascendancy reflects the importance of 'truth' to humans, hence the potential for ideas of truth to assemble support. Goldman accepts that appeals to 'truth' are used to advance claims to social ascendancy, but asserts that this does not mean truth is non-existent, or that the pursuit of truth is always concerned with that objective.[15]

If postmodernists were able to assemble extensive support for the truth of their idea that we live in a world of illusion, then the way would be open to the introduction of an alternative society. Such alternative society could only be, on their reckoning, no more than an alternative set of illusions. But certainly one set of illusions may be more agreeable than another. An alternative society of postmodern illusions would very likely be more agreeable to postmodernists than the existing society. With postmodern illusions widely supported in a society, or perhaps forcibly imposed, postmodernists would gain social ascendancy. If postmodernist illusions were the accepted understanding, postmodernists would no doubt be prominent in the new social order. They would control notions of 'truth' in the new society, as Brahmins did in India. They would shape the information interface in which the support-bargaining and money-bargaining of the society was conducted.

Large truths and small truths

It was seen in the previous chapter that the references people use in selection and interpretation of phenomena can have different scope. A 'frame' may just frame a picture; but a 'frame of reference' may comprise a theory of the functioning of a whole society. The concept of 'truth' is found in many circumstances, including those of everyday exchanges, to be too abstract and unwieldy to be of much use. 'Truth' may be more pragmatically understood as 'facts' specific to a particular event or circumstance. Facts can be identified at micro-level as being true or false, or at least as likely true or likely false, on the basis of consistency, or evidence. 'Facts', because of their specificity, tend to be more accessible and testable than 'truth'. The major natural scientific frame of reference proceeds by establishment of specific facts about material things and their relationships, though the specific facts turn out to be universal truths. Facts may be seen as 'small truths', in contrast to the broader and largely conceptual truths delineated in socio-political frames of reference. While they may be small, they have the vital quality of relevance to the transaction in hand.

Because of these qualities, facts are effective constraints on bargaining processes. If a car claimed to be five years old can be proved to be ten years old, the bargaining position of the seller is weakened. Facts accepted in the full sense of 'fact' are non-negotiable. The law of gravity is non-negotiable. The proven weight of a sack of potatoes is non-negotiable. If an immovable boulder blocks a road, a transaction involving passage along the road cannot be concluded. Facts are accepted as bounding the bargaining process when they are agreed amongst the agents concerned and, because of the specificity of facts, it is often possible to agree a range of facts that will constrain a bargaining process. People will withdraw from transactions in which they do not agree the facts on which they are based, or in which the facts are against them. If what is presented as a hundredweight of potatoes is on their weighing several pounds short, they will not buy at the price of a hundredweight. If the car they claim is five years old is deemed by the buyer to be ten years old, the seller will withdraw at the price he is offered.

The constraining effects of facts on transactions are more generally apparent in the context of consumer selection by reference to situation. Consumers in a money-bargaining system create bargaining sets by reference to their situation. If a house-buyer's family situation is such that he or she requires a house with four bedrooms, then all houses having only three bedrooms will be excluded from the bargaining set of the buyer. Companies offering only three-bedroom houses will be ruled out. The solid fact of 'three bedrooms' rules out selection. The fact derives from a 'reality' of family situation and consequent requirements for accommodation. The discounting of the three-bedroom houses is the equivalent in money-bargaining of withdrawal of support in social support-bargaining for some proposition inconsistent with an abstract frame of reference.

This constraining effect of facts means that they are important to support-bargaining and money-bargaining. Creation of an information interface consequently involves partisan engagement in the establishment of 'facts', whether or not 'absolute' or 'concrete'. Facts are developed that potentially advance the interests of certain agents, in the hope that those they are negotiating with can be induced to accept them as concrete facts and constraints on the bargaining process.

The bargaining process throws up facts of different status, even though in strict terms a 'fact' is either true or it is not a 'fact'. Colloquially, there are 'hard facts' and 'soft facts', the former reckoned to be near enough absolute, while the latter are not so secure. Searle has 'brute facts' and 'social facts'. In some cases, negotiating parties accept 'agreed facts', as a matter of convenience to the negotiations, even though they may be recognised as of doubtful quality. They become 'effective facts' – whatever their status with regard to absolute truth, they are accepted as constraints on the bargaining process. In the common theory there are 'obvious facts' that can safely be taken for granted in ordinary intercourse. People cannot be in two places at once; people cannot always be trusted.

The bargaining process is carried on by individuals and groups, who bring to negotiations their own frames of reference. Facts constitute 'truths' relevant specifically to transactions in hand, or to immediate circumstances. But facts are validated or discounted by reference to the frames of reference of those proposing or encountering them. People will assign status to the facts of others in accordance with the frame of reference they have adopted. Many 'obvious' facts will be matters of straightforward acceptance, being part of common theory and the common frame of reference. Facts of the highest status are likely to be those accepted in a scientific frame of reference, where testing is recognised as being most thorough. Natural scientific facts, at least those encountered in the normal course of social and business transactions, tend to be readily established and agreed. The point is made in bargaining processes, when someone pushing their position may say: 'It is a scientific fact that . . .' People using a frame of reference specific to and distinctive of their group are likely to see the 'facts' adduced by a rival group through its rival frame of reference as 'convenient facts' or even as 'concocted facts', the latter close to an oxymoron. The former implies at best 'selected facts', with an implication that they may not be facts at all. The 'facts' about the state of an economy based on a neoclassical analysis look different from the 'facts' derived from a socialist frame of reference. Facts are accorded different status by reference to the frame of reference in which they are identified. Each group determines for itself the adjectives it will use to describe its own facts and those of other groups.

That there can be 'facts' of different status, when the word itself seems to imply something fixed and absolute, not subject to qualification, is testament to the importance of 'facts' in bargaining systems. The word is distorted in usage for the convenience of agents of the bargaining system who wish to adopt into their arguments some of the constraint implied by facts. On its own, this might not be sufficient reason for having 'degrees of fact'. But in the last resort, the resort of philosophers and logicians, it is not possible to get beyond the content of our minds to say exactly and irrefutably what constitutes 'fact' in the strictest sense of the word. If the appointed 'authorities' doubt the existence of 'facts' then the word is open to adaptation as convenient in bargaining processes.

In *A Theory of Support and Money Bargaining* the role of the British civil service was explained in terms of a process of 'fact-formation'. The civil service was able to set bounds to political action on the basis of the facts it derived from its information and analysis. It constituted a basis of 'power' for the civil service. Politicians such as Richard Crossman and Tony Benn chafed at the foreclosure of their options by unelected civil servants. Fact-formation through the intellectual support-bargaining processes of the civil service generated facts that implied limitations on courses of political action that could be taken.[16]

The civil service exercises something like 'expert power' – a power to introduce facts into a bargaining process that depend for their authenticity on the accreditation of the expert. Economists as a group identify and sustain facts about economies and are frequently asked to interject these facts into ongoing debates over economic management. Doctors similarly sustain certain facts about diseases and disease control and are regularly asked to interject such facts into debates about health policy. Such technicians may on occasions interject something more than hard facts into the bargaining process. They may proffer as 'facts' what are more in the nature of 'opinions' in pursuit, unaware or aware, of their own conceptions of how societies should be run. Goldman cites the measurement of intelligence as a subject in which expert status has been frequently abused for personal or cultural reasons.[17]

While the risks associated with false theory and abuse of trust are apparent, it can hardly be doubted that the engagement of experts on various subjects in the conduct of support-bargaining and money-bargaining processes is beneficial. Hard facts, solid facts, facts of the highest status available, should properly bound bargaining processes. To ignore them is to risk serious adverse consequences. Responses of support-bargaining processes to climate change would be seriously deficient without the expertise of climate scientists, even if the science is sometimes inexact. Similarly, questions regarding the use of performance-enhancing drugs by athletes require the engagement of experts, even if they also raise questions about the expertise and integrity of experts. The information interface is essential to the support-bargaining process. Accurate information is essential to beneficial outcomes from support-bargaining.

Some 'facts' of geography

The use of technical expertise and 'facts' in support-bargaining is illustrated in the use of geographical facts in a sixteenth-century dispute between Portugal and Castile over the rights to trade in spices from the Moluccas. The spices of the Moluccas were the gold mines of the sixteenth century – riches beyond the dreams of avarice. To reduce the conflict between them, the two states had agreed in 1494 in the Treaty of Tordesillas that the part of the globe lying to the West of a longitudinal line drawn from pole to pole 370 leagues west of the Cape Verde Islands would be a Castilian sphere of endeavour, while to the east of that line the Portuguese would have free rein.[18] Rights to the spice trade in the Moluccas hinged on whether this line fell to the west or east of the Moluccas. If to the west, the Moluccas would be to the east of it and in the

Castilian sphere. If to the east, they were Portuguese. Everything depended on the 'facts' that could be produced by the map-makers.

The map-makers were hampered in their efforts to produce accurate maps by their dependence on the maps produced by Ptolemy in the second century AD, which underestimated the circumference of the world by one-sixth and overestimated the extent of South-East Asia, thus squeezing out the Americas and the Pacific Ocean.[19] Ptolemy's estimates had already led Fernando Magellan to try to reach the Spice Islands more quickly by heading west rather than east, putting a disastrous end to his mortal life, but earning him immortal fame. Any 'facts' derived from the Ptolemaic frame of reference were likely to be seriously awry. At negotiations in 1524 the Castilians claimed to have the better maps as a heritage of Magellan's voyage. Though Portuguese, Magellan had been employed by Castile. The leading Castilian map-maker, Diogo Ribeiro, another Portuguese in Castilian employment, had been official chart-maker for the Magellan expedition.[20] His map showed the Moluccas firmly in the Castilian sphere. Even so, the uncertainties remained so strong that it was not possible to conclude the negotiations.[21] Ribeiro produced further maps showing the Moluccas in the Castilian sphere, the latest in 1529. In that year, however, the Emperor Charles V of Castile conceded his claim to the Moluccas to the Portuguese for 350,000 ducats, with the odd reservation that he could renew his claim at any time by repaying the 350,000 ducats. Castile both relinquished its claim to the Moluccas and maintained it. The Emperor was preparing for war with France, so needed the Molucca question out of the way, and the neutrality of the Portuguese.[22]

After six further years of negotiations, it was agreed that the line of demarcation would run 17 degrees east of the Moluccas, so that the Moluccas were to the west of it, and in the Portuguese sphere of control. The parties to the agreement apparently recognised that the line they agreed upon was probably not correct, but 'agreed facts', if not 'actual facts', were necessary for their peaceful coexistence. Facts about the line separating the spheres of endeavour were recognised by both sides as critical to their negotiations. As far as the negotiations up to 1529 were concerned, it was not possible to agree the facts, so the issue was resolved under pressure of other events through support-bargaining and the payment of money. Beyond that time, substitute 'facts' were finally agreed, turning out in the end to be substantially wrong. Not surprisingly, given its origins, the line was substantially misplaced.[23] Support-bargaining creates something like facts – 'effective facts' – when negotiations require them. In some circumstances they permit resolution of bargaining situations that, without them, would reach an impasse that is more awkward than 'facts' that are not facts. An information interface is created such that support-bargaining can reach conclusions.

There is an echo of the agreement on 'facts' in the Portuguese-Castilian negotiations over rights to the Moluccas in the agreement on commitments to measures against climate change at the UN Conference on Climate Change held in Paris in December 2015. At the Copenhagen Conference in 2012 no agreement had been possible. The recognised facts regarding the likely consequences of different measures to limit global warming meant that the burdens of keeping climate change within tolerable limits were so heavy that no agreement could be reached. Politicians and those seeking to limit climate change were concerned at the prospect of a similar outcome in Paris. The solution was to 'bend' the facts. Agreement was reached on measures nominally to restrict the rise in global temperatures to less than 2 degrees and, preferably, having regard to the interests of certain low-lying island states, restricting the rise to 1.5 degrees. Amongst climate scientists, however, it was recognised that the agreed measures would not meet the stipulated targets. A report on the conference comments: 'The efforts outlined in the pledges on climate action . . . are more in line with a total warming of 3°C than one of less than 2°C, the limit that was written into previous UN documents, let alone 1.5°C'.[24] The agreement was nevertheless welcomed as a major step forward in containing climate change. Agreement can seem more important than the integrity of facts. But we or our children and grandchildren may still live to rue the day.

The 'facts' that constrain bargaining processes are generally the 'facts' that are accepted as such in the context in which the bargaining agents are working. They are conditioned by the situation in which they are used. Ad-hoc negotiating groups can agree 'facts' in the same way as different social groups agree certain understandings of what constitutes 'reality'. 'Small truths' can be as wobbly as the 'large truths'. Nevertheless, the danger remains that agreed facts will be so far different from facts that emerge from subsequent investigations or from experience that a deal negotiated on the agreed facts cannot be fulfilled or has unforeseen consequences for one or both parties.

The pursuit of truth and the pursuit of agreement

The conflict described above over the human interest in truth and the human interest in social ascendancy, the latter displayed in the pursuit of support for non-truth interests, has a parallel in debates over the pursuit of truth and the pursuit of agreement. Philosophers have debated for centuries what truth is and how it might be acquired. Some have suggested in recent decades that 'truth' can be no more than social agreement on what constitutes truth. In the context of support-bargaining, any approach to truth in the absolute sense, or to absolute reality, is ruled out. We are confined by our minds to information. Social groups generate their own understandings and acceptances of what constitutes 'truth' and 'reality'. There remain, however, strong advocates of 'truth' as something more than social agreement and 'reality' as something more than group convention. Under the rubric of 'epistemology', philosophers have debated the nature of truth and how it is best pursued.

At its inception in ancient Greece and for long after epistemology was concerned with the individual pursuit of truth. Goldman remarks, 'Traditional epistemology, especially in the Cartesian tradition, was highly individualistic, focusing on mental operations of cognitive agents in isolation or abstraction from other persons'.[25] In recent decades, it has been recognised that knowledge has a social dimension that is in many ways more conspicuous and important to the conduct of society than individual knowledge. Goldman's book *Knowledge in a Social World* is a study of what he calls 'social epistemology'.

'Social epistemology' takes into account communal influences on the pursuit of truth, but remains committed to the identification of what is truthful, under what conditions truth is likely to emerge, and where the impediments to the pursuit of truth are most likely to arise. Goldman characterises his book more specifically as an essay in 'social veritistic epistemology'. 'The main question for veritistic epistemology is: Which practices have a comparatively favourable impact on knowledge as contrasted with error and ignorance?'[26]

In his Preface Goldman writes that, 'What is missing is a general theory of societal knowledge', and commits himself to production of such a theory.[27] But early in his first chapter the commitment is to production of a theory of social epistemology.[28] Goldman notes three aspects to his social epistemology. First, it concerns investigation of the social routes to knowledge. There is a 'social path' in which individuals interact with other agents to develop knowledge. Second, it concerns the knowledge generated in some sort of group entity, such as co-workers, a political jurisdiction or an entire society. It concerns the spread of information through these group entities, though the knowing agents are still individuals. The third aspect involves dropping the stipulation that knowledge is restricted to individuals. 'Social epistemology may consider collective or corporate entities, such as juries or legislatures, as potential knowing agents'.[29] Goldman acknowledges that he rarely takes this third approach in his book. Thus social epistemology is largely a matter of how individuals go about the pursuit of truth in a social context. The concept of group knowledge and any social dynamic that might give rise to something that could be identified as group knowledge is largely excluded. 'Social epistemology' for Goldman is individual knowledge in a social context, rather than knowledge that can be specifically designated 'group knowledge'.

In the context of support-bargaining and the formation of an information interface, epistemology, the pursuit of truth, whether individual or social, is concerned with one particular interest. It is an important interest, but it competes with a variety of other interests. The pursuit of truth cannot be effectively investigated in isolation from the many interests that go into the making of an information interface. Interest must in any case, even under the constraints Goldman sets himself, be recognised as motivation, since non-truth interests are the primary impediment to the pursuit of truth.

The wider context means that Goldman's concept of social epistemology is inadequate for the study of the pursuit of truth and even more for the formulation of a general theory of knowledge. Individuals certainly seek knowledge in a social context. But the process of support-bargaining has the effect of fusing individuals into their group. It leads to the identification of a group interest and the recognition of members of the group that the group interest is their interest. The process is apparent across societies in the affiliations of individuals to different political and social groups, espousing as if they were their own the views that have been adopted by their chosen group. Thus the third of the three aspects of Goldman's social epistemology, the aspect that only rarely features, is the essential one. The idea of support-bargaining and the formulation of group interest is essential to the understanding of the pursuit of truth in human society.

Goldman's understanding of social epistemology goes little beyond the traditional individual epistemology. Others go much further. Those arguing most strongly the social nature of knowledge maintain that knowledge is not only socially acquired but that 'reality' is a social construction. What is to be regarded as 'truth' or 'realistic' is then a matter of social agreement, rather than determined by intrinsic qualities of the knowledge.

Goldman sets out to repudiate these 'world views quite opposed to the veritistic conception' – views such as 'social constructivism, postmodernism, pragmatism, cultural studies and critical legal studies'.[30] He sees these 'fashionable currents of postmodernism and (radical) social constructivism' as attempting to repudiate 'the hallmarks of traditional epistemology: the quest for truth, reason and objectivity'.[31] As was seen in Chapter 2, Goldman sees such people as suffering from *veriphobia* – they refuse to acknowledge a distinction between truth and falsity. 'When veriphobes talk of "knowledge," they do not refer, as I do, to *true* belief, but to something like institutionalized belief'.[32] The difficulties of transition from individual epistemology to social epistemology are apparent, since institutionalised belief is an extension of group belief. Group belief, or group opinion, consistent with group interest, may be organised in institutions to develop and secure the interest. '*True* belief' suggests some approach to absolute truth sustained by an individual conviction of truth. While traditional individualist epistemology set store by the capacity of individuals to probe their psyche to identify what were truly their innermost convictions, support-bargaining suggests that conviction, or confidence, itself is a matter of group support. Individual assurance depends on the support of the group. It is difficult to sustain a belief or conviction when all around are saying it is mistaken; it is easy to sustain a belief if everyone around is confirming that it is true. That is why beliefs that are plainly not true, in the sense of being inconsistent with observation and experience, are so common.

The dynamic of intellectual support-bargaining is also apparent. Political leaders have throughout history found it convenient to create foreign 'enemies'. Such enemies constitute the threat that disturbs the sense of security of the home group, and causes its members to support each other more intensively. The cohesion, and hence the combative capacity of the home group, is enhanced. 'Veriphobes' suggests a slightly manic intellectual enemy that all normal people will want to oppose. It was seen in Chapter 3 that Goldman characterises with disapproval the view he attributes to Richard Rorty that truth is 'what peers let you say'. In terms of intellectual support-bargaining, Rorty found himself lacking support in the philosophical theory group at Princeton University, suffering such discomfort that he was obliged to move to a different theory group in another university, where he could get the support he needed. It was suggested in *Support-Bargaining, Economics and Society* that intellectual support-bargaining in institutions commonly leads to the division of participants into 'right wing' groups and 'left wing' groups. Right wingers finding themselves in a left wing institutional group will find it difficult to maintain their position, and are likely to move to a more right wing environment. Similarly, left wingers will find themselves obliged to move out of right wing groups to left wing groups.[33] Philosophers, other than postmodernists, seem inclined to the right; sociologists very much to the left. Rorty had thoughts more characteristic of the left wing whilst working in a right wing institutional theory group, which partly explains why he found himself obliged to move to a different faculty in a different university. An echo of the intellectual support-bargaining over Rorty's views appears in the article by Goldman and Thomas Blanchard on social epistemology in the *Stanford Encyclopedia of Philosophy*. They write: 'His [Rorty's] notion of "social justification", it appears, simply amounted to the practice of "keeping the conversation going" (whatever this meant) rather than the classical project of pursuing "objective truth" or rationality'.[34] 'Right wingers' may designate themselves as 'conservative' or 'traditionalist', but left wingers are likely to describe them as 'reactionary'. Left wingers like to designate themselves 'progressive', but to right wingers they are 'socialist', 'communist' or just 'left wing'. Words take on complimentary or pejorative implications in accordance with their usage in intellectual support-bargaining and in manipulation of the information interface. They imply 'my group' or 'your group'. It seems essential that this sort of dynamic be understood before embarking on assessments of what is true and what is false. Language is not primarily formulated for distinctions between truth and falsehood, or the representation of reality, but for the accumulation of support for the advancement of interest in support-bargaining systems.

Goldman emphasises the importance of truth as a pervasive human objective.[35] His 'Chapter 1 confronts and rejects reasons for scoffing at truth and denying the very possibility of its attainment'.[36] He remarks that, 'Peer acceptance of one's statements might make one happy, but it does not make those statements more or less true. A consensus theory of truth seems wrong from the start, at least as an account of our ordinary concept'.[37] The impression given is of robust assertion of the existence and accessibility of 'truth' in the common sense that we know the reality of material and social phenomena. But a major part of the veritistic epistemological endeavour is the establishment of procedures by which truth is most likely to be reached. As Goldman's work unfolds, it becomes increasingly apparent that the processes by which truth emerges are inescapably the processes of group agreement. Group opinion, or the process by which group opinion is reached, becomes the touchstone of truth. He writes, 'Careful reflection on judgments of justification suggests . . . that a belief is considered justified if it is arrived at by processes or practices that the speaker (or the community) regards as truth conducive'.[38] Truth, or what is taken to be truth, is very specifically a matter of approval by a community. Claims to justification are based on agreement with regard to the truth conduciveness of the methods by which they are reached, rather than direct approval of their substance: 'Given people's interest in truth, it is relevant to classify beliefs in terms of whether they were formed by truth-conducive processes or non-truth-conducive processes'. The communal assent is diverted from the substance to the process, but remains the critical factor in acceptance of the substance.

As was seen in Chapter 3, Goldman appeals also more informally and naively to communal opinion. The quotations there ('most philosophers agree that SS-knowledge ["superstrong knowledge"] is largely unattainable'; 'Although the debate continues, it is widely accepted that S-knowledge is feasible';[39] and so on) indicate that Goldman's backstopping criterion is regularly the communal opinion on the issue. The implication is that the community determines what it will accept as truth, and how we should go about determining what is true, and that is the best humans can do. Hence the dynamic of support-bargaining is essential to the understanding of the issues associated with the pursuit of truth. Goldman is in effect saying, 'In my theory group we can identify truth'. The fate of Rorty, as described in Chapter 3, suggests that dissenters will be expelled from the theory group. That is to say, the withdrawal of support from those who disagree with the established group opinion will be so uncomfortable as to necessitate their withdrawal from the group. Those remaining can then maintain with greater assurance that they have identified the truth.

Communal opinion is readily used to uphold or confirm what is 'true' in the sense of consistent with experience of reality. But because of this function it can also be used to uphold or confirm ideas that are more easily seen as matters of opinion. Someone may say, 'That's true' to a statement such as 'Jim is selfish', or 'the rich are bloodsuckers of the poor', without any suggestion that the statements are anything more than points of view. The response is simply agreement or assent to opinion. It is 'small group truth'. The small group can believe what it finds convenient in the way of truth, to hold itself together, without any of the implications of 'large group truth', that will suggest some more fundamental truth about the realities of life. Words are adapted to fulfil functions in a support-bargaining system. They will not be confined to any fundamental 'meaning' if the associations of the word can be used to convey approval or disapproval in a support-bargaining process. People may convey 'meaning' in a statement, but they 'mean' also to advance their interests. Words are that slippery.

In the quotation above, that 'Peer acceptance of one's statements might make one happy, but it does not make those statements more or less true', the word 'happy' suggests that peer acceptance is something trivial. But something more than 'happiness' is at stake. Say, 'Peer acceptance of one's statements might make the group more cohesive', and there is a different slant on the matter. Cohesive support is crucial to the realisation of group purpose. There may be no appeal if a large group defines truth in a certain way. As was seen in the previous chapter, Kahneman identifies 'repetition' as important to the establishment of a message in people's minds. If many people repeat a particular view, it becomes difficult to dissent from it. If everyone assents to a particular faith, that faith acquires the aura of universal truth. Brahmans, as seen above, were in a position to define 'reality' in India. Goldman's 'ordinary concept' of truth is the conviction that a statement is an accurate representation of what actually is or what actually occurs, but he is unable to give this understanding of truth any basis except that of group opinion or group agreement. These imply group support assembled in a support-bargaining process. The process will only be conducive to the emergence of truth when the group assembling support has a paramount and pressing interest in truth as representation of experienced reality. Otherwise, the group may assemble support for untruths that are nevertheless conducive to the advance of the group purpose.

Nor is the 'happiness' of group acceptance just an advantage pertaining to group cohesion. Individual interest is involved. Say, 'Peer acceptance of one's statements might lead to promotion', and new significance is apparent in peer acceptance. Climbing the career ladder involves peer acceptance. People accepted by their peers become rectors, principals, masters and presidents. Support of the group will frequently be seen by people as more important than truth.

Goldman, like everyone else, uses language in intellectual support-bargaining to advance his interests. But he does not recognise the potency of language. He notes that his veritistic epistemology is criticised on grounds that, 'knowledge, reality, and truth are the products of language. There is no language-independent reality that can make our thoughts true or false'.[40] His response to this criticism is to dismiss such concerns as 'obsessions': 'The most pervasive source of social constructivism within postmodernism, perhaps, is its obsession with language as the great determiner, the determiner of both knowledge and reality'. As an example he cites Jacques Derrida's comment, quoted in Chapter 2: 'The text is all and nothing exists outside of it'.[41] Postmodernists suffer not only from 'veriphobia', but also from 'obsession'. Goldman insists that, 'the significance of language has been oversold'. He accepts, however, the more limited role assigned to language by Stephen Pinker, which separates thought and language.[42] People can have thoughts without necessarily expressing them in language. As was seen above, visual representations may also be important. Language is not all. But the separation of thought from language, though it may sink the extreme post-modernist position, does not resolve the difficulties surrounding language. Language remains the most prominent medium of the information interface, and words, figures of speech and frames of reference expressed verbally play a vital role in the assembly of support. If Goldman assembles support for his veritistic social epistemology, it is in no small measure because of the way he uses words.

Goldman specifically remarks on the political purposes of postmodernists. The quotation at note 20 in Chapter 2 extends to a Marxist reference:

'Many postmodernists, moreover, are activists whose theories are motivated by social change. Their interest is not only "to interpret daily life but to transform it"'.[43] They have the same ambiguous position as Karl Marx: whether their work is truthful, in the sense of scientific or logical, or whether the point is to change the world. Goldman asserts also that postmodernists imply that truth and reason are special obsessions of white Europeans, or even white European males, implying alignment with the concerns of 'progressive' theory groups.[44] As was seen above, Goldman does not accept the criticism that his 'veritistic social epistemology' is an instrument of social dominance. The analysis of support-bargaining and money-bargaining suggests that truth is so elusive, even when measured by consistency, that the assembly of support, implying concerns about social or intellectual ascendancy, can become the prime concern of even the most ardent chaser of truth. It is apparent also that the right–left rivalry, which in the understanding of support-bargaining is the endless and fundamental contention between individual and group, is implicated in what is ostensibly a disinterested debate over the nature of knowledge and belief. If the pursuit of truth is the pursuit of social ascendancy, then social constructivism offers delectable opportunities for turning society upside-down. Discredit their 'facts' and you discredit the group.

Postmodernists, like other groups, adopt an understanding of reality that is pertinent to their group purpose and interest. Their purpose, according to Goldman, is the transformation of society. The more strongly they can establish that society has no grasp of reality, the greater the chance of loosening the grip on power of the existing ascendant groups. It was seen in Chapter 3 that imputation of motivation, as Goldman imputes motivation to postmodernists, is a common means of manipulation of information. If postmodernists are motivated by desire for the reordering of society, the attraction of their theories is likely to be diminished. Imputation is not necessarily distortion. Many postmodernists would probably not dispute the ambition assigned to them. Few, however, would accept the imputation that they are driven by the psychological drives of 'veriphobia' and 'obsession'.

Collective intentionality and the ontological approach

While Goldman hesitates to take account of a truly social epistemology, with groups as the 'knowing agents', the arguments of John Searle, as was seen in Chapter 2, are based on an idea of 'group intentionality'. Searle straightforwardly assumes that groups can have the volition that many insist is characteristic only of individuals. In addition to an 'I intend', Searle insists that there is the 'we intend' of collective intentionality. The 'social facts' of Searle's classification of facts, and the 'institutional facts', such as money, private property and marriage, which are a sub-group of social facts, are matters of collective intentionality. Raimo Tuomela discusses collective intentionality in terms of a 'we-mode', as opposed to the 'I-mode' of individual intention, concluding that while the group is the primary acting agent and may be viewed as the intentional agent, individuals are the primary ontological agents, acting as representatives of the group.[45]

Searle notes that there have been prior references to ideas like that of collective intentionality, including those of Margaret Gilbert.[46] Gilbert suggests the concept of a 'plural subject' as the answer to the perennial problem of the relationship between individuals and the social groups to which they belong. She poses the question, 'What precisely is a social group?' The reply is essentially the subject of her book: 'The main thesis of this book will be that our collectivity concepts incorporate the concept of a plural subject . . . there is little question that plural subject phenomena are of the utmost importance in human life'.[47] Gilbert traces the debate over the relationship between individuals and social groups back to Emile Durkheim and Max Weber. Durkheim saw social groups as an identifiable type of phenomenon arising from the association of individuals. Weber accepted no concept of group autonomy or independence, arguing that individual action alone constituted human social life.[48] For Gilbert, social groups are plural subjects, and a group belief can be understood roughly as 'a *jointly accepted view*'.[49]

'Collective intentionality' serves for Searle as an essential foundation for the 'construction of social reality'. He sets his arguments in an ontological frame of reference. The scene in the Paris restaurant referred to in Chapter 4 is described as having a 'huge, invisible ontology: the waiter did not actually own the beer he gave me, but he is employed by the restaurant, which owned it. The restaurant is required to post a list . . .'[50] The crux of his enquiry is put in the following terms: 'Since our investigation is ontological, i.e. about how social facts exist, we need to figure out how social reality fits into our overall ontology, i.e. how the existence of social facts relates to other things that exist'.[51] The same question arises later on in a slightly different form: 'Hardest of all, how do we make the connection between the fundamental ontology of conscious biological beasts like ourselves and the apparatus of social facts and human institutions?'[52]

Searle tries to explain his concept of ontology through a distinction between 'objectivity' understood in epistemological terms and understood in ontological terms. In epistemological terms, the distinction between 'subjective judgement' and 'objective fact' lies in the distinction between opinion, dependent on attitudes and feelings, and facts that owe nothing to opinion. Searle gives as example of an epistemologically subjective statement, 'Rembrandt is a better artist than Rubens', and as an example of an objective statement, 'Rembrandt lived in Amsterdam during the year 1632'. He remarks that, 'It should be obvious from these examples that the contrast between epistemic objectivity and epistemic subjectivity is a matter of degree'.[53]

The 'degree' in question seems to be the extent of the opinion, or the extent to which it is possible to challenge the opinion. Anyone can dispute whether Rembrandt was a better artist than Rubens. But challenging the statement that Rembrandt lived in Amsterdam during the year 1632 means challenging a great range of received opinion. It is, in effect, a matter of support-bargaining.

No significant loss of support would be entailed in denying that Rembrandt is a better artist than Rubens. But significant loss of credibility, or significant loss of support, would be involved in questioning the statement that Rembrandt lived in Amsterdam during the year 1632.

In the ontological sense, 'subjective judgement' and 'objective fact' are regarded as involving different 'modes of existence':

> In the ontological sense, pains are subjective entities, because their mode of existence depends on being felt by subjects. But mountains, for example, in contrast to pains, are ontologically objective because their mode of existence is independent of any perceiver or any mental state.[54]

Mt Everest is an ontologically objective fact because Mt Everest exists independently of any human perception.

The ontological sense of 'objective fact' depends on confidence in the existence of some absolute reality. In two penultimate chapters Searle considers the very basic question of 'Does the real world exist?'. The anti-realist case is that we have only our own mental perceptions and understanding as a basis for concluding the existence of an external world, and there is no logical connection between those mental states and the existence of an external world. There is no logical reason to accept the existence of Mt Everest. The realist case espoused by Searle is that there exists some external reality, whether or not it is the sort of reality that we formulate in our minds:

> If one insists on a pigeonhole, one could say that realism is an ontological theory: it says there exists a reality totally independent of our representations . . . Properly understood, realism is not a thesis about how the world is in fact. We could be totally mistaken about how the world is in every detail and realism could still be true. *Realism is the view that there is a way that things are that is logically independent of all human representations. Realism does not say how things are but only that there is a way that they are.*[55]

Searle maintains that even if it turned out that Mt Everest did not exist, it would make no difference to the realist argument.[56] Like religious faith, it is an argument that cannot be resolved, or at least is most unlikely to be resolved. There is no logical reason to suppose the existence of things in accordance with our experience of them. But equally, there is no logical reason to believe in an external world that does not correspond to our experience of reality. In terms of logic, there seems little to choose between 'the external world doesn't exist at all' and 'the external world exists, but not in the way we experience it'. The latter seems to be the fall-back position when it is recognised that there is no logic to connect the experience of reality with the actual reality. But the fall-back position is, if anything, weaker than the basic position. The problem of logical connection remains, while the connection in common theory, or common understanding, is greatly weakened. If we decline to accept on logical grounds that the experience of a chair corresponds with the existence of a chair independent of our experience, we might still be inclined to accept that proposition on grounds of common theory or common understanding; its general consistency with all our experience and empirical investigations. But the proposition that something exists independent of our experience, without necessarily corresponding to our experience, does not resolve the logical problem. Nor are we inclined to accept it on grounds of consistency with common understanding of the great range of phenomena we encounter. The fall-back, Searle's understanding of realism, is less tenable that the proposition it is intended to replace.

The ontological concept of 'objectivity' requires not just an absolute reality, but an absolute reality that is the reality we experience. If the absolute reality could be another reality, then what we experience is wholly 'subjective' – a matter of human perception. Either way, ontological objectivity seems beyond human reach. An 'ontological approach' does not take us closer to answering the big ontological questions. It merely gives them a new vocabulary. That is to say, it contributes further to the information interface.

Ascribing ontological status in a modern context remains a matter of social choice. The ontological theory group will support ontological observation and explanations provided in ontological terminology. But it seems no more than a classification of what is already understood. The ontological perspective does not improve our understanding of issues relating to the existence of absolute reality or our experience of reality. For many, it makes the issues more obscure than they already are. Searle conjures up the possibility of an 'objective' reality different to anything that is suggested by our experience of reality. It suggests resolution of difficulties that are not resolved. The assertion of some reality beyond our mental range provides scope for speculation of a highly abstract kind. The ontological view can be adjusted to the understanding of phenomena arrived at in other contexts, or even to a desired understanding. We ascribe such ontological status to phenomena as makes it consistent with other information we have. Ontological status 'fits in' with the rest of the information interface, rather than providing a frame of reference so strong that phenomena are freshly illuminated by its explanatory capacity.

Searle does not say whether the statement that 'Rembrandt lived in Amsterdam during 1632' is 'subjective' or 'objective' in ontological terms. Clearly it could not be accounted 'objective' on the same basis as Mt Everest is ontologically objective. The difficulty in classification seems to arise from its hybrid mixture of social fact and brutish connection. Its 'mode of existence' is not clear. It is neither brute fact nor purely social fact. Ontology does not provide capacity to explain or account for common phenomena of this type. It merely ascribes to them a certain 'ontological status' or 'mode of existence'.

Searle's answer to his questions regarding the linkage between social facts and other things that exist, and between conscious biological beasts such as ourselves and social facts and institutions, is collective intentionality: 'Our aim is to assimilate social reality to our basic ontology of physics, chemistry, and biology . . . The central span on the bridge from physics to society is collective intentionality'[57] With collective intentionality, people can impose functions on entities that they would not otherwise have. In effect, collective intentionality deals with the hybrid 'facts'. Searle describes a screwdriver as having intrinsic properties of mass and chemical composition, but it is a screwdriver by virtue of the function people assign to it – that is, the use people make of it.[58] The existence of the screwdriver is a brute fact; its function is a matter of collective intentionality. Collective intentionality creates the hybrid. That Rembrandt lived in Amsterdam during 1632 can similarly be seen as an outcome of collective intentionality. Everyone agrees that there was a man Rembrandt who lived in a collection of buildings to which was assigned the function of 'town' and called 'Amsterdam' in a time that was 1,632 years after what is accepted as the birth of Christ. Collective intentionality constructs social reality.

Searle describes collective intentionality as the means by which 'social facts' or 'institutional facts' such as money, marriage and property are brought into being, along with the more hybrid facts of screwdrivers and cities. But there seems no reason why collective intentionality should be confined in this way. Searle might also argue that Mt Everest exists as a matter of collective intentionality, in that people have assigned to it the function of 'existing'. In that sense, Mt Everest would be a 'social construction'. The screwdriver might similarly be regarded as existing by virtue of the assignment to it of the property 'existence'. It may be that Searle doubted whether, having demanded the support of his readers for the arbitrary invention of 'collective intentionality', he could reasonably expect to retain their support for the invention of Mt Everest. But Searle was writing in the context of a fairly sharp debate, with undertones of right–left dispute, between realists and anti-realists, so that acceptance of Mt Everest as a social construction deriving from collective intentionality probably did not occur to him, since it would be inconsistent with the realist cause. Searle was arguing for 'the construction of social reality', rather than 'the social construction of reality'.

Searle summarises his idea of collective intentionality as a bridge in the 'Conclusion' of his book:

> Different cultures are different forms that an underlying biological substructure can be manifested in. But if that is right, then there ought to be a more or less continuous story that goes from an ontology of biology to an ontology that includes cultural and institutional forms; there should not be any radical break. The thesis I have been arguing is that there is no radical break. The connecting terms between biology and culture are, not surprisingly, consciousness and intentionality. What is special about culture is the manifestation of collective intentionality and, in particular, the collective assignment of functions to phenomena where the function cannot be performed solely in virtue of the sheer physical features of the phenomena. From dollar bills to cathedrals, and from football games to nation-states,

> we are constantly encountering new social facts where the facts exceed the physical features of the underlying physical reality . . . The biological capacity to make something symbolize – or mean, or express – something beyond itself is the basic capacity that underlies not only language but all other forms of institutional reality as well.[59]

It was argued in Chapter 2 that we construct neither social reality nor reality of any other sort, but an information interface. In Chapter 4 it was argued that support-bargaining created the social and legal context – the 'huge, invisible ontology' – in which a Paris waiter served a glass of beer. In Chapter 3 it was argued that the 'norms' that are so much a part of sociological explanations are outcomes of support-bargaining. In *The Evolution of Economies* it was argued that the 'institutions', including money, weights and measures, laws and regulations, identified by institutional economists as the means by which economies are made to function are also creations of support-bargaining.[60] In this chapter it has been suggested that group support-bargaining creates the concepts of reality that a group will accept in order to function according to its agreed purpose. So here it is suggested that support-bargaining constitutes the dynamic behind collective intentionality and the assignment of functions. An information interface created through support-bargaining for the assembly of support generates collective opinion, collective purpose and collective intention. 'Social facts' derive from support-bargaining. The psychology and motivation of collective intentionality is that of support-bargaining. 'Rembrandt' is Rembrandt because a group, his family, agreed through support-bargaining that a certain individual should be referred to in that way; a group of residents of a certain location, in the course of their social and political support-bargaining, agreed that a prominent aggregation of buildings in their location would be referred to as 'Amsterdam'; Christians, who comprised nearly all Europeans for something like fifteen hundred years, agreed that when Rembrandt lived in Amsterdam it was 1,632 years after the birth of Jesus Christ. Support-bargaining generates these agreed names, concepts and understandings, and so long as the defining groups are sustained the names, concepts and understandings are likely to be sustained. Tuomela touches on the dynamic of support-bargaining when he writes that individuals:

> tend to share goals, values, beliefs, and standards with others in their social groups, and collectively act on the just mentioned factors, often with the motive of getting approval from others by the right kind of behaviour. Indeed, seeking approval and imitation are often mentioned as motivational factors leading to sharing and to conforming behavior.[61]

Support-bargaining does not so much create a bridge between physics and chemistry on the one hand and social facts on the other. It conceives the creation of an information interface in which phenomena are accounted for in mentally manageable forms. It does not so much create 'symbolism' that goes beyond brute facts; it reduces everything to the forms in which phenomena can be assimilated in the human brain and communicated between human brains.

Ontology and information

Support-bargaining involves the creation of an information interface and is carried on within the information interface it creates. The manoeuvres of support-bargaining for assembly of support centre on the arrangement of information. The construction of the information interface includes cues as to how its elements are to be understood, or the status that is to be assigned to them. We cannot know their 'mode of being' or their 'state of existence'. We can only have information. The information may suggest to us a certain mode of being or a certain state of existence, but that is as far as it goes. The idea of support-bargaining and money-bargaining and the creation of an information interface implies an 'informationist ontology'.

The status assigned to different experiences is strongly influenced by the way information is received about them. Information derived from perception is generally assimilated with greater conviction than information derived from testimony. Perceptual experience is uniquely convincing with regard to the existence of material things. Searle's 'brute facts' are facts about material things, known by perceptual information, and giving us special conviction with regard to their existence independently of our minds. We are pretty sure that they continue in being when we are not there. All the evidence points that way. Our experience consistently suggests that they are always present, whatever we are doing or observing. But we cannot be sure in any absolute sense. The conviction of 'brute facts' arises in large part from the particular qualities of perceptual experience.

'Social facts' have a different status. They are known from testimony. We are informed that a group of buildings is referred to as 'Amsterdam', an understanding that a particular process of communal support-bargaining has resulted in agreement to call that group of buildings 'Amsterdam' in the information interface. We can communicate about the group of buildings by using the name 'Amsterdam' settled by testimony within the group. We know the buildings by perceptual information; or at least, we are confident that by placing ourselves in a certain location, we would see a group of buildings which has been named 'Amsterdam'. Similarly with Mt Everest. We are pretty sure of the existence of Mt Everest, because those who have positioned themselves appropriately claim with great assurance to have had visual encounter with a big mountain which has been named Mt Everest through communal accord. We have seen photographs of Mt Everest that give us perceptual information about the big mountain only a little less convincing than an actual sighting of it. As regards Valhalla, Camelot or Shangri-La we have only testimonial information. Their ontological status, their mode of being, as understood through the information interface, is something different to that of Amsterdam or

Mt Everest. Testimonial information, or socially agreed concepts and labels, are overlaid on perceptual information relating to material things, giving a hybrid compilation of 'brute facts' and 'social facts'.

Support-bargaining assigns status through its creation of an information interface. Its assignations of status are strongly influenced by the way in which people derive information from their experiences. Information derived from perception, particularly visual perception, is likely to be accorded the particular status of being that implies a degree of permanence and high independence from the faculties of the perceiver. They are understood as having an existence independent of the human mind. What is known from testimony is not accorded the same status. It is understood as being shaped much more by the interests expressed and advanced in the support-bargaining process. It is potentially 'contaminated' by the advance of interests. It lacks the peculiar conviction of information derived from direct perception. The 'ontological approach' has to be understood in this context of the construction of an information interface by support-bargaining, and the assignment of status to phenomena through that process. It has to take account of the way information is acquired about different phenomena, and the impact this has on the assessment of ontological status.

In the case of the naming of 'Amsterdam', the subject of the naming is present prior to the naming. But in many cases the status of testimonial information is strengthened by providing perceptually intelligible renditions of the testimonial information. Christian faith is rendered more intelligible and given greater conviction by the construction of churches and cathedrals that can be known from perceptual information. They are expressions of faith otherwise conveyed in testimonial form translated into a form that is accessible to perception and hence imparts the conviction of perceptual information.

The conviction associated with visual information is not necessarily a conviction of permanence. 'Marriage' is given perceptual form by ceremonies and special attire with high visual impact. The idea of 'royalty' is similarly expressed in ceremony, with the participants garbed in ceremonial robes and riding in ceremonial carriages.[62] Parliaments assemble with formal procedures and dress. Even in societies of highly educated and sophisticated people perceptual information is important to conviction. Perceptual encounter with reality has a vivid quality lacking in testimonial information.

Natural science and the information interface

It was seen above that different groups adopt different understandings of what constitutes truth and how it is to be arrived at in the context of their activities. In common society truth is a pragmatic matter of trusting proven sources of information and keeping an eye out for swindlers. In legal practice truth is sought through various conventions regarding assessment procedures and the admissibility of evidence. It was seen that the most rigorous conditions surrounding the discernment of truth are those adopted by natural scientists.

'Scientific method' has been developed to ensure that, as far as possible, given human limitations, only truthful findings are added to the body of accepted scientific knowledge.

Goldman notes that the postmodernists and others who question the status of scientific knowledge allege that its 'truth' is based on no more than a set of conventions and consequently has no greater claim to veritistic value than other claimants to truth.[63] What is then critical to the acceptance of findings as scientific knowledge is that they accord with the conventions and are endorsed by the guardians of the conventions. Bruno Latour describes science as a form of argument from authority. Certain persons or institutions become established as 'authorities' in the field of natural science, and are able to ordain what shall be recognised as scientific knowledge. Goldman quotes a passage from Latour indicating that the scientific determination of truth is a matter of assembling allies to endorse the proposition under investigation.[64]

Goldman recognises these social processes, but understands them differently. Rather than seeing them as indicative of the predominance of social factors in the establishment of scientific truth, he suggests that the preponderance of numbers is a measure of truth: 'the relative number of allies and enemies might be taken as a measuring rod of the truth of the claim'.[65] The greater numbers are conceived as evidence for the truth of the view of the preponderant side. Even if Latour's account of authorities determining the acceptance of scientific findings is correct, it does not, in Goldman's view, invalidate the veritistic approach, since the authorities can be relevant to the search for scientific truth.[66]

In accepting relative numbers as a measure of truth, Goldman is nevertheless accepting that truth may be a matter of agreement, or at least what is accepted as truth may be a matter of agreement. Even unanimous agreement is not necessary to the acknowledgement of truth, merely 'the preponderance of numbers'. As has been seen, he understands the main question for veritistic epistemology as being concerned with the practices which have a comparatively favourable impact on knowledge. But he identifies 'veriphobes' as those who regard truth as an institutional matter, rather than a matter of 'true belief'. He increasingly comes to accept that 'truth' is a matter of communal assent and that the 'practices' that lead to it can only be the practices that lead to communal assent. He effectively abandons the idea of 'true belief', since it is not possible to identify any such thing, or any process that leads infallibly to it. He becomes himself a 'veriphobe', seeing truth as a matter of agreement, or a matter of institutional assent. The practices are, according to present arguments, a matter of intellectual support-bargaining. The practices which identify truth are the processes of intellectual support-bargaining. The fallibility of the processes is evident from the many different understandings of truth. Each group comes up with its own understanding of truth, commensurate with its purposes. Each understanding is connected with the interests of the group, which in some cases can be seen as the need for cohesion of the group. The dynamics of intellectual support-bargaining suggest reasons why some procedures are more likely to approach the truth than others.

Goldman notes that Robert Boyle, the seventeenth-century pioneer of experimental science and a founding member of the Royal Society, drew a parallel between the legal requirement for the confirmation of evidence by multiple witnesses and the scientific requirement for testimony from several sources with regard to the outcome of scientific experiments. Goldman recognises that the pursuit of veritistic value is enhanced by the testimony of multiple witnesses: 'More precisely, in my terminology, the practice of relying on multiple-witness testimony has more positive veritistic value than the practice of relying on single-witness testimony'.[67] Boyle suggests that the legal concept of truth is applicable also in the scientific sphere.

Goldman argues that the veritistic approach is better than the postmodernists make it seem. The search for truth can and is still carried on amidst the distractions of psychological bias, misperception, the pursuit of interest and the influence of authority. The outcomes of scientific endeavours are nearer to the truth, more likely to be accurate, more truthful and more dependable than the strictures of the postmodernists make them appear. But he does not establish that the postmodernists are wrong. The differences between himself and the postmodernists are matters of emphasis, matters of degree, and not matters of substance. He concludes by conceding their case: 'I am attracted to standard forms of realism in philosophy of science, but I am also sensitive to the difficulties and intricacies of attempting to defend realism over anti-realism in satisfactory detail'.[68] The identification of 'true belief' has to be abandoned. This sensitivity leads him to the position:

> Instead of making categorical or absolute claims about the veritistic success of science, or its rate of veritistic improvement, I shall restrict my defense of science to its *comparative* veritistic performance: how well it performs, or has performed, in comparison with rival, non-scientific practices that try to tackle the same questions.[69]

The alternatives against which science is put to the test fall into four groups: elves, gremlins, leprechauns and the like; agents of witchcraft and sorcery; astrological theories; and deities of many kinds.[70] In effect, Goldman allows himself to be driven from the field. He is prepared to defend no more than the weakest case for science. The special status of natural science is vindicated if it is superior to fantasies, or better say, superior to modes of explanation that will not recognise evidence that fails to corroborate the explanations.

Goldman distinguishes between the theoretical status of science and the empirical status of science. While he suggests that science is not inferior in the theoretical domain, he claims it is superior in the empirical domain. The distinction is not sharp, since the non-inferiority of science in the theoretical domain is held to be proven by reference to its 'track record', while the empirical superiority of science is argued on the same basis. Science has superior capacity for predicting outcomes than any of the rival theories. As noted in Chapter 3, the basic appeal is to group opinion: 'How can (CSS) [comparative scientific superiority] seriously be doubted?'

Goldman provides a list of what he describes as 'some central facets or dimensions of science that seem veritistically significant'.[71] His six factors may be summarised as follows:

1. An emphasis on precise measurement.
2. A systematic and sophisticated set of inferential principles.
3. The marshalling and distribution of resources.
4. A system of credit and rewards that provides incentives for workers to engage in scientific investigation.
5. A system for dissemination of scientific findings and theories.
6. The use of domain-specific expertise in decisions on dissemination and resource allocation.

Factors 3, 4 and 5 are all administrative or managerial factors. They are the sort of factors that contribute to the success of many areas of human endeavour, including an economy. Factor 1 is perhaps most specifically related to scientific pursuit. Factor 2 suggests the importance of logical reasoning and mathematical techniques. Factors 1, 2, 5 and 6 might be regarded as together implicitly identifying the importance in science of precise recording of results. Latour and Woolgar note that much scientific activity is in the end reduced to a written text.

The recording of scientific work is connected to a further factor which Goldman does not list. Scientific method emphasises the importance of replication of scientific findings. This can only be done if experiments are recorded precisely, including records of the conditions in which they were carried out. As has been seen, Goldman endorses Boyle's assertion of the importance of multiple witnesses in establishing the truth of scientific findings, but does not include it in his list of the factors he sees as important to the veritistic superiority of science. Replication is different to the use of multiple witnesses in legal proceedings. In a trial, multiple witnesses are witnesses to the same single event. Scientific method requires replication of phenomena as precisely as possible by different agents, and the same observations recorded about them. This imposes limitations on the application of scientific method, since not all phenomena can be replicated with the necessary degree of precision. It also makes scientific method different from legal proceedings and potentially enhances the probability that the communal conclusion reached will be the truth about the phenomena in question. Natural scientists have established their understanding of what will be accounted 'true' or 'realistic' according to their purpose and taking account of the characteristics of the phenomena that are the objects of their enquiries. Goldman's weak defence of natural science is partly a consequence of neglect of this vital aspect of natural scientific enquiry. He confines his list of veritistically significant practices to *social* practices, but this would not be good reason for excluding the replication required by the scientific community.

It has been seen that the pursuit of truth in general is necessarily a matter of support-bargaining. The information interface is formed as part of the process of support-bargaining. Scientific endeavour involves intellectual support-bargaining – that is, support-bargaining within and amongst institutions specifically established in societies for the pursuit of the truth about the world. The more secure forms of information are those which are derived from perception. These perceptions very prominently involve material objects. The consistency experienced in perception gives rise to the idea that what are perceived are permanent elements of a reality external to the perceiver – the 'absolute reality'. The apparent stability of the material objects makes it possible to carry out replicative tests on them to see how they perform in different circumstances. It also makes possible observation of the same phenomena, in all important respects, if the recording is full and precise, by different observers. If all come to the same conclusions regarding the nature of the phenomena under observation, then the probability rises that the experienced reality is that of absolute reality, or some reality that is independent of the observers.

The value of such procedure with regard to the pursuit of truth is called into question if the observers are connected. If people are using the same frame of reference, they will be inclined to see or interpret things in the same way, and overlook or ignore phenomena that do not fit their adopted frame. Goldman notes that Boyle tried to offset this potential detraction by preaching against the influence of authority.[72] People subject to the same authority are likely to evaluate in accordance with the wishes of the authority. The 'scientific revolutions' studied by Thomas Kuhn take place when the scientific community adopts different frames, or paradigms, and interpret differently the phenomena they observe.[73] Many of the phenomena that are the basis of perceptual experience seem stable, but the perceptual process involves selection and exclusion, and different imputations regarding the unseen dynamics associated with what is perceived. We impute force, friction, energy transfer, causation to observed phenomena, but do not actually see them. Since Einstein, 'gravity' is a phenomenon consequent on the curvature of space, rather than, or as well as, a force.

Replication, or repetitive testing, is an important point of distinction between science and the non-scientific alternatives considered by Goldman. Not everyone sees elves and goblins. Not everyone recognises the efficacy of astrology. Even though most people are devoted to some particular god or gods, they almost invariably reckon other people's gods to be false. Repetitive testing is clearly a means of ensuring that individuals are not free in a scientific context to pursue their own fantasies or their own interests. That is why those parts of the information interface that are established by scientific method are likely to be the most dependable of the whole information interface. Applied science has taken people to the moon and equipped them with smartphones.

It was noted above that 'facts' constrain bargaining positions in common circumstances. Time and space, and the consequences of gravity, are accepted as constraints. People will not normally support ideas that imply people or things can be in two places at once, or that a car can cover thirty miles in a minute. The implication is that as 'facts' become less secure, as truth and reality become less well defined, support-bargaining will become more prominent. This process can be seen very clearly in the debate over climate change. Scientists sought to establish the reality of climate change on firm scientific foundations, but were hampered by deficiencies of data and the complexity of the factors that interact to create weather patterns. A big gap was apparent in the scientific information interface relating to climate issues, and the gap was filled by assembly of support for and against the reality and causes of climate change. Important interests opposed the theory of climate change, portraying it as a theory designed to discredit and restrict business development. Threats of climate change have been used to assemble support for the broader 'green' or 'environmental' movement that advocates greater control over the activities of businesses. If the 'facts' of an issue are not sufficient to constrain the bargaining process to the point of determining, to the satisfaction of all, what should be done, then the determination is made on the basis of persuasive assembly of support. In the social sciences, the phenomena at issue are even more complex than those relating to climate change, and the interests involved are often more immediately pressing, so support-bargaining becomes much more prominent.

There is a further dimension to replicative testing. The outcomes of science are familiar in everyday life. A constant stream of scientific innovations has changed the human way of life, particularly following the example of Isaac Newton and other scientists of his era, and the initial codification of the methods of science in Europe in that era. Everyone has been able to test the outcomes of scientific endeavour. Everyone knows that an iPad performs remarkable functions that are the results of scientific research. Science and scientists have assembled extensive support in Western societies because everyone has been able to test, albeit in an informal manner, the outcome of their work. There are multiple witnesses to repetitive tests of the efficacy of these forms of scientific endeavour. Such tests advance communal faith in the veracity of information disseminated to the information interface by agencies committed to the use of scientific method.

Goldman would probably claim that such support had 'veritistic value'. If support is a 'measuring rod' of truth, then it would have veritistic value. But its veritistic value is diminished by the standards accepted in the common theory group. Popular support is accorded on a loose, pragmatic basis. Everyone knows that an iPad is very functional, and functions as if it exists independently of all perception of it. The popular experience of the reality of technology confirms that scientists have understood reality. And the experience of that reality is so consistent as to suggest an absolute reality. But back in the strict world of scientific endeavour, within the sharply defined groups of natural scientists, it is not possible to claim that the experienced reality corresponds to an absolute reality. That is a leap that natural scientists will not take.

It was noted in Chapter 2 that Stephen Shapin suggests that the strict world of scientific endeavour may have originated in the social world of gentlemanly conduct. Early in his book Goldman rejects what he sees as Shapin's acceptance of a loose notion of truth.[74] Goldman rejects the idea that truth is 'accepted belief' rather than the 'true belief' that he regards as essential to the notion of truth. As has been seen, however, Goldman's confidence in the search for 'true belief' wanes in the course of the book to the point where he finds himself obliged to abandon the notion of true belief. As has been seen also, different groups within societies create their own standards with regard to what shall be regarded as true, or realistic. According to Shapin, the commitment to truth-telling in a certain social grouping came to be applied to questions about the experience of the physical world. The essential qualification for the status of 'gentleman' was possession of land and the rental income derived from it.[75] 'The recognised facts of economic circumstances were taken substantially to distinguish the gentle from the nongentle'.[76] A gentleman had no need to compromise over the truth to obtain money. The sanction on those breaking the commitment to truth was that of support-bargaining – withdrawal of support. That same threat of withdrawal of support by other members of the scientific community, coupled with the support accorded to those who act in accordance with the recommended behaviour, and the honour accorded to those who achieve conspicuous success through actions that accord with the recommended behaviour, constrains the behaviour of most modern scientists.

Natural scientists today are perhaps even less inclined to claim absolute knowledge than their counterparts a few decades back. The scientific information interface now includes some elements that particularly call into question the link between the experienced reality and the absolute reality. It seems that our experience of reality may, after all, leave us with an imperfect understanding of the nature of reality. The common understanding of space and time is not consistent with the theory of relativity. Space and time warp at speeds approaching the speed of light. The acceleration of large masses produces pulses across space, or gravity waves, recently detected. Fundamental particles do not behave in accordance with the common understanding of the behaviour of things. 'Quantum entanglement' implies that fundamental particles adjust their state to accommodate changes in other fundamental particles at great distances from them, and whatever communication is necessary to the adjustments is faster than the speed of light. The state of particles may depend on the presence or absence of an investigator – the act of measurement itself may influence the state of the particles observed. Fundamental particles seem to behave more in accordance with laws of probability rather than the laws of physics that apply to physical forms of common experience. Information derived about phenomena that are beyond our direct perceptual experience conflicts radically with the understanding derived from our perceptual experience. Physicists, at least those engaged in these fields, have been obliged to revise ideas regarding our direct access to the external world. Much natural scientific information still needs to find its correct 'interpretation' – the interpretation that will render all information consistent.

Even the comforting thought that the behaviour of fundamental particles may be intrinsically different from what is encountered in more familiar phenomena cannot be sustained when there is evidence from quantum biology that birds depend on a quantum effect to align their flight with the earth's magnetic field. Peter Hore describes research on a quantum mechanism that might perform the functions of a magnetic compass and enable a bird to align itself on a course to its intended destination.[77] Hore notes that the relevant experiments need to be repeated – 'independent replication is the gold standard in scientific research'.[78] The internet suggests several other technologies in which quantum effects are employed, including smartphones, lasers and levitating trains.

It is not possible to comment usefully on the substance of these scientific findings without being part of the theory groups that are pursuing them, but they nevertheless cannot be overlooked in the present context, since they plainly bring into question the conceptions of reality adopted in common understanding. It seems almost an act of intellectual perversity to deny that material objects exist. Dr Johnson celebrated that view by aiming a boot at a stone and proclaiming, 'Thus I refute it!' But the encounters with reality experienced by quantum scientists seem to suggest that our everyday experience of reality may be significantly removed from the truth. Common conceptions of reality are derived from everyday experience of reality, but they are not consistent with the particular encounters of quantum scientists with reality. Theory groups investigating these phenomena find themselves obliged to adopt new concepts of reality.

Maps as information interface

As noted above, the role of language in describing or defining reality has been a matter of intense debate. In the extreme, as in the quotation at note 41 above, knowledge, truth and reality have been regarded as products of language. Goldman asserts that 'veriphobes' are 'obsessed' with language. Its significance, he argues, has been greatly exaggerated. The role of language in the creation and manipulation of the information interface was strongly emphasised in Chapter 3. Words and figures of speech are used to shape the information interface in such a way as to assemble support for interest. It is suggested that language gives every indication of having been itself created for use in support-bargaining.

Pictures and images present an alternative to language, and hence a potential means of escaping from the manipulation that is inherent in the use of language. Maps in particular are understood as providing a scalar representation of reality. Scaled up, a map would become the reality in spatial essentials. Maps establish an information interface that is supposed to fit very precisely with the experience of reality. Both maps and the experience of reality they represent are known from perceptual information. The map is a matter of visual perception. The experience of topographical reality is visual and tactile information. Both have the high levels of confidence commonly associated with perceptual information. Yet the map is, at the same time, testimonial information, in that it reports on the nature of the reality it represents. The visual codification of information in maps gives opportunities for the manipulation of the geographic information interface, whilst maintaining the vivid and compelling form of perceptual information.

Maps are made in response to the requirements of users. They are made and sold by companies in money-bargaining systems, and consequently must meet the situation-related requirements of potential buyers. The most common use is in guidance for travellers. People buy maps of their home location and maps of the places they are going to visit. The chief requirement of such maps is that they provide reliable guidance in getting from one place to another. In this case, there is a prominent interest in the accuracy of maps. What is portrayed on the page must be consistent with what is experienced as the reality of travelling. 'Truth' about terrain and routes is a prominent interest of those buying maps, and those making maps consequently give high priority to the accuracy of maps.

The greatest advances in the accuracy of maps came in the sixteenth and seventeenth centuries when first the Portuguese and Castilians, then the Dutch, were developing global trade routes, particularly the routes connecting Europe with the Spice Islands. The difficulties encountered by Magellan in his search for a westward route to the Moluccas were referred to above. The Kings of Portugal and Castile were the instigators of exploration and trade voyages, so political rivalries were prominent. But the paramount importance of good maps and charts in moving securely and rapidly around the world's trading posts was early recognised. The prospect of wealth, and the political ascendancy it can secure, concentrates minds. Both the Portuguese and the Castilians established organisations for the training of navigators and the preparation of maps and charts.[79] The Dutch in the seventeenth century brought a strong commercial dimension to map-making. There was competition not just over global trade, but over provision of the maps that were essential to the trade. The Dutch extensively displaced the Portuguese as the Vereenigde Oostindische Compagnie (VOC), or Dutch East India Company, became the leading international trading organisation. The mariners of the VOC brought back the charts they prepared and used on their voyages for use by the map-makers assembled by the company at its headquarters in Amsterdam. Many of the best map-makers of the era were employed by the VOC.[80]

Improvements in printing and engraving techniques meant that maps could be reproduced at low unit cost in substantial quantities. The activities of the VOC stimulated extensive public interest in international trade and far countries, not least because shares in the VOC were publicly traded.[81] Ordinary people, not just kings and emperors, had an interest in the success of international trade ventures. So it was possible to sell low-price maps in the volume necessary to establish viable formats for map-making companies. Other map-makers competed with those of the VOC. Jerry Brotton remarks that, 'The Portuguese had introduced the scientific craft of modern mapmaking, but it was the Dutch who turned it into an industry'.[82] The feedback in the form of maps and charts prepared and used by the mariners of the VOC meant increasing accuracy.[83] When there is a pressing interest in truth, truth is built into the information interface.

While the users of maps want accuracy, they also want convenience. In map-making these are conflicting requirements. The users of maps want maps that they can set out flat on a table in a cabin or study, and which can be stored in drawers or folders. When the maps in question cover just a small area there is little problem. The world is large enough to be near enough flat over small distances. But it is nevertheless spherical. Over large distances this becomes a matter of major importance. Substantial loss of accuracy is necessarily incurred in translating a spherical world into flat maps. Many different 'projections' are available for this translation, each accommodating different situations and interests of the users. The most famous, and the most widely used, is the projection of Gerard Mercator, published in 1569.

The Mercator projection owes its prominence to its usefulness to mariners. Existing maps, before Mercator, enabled mariners to plot courses that were near enough correct over short distances, like the distances generally covered by traders within the Mediterranean basin. But for journeys of global reach the existing maps could lead mariners well away from their destinations. The Mercator projection made it possible to take a bearing directly from the map that could be held over long distances and take a ship to its intended destination. A straight line drawn on a Mercator map from origin to destination has a constant angle to lines of longitude, or constant bearing, which mariners can use to set their course. The price of the convenience is that the projection involves the increasing north–south separation of lines of latitude, and the increasing east–west separation of lines of longitude, as north or south latitude increases. In consequence, the countries of higher latitudes appear much larger in relation to countries of equatorial regions than is apparent from actual measurements of area.[84] True bearings are represented at the cost of true areas. An essential 'truth' for travellers was provided at the cost of essential truths about the relative size of continents and regions. Brotton remarks: 'Mercator's 1569 projection may be the most influential map in the history of geography, but it was also one of the most peculiar'.[85] The polar regions stretch right across the map. Greenland looks the same size as South America, but is actually only one-eighth the size of it.

The translation of a spherical world to two-dimensional maps introduces one distinct and inevitable sort of distortion. The translation of real topography to a page introduces inevitable distortions of selection and omission. In a sense, Mercator was choosing to represent the particular quality he saw to be a requirement of mariners, even if it meant omitting other valuable information. Maps for particular groups of users very commonly select certain features for inclusion, while omitting others. Maps have small space in which to incorporate the reality of the world they are mapping. 'Tourist maps' include sites of interest to visitors. Henry VIII, fearing an invasion from France, commissioned maps of the English coast showing locations where landings were feasible. Brotton notes the introduction of 'thematic maps' portraying different geographical features, including geological strata, climate and vegetation.[86]

Maps and causes

While much of an information interface comprises information responding to known or potential interests of users, particularly in the context of a money-bargaining system, there is also, as was seen in Chapter 3, a large volume of information that is provided to advance directly the interests of the providers. One prominent concern of providers of information, particularly those engaged in support-bargaining rather than money-bargaining, is the establishment of a frame of reference that, if extensively used, will ensure that people observe and interpret what they observe in ways conducive to support of the interests of the provider. While Mercator incorporated features required by his potential clients, other map-makers were more concerned to disseminate maps that promoted their own interests. They imposed on maps the particular features around which they sought to assemble support. One of the earliest and most celebrated of this kind of map is the Hereford mappa mundi, produced around the year 1300. It is not known definitively what the map was for,[87] but it seems primarily a confirmation of Christian belief in the form of a map. Brotton comments:

> This is not a map as we understand it in any modern sense. Instead it is an image of a world defined by theology, not geography, where place is understood through faith rather than location, and the passage of time according to biblical events is more important than the depiction of territorial space.[88]

According to Ezekiel, God said he had put Jerusalem in the midst of the nations, so that is where it is placed on the map. The map-makers select biblical locations as the most relevant to their story. Mount Ephraim, the Mount of Olives and the Valley of Jehoshaphat surround Jerusalem. Further out are various other locations and scenes of biblical and mythical events. In a roundel at the top is the Garden of Eden.

The mappa mundi identifies three major centres of pilgrimage and records the towns on the routes to the shrines. It also draws on the experience of pilgrims to the Holy Land to record place names.[89] It was not, however, anything like a 'tourist map'. As Paul Harvey states, the map, and mediaeval land maps in general, were not intended to help anyone get from one place to another.[90] Furthermore, the representation of biblical events is only part of the information on the map. Harvey concludes that biblical instruction was not the compiler's chief concern. Most of the general information on the map comes from classical and later Latin authors.[91]

Modern encounter with the mappa mundi produces what is probably no more than a faint echo of its impact when it was produced. It is marked on a whole calf-skin that was originally creamy white but is now much darkened. The colours have faded. The mappa is displayed in dim light to impede further deterioration. It is extraordinary now for its revelation of the mediaeval worldview, literal and figurative, rather than for its visual impact. A note in the bottom left corner of the map discreetly informs us that its maker was Richard of Haldingham or Sleaford, by requesting that we pray for him, that he may be granted eternal bliss. The map is one amongst more than one thousand world maps surviving from the mediaeval period.[92]

The map confirmed the accepted frame of reference. Ordinary people looking at it would have no reason to doubt the representation. The visual impact of the map when first drawn would have reinforced the message it carried. People would see confirmation of what the clergy told them. The clergy were 'people who knew' and the map proved the accuracy of their knowledge. It constituted an information interface in visual codification that confirmed the truth of Christian faith in its association with the disposition of global territory.

There is, of course, no cartographic objection to placing Jerusalem at the centre of the map. No place or region has greater claim to be regarded as the centre than any other. Londoners and visitors to London buy maps of 'London and its environs' with London in the centre of the map. Similar maps are produced for most other substantial towns and cities. A map of 'Jerusalem and its environs' responds to similar interests. What is of central importance depends on the situation and understanding of the maker or user. The problem with the map, to unchristian eyes, is the justification for placing Jerusalem at the centre. It confirms Jerusalem as the centre of the world, not just as a matter of convenience, but as a matter of divine design. The map is more an illustration of a story than a topographical map. The information codified in language in the Bible is re-codified visually in the map.

Outside the Christian frame of reference everything is odd or awful. All sorts of strange creatures and variations on humanity, both of physique and behaviour, adorn the borders of the map. What the frame of reference does not explain is open to the wildest conjecture. Those outside any spiritual frame may regard faith itself as the wild conjecture that fills the mental spaces where questions cannot be answered for lack of a settled frame.

Six hundred years later, Halford Mackinder, one of the leading geopolitical theorists of the twentieth century, consciously drew inspiration from the mappa mundi.[93] Mackinder was one of the founders of the London School of Economics and a Scottish Unionist Member of Parliament.[94] In the early years of the century he was concerned with the significance and potential of the British Empire. In his book *Britain and the British Seas*, published in 1902, he published a map to illustrate Britain's command of the world's seas. The map placed Britain at the centre of a world map to demonstrate how, 'the five historic parts of the world are accessible from its waters'.[95] He developed his ideas on global strategy further in 1904 in an illustrated talk to the Royal Geographic Society. The 'heartland' of power lay in the land power of Eurasia rather than with the sea power of Britain. His thesis was illustrated with a world map captioned 'The natural seats of power'.[96] A land-based 'pivot region' stretches from Wirballen in the west, in modern Lithuania, to Vladivostock in the east. The natural resources available to the dominant powers of this region would put them in a position to challenge the sea-based power of Britain. The United States appears mainly as an eastern presence, in accordance with Mackinder's view that it would influence Europe mainly through Russia, rather than by direct engagement with the European balance of power.[97] According to Brotton, Mackinder's geopolitical assessment influenced global strategists throughout the twentieth century. Brotton remarks that,

> With the benefit of historical distance, we can see that Mackinder's 1904 map is in fact a manifestation of the same kind of ideological geometry that inspired the Hereford *mappa mundi*; the providential mission of empire had replaced the pursuit of organized religion.[98]

Mackinder was shaping the information interface to assemble support for his view of the position of the British Empire and the emerging threats to it. His maps and text seek support for his assessment and its implications. The maps he uses give perceptual information that confirms his textual arguments. The 1902 map provides a projection that might be called, 'Britain and its environs'. His maps are also selective. The 1902 map portrays Britain as having access by sea to the five historic parts of the world. The seas around Britain are shown as open, even though ice to the north blocks access by sea in that direction to many parts of the world almost as surely as would land. In the 1904 map, in which Mackinder is seeking to demonstrate the land power of the controllers of the Eurasian land mass, the northern sea is shaded and marked 'Icy Sea', implying that that expanse of sea can be disregarded for strategic purposes.

The most notorious modern incidence of the use of maps to promote causes was the publication in 1973 by Arno Peters of a new global projection that he claimed would liberate the developing world from the eurocentricity of map-making. The focal manifestation of this eurocentricity was the exaggeration of the area of Europe in relation to equatorial countries that occurs in the Mercator projection. The Peters projection was an 'equal area' projection. The idea of eurocentricity encompassed other issues besides mapping. Governments of developing countries and their supporters had long argued that a European frame of reference belittled the capacities and achievements of developing countries. The contention between developed and developing countries has many themes, including rich versus poor, powerful versus weak, exploiters versus exploited, capitalists versus socialists, assailants versus victims, colonisers versus colonised and individualism versus communal cooperation. In some respects it has characteristics of the right–left divide that is fundamental to support-bargaining. Peters gave his projection a strong ideological context by presenting it as righting wrongs perpetrated by European colonial interests against the indigenous people of their colonies.[99]

Agencies engaged with the cause of developing countries in international support-bargaining took up the Peters projection with enthusiasm. The United Nations in particular adopted it and circulated numerous copies. Governments and aid agencies gave it their vociferous support. Professional cartographers, however, were outraged. Peters, who was not a professional cartographer, was accused of exploiting the political significance of the issue for his own personal advantage. His projection was ridiculed by distinguished cartographers and geographers.[100] There were significant technical errors. It did not do what it was claimed to do. Other cartographers had produced better maps to represent true area. The Peters projection was almost identical to the earlier Gall projection.

Brotton sums up the position in emollient terms:

> Peters's methods were suspect and his world map made unsustainable claims for greater accuracy, but his work revealed a more important truth about mapmaking: by arguing that all maps and their projections are either deliberately or inadvertently shaped by their social and political times, the 'map wars' ignited by Peters forced mapmakers to concede that their maps had never been, nor ever could be, ideologically neutral or scientifically 'correct' representations of the space they claimed to depict. Peters asked both cartographers and the general public to confront the fact that all maps are in some way partial and, as a consequence, political.[101]

Brotton gives Peters his support for the new projection, not on the grounds that it portrays the truth about global topography in a way that had not been done before, nor on the grounds that it advances the cause of developing countries, but because it brings to the forefront ethical issues in map-making. Peters is portrayed as a grand moralist rather than a poor map-maker or a political propagandist. He is a 'postmodern' map-maker, pointing out unpalatable truths to traditionalists. The distortions introduced by Peters are justified as demonstrations of the way in which maps are universally distorted to advance interests. But if Peters had genuinely had such high moral purpose, he would have felt obliged to warn people of the defects of his projection.

That some distortion is inevitable in a two-dimensional map of a three-dimensional world does not mean that any distortion is acceptable. There is unavoidable distortion, but there is also distortion contrived to advance interests. Maps can be used to disseminate geographical information to the information interface, but they can also be used to advance certain interests distinct from geographical facts.

A standard eighty-page Bartholomew atlas for schools published in Britain in 1954 has only one map using the Mercator projection – a two-page world map marked with shipping routes. The atlas includes also a two-page 'Recentred Sinusoidal Equal Area Projection' of the world. The same projection is used for four further maps on two pages showing geology, mineral resources, soil distribution and land utilisation, and a further nine maps on three pages showing production of various commodities. In the Vegetation Supplement the Sinusoidal projection is used for a further two maps on one page showing rainfall and climate. Lambert's Zenithal Equal Area Projection is used on several pages for maps of continents, parts of continents and regions. Gall's Projection is used on two pages for a world map of natural vegetation and ocean currents, and in four maps on two pages showing aspects of world climate. The Atlas also includes a 'Regional Projection' centred roughly on the North Pole designed to show good directional relationships between the North Temperate Zone and the Southern Hemisphere, which is also near-equal in area representation.

Young British minds would not have been misled by their atlases. But they may have been misled by their wall maps. The Mercator projection was widely favoured for display on classroom walls. The requirement for accurate bearings that is of prominent importance to mariners is not operative in the case of wall maps. But the Mercator projection seems aesthetically more attractive than the alternatives, and even seems more sensible. An equal area projection, such as the Gall projection, makes the world look as if big chunks are missing. On its own, the preference for the Mercator projection is hardly evidence of a concerted effort to belittle the countries of the developing world. The conventions of map-making introduce other features which might, if people were so inclined, raise factions against them. The southern hemisphere might protest that it was always put 'under' the northern hemisphere. Australians and New Zealanders might protest at being always 'down under'.

Maps, manipulation and theory-making

The information interface codified through visual media is clearly created under the same impulses as that part of the information interface codified using language. People make maps for the advancement of their situation-related interests, whether this is seen in terms of assembling support for an interest or whether it involves persuading others to buy maps for money. Map-makers manipulate their products in the way language is manipulated to incorporate features that will advance interests. In the context of money-bargaining, the common requirement of potential buyers is accuracy. Travellers want to be sure that their experience of reality will be consistent with the understanding of that reality conveyed by their maps. Their 'situation' implies an interest in getting from A to B, and a feature that enables them to do so is central to their bargaining sets. 'Truth' in the sense of experience of reality consistent with its representation is of central concern. Furthermore, the perceptual nature of their experience of reality convinces them that their experience of reality is experience of an absolute reality, to the extent that very few will bother their heads as to whether a hill or a road actually exists independently of the information they have in their minds. Travellers feel that their perceptual experience of reality is good enough evidence for the actual existence of a world beyond their minds.

Nevertheless, even with a commitment of map-makers to accuracy and 'truth', there arise distortions. Manipulation, albeit benign and incidental, may be necessary. If long-distance seafarers demand a map from which they can easily read off their bearing from A to B, and which they can spread out on a cabin table, they must be provided with a map prepared on Mercator's projection. They must accept the distortions of area that necessarily accompany the convenience of a flat sheet.

The requirements of travellers result in further distortion. A traveller wanting to go from London to Birmingham will not want maps that show the route from Delhi to Lucknow. A provider of maps must provide just the maps that meet the locational interests of potential buyers in a particular locational situation. The standard Bartholomew Atlas referred to above has ten pages devoted to the British Isles and a further eleven pages devoted to Europe. Africa is covered in three pages. Although it seems unlikely that users of the Bartholomew Atlas would derive distorted information from the prominence of the Mercator projection, it is quite probable that they would derive distorted information about the relative importance of the British Isles from the relative number of pages devoted to it. African users of a British atlas might feel aggrieved at the limited coverage of their continent. But an atlas produced for the African markets would give comparable prominence to Africa. Asian and American users of a British atlas, and even non-British European users, might also wonder at the prominence given to the British Isles. But they would normally be using their own atlases, incorporating features related to their own locational interests. For the most part, people consider their own locations more important than far-away places, whatever the arguments for equal representation, and their budgetary outlays will reflect this assessment. On this basis, it is commercial concerns, rather than concerns for ascendancy, that give rise to the representations of the world encountered in atlases.

While travellers as map users have a primary interest in accuracy and truth, the same is not necessarily true of the providers of maps. Map makers have pursued their own causes in the formulation of their maps. The visual form of their maps has been contrived to advance certain understandings of the world favourable to their interests. It is in this context that manipulation of information is most apparent. Knowing how things are in the uncomplicated way of travellers, or knowing by systematic topographical survey, makes it possible to identify circumstances in which map-producers are representing reality in a way that it is not. The mappa mundi translates the information conveyed linguistically in the Bible to the visual context of a map, reconciled with the sketchy information held at the time on the actual physical dispositions of continents, seas and settlements. Mackinder portrays geographic reality in a way that supports his interest in certain strategic arguments related to the continued ascendancy of the British Empire. Peters adapts cartographical techniques to advance arguments regarding the subordination of the developing world to the interests of the industrialised world. These contrivances make clear how analogous linguistic codification can manipulate information so as to disseminate false understandings of issues. As with the map-making, the manipulation can be gross or subtle, conscious or unconscious, but the scope for manipulation in social theory-making is far greater than in map-making because the experience of the reality itself imposes much less constraint on theoretical speculation. There are fewer 'facts' to anchor and constrain theoretical speculation in the social sciences. The theories themselves crucially condition what is perceived and selected, and how it is interpreted.

Experience with maps confirms also the essential condition for the emergence of 'truth'. Information disseminated to an information interface will be truthful, in the sense of being highly consistent with experience of reality, when the disseminators have a primary interest in disseminating the truth. This occurs most prominently in the context of the provision of maps for travellers, who have a prime interest in the accuracy of maps. Maps gained most rapidly in accuracy when they were required by mariners for passage around the world in pursuit of trade. The trading companies themselves strove to produce accurate maps that would ensure the most rapid passage possible to the locations where they wanted to trade. Commercial map-makers were obliged to provide what their clients wanted, and they wanted as a priority the feature 'accuracy'. When this interest of clients in 'truth' was not paramount, map-makers pursued other interests.

Distortion is inseparable from the codification of experience in the form of information. The visual codification of map-making introduces distortions as significant as those of linguistic codification, though since map-making is concerned with phenomena of a very material and visible type the 'realities' they are supposed to represent are understood with much greater assurance than many of those that are codified in language. The phenomena captured in map-making are very stable over time and generally have a similar impact on all observers, so that it is easy to conceive them as existing independently of observation. It is nevertheless apparent that the visual codification used in map-making affords opportunities for its users to distort maps to advance their interests. Richard of Haldingham, Mackinder and Peters all took advantage of inherent scope for manipulation of information to advance their interests. It illustrates the way an information interface is created with different codifications to assemble support for bargaining advantage in a system of support-bargaining and money-bargaining.

The mathematical distortions of neoclassical economic theory are analogous to the cartographic distortions of the mappa mundi. The mathematics of the model gives it some of the 'absolute' status that faith accorded to the mappa mundi. It is centred on a concept of 'rational man' in much the same way as the mappa mundi is centred on Jerusalem as the centre of its faith. People using the neoclassical model keep getting lost because it was not designed to provide a realistic account of the functioning of economies, but as a mathematical diversion.

There is a parallel also with Mercator's projection. Mercator's projection provided the convenience of flat sheets of paper instead of curved surfaces, or a globe. The flat sheets were of particular value to navigators, since they showed the true bearings a ship should steer to reach its destination. The area distortion that accompanied this flattening was of minor importance as far as navigation was concerned. Neoclassical economists enjoy the convenience of a mathematical model that can be investigated in the confines of a study. With regard to the content of the model, they argue that if you want guidance on the essentials of the working of a competitive economic system, you have to accept certain simplifications, and hence a degree of distortion. The essential guidance, that competition can refine by selection and rejection, has generally been accepted. But the model catches only a small part of the dynamic of economic competition, at the expense of extreme distortions. No supplementary linguistic codification can make good the distortions. Users of the Mercator projection disturbed by its distortions can revert to a globe for accurate representations of area. But those disturbed by the distortions of the neoclassical model have little or no alternative, given the importance of a 'mainstream' theory group. Physical travellers using the Mercator projection arrive where they want to go, but the neoclassical projection provides such a distorted account of the real world that it frequently leads its users astray. The idea of support-bargaining and money-bargaining, and the creation of an information interface, offers an alternative with the authenticity of a globe.

The symmetry connection

The postmodernist argument against the existence of an external world rests on the lack of any logical connection between our experience and an external world. There is no set of secure premises and logical argument that can lead us to an incontestable conclusion that the external world exists independently of our minds. Logic seems distinctively a matter of mental processes, so that it is hardly conceivable that it could prove anything that is not a matter of mind. Logic is a matter of words and words, being within the mental domain, cannot take us beyond that domain. The postmodernists have an apparently secure position.

But a map has a form that links it to the land it represents. While there may be no apparent logical connection, there is a connection in the patterns or shapes formed by the map and the patterns or shapes of the land. We have visual understanding of both the contours of the map and the contours of the land. There is a connection through symmetry between the map and the land it is supposed to represent.

Common theory has very firm ideas about the external world: it is plain daft to suppose that it does not exist much as we see and experience it. Academic logic is irrelevant. We just know that trees and stones exist as something other than information. The question then is, 'on what basis do people have such firm convictions?' when the cleverest people can find no good reasons for such conviction. It was suggested in Chapter 2 that people use a 'makeshift' scientific method to sift truth and reality from what is false and imaginary. They engage in repetitive observation and have repetitive experience, and they attend to the reported observations and experience of others. Where they perceive consistency, they accept truth and realism.

Consistency is a matter of 'fitting together'. When observations, experience and reports are consistent they 'fit together'. They form a regular pattern, or are symmetrical. The map fits the land. The jigsaw fits together. The conjecture here is that people's assurance regarding the existence of an external world derives from their sense of symmetry. The patterns perceived in their minds are reckoned correspondent to symmetries of the external world. Symmetry pervades our mental processes and formulations, and pervades also the external world as we know it. The pervasive symmetry gives us grounds, very sure grounds as far as ordinary people are concerned, for believing that the external world exists much as we experience it. When we say something is consistent with something else, we imply a symmetrical relationship between them.

It is then necessary to reconsider postmodernist understanding of logic. It is seen as an independent and ascendant phenomenon of our minds. Logic rules. But logical conclusions are consistent with premises. What is logical is consistent; what is illogical is inconsistent. Logic is then a matter of consistency, and hence logic itself is a matter of symmetry. Establishing a link by symmetry of minds to an external world is potentially establishing also a logical link. Postmodernists miss this wider context of the exercise of logic.

Symmetry provides the connection between minds and matter, giving an apparently seamless link between the understandings formed in our minds and the characteristics of the world beyond our minds. The characteristics we recognise include characteristics captured in the mathematics of symmetry, or symmetry group theory. It includes also the characteristics brought to light by natural science, including the symmetry that led to the promulgation of relativity theory and the principles of quantum mechanics. It includes the characteristics of crystalline structures. It includes the symmetry we see in landscapes, trees, flowers and all other emanations of nature. The connection is made in the information interface, so that the 'information' forms an 'interface' between symmetries of mind and symmetries of the external world.

Our minds work on symmetry and are governed by symmetry. Ian Stewart and Martin Golubitsky have suggested that the early survival of the human species depended on our sense of symmetry.[102] When we draw, paint, compose music or write stories, we impose symmetry on our creations. People recognise and enjoy the symmetries that are produced. The sense of symmetry plays the vital role in support-bargaining and money-bargaining of enabling us to fit potential acquisitions to an existing situation. Humans judge what is fitting to their situation using a sense of symmetry. Formation of the bargaining sets described in Chapter 4 in the context of consumer choice is an exercise in symmetry.[103] The evolution of societies and economies is conditioned by the requirement that change should be seen as symmetrical to an existing order. 'Revolutionary change' imposes new concepts of symmetry. Through symmetry, the human mind, and its emanation in support-bargaining and money-bargaining, is connected with the characteristics we recognise in our experience of the external world.

It was suggested in *Support-Bargaining, Economics and Society* that the shared human sense of symmetry is important to the formation of groups.[104] In the theory of support-bargaining and money-bargaining, groups are formed as a consequence of the need of all individuals for support from those around them or associated with them. Groups form on the basis of shared situations or shared understanding. A shared sense of symmetry means that people are naturally inclined to see things in the same way. This facilitates the process of group formation. At the same time, the sense of symmetry is malleable – people do not always see the same patterns. Apparent symmetries can be adopted that relate to particular interests. The falling apart of groups, or the failure of groups to form, may be in part a consequence of differences over perceived symmetries. The support-bargaining and money-bargaining process creates the information interface, so that the shared sense of symmetry, and disputes over perceived symmetries, will be reflected in the content of the information interface. We try to 'make sense of the world' or 'set our minds at ease' by shaping the information we have into symmetrical forms. We codify information in accordance with symmetries. The frames of reference described in Chapter 3 summarise patterns of behaviour, or symmetries in behaviour. We cannot understand or grasp a jumble of disconnected items of information, but we can grasp patterns that involve the most complex interactions.[105]

It has been argued as something of fundamental importance that our minds deal only with information and hence we can have no sure knowledge of what is beyond our minds. This conjecture of a symmetry connection rests on the propensity of our minds to evaluate its information on the basis of perceived patterns, and the propensity of the real world as experienced and as encountered in natural scientific investigations to display symmetry. It is conjectured that this common symmetry derives from the biological matter that constitutes our brains and generates what we are aware of as information. The 'grey matter' of our minds is necessarily the same order of material that supposedly constitutes an external world independent of our minds, and must carry the same symmetry characteristics as that other material. We are governed by the same kinds of particles that constitute the supposed existence of mountains, trees and stone, so that the symmetries perceived in our minds are linked with the symmetries of mountains, trees and stone. In some cases, the symmetry of our mental activity can be directly associated with the physical symmetries of receptor organs. Stewart and Golubitsky record that 'Our visual cortex . . . is composed of layer upon layer of cells, with remarkable internal symmetries related to the detection of orientation'.[106] We share in our biological being the material constituents of the external world and the symmetry that is characteristic of them. Our mental predilection for symmetry derives from our biological constitution, and thereby connects our minds with what we understand as an external world. The 'grey matter' of our minds generates the symmetries of our information interface; it is of the same material as the external reality that we suppose to exist; it exists itself as an observable external biological reality. The symmetry seems to originate in the quantum symmetries that determine the characteristics of matter. It is connected also with the conservation of energy, in that symmetrical forms commonly minimise the use of energy.[107] For example, the lines that make a car aesthetically pleasing tend to be the lines that are most aerodynamically efficient. The absence of an external world in much the same form as that in which we recognise it would involve a breach of universal symmetry. There is no phrasing that can adequately express the improbability of such a circumstance. Even probability may be contingent on symmetry. We are part of a 'big picture' and the picture cannot be spoilt. The sense of symmetry gives people the conviction that their mental experience derives from what exists beyond their minds.

Notes

1 Spread, Patrick, 2013, *Support-Bargaining, Economics and Society: A Social Species*, Abingdon: Routledge, pp. 4–12, 162–3, 168, 254–6.
2 Goldman, Alvin I., 2003, *Knowledge in a Social World*, Oxford: Clarendon Press, p. 19.
3 Searle, John R., 1996, *The Construction of Social Reality*, London: Penguin, p. 26.
4 Searle, 1996, p. 27.
5 Searle, 1996, pp. 23–6.
6 Searle, 1996, p. 190.
7 Berger, Peter and Luckman, Thomas, 1991, *The Social Construction of Reality*, London: Penguin, p. 134.
8 Berger and Luckman, 1991, p. 138.
9 Berger and Luckman, 1991, p. 135.
10 Berger and Luckman, 1991, p. 137.
11 Berger and Luckman, 1991, p. 137.
12 Berger and Luckman, 1991, p. 136.
13 Goldman, 2003, p. 33.
14 Foucault, Michel, 1977, *Discipline and Punish: The Birth of the Prison*, London: Allen Lane.

15 Goldman, 2003, pp. 34–7.
16 Spread, Patrick, 1984a, *A Theory of Support and Money Bargaining*, London: Macmillan, paras 6.70–102, etc.
17 Goldman, 2003, p. 34.
18 Brotton, Jerry, 2013, *A History of the World in Twelve Maps*, London: Penguin, pp. 186–7.
19 Brotton, 2013, p. 195.
20 Brotton, 2013, p. 195.
21 Brotton, 2013, p. 207.
22 Brotton, 2013, p. 211.
23 Brotton, 2013, pp. 211–13.
24 *The Economist*, 2015, 'The Paris agreement marks an unprecedented political recognition of the risks of climate change', 12 December. Available at: www.economist.com/news/international/21683990-paris-agreement-climate-change-talks. Accessed 2 February 2017.
25 Goldman, 2003, p. 4.
26 Goldman, 2003, p. 5.
27 Goldman, 2003, p. vii.
28 Goldman, 2003, p. 4.
29 Goldman, 2003, pp. 4–5.
30 Goldman, 2003, p. 7.
31 Goldman, 2003, p. viii.
32 Goldman, 2003, p. 7.
33 Spread, 2013, Chapter 4: Power elites and pluralist democracy, see esp. p. 74.
34 Goldman, Alvin and Blanchard, Thomas, 2016, 'Social epistemology', in Zalta, Edward N. (ed.), *The Stanford Encyclopedia of Philosophy*, Summer Edition, 1. Background, para. 2. Available at: http://plato.stanford.edu/archives/sum2016/entries/epistemology-social.
35 Goldman, 2003, p. 3.
36 Goldman, 2003, p. 5.
37 Goldman, 2003, p. 12.
38 Goldman, 2003, p. 29.
39 Goldman, 2003, pp. 23–4. See notes 24–28 in Chapter 3.
40 Goldman, 2003, p. 17.
41 Goldman, 2003, p. 17.
42 Goldman, 2003, pp. 18–19.
43 Goldman, 2003, p. 19. Goldman's reference: Huyssen, Andreas, 1986, *After the Great Divide: Modernism, Mass Culture, and Postmodernism*, Bloomington: Indiana University Press, pp. 157–8.
44 Goldman, 2003, p. 12.
45 Tuomela, Raimo, 2013, *Social Ontology: Collective Intentionality and Group Agents*, Oxford: Oxford University Press, p. 2.
46 Gilbert, Margaret, 1989, *On Social Facts*, Abingdon: Routledge. Searle also cites: Bratman, Michael, 1992, 'Shared cooperative activity', *Philosophical Review*, Vol. 101, No. 2, pp. 327–41; and Tuomela, Raimo and Miller, Kaarlo, 1988, 'We-intentions', *Philosophical Studies*, Vol. 53, No. 3, pp. 367–89.
47 Gilbert, 1989, pp. 2–3.
48 Gilbert, 1989, p. 2.
49 Gilbert, 1989, pp. 17, 20. Original emphasis.
50 Searle, 1996, p. 3.
51 Searle, 1996, pp. 5–6.

52 Searle, 1996, p. 29.
53 Searle, 1996, p. 8.
54 Searle, 1996, pp. 8–9.
55 Searle, 1996, p. 155. Original emphasis.
56 Searle, 1996, p. 156.
57 Searle, 1996, p. 41.
58 Searle, 1996, p. 8.
59 Searle, 1996, pp. 227–8.
60 Spread, 2016a, *The Evolution of Economies: Money-Bargaining, Economic Change and Industrial Revolution*, Abingdon: Routledge, pp. 71–4, etc.
61 Tuomela, 2013, 10.
62 On ceremony, see Spread, 2013, pp. 238–40.
63 Goldman, 2003, p. 221.
64 Goldman, 2003, p. 226. Goldman's reference: Latour, Bruno, 1987, *Science in Action*, Cambridge MA: Harvard University Press, p. 31.
65 Goldman, 2003, p. 228.
66 Goldman, 2003, pp. 229–30.
67 Goldman, 2003, p. 223.
68 Goldman, 2003, p. 244.
69 Goldman, 2003, p. 247. Original emphasis.
70 Goldman, 2003, p. 249.
71 Goldman, 2003, pp. 250–1.
72 Goldman, 2003, p. 223.
73 Kuhn, Thomas S., 1970, *The Structure of Scientific Revolutions*, Chicago: Chicago University Press. First published 1962.
74 Goldman, 2003, pp. 7–8.
75 Shapin, Steven, 1994, *A Social History of Truth*, Chicago: University of Chicago Press, pp. 48–52.
76 Shapin, 1994, p. 49.
77 Hore, Peter, n.d., 'The quantum robin', *Navigation News*. Available at: http://hore.chem.ox.ac.uk/PDFs/The_Quantum_Robin.pdf. Accessed 12 August 2015. See also Solov'yov, Ilia A.; Ritz, Thorsten; Schulten, Klaus and Hore, Peter J., 2014, 'A chemical compass for bird navigation,' in Mohseni, Masoud; Omar, Yasser; Engel, Gregory and Plenio, Martin (eds), 2014, *Quantum Effects in Biology*, Cambridge: Cambridge University Press.
78 Hore, n.d., 'The quantum robin', p. 17.
79 Brotton, Jerry, 2013, *A History of the World in Twelve Maps*, London: Penguin, p. 200.
80 Brotton, 2013, p. 261–6.
81 Brotton, 2013, p. 263.
82 Brotton, 2013, p. 264.
83 Brotton, 2013, pp. 280–90.
84 Brotton, 2013, pp. 249–54.
85 Brotton, 2013, p. 247.
86 Brotton, 2013, p. 343.
87 Harvey, Paul D.A., 2002, *Mappa Mundi: The Hereford World Map*, Hereford: Hereford Cathedral, p. 14.
88 Brotton, 2013, p. 89.
89 Brotton, 2013, pp. 106–7.
90 Harvey, 2002, p. 53.
91 Harvey, 2002, p. 42.
92 Harvey, 2002, p. 21.

93 Brotton, 2013, pp. 368–9.
94 Brotton, 2013, p. 346.
95 Brotton, 2013, p. 357.
96 Brotton, 2013, p. 363.
97 Brotton, 2013, pp. 358–65.
98 Brotton, 2013, p. 367.
99 Brotton, 2013, pp. 378–9.
100 Brotton, 2013, p. 380.
101 Brotton, 2013, p. 385.
102 Stewart, Ian and Golubitsky, Martin, 1992, *Fearful Symmetry: Is God a Geometer?* London: Penguin, p. 257.
103 On symmetry and consumer choice, see also Spread, 2013, pp. 244–7.
104 Spread, 2013, p. 232.
105 Cf. Spread, 2013, p. 235–6, 238–9.
106 Stewart and Golubitsky, 1992, p. 257. See also Spread, 2013, p. 230.
107 See Spread, 2013, pp. 245–50 and associated references.

7 Media theory and the information interface

One reason why theorists such as ontologists and economists have been able to dispense with ideas of an information interface and supposedly deal directly with reality is perhaps that theories about the role of information in society have been limited in the explanations they provide. A clear and convincing account of the role of information in political, social and economic affairs would have made it more difficult to sustain the simple idea of information as direct representation of reality. The leading academic theory of media seems to have no understanding at all of information. This chapter considers media theory in the light of a support-bargaining and money-bargaining process carried on by reference to an information interface created as part of the same process. The agents of support-bargaining and money-bargaining systems purvey information with a view to advance of their interests.

This may be information of a relatively simple kind, presenting some benefit that is expected to fit the situations of those who come across it. One political party informs people that it will promote rapid expansion of employment, anticipating that such a commitment will bring support to the party. Another political party informs people that it will raise benefits to the disadvantaged, in the expectation that people will give support for provision of this kind. In the money-bargaining network the information provided may be yet simpler. One company informs potential buyers that its refrigerators are of the highest quality and guaranteed for five years. Another company informs buyers that its refrigerators incorporate the latest technology and are guaranteed for ten years.

The more complex form of information is that which establishes an understanding of situation in the information interface, so that people accepting the situation as set out in the information interface will be inclined to make certain selections relative to that understanding. Political parties endeavour to ensure that their understanding of the economic situation is of such a kind that their favoured policies and programmes seem the natural and necessary measures to improve the situation. A right wing party will emphasise economic growth, investment and incentives, while a left wing party will emphasise inequality and social deprivation. At a more abstract and theoretical level parties will advance ideas of 'free enterprise' and 'socialism' as the frames of reference in which their policies can be seen as of vital importance to an electorate. Companies will also endeavour to establish concepts of situation in the information interface that are conducive to purchase of their products. One company may present images in its television advertisements of a secure and homely family enjoying a conventional way of life, featuring, of course, a refrigerator from the company. Another company may present images of a contemporary family with a lifestyle based on enjoyment of the latest technology, exemplified, of course, by a refrigerator from that company.

All this information is subject to manipulation, including selection and omission. A left wing party, for example, may neglect to disseminate information about the implications of its programme for taxation. An independent testing agency may conclude that a refrigerator claimed by its maker to be of the highest quality is more than normally subject to faults.

In the circumstances outlined above, the information interface will be filled with confused and in some cases conflicting information. The economic and social situation may be a matter of slow growth and low investment, or it may be a matter of social disadvantage. Parties will be inhibited in their assembly of support by the contrary messages of others. Plainly, if one party can control what goes into the information interface, it will be easier for it to assemble support. Similarly, if one company can control what goes into the information interface, its sales prospects will be greatly improved. Hence control of the information interface is important to the advance of interests. Control of the information interface means the capacity both to purvey information conducive to the interests of the controller and suppress information that is detrimental to its interests. If providing certain information is advantageous to one agent, suppressing that information will often be advantageous to another.

There is consequently a long experience of agents of bargaining systems trying to suppress or impede the circulation of information that is detrimental to their interests. The maintenance of some degree of control over information constitutes an essential part of the exercise of power. In the extreme, the exercise of anything like absolute power requires something like absolute control of the information interface.

The exercise of power is associated most readily with violence, or a preponderant capacity for violence. So it is that those having political power, with a preponderant capacity for physical violence, have used their violent capacity to control information. Those who oppose government may be beaten up, locked up, impoverished or even killed. People soon learn that speaking their minds can be dangerous; that safety lies in speaking in accord with government. Historically, control of information by these means has been common. Germans in the Nazi era, the citizens of the Soviet Union and the citizens of the People's Republic of China under Mao Zedong learnt to control their tongues in accordance with the ideology of their rulers. All found it necessary to assent to the situations of their nations as portrayed by their rulers. Since in all these cases little alternative information was available, many people came to believe that what they were told was incontrovertibly true. The tradition is maintained today in many parts of the world. A 2016 survey of Russia in *The*

Economist comments that, 'The two main pillars of the Soviet state, propaganda and the threat of repression, have been restored'.[1]

Power established through a support-bargaining system has different implications for the information interface, since support-bargaining systems can only function with extensive freedom for the dissemination of information. Power in a democratic system necessarily involves constraints on the capacity of the powerful to control the information interface. Nevertheless, a governing party will have certain advantages regarding access to information. It will normally have access to extensive sources of information through a civil service, including an intelligence service, which are not available to other agencies. To some degree, it can select the information that is disseminated to the public information interface, and what is withheld. A government has considerable scope for determining what information reaches the information interface, even though it has no monopoly of power, but is rather engaged in a contest for political ascendancy.

Other agencies will similarly be in a position to assert some degree of control over the public information interface in the spheres in which they have unique access to information. In a money-bargaining system, companies know better than their potential customers the specifications and qualities of their products, and can to a large extent control what their potential customers learn about their products.

Earlier authoritarian regimes did not generally have such all-embracing ideologies as those of the Nazis, the Soviet Communist Party or the Chinese Communist Party to provide a filter or reference by which appropriate and inappropriate information could be recognised. They did, however, have religious doctrines, which, while not commonly understood as ideologies, perform a similar function. Religious doctrines provided the frames of reference by which people selected what was relevant to them and interpreted what they selected. Mediaeval monarchs in Europe ruled in alliance with the Catholic Church. The monarch guaranteed the Church certain privileges, including landholdings, wealth and participation in government, while the Church ensured that the information propagated to the people through sermons and religious tracts maintained acceptance of the existing order as something ordained by god and not to be disturbed. Without alternative information, people had no means of assembling support against the existing order. The Church's monopoly of information ensured that people came to assume the information they had was incontestably the truth about the world and their rulers. In France the phrase 'trône et l'autel' summed up the alliance that maintained order in the land, assuring that the information interface did not contain information detrimental to the established order. The government, in the form of the monarch, attended to the application of armed force and the threat of armed force against insurrection, while the Church was expected to ease the stresses by establishing an information interface that gave supernatural justification for the role of the monarch. Minds set in a certain way posed a threat to government, but set in another way would ease the difficulties of government.

'The sword and the pen' encapsulates the secular understanding of the combination of political and intellectual support-bargaining that is necessary to social order. The sword must establish a level of order in society that makes it possible for the pen to perform. The 'pen' must establish an information interface that makes it unnecessary to wield the sword in actual violence. Actual violence for the establishment or protection of the state is much less needed if people have absorbed information conducive to the rule of a particular agency.

The exercise of power normally involves attention both to the daily necessities of life and to the pleasures of high living. Material benefits are important to the maintenance of support. Those who would be powerful must have revenues for deployment in their cause. The Catholic Church gained revenues from its land and donations of the faithful, including money bequeathed in wills. Not unnaturally, given the opportunities and temptations of power, and the pleasures of high living, the Church found its revenues less than sufficient for its ambitions. Individual priests in the Middle Ages had discovered that the faithful were ready to pay for 'indulgences' that reduced the period of time they or their deceased relatives would be obliged to spend in purgatory. The Church itself came to recognise such sales as valuable additions to its revenues. The programme expanded in the fifteenth century. It even had an advertising jingle. One Franciscan friar, selling indulgences, proclaimed:

> As soon as the coin in the coffer rings,
>
> the soul from purgatory springs.[2]

The sale of indulgences became the focal cause that brought about the most profound change in Christendom. It resulted in the break-up of the monopoly of the Catholic Church on provision of information relating to the Christian faith.

Martin Luther's Ninety-Five Theses of 1517 were prompted by outrage at the sale of indulgences by the Church. The Reformation gave birth to many alternative churches, and many alternative sources of information about the world, the place of people in it, and the rights and wrongs of rulers. The information interface expanded with new and challenging information. Support could move from group to group in accordance with the attraction of their posted information. 'The pens' took issue with each other within Christianity, their dissension inevitably spilling over into armed confrontation as their writing assembled support behind different factions.

The role and influence of communications media are dramatically apparent from this period. The printing press, in the form of the Gutenberg press, introduced around 1440, dramatically reduced the unit costs of disseminating written information, and made possible the wide propagation of all this new information. It became feasible to format companies for the provision of written information.[3] It may or may not be true that Luther's Ninety-Five Theses were pinned to the door of a church, but it is certainly true that they were disseminated across Europe in printed form. The Catholic Church attempted to limit the consequences of subversive information by introducing the 'Index Librorum Prohibitorum', the 'Index of Prohibited Books', which listed material that its members should not read. The first version was published in 1559. Remarkably, given the changes in Christendom, it was only abandoned in 1966.

The mediaeval Church's monopoly of information was exercised partly by limiting access to what was universally regarded as essential information. The Bible was available in Latin, but not available in vernacular languages. William Tyndale, the translator of the Bible into English, was executed for his pains, though his work later formed the basis for the King James' version of the Bible in English. While ordinary people could not read the Bible themselves, they were dependent on the clergy for interpretations of what the Bible said. Making available an English version meant opening up the Bible to the interpretations of lay people, or at least those among them who could read. An essential part of the information interface became accessible to a wide public.

Across Europe disagreements ran so strongly over the new information that they could not be settled by support-bargaining. The Catholic Church mounted a 'Counter-Reformation' to recover its lost ground. Vital interests were at stake – the sort of interests that cannot be settled by support-bargaining.[4] Armed conflict was rife across the European continent in the early seventeenth century, stemmed at last by the Peace of Westphalia in 1648. In England a two-phase civil war was fought between 1642 and 1647 over the rights of a monarch, though with fundamental religious implications, since the main right in question was the divine right of a monarch to rule. In England the horrors of civil war seem to have prompted people to accept more widely a support convention, whereby support substitutes for violence. The scope of 'vital interests' was allowed to contract. In Europe the Peace of Westphalia ordained that the ruler of a state would have the right to specify the religion of the state, though other Christian faiths were to be tolerated.

Once a support convention is adopted as the basis of governance of a society, the information interface gains in significance, variety and prominence. People and factions are obliged to argue their cause rather than fight for it. The idea of 'free speech' becomes less outrageous, less damaging, less threatening. It begins to be acceptable. It also becomes more expedient, in that if the sanction of violence, or the quasi-violence of physical intimidation and threat of imprisonment, is dropped, it is difficult to suppress the expression of alternative opinion. People think twice about stating opinions that might get them imprisoned, beaten up or burnt at the stake, and are likely to desist. People will also think twice before saying what they know will attract disapproval and make them unpopular, but they are more likely still to say it if those are the sole sanctions. If some disapprove, others may nevertheless give their support.

With relief from the threat of violence, the expansion of intellectual support-bargaining becomes possible. The 'pen' part of the struggle for ascendancy may be seen as shorthand for the process of intellectual support-bargaining. This, as has been seen, is the process by which support is assembled for different ideas, and most particularly for the theories, or frames of reference, by which a society understands its basic circumstances. It functions most freely in circumstances of peace and freedom, implying that the sword is at least sheathed. In modern Western societies it is a major factor in the assembly of support. Policies and programmes in housing, economic advance, welfare, foreign trade, foreign relations, defence, education and health are extensively debated, nationally and locally, to see what support is available for the many different proposals, and how proposals might be modified to increase the support assembled behind them. The process determines what frames of reference will predominate in the information interface, and hence the sort of information that will be posted to the information interface and recognised by those using the interface. In short, it determines what the everyday support-bargaining and money-bargaining systems use as their raw material. There remains heated rivalry over control of the information interface, but it is recognised also that no single agency can be permitted to control the creation of the information interface.

Intellectual support-bargaining and the creation of the information interface are motivated by the pursuit of interest. Issues of truth, realism and falsehood take second place to the pursuit of other interests. In general, humans have a strong interest in establishing the truth, because falsehood often has serious ill consequences, for its perpetrators as much as for those who adopt it. But there is still much advantage to be gained from dissemination of falsehood and, if not outright falsehood, then the dissemination of information that is less than the whole truth. There is an interest in truth, and there is interest in social advantage. The truth may be so prominent and pressing as to outweigh any social disadvantages attaching to it. In some cases truth and social advantage coincide. But in other cases social advantage is sought despite the truth. Most commonly truth is compromised by selection and manipulation of information. The truth about climate change is of major importance to all humans, but early uncertainties over the precise nature of the truth about climate change gave rise to extensive support-bargaining for the protection and advance of business and political interests, involving extensive manipulation of information.

Those disseminating false information are at risk of serious social discredit, the extensive withdrawal of support, if the falsehood is revealed. This constitutes a significant deterrent to the provision of false information. But there is extensive tolerance of the manipulation of information for the advance of interests. It is so much part of the support-bargaining and money-bargaining process that people learn to live with it. It is impossible to identify reliably all the misinformation that is put about, especially when the manipulation includes selection and omission of information. The whole truth and nothing but the truth is beyond human grasp. As remarked previously, our psychology has evolved for the advance of interest rather than the pursuit of truth. It was seen in Chapter 3 that information can be manipulated to advance interests through inflections of language or word selection, and by the attribution of motivations. The more an agent is in control of a society and the creation of the information interface, the less chance that agent has of being caught in the dissemination of false or misleading information, and the less likely it is to suffer the consequences of disseminating such information. So the more a particular agent controls the information interface, the more false and misleading information is likely to be established in the information interface.

The information interface is of central importance in support-bargaining and money-bargaining, since it forms the basis of transactions. It identifies the situations by which interests are understood, and the benefits by which interests can be met. Because of this, the technologies by which the information interface is created are of great importance. Some make it easy to disseminate information so that it is widely accessible. Some make it difficult. Some facilitate the close control of the information interface. Some make it difficult to control. The Gutenberg press is widely recognised as a technology that radically changed the parameters governing dissemination of information in Europe. But because the information interface is created through the support-bargaining and money-bargaining process that uses it, it is the relative bargaining positions, or degrees of ascendancy, or degrees of power, that are most fundamental in determining control over the creation of the information interface. Given the necessary degree of ascendancy, a government can control the usage of the technology that is used in the creation of the information interface. In a democratic society, or a full support-bargaining society, no one agency will have sufficient ascendancy to control what is disseminated to the information interface. The information interface will include a wide range of information variously manipulated in accordance with the interests of the various agents.

Media theorists and the significance of media technology

The idea of support-bargaining and money-bargaining thus conceives a competitive process for the establishment of an information interface through which interests will be pursued in the bargaining process. The bargaining process runs on information, so that establishing information of a certain type is crucial to the success of any agent. With the emergence of a support convention, and corresponding reductions in violence, intellectual support-bargaining gains in importance as the means of assembling support. While support-bargaining of all kinds – political, social and intellectual – requires media of communication, intellectual support-bargaining is scarcely conceivable except in the context of the media of communication through which it is conducted. From speech through writing, printing, typing, radio and television to the internet, the media of communication have been inseparable from the intellectual support-bargaining process. The subtle distinctions that can be made with such media are used in the assembly of support in intellectual support-bargaining.

While intellectual support-bargaining depends on the information conveyed by media, the most prominent academic theories of the function of media, the theories of the Toronto School, have made the technology of the media the centre of attention. In Harold Innis it is the characteristics of the media – papyrus, parchment, paper, print, radio – that determine the nature of a society. Changes in the use and availability of the media bring about consequential changes in the societies in which they are used.[5] Innis seems significantly incomplete. Marshall Poe's *History of Communications* is largely an attempt to give substance to Innis' arguments about the relationship between media and society. In Marshall McLuhan 'the medium' is even more strongly the focus of attention, eclipsing the content of the communication. Poe sees McLuhan's theories as the starting point of modern media theory: 'Any discussion of media theory must begin with Marshall McLuhan, if only because he coined its most famous expression – "the medium is the message"'.[6] With apparent paradox, Poe sees McLuhan as separating medium from message and thereby establishing the starting point for the central programme of modern media studies.[7] McLuhan's theories thrive on paradox and ambivalence.

The writers of the Toronto School are cited as of particular importance in the development of interdisciplinary theories of the media by Asa Briggs and Peter Burke in their brief coverage of media theory in *A Social History of the Media*:

> Contributions were made from economics, history, literature, art, political science, psychology, sociology and anthropology, and led to the emergence of academic departments of communication and cultural studies. Striking phrases encapsulating new ideas were coined by Harold Innis (1894–1952), who wrote of the 'bias of communication'; by Marshall McLuhan (1911–80), who spoke of the 'global village'; by Jack Goody (1919–), who traced 'the domestication of the savage mind'; and by Jürgen Habermas (1929–), the German sociologist, once associated with the Frankfurt School, who identified the 'public sphere', a zone for 'discourse' in which ideas are explored and views expressed.[8]

As remarked above, the means by which information is disseminated influence what is disseminated. There are two aspects to this, the first specifically related to the medium by which information is disseminated and the second related to the social and political circumstances in which dissemination takes place. With regard to the first aspect, a message conveyed on paper, for example, may be formulated differently from a message conveyed by word of mouth. The paper medium gives opportunity for conveyance of a more intricate message than is generally possible by word of mouth. On the other hand, the rhetorical tones that can be used in word of mouth may convey a more persuasive message. Word of mouth is normally ephemeral and its content may be affected by this characteristic. The content of speech will be adjusted to the circumstances of the immediate audience. Written messages can be disseminated widely. Print technology permits the reproduction of messages and their dissemination to a wide range of people. The content will be adjusted to take account of the circumstances of the people likely to read it. McLuhan gives the influence of 'electric' media technologies great prominence, not on account of their content or the range of their transmission, but because the technology has an unrecognised yet intrinsic quality that gives it social impact.

As regards the second aspect, certain technologies are more difficult to control than others. A government can establish an effective monopoly of information when it controls the supply of a raw material essential to a technology of communication. Innis notes that control over the supply of papyrus after the conquest of Egypt gave the Romans something like monopolistic control over the dissemination of information.[9] Printing presses, being small and movable, can be difficult to control. But a government determined to do so can impose such draconian punishments on the installation of unauthorised printing presses that their use is effectively terminated. The internet is difficult to control. High intrusion into freedom of expression is necessary to control the dissemination of information over the internet. Authoritarian states lacking the Western commitment to freedom of expression find ways of constraining the information available over the internet. McLuhan's emphasis on the intrinsic importance of technology as disseminator of hidden messages means that he recognises no issues concerning media control.

The influence of technology on output and the facility with which different technologies can be controlled by governments is not unique to media technology. Technologies for the production of most products influence the characteristics of the product. Some technologies for the production of textiles produce highly durable and close-meshed material, while others produce fragile and loose material. Governments wishing to control the production of alcohol will find it easier when the technology in use requires a large scale of operation and hence a small number of producers. Many small producers devoted to 'moonshine' are hard to control.

As in all other industries, the cost characteristics of the technology used are of paramount importance in the media. Companies use technology to establish viable formats – formats in which the unit cost of production at a certain level of output is such that a price for the service can be established that results in profitable sales of all the output. Where the dissemination of information is open to private initiative, these format considerations are of the highest importance, and the cost characteristics of the technologies available have corresponding importance. Media technology plays a central role in the format of media companies. A company producing television programmes in the twenty-first century and a printer of the fifteenth century using a Gutenberg printing press both convey information, and are both dependent on the cost characteristics of their technology for the viability of their enterprises.

Much of the importance of media technology thus lies in the importance of technology to industry in general. Media technology is nevertheless exceptional, first because information is of such central importance to a society and, second, because of its intricacy. Information can be almost infinitely tailored to the requirements of audiences, so that its delivery requires technology that can convey intricacy to an exceptional degree. Awareness of the suitability of different media technologies to different types of information and different audiences will affect the technologies chosen by those who wish to disseminate information.

Well before Innis and McLuhan the significance of media technology in intellectual support-bargaining was identified and eloquently explored by Victor Hugo in *The Hunchback of Notre Dame*, published in 1831.[10] Book V seriously interrupts the flow of his narrative to argue the role of stone and architecture in the transmission of ideas and the effects of their displacement by the invention of the printing press in the fifteenth century. It is not tied in with the story of Quasimodo and la Esmeralda, though their story centres on the great stone structure of Notre-Dame de Paris. The original French title was simply *Notre-Dame de Paris*, implying even more strongly a focus on the structure. Hugo was apparently displeased by the English title.

Hugo's point is that 'The book killed the edifice'. In the words of his fictional archdeacon, 'This will kill that. The book will kill the edifice'.[11] Hugo argues that the stone and architecture that constituted the media of civilised expression for centuries were displaced by the invention of the printing press. Stone imposed on what could and could not be expressed. Architecture was the mode by which artists and society in general expressed their ideas and aspirations. With the advent of the printing press there was:

> a presentiment that human thought, in changing its form, was about to change its mode of expression; that the dominant idea of each generation would no longer be written with the same matter, and in the same manner; that the book of stone, so solid and so durable, was about to make way for the book of paper, more solid and more durable. In this connection, the archdeacon's vague formula had a second sense. It meant, "Printing will kill architecture."
>
> In fact, from the origin of things down to the fifteenth century of the Christian era, inclusive, architecture is the great book of humanity, the principal expression of man in his different states of development, either as a force or as an intelligence.[12]

The intelligence extended beyond religion. Hugo cites examples of exotic and lewd stonework in churches that reflect 'the liberty of architecture'.[13] He comments, 'This liberty goes very far. Sometimes a portal, a façade, an entire church, presents a symbolical sense absolutely foreign to worship, or even hostile to the church'.[14] He continues, 'In this manner, under the pretext of building churches to God, art was developed in its magnificent proportions'.[15]

He concludes:

> that architecture was, down to the fifteenth century, the chief register of humanity; that in the interval not a thought which is in any degree complicated made its appearance in the world, which has not been worked

> into an edifice; that every popular idea, and every religious law, has had its monumental records; that the human race has, in short, had no important thought which it has not written in stone.[16]

Printing ends all that. Its qualities have new implications for intelligence and ideas:

> The invention of printing is the greatest event in history. It is the mother of revolution. It is the mode of expression of humanity which is totally renewed; it is human thought stripping off one form and donning another; it is the complete and definitive change of skin of that symbolical serpent which since the days of Adam has represented intelligence.[17]
>
> In its printed form, thought is more imperishable than ever; it is volatile, irresistible, indestructible . . . It passes from duration in time to immortality. One can demolish a mass; how can one extirpate ubiquity?'[18]

Hugo notes other characteristics of printed material. It is simple, convenient and practical. It does not involve bulky baggage. It does not require four or five other arts, tons of gold, a mountain of stone, a forest of timber, a nation of workmen. 'A little paper, a little ink and a pen suffice'.[19] (Though printing requires something more than a pen – Hugo seems to forget momentarily that he is concerned with the printing press.) He notes also that the power exerted over other modes of expression by the dominance of architecture is eroded by the change to printing:

> Nevertheless, from the moment when architecture is no longer anything but an art like any other; as soon as it is no longer the total art, the sovereign art, the tyrant art – it has no longer the power to retain the other arts.[20]

Architecture, for Hugo, controlled the information interface. The printing press deprived it of its controlling authority.

Hugo emphasises also the economic advantages of the printing press:

> Let the reader make no mistake; architecture is dead; irretrievably slain by the printed book, – slain because it endures for a shorter time, – slain because it costs more . . . A book is so soon made, costs so little, and can go so far.[21]

Stone and architecture dominated the expression of ideas for centuries. The durability, ubiquity, convenience, cost and accessibility of the printed book mean that it displaces architecture in the expression of intelligence. 'The human race has two books, two registers, two testaments: masonry and printing; the Bible of stone and the Bible of paper'.[22] The change is regarded as having profound implications for human ideas and their expression – in other words, for the creation of the information interface.

Neither Innis nor McLuhan make reference to Hugo's thesis. It is relevant to Innis' work as plainly a similar theme, though Innis might insist that he is concerned with social science, and need not concern himself with fictional writing. McLuhan also follows a similar theme. He extols the impact of 'electric' media much as Hugo extols the impact of printing, albeit in convoluted style. He was a specialist in English literature and specifically places his theories in a cultural, including literary, context. A classic text of French literature might reasonably come within the scope of a theory written in that context, especially a Canadian theory. Hugo's thesis might be expected to feature as a precursor of McLuhan's own.

Harold Innis: media of space and time

Harold Innis echoes Hugo's ideas, though not with the same facility. Innis spent his early career as an economic historian, writing about the emergence of Canada's staple industries – wheat, timber, furs, metals, pulp and paper – and their impact on Canada as a nation and society. His study of the pulp and paper industry in particular, with its extensive consequences for Canadian development, stimulated his concern for the effects of media more generally on government and social circumstances. Just as the prominence of the pulp and paper industry in Canada gave Canadian government and society a certain stamp, so different types of media caused societies at other times and in other places to develop in certain distinctive ways.

Innis' central thesis is that media have either a time bias or a spatial bias, and the predominance of a medium of one type or the other has effects on the society concerned. A temporal medium tends to sustain a more egalitarian and spiritual type of society, with decentralised governmental structures. A spatially biased medium generally gives rise to a more centralised and hierarchical form of government. Stability depends on the emergence of a balance between the spatial and the temporal. Innis' message is that the United States is a society of excessively spatial orientation, due to the predominance of the newspaper medium and neglect of the oral tradition. Innis regards the oral tradition as of fundamental importance to the health of societies. On page 1 of *Empire and Communications* he writes: 'It is suggested that all written works, including this one, have dangerous implications to the vitality of an oral tradition and to the health of a civilization.'[23] Radio is not regarded as part of the recognised oral tradition, because it is 'mechanized'. Near the end of his text he writes: 'The limitations of mechanization of the printed and the spoken word must be emphasized and determined efforts to recapture the vitality of the oral tradition must be made'.[24]

The spatial and temporal character of media is identified as follows:

> The concepts of time and space reflect the significance of media to civilization. Media which emphasize time are those which are durable in character such as parchment, clay, and stone. The heavy materials are suited to the

> development of architecture and sculpture. Media which emphasize space are apt to be less durable and light in character such as papyrus and paper. The latter are suited to wide areas in administration and trade. The conquest of Egypt by Rome gave access to supplies of papyrus which became the basis of a large administrative empire. Materials which emphasize time favour decentralization and hierarchical types of institutions, while those which emphasize space favour centralization and systems of government less hierarchical in character.[25]

In practical terms the distinction seems to rest largely on durability and transportability. The temporally biased media are durable. The spatially biased media are those which are easily transported. For most of the periods which Innis cites in relation to his theory the movement of information required some form of transport. Communications required an infrastructure of roads, tracks, rivers and oceans and the runners, horsemen, carriages and ships that would use them.

The spatial dimension introduces considerations of economic geography, both physical and cost-related, into the influences on social development. Innis notes early in *Empire and Communications* the importance of the North American river systems to the development of the continent, and of the St Lawrence and Hudson Bay to Canadian development in particular. Graeme Patterson suggests that the waterways were a more important origin of Innis' ideas than the pulp and paper industry,[26] though this aspect of Innis' work 'escaped most of his readers'.[27] Innis, however, covers extensively the impact of media on ancient Egyptian society, with scant attention to economic geography. By concentrating so strongly on the effects of media technology he seems to have underestimated the importance of the Nile in determining the character of Egyptian society. Readers may not have recognised the importance of the waterways of North America to Innis' thought, but Innis may not have expressed his thought on the subject with sufficient emphasis.

The importance of transport and transportability is critical to Innis' thesis that the civilisation of the United States is excessively spatial. Newspapers are easily transported, giving the United States its spatial orientation. The weakness of Innis' classification in terms of 'temporal' and 'spatial' media is apparent in that newspapers are in a way as durable as stone. To Victor Hugo, print was immortal because it was ubiquitous. 'How can one extirpate ubiquity?'

The weakness is apparent also in that neither temporal nor spatial bias can be regarded as the most important influence on society in the United States. The sheer volume and variety of information disseminated by newspapers at the time Innis wrote, supplemented by radio, contributed to the distinctive vivacity of the society. The old societies referred to by Innis in development of his thesis disseminated very little information, whatever its bias. The oral tradition could never come close to the volume of information purveyed by newspapers and radio. Support-bargaining and money-bargaining operate on the basis of an information interface, and the more extensive the interface, the greater the intensity of support-bargaining and money-bargaining is likely to be. The extensive information interface developed in the United States through newspapers and radio was a major factor behind the rapid economic development of the country.

The distinction between temporal and spatial character does not satisfactorily cover printed material; nor does it satisfactorily cover speech. The 'oral tradition' is of great importance in Innis' understanding of the strength of ancient civilisations and the weakness of modern American civilisation, but it is difficult to give it temporal or spatial character. Relays of messengers might give oral communication a kind of spatial identity. But for the most part speech is ephemeral, so that it has neither temporal character, at least in the sense of durability, nor spatial character. Speech on radio can be recorded and rendered durable, giving it temporal character. It can also be widely transmitted, giving it spatial character. Newspapers have also, as has been seen, both spatial and temporal characteristics.

Radio is, as in the quotation above, regarded as 'mechanized' speech and consequently not properly part of the oral tradition. Radio certainly does not sustain the oral tradition in its pure form, but it can still transmit with a rhetorical impact that is the essence of the oral tradition. Radio can still persuade by use of spoken language. And, just as important, radio greatly extends the use of speech for the transmission of information. In many ways radio extends and enhances the old oral tradition. It is perhaps because of these unacknowledged qualities of radio that Innis sees radio as being in competition with newspapers. He makes one of those giant leaps across a causative chasm that were later indulged to extreme by McLuhan. Innis remarks that, 'The Second World War became to an important extent the result of a clash between the newspaper and the radio'.[28]

The identification of a medium as temporal or spatial may depend also on the particular circumstances in which it is used. Innis gives papyrus a spatial character, because it is light and transportable. But he also notes that papyrus is fragile, so that it does not fare well when transported over rough terrain. It requires river or ocean transportation.

> In contrast with papyrus, which was produced in a restricted area under centralised control to meet the demands of a centralized bureaucratic administration and which was largely limited by its fragile character to water navigation, parchment was the product of a widely scattered agricultural economy suited to the demands of a decentralized administration and to land transportation.[29]

Papyrus has spatial character when the transport infrastructure favours its movement. Only then can it produce the sort of centralised administration that Innis sees as consequent on a medium with spatial character. Parchment is classified as having temporal characteristics, on grounds of its durability, and consequently likely to give rise to decentralised government. But in the quotation above he gives it a spatial characteristic – suitability to land transport – and agricultural origin, which also suggests spatial character. Yet he still deems it suited to decentralised administration, rather than the centralised administration that is normally consequent on a medium with spatial characteristics. The temporal/spatial character of a medium may depend on the particular circumstances of its employment. The social consequences may depend not just on temporal/spatial character, but on factors relating to the availability of the material from which the medium is made. Local availability of the raw material for a medium tends to promote local, or decentralised, government. It appears also from the above quotation that papyrus met the requirements of a centralised administration, rather than itself promoting centralised administration.

Monopoly in media

Spatial character is largely a matter of ease of transport. Temporal character is largely a matter of durability. The characterisations are too confined to do justice to the way in which characteristics of media influence their role in society. There are many other characteristics of media that influence their role. Innis largely drops his temporal/spatial characterisation when he deals with other factors pertaining to the social impact of media. Of particular importance are various factors, including supply of materials, ease of writing, and costs of production, that facilitate the emergence of media monopolies controlled by particular groups, or by a governing group. Innis recognises media monopolies of various kinds as of paramount importance at different times and in different places, but they do not sit easily in his temporal and spatial classification of media. This potential for monopoly arising from characteristics of media has direct relevance to the creation of an information interface through support-bargaining and money-bargaining and the potential for any single group to exercise control over the content of an information interface.

Empire and Communications is full of references to the monopoly of communications and breaks in the monopoly of communications. Innis was an admirer of Adam Smith,[30] who had strong opinions about monopoly. It might be said that the book is about the opportunities for monopoly of communications that arise with different media of communications. It is then something like a book about the control of the information interface. Different agencies develop different bargaining positions with regard to the purveyance of information, and can take advantage of their bargaining strength. The aim of any agency is to govern entirely the information that reaches the populace. Innis sees it as a tussle between the state and religious orders for ascendancy in propagation of information. Certain media, such as parchment, tend to give advantage to monastic agencies. Other media, such as paper, give advantage to the state. As in the industries of the money-bargaining system, certain characteristics, often related to technology, can bring about strong bargaining positions and in some cases monopoly bargaining positions. Media technology thus presents opportunities for support-bargaining agencies to assemble support and advance their bargaining positions through enhancement of their control of the information interface. Some idea of Innis' approach to monopoly may be derived from the following extracts:

> Inability [of monarchy and priesthood] to maintain the fusion and to develop a flexible religious and political organization was in part a result of a monopoly of knowledge which had been built up in relation to the papyrus roll and a complex system of writing . . . Dependence on stone as a medium provided the background of an absolute monarchy, but its monopoly position invited competition from papyrus and the development of a new monopoly dominated by religion and control over writing in the complex hieroglyphics . . . Monopoly over writing supported an emphasis on religion and the time concept which defeated efforts to solve the problem of space.[31]
>
> The monopoly power over writing exercised by religious institutions in Egypt and Babylonia was destroyed by the development of a new simplified type of writing which became the basis of new developments in communication and political organization shown in the Assyrian and the Persian empires.[32]

Supply characteristics of media such as papyrus and stone and the complexity of writing lent themselves to monopoly of information provision. Changes in the supply of papyrus affected monopoly positions and changed the societies experiencing them. Changes in writing had similar effects. Innis associates the changes in writing with his time concept, but the association is not based on a quality of the medium, but on the advantages derived by religion from a monopoly over writing. Diverse characteristics of media and the modes adopted for writing on them, not just their temporal status, offered opportunities for monopoly, or destroyed monopolies already created.

The process has to be seen in the context of the more general struggle for ascendancy. Authoritarian governments normally suppress information contrary to their interests simply by banning it, on pain of imprisonment or death. Whatever the media technology, such suppression is generally effective. Anyone disseminating information contrary to the interests of a ruling group risks arrest, whether he or she disseminates the information on parchment, papyrus, stone or paper, and whatever the complexity of the writing. Even now, when the internet makes it easier to circulate information than ever before, and the right of authorities to censor information is not taken for granted globally, authoritarian states are still able to censor the information reaching their people. Religious organisations have used similar means to suppress information adverse to their interests. The Roman Catholic Church excommunicated men like Martin Luther who challenged their authority. Luther narrowly escaped being burnt. Anyone reading anything on the 'Index' risked being asked to explain themselves to the Inquisition. Those who criticise Moslem faith today risk condemnation and even death from Islamic authorities. These contending political and social interests seek control of the information interface as central to their continued command over the levels of support that give them ascendancy in their communities. The technology of communications makes their task easier or more difficult – generally more difficult as the technology has evolved – but it is the support-bargaining process that drives the evolution of societies and gives them their character, rather than media technology in itself. The media technology is the means to the end, or the means by which certain functions are performed.

The social stability that Innis sees as achieved by a mix of temporal and spatial media is more the social stability that is achieved when 'the pen' assembles support that is consistent with the interests of 'the sword' and the sword provides the sort of protection under which the pen can pursue its concerns. Both have sought to control the information available in their sphere by developing strong bargaining positions in support-bargaining and money-bargaining systems. Both have aspired to monopoly positions in the provision of information. So long as they stick to their agreed spheres, and do not contradict one another too directly, there can be stability. It is the harmonisation of political support-bargaining and intellectual support-bargaining. The state is concerned with political support-bargaining, the church with intellectual support-bargaining, with important cross-currents. The nature of the media available is important to the efficacy with which each agent can achieve its purposes, but the media as technology are not the prime determinant of what is communicated. The media can facilitate or impede, but how they are used is mostly determined by ascendant groups. Innis is more to the point when he writes about monopoly of media than when he attempts to give media temporal and spatial character and derive from that a conflict between the state and religious groups. There is little idea of information as the critical requirement, but there is an idea that something is being monopolised, and being monopolised by one faction is being denied to another, and thereby stamping society with the character of the monopolists.

Characteristics of media: codification and transmission

In *The Evolution of Economies* a distinction is made between the codification of information and its transmission.[33] The nature of media is more apparent in the context of the codification of ideas and their transmission in codified form than through temporal and spatial characteristics. Codification and transmission identify the processes by which ideas are disseminated as information in an information interface, and hence how they influence the character of a society.

Transmission covers the transport systems that are essential to the dissemination of material media. This is the facet of media by which Innis mainly distinguishes their spatial dimension. Transmission covers also the later dissemination of information by electronic means, whether wired or wireless. Different forms of transmission have different costs. A transport infrastructure is expensive. Stone can be transported, but at substantial cost. Newspapers can be transported at low unit cost by rail. On the basis of 'cost per unit of information', digital transmission costs are very low.

Codification covers the expression or recording of the information itself. Information can be codified in spoken language or codified in written language on paper, parchment, papyrus, stone, or other materials, depending on availability and convenience. It can be recorded in complex hieroglyphics or with a simple phonetic alphabet. Technology means that writing entered on a keyboard can be converted into digital form, and transmitted in the same form. The durability of the material used may have some implications for its survival over time, but digital material survives in digital format, and newspapers, as Hugo suggests, have capacity for survival due to their ubiquity. Speech can perhaps be regarded as the most basic codification. It comes so naturally that it seems scarcely appropriate to regard it as a 'codification process'. But the codification is immediately apparent when we encounter someone speaking in a language whose codes we have not learnt. In societies in which few could read or write, the only linguistic codification intelligible to the majority would be speech. The 'oral tradition' would necessarily be important in such societies.

There are, as outlined in *Support-Bargaining, Economics and Society*, close links between the formation of ideas and language, so that sharp distinction of thought and language is probably not appropriate.[34] But language is still recognisably the codification of thought. Complex language is amongst the most outstandingly distinctive features of the human race. Up to about 1500 in Europe the information contained in the Bible was codified in Hebrew, Latin or Greek. As was seen, written codification in such languages gave those conversant in them strong bargaining positions as sources of certain essential information regarding the nature of deity. In the last sixty years or so economic theory has been increasingly codified in mathematical terms, giving mathematical economists strong bargaining positions as sources of essential economic information.

In an odd reversal of the normal sequence of codification, the thinking of economics, the concepts of neoclassical economics, have been adapted so that they can be codified in mathematical terms. As was seen in Chapter 4, the mathematical codification of economic relationships has distorted the understanding of the relationships. The requirements of mathematics have dictated what is thought. In the same way, it can be seen that language influences the way people think. Language lays down certain forms of expression, and thoughts tend to mould to the forms of language. It was suggested in *Support-Bargaining, Economics and Society*, and in Chapter 3, that the common linguistic form of an agent performing some action – the subject noun and active verb formulation – has given rise to personification as a common mode of thought.[35] Some linguistic philosophers, cited by Goldman and mentioned in Chapter 6, have understood this imposition of language on thought as being absolute; the total conditioning of thought by language. There is an implicit claim in neoclassical theory that mathematics has universal authority, whatever other observations suggest.

Access to techniques of codification confers bargaining strength. Ability to transmit information over distances extends bargaining sets and confers bargaining strength in the extended bargaining sets. Capacity to codify and transmit information hence gives influence and potentially a degree of control over the creation of the information interface, and hence influence and potentially a degree of control over a society. The distribution of capacity to codify and transmit, either as a matter of the natural occurrence of materials, or some other natural factors, or as a matter of social contrivance, or support-bargaining, dictates the strength of the bargaining positions of those who have such capacities, or the degree of monopoly they achieve. These factors, more than any temporal or spatial character of media, lie behind the influence of the media on their societies.

As with transmission, different codification processes also have different cost implications. The impact of the Gutenberg press derived from the reduction of costs it achieved relative to those of copyists. Cost is of particular importance with regard to social impact, whether in relation to codification or transmission. The Gutenberg press sparked an 'information revolution' because of its cost characteristics, and the internet has sparked another. An 'information revolution' was essential to the 'industrial revolution', because support-bargaining and money-bargaining run on information. The major expansion in economic and political activity that constituted the industrial revolution required commensurate expansion in the availability of information.[36] Low cost means that the monopolies of the rich, especially rich governments and rich religious organisations, are at risk. Almost anyone can disseminate their opinions.

Innis' analysis suggests that the different media impose temporal or spatial characteristics on a society, dictating whether it will have a centralised or decentralised governing structure and whether religious orders will flourish. Innis' analysis moves from era to era with confusing facility, so that the precise media available at any time is seldom clear. But it seems that much of the time state and church could select the medium they used, and would select the medium that best suited their purpose. One available medium did not necessarily dictate what they could do. They could choose the type of codification and the type of transmission that best suited their purpose. A monastic order would opt for the sort of medium that would preserve their scriptures for succeeding generations of monks. Durable codification is required; spatial transmission is of little or no importance. The administration of an empire, however, is likely to require transmission of information over distances. It has to be codified in a form that can be rolled or folded and put into a protective container. It must withstand the rigours of transmission by runners, riders or water transport. The end, or the function, dictates the means, the medium, that is chosen.

Innis' derivation of ideas on communications from his studies of the Canadian pulp and paper industry has a parallel in the derivation of Victor Hugo's ideas on the impact of media from his contemplation of Notre-Dame de Paris. Both evolutionary chains are rather narrow, in that they take a particular starting point and pursue its implications, with little regard for other aspects of the societies in which they are placed. They stress too much the influence of their inspiring origins. Christian scriptures seem more important to European civilisation than the great cathedrals. The cathedrals are impressive, but their impact, and the significance of their decoration, depend to a degree on some acquaintance with the scriptures. They are embellishments of ideas established through other media. Their function is to illustrate, persuade and inspire. They are not the whole story, or a story in themselves. The essential ideas were codified in writing before they were re-codified in stone. Furthermore, it was the ideas that were codified, rather than the medium of codification, that impacted society.

In the same way, Innis' thesis exaggerates the role of temporal and spatial characteristics of media as influences on the character of societies. The main factors formative of societies are something else. States and churches take advantage of the opportunities for codification and transmission of their ideas. The options influence the formation of the information interface, and hence the character of societies, but they are not the primary influence on social order. Societies evolve through a process of support-bargaining and money-bargaining, which brings into play a great number of influences. The role of the media becomes apparent only with the identification of the importance of the creation and use of an information interface as an essential part of the process of support-bargaining and money-bargaining.

Poe's follow-up to Innis

Marshall Poe recognises the value of Innis' fundamental idea regarding the effects of different media on the social and political character of societies, but regrets the style of exposition. He endeavours to provide a more detailed and better substantiated account of the effects of different media on their societies, ranging from the spoken word, through manuscript writing and the printing press, to audio-visual media (radio, television, telephones, etc.) and the internet. He identifies first the character of the 'networks' that each medium gives rise to – whether it is, for example, dialogic or monologic, extensive or intensive. He then identifies what he takes to be fundamental human traits or needs – for example, need for power, or secrecy, or human curiosity. From the combination of media network attributes and human needs he identifies consequent social practices – for example, equalised or hierarchicalised, hedonised or economised – and cultural values – such as egalitarianism or elitism, hedonism or asceticism.

Poe encounters difficulties similar to those of Innis, though he recognises them himself. Starting from particular types of media, it is difficult to derive clear-cut identification of social practices and cultural values. The great variety of societies that arose in the manuscript era, the period dominated by manual writing, and in the era of print suggests that a particular medium can give rise to many kinds of society. Poe writes at one point that, 'Taken together, we argued, these [media] attributes predictably led to the formation of certain sorts of media networks in the Manuscript Era, and these networks predictably led to the evolution of certain social practices and rules'.[37] So the links are held to be so strong as to make possible firm predictions regarding the nature of society that will arise. But this assertion is followed immediately by the comment: 'We need to keep firmly in our minds that writing doesn't always produce these effects or, where it does, always to the same extent'. In other words, the linkages are not so strong as to make prediction possible. This comment on the manuscript medium is echoed in a comment on print medium: 'Of course, print doesn't necessarily nurture these effects, or, when it does to the same degree'.[38] Almost exactly the same phrasing is used with regard to audio-visual media and the internet.[39] If the consequences of each media type for social practices and cultural values are uncertain, the consequences when all the media are operative at the same time would seem to be anyone's guess. It may be, moreover, that factors other than the prevailing media type are important in determining social practices and cultural values.

Poe's conclusion is perhaps stronger than his analysis justifies:

> Organized interests – churches, states, parties, corporations – have tried to rein in print for centuries. They have done so in the pursuit of godliness and godlessness, democracy and domination, liberalism and conservatism, capitalism and communism. But nowhere have they ever really succeeded. In almost every case, print did what print naturally does. This is part of the reason why modern societies from North Korea to the United States, all look 'modern' as regards print. They uniformly have large, diversified print industries. Some are government-run and others private, but all are nominally devoted to enlightening and entertaining 'the people'.[40]

The evidence is rather that churches, states, parties and corporations have used the media to further their ends or objectives. The objectives were shaped by dominant social groups in political and intellectual support-bargaining. In some cases, political parties saw that their objectives could only be achieved through total control of their societies and, as necessary adjunct, total control of the information interface. Such parties brought the media under their direct control, as in the Soviet Union, China and North Korea. In other societies, intellectual support-bargaining produced more complex forms of government that kept some sort of balance between the freedom of individuals and the dominance of the group, as expressed through government. These objectives implied freedom of individuals and organisations to post information to an information interface, as the means by which citizens could know the situation and identify their interests. Print may have done what it 'naturally' does. Poe assesses it under eight headings, starting with 'Accessibility', 'Privacy', Fidelity'.[41] But Poe's analysis makes clear that what it might 'naturally' do with regard to the state of society is not predictable. It can lead to almost any sort of society. It produces cultural values that include egalitarianism, hedonism and pluralism. It also produces values of dictatorism and collectivism.[42] Print did what the organisations involved made it do. In some societies it was made to push the party line. In other societies it produced a great variety of different information calculated to advance different interests. 'Enlightening and entertaining the people' are not the first words that spring to mind for the aims of North Korean authorities. Accepting such a phrase under the qualification 'nominally' merely underlines a lack of awareness of the systematic use of the information interface to deceive, or a decision to ignore such use. Print media in North Korea, along with all other media, are devoted to maintaining the ascendancy of the ruling group.

The printing press is a means to an end. It makes it more difficult to meet some ends; easier to meet others. It undoubtedly facilitates the functioning of an open support-bargaining society, since free flows of information and the creation of an information interface are essential to such societies. But the existence of printing presses is not sufficient to bring about such a society. The exercise of violence, outcomes of political support-bargaining, and support assembled through intellectual support-bargaining will determine whether printing presses are permitted in a society, who can own and operate them, and what sort of material they can disseminate.

Poe is aware, more than Innis, of the 'other factors' that impinge on the state of society and its values. In his coverage of the 'age of speech' he refers to 'big men' and 'little men' as a shorthand for the 'political' influences that lie outside the scope of his analysis. In the coverage of the manuscript era he refers to 'princes and priests' or to 'the elite'. The precise role of these people is not defined. According to the present thesis, it is not possible to give a satisfactory account of the exercise of power without an understanding of support-bargaining.

Poe nevertheless provides an account of the emergence of print to a dominant role amongst media in the West by reference to external factors.[43] He suggests that it was not the invention of the printing press in Europe by Gutenberg that brought in the print era. The various components of the technology of printing – stamping, movable type, mechanical presses, stable media – had been known for decades and in some cases for centuries. They had also been combined in various forms for the purpose of printing. What caused the emergence of the printing press to its dominant role was, according to Poe, the 'pull' exerted by three factors: the emergence of capitalism, the growth of bureaucracy and the growing inclination of ordinary people to read religious texts. These interests nurtured skills in reading and writing and a demand for printed material. Mercantile capitalism required, 'catalogues, contracts, sureties, indemnities, orders, delivery schedules, transit papers, bills of lading, inventories, receipts, invoices, account books, tax documents, bank statements and so on'.[44] The development of mercantile capitalism was led successively by the city states of Italy, the Dutch Republic, and London. The presiding authorities encouraged such developments because of the revenues they provided to the public budget.[45] Similarly, bureaucracy required, 'laws, regulations, guidelines, directives, writs, summons, warrants, reports, white papers, memos, registers, indexes, and so on'.[46] Religious groups were coming round to the idea that their adherents should be able to read, even if they were strongly inclined to control what they read. Poe records that even Martin Luther, 'went back and forth on the issue of whether every believer was "priest" enough to interpret scripture in his or her own way'.[47] But once broached the idea was accepted and unstoppable. The demand for written material gave rise to Gutenberg's printing press and the spread of its usage across the relatively free world.

Poe recognises, in effect, that the printing press evolved as a technology. It existed in various forms well before Gutenberg set up his press.[48] Finding a suitable ink seems to have been a major concern of Gutenberg. This is the pattern subsequently experienced in the industrial revolution in Britain. Technologies existed in various forms and were gradually refined. The refinement included most importantly the emergence of a technology with unit cost characteristics that made it possible to use it in viable company formats. The vendor sets identified by Poe, relating to merchant capitalism, bureaucracy and religious texts, provided the opportunities for establishing viable businesses. If the budgets of a sufficient number of capitalists, bureaucrats and religious readers were of a size to accommodate the price of material implied by its unit cost of production utilising the new technology of the printing press, then a printer could make a living. Subject to his or her assessment of the risks of ending up in confinement, on a rack, hanging from a gibbet, or burning at a stake, the prospect of profit would be attractive. It proved to be of sufficient attraction to sufficient numbers to bring about a revolution in the dissemination of information and the growth and content of the information interface.

Poe sees the new requirements for printed materials amongst mercantile capitalists, bureaucrats and religious readers as emerging from the general course of social change. But low-priced material from printers would itself have attracted new readers and stimulated demand for instruction in reading. The new demand would in part have been a consequence of the commercial effort put into the production and sale of printed texts. Printers would then, as now, have the commercial instinct to adapt their output to the circumstances and tastes of their vendor sets. As well as the 'pull' of demand, there would be the 'push' of printers selling their services. There is no 'product' that can be so readily adapted to the requirements of potential buyers as information.

The same revolution did not happen in East Asia, where the technologies of the printing press were largely available. Poe attributes the failing to the lack of demand for reading material of the type he identifies in Europe. He writes:

> Millions and millions of texts were printed and found their way all over East Asia. Yet there was no "Print Revolution" in East Asia. In Europe, the introduction of print was associated with a massive increase in the amount of text produced, in the speed with which texts circulated, and in the proportion of the population that could read them. In East Asia it was associated with none of these things. Why the difference?[49]

Poe suggests that the difference was the expanding demand in Europe from merchant capitalism, bureaucracy and religious people. But it may also be that the proliferation of money-bargaining organisations formatted for the profitable production of printed texts was more tolerable to governments in the West than to those of East Asia. In East Asia, the risks for printers of confinement or worse were perhaps too high to permit the emergence of a print revolution. This factor is the more important if it is recognised that the printers themselves were instrumental in Europe in generating sales of printed material. If printers in East Asian societies had had the freedoms of Western printers, they might have generated comparable expansion in reading through the provision of interesting, useful, instructive and entertaining texts at prices that could be accommodated in the budgets of potential buyers.

Understood in this way, the emphasis with regard to the origins of the print revolution is thrown back again onto Gutenberg and his printing press. The press made it possible for printers to offer products at such low cost that they stimulated a major expansion in reading, literacy and use of printed material. The basic technology may have been around for many years before, but the Gutenberg press marked an evolution of the technology to a form in which the production of printed texts became a profitable business proposition.

Marshall McLuhan: medium and messages

McLuhan is the 'star' of media theory, with an ascendancy that seems unmatched in any other sphere of enquiry. McLuhan's theories are encapsulated in the arresting comment, 'The medium is the message'. His message seems bound up in the interpretation of this remark. He himself clearly attached great importance to it. It is the title of the first chapter of his book *Understanding Media*.

Followers and opponents of McLuhan have debated its meaning. For a statement that is central to the work of a writer so ascendant in his field there is remarkably little agreement on what it means. That would probably have pleased McLuhan. His theory is set out in such a way as to suggest he is not primarily concerned with provision of a clear account of the functioning of media. Rather he is making assertions and looking for reactions – what one might call 'poking around'. He is the 'provocateur'. The technique has proved remarkably successful in arousing interest and assembling support, but not successful in advancing the understanding of media. The weaknesses of McLuhan's theories become plainly apparent in the context of support-bargaining and an information interface.

Sidney Finkelstein interprets McLuhan as maintaining that the content of a communication, in the common sense, is of no importance:

> 'The medium is the message' means, to McLuhan, that, in any form of communication or artistic expression, what is consciously or purposefully 'said' is of no importance. Equally unimportant is 'the way it is said'. Important only is the medium through which it is said.[50]

Finkelstein continues immediately to explain what he regards as McLuhan's essential thesis:

> A medium is also a technology and creates a new environment. Thus it alters the mind and senses of the people in that environment. This alteration is the real message, the only message that counts.

Graeme Patterson challenges Finkelstein's understanding of the significance of content as common but wrong:

> The necessity of distinguishing form from content underlay his famous slogan 'the medium is the message' which, contrary to the opinion of many, did not mean that content is of no importance. It meant rather that content itself should be thought of as form, the content of any medium being always another medium.[51]

Thus, the content, or what is normally taken as the message, is a medium. So it seems that 'the medium is the message', but also, 'the message is a medium'.

As has been seen, Poe regards McLuhan as the starting point for media theory, mainly on the strength of his expression, 'the medium is the message'. Yet Poe, contrary to this expression, sees McLuhan's originality as lying in his separation of the medium from the message:

> He separated the medium from the message and, in so doing, founded the central program of modern media studies, that which attempts to describe and explain the effects of media on the human mind and human groups.[52]

The comment asserts separation of media from message. It also suggests a focus of media study on psychological impact, rather than on the social impact of media activity. Media have an impact on the way people think; forget the impact that media reports have on societies. People do not consciously receive messages in the ordinary way; rather 'messages' deriving unrecognised from media technology affect their psychological condition. There are thus markedly different accounts of what is meant by 'the medium is the message' and its significance.

McLuhan would presumably not be concerned at such confusion. In the first paragraph of his first chapter he states:

> it is sometimes a bit of a shock to be reminded that, in operational and practical fact, the medium is the message. This is merely to say that the personal and social consequences of any medium – that is, of any extension of ourselves – result from the new scale that is introduced into our affairs by each extension of ourselves, or by any new technology.[53]

McLuhan thus introduces at the outset aspects of his characteristic exposition. Positions are imputed to others that they do not hold – we cannot be shocked to be reminded of something we did not have in mind. He asserts as obvious, or self-evident, what is highly dubious – a medium is not immediately recognisable as an extension of ourselves. And he is vague to the point of vacuity – a 'new scale' is nothing when defined as arising from each extension of ourselves. Clearly, McLuhan either does not intend to communicate clear ideas, or is not capable of doing so, or does not have any.

McLuhan does not hold, as Finkelstein suggests, that content has no importance. It has no importance in the way that it is normally understood as important – that is, in conveying information about ideas, activities or events. But it is important as a distraction: 'Indeed, it is only too typical that the "content" of any medium blinds us to the character of the medium'.[54] 'Content' is not only another medium, as Patterson has it in the above quotation, but is also a distraction.

McLuhan refers to Cubism as illustration and elaboration of his thesis regarding the impact of technology:

> Cubism, by seizing on instant total awareness, suddenly announced that *the medium is the message.* Is it not evident that the moment that sequence yields to the simultaneous, one is in the world of the structure and of configuration? . . . Specialized segments of attention have shifted to total field, and we can now say, 'The medium is the message' quite naturally. Before the electric speed and total field, it was not obvious that the medium is the message. The message, it seemed, was the 'content,' as people used to ask what a painting was *about.*[55]

The conventional view of the importance of content is castigated as a dangerous diversion from the real effects of media. The 'content' is another medium that heightens the impact of the primary medium:

> Our conventional response to all media, namely that it is how they are used that counts, is the numb stance of the technological idiot. For the "content" of a medium is like the juicy piece of meat carried by the burglar to distract the watchdog of the mind. The effect of the medium is made strong and intense just because it is given another medium as 'content'.

Much later, McLuhan confirms the concept of two mediums, a technological medium and a content medium. He remarks: 'Except for light, all other media come in pairs with one acting as the "content" of the other, obscuring the operation of both'.[56] He conceives electric light as a medium without content,[57] but performing the same function as a communications medium:

> If the student of media will but meditate on the power of the medium of electric light to transform every structure of time and space and work and society it penetrates or contacts, he will have the key to the form of power that is in all media to reshape any lives they touch.[58]

But an electric light is not a medium in the sense of communications medium. It does not have content, in the sense of imparting information about ideas, activities or events. It is a technology with a function, or end; that of producing light.

We are dealing with two 'mediums' and two 'messages'. A 'medium' in usage 1 and a 'message' in usage 1 are getting mixed up with a 'medium' in usage 2 and a 'message' in usage 2. The 'medium' in usage 1 is a technology; in usage 2, it is the medium of content. The 'message' in usage 1 is a psychological impact of technology, affecting the behaviour of those experiencing it, while the 'message' in usage 2 is the message of what is commonly regarded as content. Combining the medium as technology in usage 1 and the message in usage 1 as the psychological impact of technology gives the sense identified by both Finkelstein and Poe. Media technology has a psychological impact that can be construed as a 'message', affecting the behaviour of those experiencing it.

This sense clashes with the common sense of a medium as technology in usage 1 conveying a message in usage 2 as content. A message is codified in a certain medium for transmission to its intended audience. Since this is the normal understanding of a medium and its function, the comment that 'the medium is the message' seems odd. McLuhan, however, regards this 'content' message, usage 2, as a distraction from what is important, the psychological impact of the technology. He uses the analogy, as quoted above, of a guard dog distracted by a juicy steak while a burglar goes about his business.

McLuhan contends that there is a content medium, a usage 2 medium, corresponding to the content message, the usage 2 message. He asserts that:

> The effect of the medium is made strong and intense just because it is given another medium as 'content'. The content of a movie is a novel or a play or an opera. The effect of the movie form is not related to its program content. The 'content' of writing or print is speech, but the reader is almost entirely unaware either of print or of speech.[59]

The medium is here elided with the content. A novel, a play and an opera would all be commonly understood as media. Information is codified in writing, in speech or in music and transmitted in the adopted medium to an audience. It is easy to confuse content with medium. Language melds with ideas and information. If questioned about the content of a movie like *Gone with the Wind*, the straightforward answer would be that it is a story about romance, civil war and family tragedy in the Southern States of America. But the answer could conceivably be that it is the novel *Gone with the Wind*. The film derives from the novel, so in a sense the 'content' is the novel. The content of a book is, in a very literal sense, 'print'. When Polonius asks Hamlet 'What do you read, my lord?' Hamlet, feigning madness, or winding up Polonius, replies, 'Words, words, words'. Polonius follows with: 'What is the matter, my lord?' And Hamlet tells him what the words are about. McLuhan exploits the ambiguity of 'content'. Recast in the context of 'messages', or 'information', it is clear that the significant content is the information that is imparted by the film. The message of the novel is the information and ideas about romance and civil war in the Southern States. This message is re-codified in pictures and sound in the film.

McLuhan contends that the novel, the play or the opera that he describes as the content of a movie constitute a content medium. But that is only so if 'content' is understood not as message or information, but as a literal kind of content. It is content as 'words, words, words', rather than content as 'matter'. If Hamlet is being perverse, so too is McLuhan. The 'message' of the film is the information and ideas it imparts to its audience. There is then no second medium, a usage 2 medium, carrying content. What McLuhan conceives as the content medium is an alternative codification of the information that is to be transmitted.

McLuhan seems to suggest also that the 'content' of writing or print is speech, so that writing or print carries a second medium associated with content. But here again the word 'content' is used to mislead. The content, in the sense of message, or information, conveyed by writing or print is what the language of the writing means according to the agreed conventions of linguistic codification. Writing may be read out aloud; it can be translated into the medium of speech, which is to give it a different codification. But the information imparted will be much the same, with allowance for the different inflections of meaning that can be achieved with speech. The message can be discerned either by reading the writing or listening to the speech.

Message and information

McLuhan can fade the 'usage 2' sense of message into next to nothing, a mere distraction, because he has no idea of the role of information in the advance of political, social and economic interests in a bargaining society. He has no conception of the dependence of all agents of a bargaining system on the acquisition of information for evaluation of their own position and advantage and the dissemination of information that will persuade others to sympathetic acceptance of their interests. The 'message' substitutes for 'information', but the word 'message' does not carry the implications of 'information'. The word 'content', which might be understood as 'information content', is ambiguous, as used by McLuhan, as to whether it refers to information content or medium content. A 'message' is information that is already codified and ready for transmission, or already transmitted. It is both 'writing' and 'information'. It is possible for people to receive a message without receiving information. If they received a message and lost it, they would not receive the information it contained. If they received a message not intended for them, they would probably receive information that was irrelevant to them, and would perhaps not understand it, or would ignore it.

'Information' is being confused with its codified form; information imparted is being confused with the codified message which carries it. 'Words, words, words' may be confounded with the information they carry. Information can be codified in various media, including speech, print, film, radio and television. Each is used according to the purposes and capacities of those wishing to send information. Each has implications for the creation and control of an information interface. Each offers different opportunities for the manipulation of information. Like all technology, each has implications for the conduct of support-bargaining and money-bargaining. But their essential function is the codification of information for transmission to others. The failure to understand the role of 'information' and the failure to distinguish information from its codification means that McLuhan has nothing to go in his messages, except the ambiguous 'content'. He avoids use of the word 'information' because his thesis requires that he avoids its implications. People will be interested to hear that a new supermarket has opened in their vicinity, that there is a forecast of rain and floods for their neighbourhood, that a favourite film star will shortly be on screen at their local cinema, or that their income tax is to rise by ten per cent. They will receive much the same information whether they receive it from a neighbour, a newspaper, from radio or from television. If, when they receive the information from radio or television, they are told that the information is of no account, a mere distraction, while the media technology is changing their sensibilities, they may wonder whether the people at the universities are as clever as they are reputed to be. McLuhan treats messages not as imparting information, but as themselves the objects of transmission and reception, becoming media themselves. With that kind of preconception, it is easy to dismiss 'content' as mere distraction.

That McLuhan can write of 'understanding media' with little or no reference to 'information' is a consequence of the general lack of recognition of the functioning of support-bargaining and money-bargaining systems and their creation and use of an information interface. Information is often treated as factual, or neutral with regard to interest. If it is not so, it is simply because bad people are providing it. It is also commonly treated as unitary, a kind of commodity, a 'product' devoid of variety. With that understanding, it is easy enough to confound information with a 'message' or a medium. The nature of information becomes apparent only with the idea of support-bargaining and money-bargaining and the creation of an information interface. Information is of infinite variety, and the particular variety that is important to any agent is that which is relevant to the circumstances of that agent. Information has to be relevant to interests, deriving from some understanding of physical and social situation, or from a theoretical frame of reference. A buyer in a money-bargaining system requires information about the features of a product relative to his or her understanding of their situation. Information is thus extremely diverse.

McLuhan's insistence that the content of a film is a novel, a play or an opera seems to derive from his desire to separate 'electric' technological media from other media. The 'electric' media technology conveys a psychological message which other media do not. The movie medium is electric technology and separate from the novel, play or opera that, according to McLuhan, are its medium content. McLuhan did not separate the medium from the message, as Poe contends. He elided medium and message by insisting on a psychological message inherent in a technology, a usage 1 message necessarily bound up with a technological medium.

Yet Poe is right in the sense that McLuhan separated technological medium and inherent psychological message from the ordinary understanding of a medium used to convey a message carrying information. McLuhan associates medium with a technological medium message, and in doing so dissociates medium from the information it conveys. The distinction led to attempts to 'describe and explain the effects of media on the human mind and human groups'. McLuhan 'focused scholarly attention on the media themselves – talking, writing, printing, electronic signals – as opposed to the information the media convey'.[60] It is breathtaking that such a device could so distract scholars that they ignore the manifest impact of the transmission of information on the state of societies. While neoclassical economists assume 'perfect information', media scholars ignore information almost entirely, or mistake it for something else. The nature of information has flummoxed social scientists.

The difficulties McLuhan has in sustaining his argument over the importance of technology and the irrelevance of information are apparent in his treatment of the 1960 Nixon–Kennedy television debates. Some say the debates cost Nixon the presidency in that year. McLuhan recognises that different presentation of Nixon, along the lines of the 'doggedly creative and modest performer' on the piano that had been presented in an earlier TV appearance, might have altered the result: 'A few timely touches like this would have quite altered the result of the Nixon–Kennedy campaign'.[61] That is, a different selection and different manipulation of information concerning the personality of Nixon would have changed the information disseminated to the information interface and changed the distribution of support between Nixon and Kennedy. McLuhan's own account seems initially to make clear that it was not a matter of the technology by which the debate was transmitted, but a matter of how media people manipulated the information that was transmitted. It seems to illustrate the point that it is the information conveyed by the technology that is important, and not the technology itself. But rather than acknowledge an explanation so destructive of his whole thesis, McLuhan produces a curiously artificial and evasive argument. He argues that television is a 'cool' medium, rather than a 'hot' medium, like newspapers or radio. A 'cool' medium is not suited to the portrayal of controversial topics, but is rather suited to involvement 'in *depth*'.[62] Hence Nixon as a sensitive pianist would be more attuned to the technology than Nixon the abrasive confronter of issues. Presenting Nixon as a sensitive pianist would have got a better reaction from viewers, because it would have been better attuned to the characteristics of the medium. But even if it were true that television had this characteristic, the important factor would still be the sort of information about Nixon that was transmitted. The medium might help in the acceptance of the information by its audience, just as poetry helps to promote acceptance. It would be open to a media person wanting to discredit someone like Nixon to present information suggesting an abrasive and confrontational personality in a medium that was unsympathetic to such a style. Different media offer different opportunities for manipulation, but it is still the information conveyed that is important in achieving desired results from a transmission. The information it contains is what is important about any message.

McLuhan was not the first to recognise that a medium has an impact, or conveys a message, independently of the information in the message it transmits. Victor Hugo's understanding of the role of stone and architecture makes the point very clearly. There is, and perhaps always has been, a strong recognition that the media by which information is conveyed affects the way people react to it. Speech, particularly in the form of rhetoric and debate, was recognised as having a crucial effect on what was conveyed, especially with regard to the interpretation of what was conveyed. Poe quotes Plato extolling the virtues of dialectic, or debate, over writing.[63] Innis cites Socrates as the great exponent of an oral tradition disrupted by writing. The medium of expression had an effect, independent of the information consciously purveyed.[64] Innis notes the influence of writing on thought: 'Writing enormously enhanced a capacity for abstract thinking which had been evident in the growth of language in the oral tradition',[65] though he later refers to the written tradition as a 'dead hand' at certain periods.[66] In all matters where means are used to an end, the means themselves affect both the people using the means and the end they seek. The technology used in an industry affects the output of an industry. It also has a psychological impact. Railways and air travel are widely recognised as having affected our sense of space. Electric lighting drove back 'the forces of darkness'. The industrial revolution changed the individual and collective psychology of the nations which experienced it. Everything around us affects us psychologically. As described in Chapter 3, our psychology steers us along without our being conscious of it. It would be exceptional if media technology had no psychological effects. But it is invariably the case that the psychological effects of technology are seen, if they are seen at all, as subordinate to its output. In the case of communications media, it is the information they convey that is important. Their importance arises from the importance of information to the conduct of societies. McLuhan certainly gave an original account of the relationship between media and what they convey, but his account depends on deep ignorance or total disregard of the role of information in societies. The survival and prominence of his theories is no doubt partly attributable to the distinctive impact that the 'electric' media do have, but there is a better explanation of their impact.

The distinctive impact of 'electric' media

The distinctive impact of 'electric' media derives from their presentation of information in the form of perceptual information. Film and television utilise our visual sense, which we commonly use when accessing directly the real world of experience. Film and television make testimonial information into perceptual information. While we assimilate testimonial information with caution, we assimilate perceptual information with conviction. The content of films and television is easily and confidently assimilated, even though it is testimonial information. Print is recognised as testimonial information and assimilated with more difficulty and greater reservation. What McLuhan interprets as the impact of 'electric' media technology is the impact of perceptual information, very like that which we encounter in seemingly direct experience of reality, but artificially produced. Testimonial information is experienced as perceptual information. It opens up new scope for conveyance of information, new scope for manipulation, new scope for establishing in the information interface information conducive to the interests of those controlling the media. It constitutes a new 'perceptual–testimonial' category by which information is assimilated. McLuhan confuses these effects of different forms of information codification and transmission with a psychological impact of technology. His focus on technology and neglect of the idea of information cause him to miss these important distinctions.

One central issue for McLuhan concerns the 'wholeness' of the experience associated with the electric medium. He attributes the sense of 'wholeness' to the technology of the medium itself, particularly its speed.[67] He emphasises the 'fragmentary' nature of non-electric media and contrasts it with the 'wholeness' of electric media, but the 'wholeness' is only a consequence of the speeding up of the fragmentary images. The sense of 'wholeness' derives from the facility with which perceptual information is assimilated and the confidence we have in it, rather than anything specifically technological. We assimilate written information in, as McLuhan says, a linear process. We also take it in, as Poe says, with some effort. It does not come naturally.[68] We are also more suspicious of testimonial information than we are of perceptual information. Our evolution equipped us to receive visual information and interpret it instantaneously and with confidence, as a condition of our survival. We take in whole scenes, whole situations, because we are equipped to recognise patterns. Our brains give it the 'stamp of approval' that is peculiar to perceptual information. That is what makes the electric media so special. The medium is not the message. It is just that the message, the content, the information, transmitted as moving pictures, is very readily taken in by us and assimilated with much more confidence than information received from a print medium.

This ease of assimilation of the visual media leaves us more open to the manipulation of information than we are with written information. We treat the cinematic images with the same confidence as we treat 'real' visual information. We trust our senses. We trust 'the evidence of our own eyes', even though it is evidence that someone has chosen to put before our eyes. With printed information, as was seen in Chapter 3, information is manipulated by choice of words and by imputation of motivations to agents of the bargaining system. In film and television there is a whole new range of opportunity for the manipulation of information. Cameras frame, select and exclude. What they frame and select can be designed to create favourable or unfavourable associations in the minds of viewers. They can rest on a scene or move rapidly on. They can be close-up or panoramic; angled up for one effect, angled down for another. It is the job of actors to make us believe what is not true. Boundaries between real life and fiction are blurred. Fiction and fact are blended, with the fiction used to assemble emotional support for dubious fact. We can be made to experience the purest fiction as if it were real life, and such skills are used in the propagation not just of the purest fiction but to assemble support relating to matters of real political and social significance and outcomes accordant with the interests of the agents controlling or commissioning the transmissions. Sophisticated viewers may retain an idea of whether they are watching fiction or a genuine attempt to present documentary evidence of real life. They may consciously withhold their support from ideas encountered in presentations they identify as fictitious. But even sophisticated viewers may find that in the course of time they are not certain whether some event or report was real or fictitious. They may find themselves supporting certain ideas because they were associated with 'the good guys' in some fictional representation. Ordinary viewers will give what they see through the media much the same credence as they give to what they see when they walk down the street. They will rarely agonise over what is fact, what is fiction and what is misleading.

Perceptual information and its assimilation prominently involve the identification of patterns. Our sense of symmetry enables us to understand and evaluate symmetric forms very rapidly and with conviction. McLuhan's ideas of pattern, 'total field', holism and other qualities relating to the 'wholeness' of experience are plainly related to the sense of symmetry. McLuhan contrasts the 'integral configuration', 'pattern' and 'conjunction' of the electric media with the 'fragmentary' and 'sequential' characteristics of older media.[69] Movies produce instantaneous understanding of the world, in contrast to the laborious assimilation of the texts of written media. In movies, one can 'see at a glance' what is going on, rather than having to piece together a full picture as a sum of separately imparted fragments. It was suggested in *Support-Bargaining, Economics and Society* that a part of our minds functions as a 'symmetry computer', enabling us to assess how our observations and experience fit together.[70] These symmetry computers readily go to work on movies. This is the dominant natural mode of selection and understanding of humans since they emerged as a species. The electronic media have given it greater scope. They have also made it possible for testimonial information, including highly manipulated and false information, to be given the symmetrical visual forms which are most easily assimilated by humans and carry most conviction with humans.

The importance of the sense of symmetry is apparent also in McLuhan's references to Cubism. 'Total awareness', the 'simultaneous' and 'total field', as in the quotation above at note 55, suggest the immediacy of the recognition of symmetry. McLuhan insists that it is this 'total awareness' that is important, not the 'content' of the painting. People should not ask what the painting is *about*, what information it conveys. McLuhan is perhaps right – art needs to have impact through its symmetries, rather than through the information it conveys. But he was surely wrong to imply that concern for the information conveyed was old fashioned. Certainly nowadays all the avant-garde visual art comes with copious instruction on the enlightenment it brings to society. Such information seems even to substitute for symmetry.

Visual impact and the medium of stone

McLuhan refers extensively to artists and writers. If he had studied Victor Hugo he would perhaps have found a better explanation of the impact of electric media than its technology. Notre-Dame de Paris has a visual impact analogous to that of film. It is 'wholeness' and instantaneous understanding. It conveys testimonial information about the nature of Christianity and religious faith through the visual sensations excited by the cathedral and its sculpture. We experience the conviction peculiar to information received through visual sense. Christ and the saints, angels and devils, and things we would rather not talk about, are all there, just as we think, expect or fear. Perhaps more than anything, it is symmetry. The architects of the great cathedrals knew the importance of pattern or symmetry in the human assimilation of messages. We recognise symmetry, even broken symmetry, as 'truth'. The cathedrals are chock-full of awesome symmetries that leave the human mind struggling to absorb the enormity of the truth it is encountering. That response reinforces the message of the awesome divinity of God as portrayed in the scriptures. The symmetries reinforce the message and the conviction. It is used for that purpose by the architect, the media manager, who creates the building. Ecclesiastical authorities used buildings and their symmetries to drive home the assertions of their faith. The cathedrals manipulate information to a purpose just as do television programmes and films.

Oddly, given McLuhan's neglect of Hugo's ideas, if any sense can be made of 'the medium is the message', it is in the context of the great mediaeval cathedrals. They were created to convey a very specific message, or unitary piece of information: the truth of Christian faith. The medium conveys a message, and the message can be conceived as just the one piece of information about the Christian faith. There is an integration of medium, message and unitary information. The cathedrals constitute themselves a part of the information interface, expressing in visual form a frame of reference that their constructors wanted others to adopt. The electric media do not achieve this. Their technology was developed to convey many messages, with a great variety of information. The translation of testimonial information into perceptual information, on which their impact depends, is not specific to any element of the information they convey. The medium is not integrated with messages and the information they contain, even if it presents all information in perceptual form. Hugo maintains that the cathedrals conveyed information about much more than Christian faith, but the overwhelming predominance of the Christian message is apparent. Hugo argues that the book will kill the edifice because of its durability, ubiquity and cost advantages, but the real advantage of print lies in the great variety of information it can convey. The edifice is specific to its message; print is a means for the conveyance of a great volume and variety of information. The electric media have similar capacity.

Control of the media

The importance of information to the advance of interests implies importance of control over the dissemination of information. Lacking understanding of information, McLuhan has no understanding of the importance of its control. The very vehemence of his opposition to anything that suggests the importance of control over the media is perhaps indicative of concern that he might have missed something. As was seen above, he dismisses the idea that the importance of the media may lie in how they are used as 'the numb stance of the technological idiot'. General Sarnoff is McLuhan's technological idiot. He quotes with scorn a comment of General Sarnoff to the effect that technology is not in itself good or bad; its value depends on how it is used. General Sarnoff clearly meant that it is the information that is disseminated by the technology, and beyond that the people who determine what is disseminated, that is the critical factor in determination of what is 'good' or 'bad' about technology. Those who determined what information would be purveyed through the Nixon–Kennedy debate clearly had significant scope to influence the outcome of the US presidential election. It was suggested in *The Evolution of Economies* that the media industry, though relatively small in monetary terms, played a role in the industrial revolution in Britain comparable with that of the largest industries.[71]

McLuhan's emphasis on technology seems wilfully to dismiss the overwhelming importance of the function of media and media organisations in providing information that influences the distribution of support in societies and hence influences the conduct of societies. Media organisations disseminate information to the information interface where it is used by agents engaged in support-bargaining and money-bargaining. Those disseminating information use all the resources at their command to get their information established, accepted and used by the agents they wish to influence in the way they wish to influence them. McLuhan effectively diverted attention from the media as people and organisations to the medium as impersonal and unaccountable technology. The subsequent study of media has, as Poe implies, followed McLuhan in pursuing the psychological impact of media technology rather than evaluating their role as purveyors of information in society.

The diversion was welcomed in particular by those who controlled the media. McLuhan received support across the media industry. The theory was well aligned with their interests, particularly those of advertising agencies. It relieved them of responsibility for the information they conveyed. The job of advertising agencies is to manipulate the information interface in the interests of their clients. Questions regarding the accuracy of claims about products or policies made by advertising agencies on behalf of their clients were irrelevant when understood in the context of McLuhan's theories. They imply that media people can disseminate whatever information suits them, even if it is known to be false, because it is no more than a diversion from the real message conveyed by the media technology. It is an open invitation to the creation by media organisations of an information interface full of false information. McLuhan lauds advertisements as 'by far the best part of any magazine or newspaper'.[72] The 'good news' of advertisements is more important than the 'bad news' that is standard media fare. It is more important that news be responsive to human concerns for happiness and reassurance than that it convey 'truth' and exclude what is 'false' or 'misleading'. McLuhan's theory placed responsibility for the impact of media on the technology, rather than on those responsible for the information it conveyed. Hence McLuhan's theory was puffed by the media about which he wrote. McLuhan was a 'cover story' for *Time* and *Newsweek*, the two leading American news magazines of the time. Advertising executives were prominent enthusiasts for his cause. The content might be confused and dubious, but it freed media people from conventional fetters of honest dealing. It gave what was apparently scholarly endorsement of freedom to manipulate the information interface in accordance with their interests.

Media, money and technology

The interests of media people and media organisations lie partly in the dissemination of information that will assemble support for political and social causes which they approve of, and alienating support from those they do not approve of. But their major interest is necessarily the sustained operation of their organisations. Since they are nearly all private organisations, this means meeting the viability condition for money-bargaining agencies: revenues in excess of costs. Revenues from sales, subscriptions and advertising must cover the costs incurred in providing media services.

McLuhan's concern with technology, and lack of understanding of information, mean that he has acute difficulties in incorporating monetary considerations into his theories. McLuhan insists, as is apparent from the quotation at note 53, that media are an extension of ourselves. He asserts rather lamely that money also is an extension of ourselves: 'Money has reorganised the sense life of peoples just because it is an *extension* of our sense lives'.[73] His chapter on money imputes various qualities to money, but does not associate concern for money with media technology or the profitability of media organisations. As with other companies, the formats of media organisations depend on technology. The 'electric' media became established because it was possible to use the technology as the basis for viable businesses. For the media, the essential message lies in the company accounts. This affects the information that is posted to the information interface, and hence the way a society carries on its affairs. As was seen in Chapter 5, people are alerted by threats, so that threats of some sort are the best way of attracting attention and promoting sales. People are attracted by sensational news, and consequently there is inclination to make information sensational. People are not necessarily attracted by stone-cold sober truth. McLuhan makes the technology an impartial and impersonal conveyor of messages, but the technology is operative at the behest of its owners and controllers. Where the cameras are taken, and what they are pointed at, are dictated by those who run media organisations. Their primary concern is the commercial viability of their organisations. Accuracy and integrity of the information conveyed is a matter of subordinate concern. McLuhan's theories lightened that burden on those who conceived it as a burden. The commercial pressures on most media organisations, considered further in the following chapter, mean that many are inclined to take as much liberty over accuracy and integrity as they think they can get away with.

This monetary or commercial aspect of media operations has a most fundamental effect on societies, subsuming the importance of technology through its role in viable formatting. It affects capacities for the dissemination of information and for the control of information. The controllers of media organisations can communicate what they wish, within the constraints of the viability condition. The rest find it more difficult to get attention for their views and opinions. The contrast can be accentuated or diminished by technology. Purveyance of information using stone is largely confined to wealthy organisations. All but the poorest can convey information on the internet. Once the printing press made possible the establishment of viable businesses in the dissemination of information and amusement the information interface expanded rapidly and the bargaining business of societies, support-bargaining and money-bargaining, expanded along with it. The purely technological characteristics of media technology are important, but its cost characteristics are of primary importance in determining the level of usage. McLuhan's failure to assess these commercial influences in his account of the media is a further consequence of his narrow attention to technology as the determinant of the impact of media.

In the Western world, printing and publishing based on the printing press was extensively given free rein. The newspapers and radio stations that gave the United States such vitality arose because there were few government constraints on their operation as profitable businesses. The greatest profitability was found to lie in operations on a large scale. In some countries, governments suppressed the use of printing presses, stifling the dissemination of information and hence stifling the support-bargaining and money-bargaining through which societies evolve. The effects of such suppression have proved durable.[74]

The 'guru' approach

McLuhan does not use evidence in the way that scientists use evidence. Nor does he attempt to establish the strong and regular, apparently causative, links that do duty as evidence when the phenomena at issue are not of a kind amenable to strict scientific method. McLuhan favours rather the intuitive artistic approach, trusting in the sensual and unexamined. He works in a cultural context, especially artistic and literary. It is an avowedly 'modernist' approach, with frequent references to modernist authors and artists.[75] Poe remarks, 'McLuhan, then, was not really a theorist in any straightforward empirical sense'.[76]

Finkelstein puts it more strongly. He argues that McLuhan has no regard for facts, choosing quite consciously to speculate freely and confuse fact with fiction.[77] McLuhan, according to Finkelstein, is 'an expert in setting the half-truth to work'.[78] McLuhan is reported as replying to unsympathetic questioning on television by a prominent professor, 'You're not trying to explore anything with me. You're exploring my statements, not the situation. I'm not interested in my statements. I don't agree with them. I merely use them as probes'.[79] McLuhan justifies 'somewhat devious means of diagnosis that have to be used to pin down the actual form and impact of a new medium' by reference to a quotation from the crime novelist Peter Cheyney to the effect that a crime investigator wades through the lies that people tell to reach a logical conclusion.[80] McLuhan effectively claims freedom to manipulate the information interface in accordance with the requirements of his theory. It is 'artistic freedom' in the self-indulgent sense.

This takes McLuhan into the 'guru' category of theorists. 'Guru' is, according to Wikipedia, a Sanskrit word meaning teacher, guide or master, but having in the Indian tradition the additional character of being someone who is trusted and revered. A 'guru' may be seen as a teacher of truths that are beyond science, dealing chiefly with religious or philosophical issues. In the Western context, however, the term is often applied, with more than a hint of mockery, to scientists, particularly social scientists, who are regarded as 'not quite right', populist rather than scholarly, or even close to fraudulent. Business theorists pushing the latest turn-around programme for failing businesses, or the several principles of effective leadership, may be referred to as 'gurus'. Economists over-exposed in the media may be referred to by their more reticent colleagues as 'gurus'. The term has been applied to McLuhan, perhaps as much in exasperation as in mockery. Beyond gurus are charlatans, who are explicitly fraudulent.

'The medium is the message' has all the character of the teachings of a 'guru'. As has been seen, it confuses the meaning of words to make an impact. The mind does a 'double take' as it tries to distinguish meaning in the use of familiar words in unfamiliar expressions. It may mean something, but it may mean nothing. We know the meaning of 'medium' and the meaning of 'message', but a medium, though it may carry a message, does not constitute a message. Yet the association between a medium and a message means that the sentence has the possibility of meaning. It may even be wise. It has the kind of 'guru' mysticism of 'the sound of one hand clapping'. The play of words throws the mind out of its common course. Such gnomes are not difficult to invent: 'There is sunlight in darkness'; 'A picture is the porthole of the human psyche'; 'The nail threatens the hammer'; 'Silence is cheating'; 'If Mount Everest did not exist, logic could get you to the top'; '"All's well that doesn't happen" is a play by William Shakespeare that he never wrote'. Such statements use words that have meaning, but the words are used in a context that seems inappropriate to their meaning. They present apparent contradiction, paradox or odd juxtaposition. They may affront common theory. They may, on occasion, reveal something – the 'porthole' has a point, though it is perhaps not truly gnomic. The Everest conjecture is for postmodern existentialist logicians. '"All's well . . ."' is for transcendental realists. They are the verbal equivalent of the Escher drawings that warp perspective to present plausible images of impossible stairways and structures. The really memorable gnomes, like that of McLuhan, require a rare talent in a teacher to recognise the particular susceptibilities of a class. Such statements are not used in empirical science, where the concern is for clarity and precision of meaning, and a clear relationship to the experience of reality, but on the fringes of science they assemble support, and consequently have significance in intellectual support-bargaining. When whole books are written in gnomic style, there are inevitable difficulties for those who cannot sit at the feet.

The phrases 'the construction of social reality' and 'the social construction of reality', discussed in earlier chapters, have a gnomic element, which has been part of their appeal. 'Construction' suggests something solid, like house-building; it had not hitherto been used in connection with social intercourse. 'Reality' and 'social reality' are not at first take the sort of things that would be 'constructed'. It seems to suggest that Mount Everest is constructed like a house by means that could not possibly perform that function. The word-play challenges mental response, as it does in 'the medium is the message' and the other gnomes cited above. Bruno Latour and Steve Woolgar concluded that the word 'social' in 'social construction' as they had used it had become meaningless. Other theorists of 'social construction' might have come to the same conclusion. The theory of support-bargaining makes apparent how a society can create an information interface that constitutes an effective 'reality'. It is because such phrases as 'the social construction of reality' have some underlying element of accurate observation that they have not been universally dismissed as nonsense, but rather found worth further thought. Nevertheless, the idea of 'social construction' arises from the same ignorance of information and the information interface as underlies McLuhan's speculations on media technology.

With regard to social impact, the assembly of support is the important factor. In intellectual support-bargaining over media issues, the followers of McLuhan are potent players. His theories have been institutionalised in academia. 'Gurus' are usually understood as operating on the fringes of science or what might be called 'disciplined' investigations. But in the case of McLuhan, theory that has all the hallmarks of the 'guru' in the pejorative sense has become established as mainstream.

McLuhan found notable support in the 'hippy' movement prominent in the fifties and sixties. McLuhan writes of media being 'hot' or 'cool'. One chapter is titled 'The print: how to dig it'.[81] These terms were part of the vocabulary of the hippy movement, adopted from jazz and pop music. McLuhan gave the movement the phrase 'global village'. Changes in human work and human relationships are associated with the move from the 'fragmentation' of mechanical technology to the integral character of the new automation technology. The movement dreamed of an alternative society offering greater scope for personal fulfilment in a kinder and gentler society than the existing social order. It was youthful and idealistic, open to elaboration of its principles. McLuhan's theories perhaps confirmed the wisdom of its detachment from the informational complexity of modern life. If someone else claimed to have done the hard thinking, then it was only necessary to become a disciple.

McLuhan voices something of the movement's opposition to the conventional social order in forceful terms, as quoted above: 'Our conventional response to all media, namely that it is how they are used that counts, is the numb stance of the technological idiot'.[82] Conventional people like General Sarnoff do not just have questionable opinions, but have opinions so idiotic as to justify abuse. To use the expression of a General to discredit a commonplace idea suggests an assumption that anything said by a military man is likely to be discreditable, and an expectation that readers will share the assumption. Questions over the 'military–industrial complex' were prominent at the time in left-wing debate, initiated in particular by C. Wright Mills's account of *The Power Elite*.[83] In his analysis of the effects of the phonetic alphabet McLuhan later remarks, 'That is the reason why our Western industrial programs have quite involuntarily been so militant, and our military programs have been so industrial'.[84] The idea at issue is whether it is the information that is conveyed to the information interface and the instigators of its conveyance that are important, or whether it is simply a matter of the psychological impact of the technology. Without an understanding of information and its manipulation, McLuhan cannot provide a satisfactory analysis.

McLuhan's theories may be seen as part of the tradition of contrarian theory designed to assemble support for the break-down of existing social structures, accompanied by promises of an 'alternative society'. It was suggested earlier, in Chapter 2, that postmodernists challenge conventional assumptions about the nature of reality in order to call into question the conventional political and social order, as a prelude to the establishment of a new order. Support for the existing order can be undermined by dismissal of its 'ideas', 'facts' and theories. In some cases supporters, like the adherents of religious movements, prefer to put their faith in leaders and teachers, rather than in theories supposedly overconstricted by demands for evidence. Each group determines for itself through support-bargaining what it will regard as 'reality' and 'truth'.

Consequences of the Toronto School

McLuhan argues that any information content of messages is mere distraction from the influence of technology. But his position is a consequence of the lack of understanding of the role of information in a support-bargaining and money-bargaining society, and the part played by the creation of an information interface in such societies. Media are presented as technologies, sufficient in themselves. With that understanding, it is apparent that the Toronto School has distracted attention from critical aspects not just of the media but of the functioning of societies.

For Innis, the media such as stone, papyrus and parchment produce certain effects on social structures and practices through their character as 'spatial or 'temporal' media. For McLuhan, the importance of the media lies in the messages imparted unrecognised by their technology. In the case of 'electric' media, they have a powerful psychological impact arising from 'wholeness' or presentation of a 'total field'. In McLuhan's account they are little more than an electronic art gallery that stimulates certain psychological reflexes in an unsuspecting clientele. The Toronto School makes no attempt to unravel the complexities of 'information', preferring to concentrate on supposed effects of technology.

The distraction from information means also distraction from the part played by media in the competition for social ascendancy in all societies. Media organisations disseminate information of a kind that assembles support for certain groups and erodes support from others. The different technologies affect the opportunities for creation of the information interface. The Gutenberg printing press in Europe radically affected the dissemination of information and radically affected the state of European society. But while different technologies give rise to various opportunities, media organisations are subject to control by politically ascendant groups. Authoritarian governments control the media and the information they disseminate as an essential part of the retention of support. Even today, when internet technology gives exceptional scope for the dissemination of information, authoritarian governments find it possible to impose control. In open bargaining societies, or 'democracies', a diverse press is recognised as essential for the dissemination of the great variety of information necessary to effective support-bargaining and money-bargaining.

Innis recognises the opportunities that arise from different media technologies for various forms of media monopoly, and hence opportunities to gain social ascendancy. Supply of materials such as papyrus, or techniques of writing, can create circumstances of monopolistic supply, which can be exploited by ascendant agencies to establish and consolidate their positions. With this, the Toronto School comes nearer to realistic understanding of the role of media in societies. But the general influence has been to divert researchers and scholarly commentators such as Poe from the processes by which the media have such impact on the governance of societies.

The Toronto School suffers also from lack of general understanding of the role of technology. Media technology is central to their explanations of how media influence society, but there is no understanding or consideration of how non-media technology influences society. Technology influences the nature and performance of products and services in virtually all industries. It influences the scope for monopoly, just as it does with media technology.

The exceptional importance of media technology arises from the nature of information – its importance to social exchange and the intricacy of the information required for such exchange. Serious people will think that enough to distinguish it, but its capacity for intricacy means that it can also be marvellously entertaining.

The general influence of technology is particularly important with regard to the use of technology in companies for the format of viable businesses. Technical and cost characteristics of technology form the basis for the establishment of viable business formats. Media technology is no exception. Technical and cost characteristics of media technology determine which technologies go into widespread use in societies. The treatment of technology by the Toronto School obscures this aspect of technology. The impact of the Gutenberg press was due as much to characteristics that made it a sound investment for viable businesses as to its purely technical characteristics, which seem to have been fairly common knowledge at the time of Gutenberg's innovation. Once the printing press became a vehicle for making money, its use naturally spread, so that a far greater volume of information became available than ever before. As part of that expansion, the investors in printing presses tailored their products to potential buyers, shaping the information they provided to the circumstances of potential buyers. They provided serious political and religious information to some, while to others they provided entertainment. The Toronto School lacked a satisfactory frame of reference by which to evaluate the commercial aspects of the provision of information. Economic theory offers no help, having no concept of the function of companies in a money-bargaining system. The School's own understanding of technology was too narrow to cover cost considerations in anything more than lightly descriptive terms.

It is apparent to common observation that the media play a role in any society closely connected with the exercise of power in the society. The information they convey assembles support for, or repels support from, many different causes. It forms the basis for decisions across societies in political, social and economic affairs. It creates an information interface by which transactions are conducted in both support-bargaining and money-bargaining. Issues of national and global importance are influenced, if not determined, by media coverage. Following McLuhan, writers on media, including Poe, concentrate on the technological characteristics of the media and cover only incidentally the vital part they play in the dynamics of governance and monetary exchange through their dissemination and manipulation of information. The theories fail to provide a frame of reference that generates adequate explanations and understanding of media phenomena.

The following chapter investigates the role of the media in a modern democracy, with particular reference to some very contentious media behaviour in Britain, as illustration of the functioning of the media in the context of the contested creation of an information interface in a support-bargaining and money-bargaining system.

Notes

1 *The Economist*, 2016c, '"Inside the bear", Special Report on Russia', 22 October, after p. 44, p. 4.
2 Quoted in 'Martin Luther', *Wikipedia*. Accessed 11 September 2015.
3 Spread, Patrick, 2016a, *The Evolution of Economies: Money-Bargaining, Economic Change and Industrial Revolution*, Abingdon: Routledge, pp. 295–6.
4 On vital interests, see Spread, Patrick, 2008, *Support-Bargaining: The Mechanics of Democracy Revealed*, Sussex: Book Guild, pp. 373, 378, 447–8, 451; Spread, Patrick, 2013, *Support-Bargaining, Economics and Society: A Social Species*, Abingdon: Routledge, pp. 39–40, 70.
5 Innis, Harold, 1950, *Empire and Communications*, Oxford: Oxford University Press.
6 Poe, Marshall T., 2011, *A History of Communications: Media and Society from the Evolution of Speech to the Internet*, Cambridge: Cambridge University Press, p. 2.
7 Poe, 2011, p. 3.
8 Briggs, Asa and Burke, Peter, 2009, *A Social History of the Media: From Gutenberg to the Internet*, Third Edition, Cambridge: Polity Press, pp. 1–2.
9 Innis, 1950, p. 7.
10 Hugo, Victor, 2015, *The Hunchback of Notre Dame*, Waxkeep Publishing, Kindle Edition. First published 1831.
11 Hugo, 2015, loc. 2861–67.
12 Hugo, 2015, loc. 2874–80.
13 Hugo, 2015, loc. 2935–41.
14 Hugo, 2015, loc. 2941–47.
15 Hugo, 2015, loc. 2947–53.
16 Hugo, 2015, loc. 2978–84.
17 Hugo, 2015, loc. 2990–96.
18 Hugo, 2015, loc. 2990–3002.
19 Hugo, 2015, loc. 2996–3008.
20 Hugo, 2015, loc. 3009–21.
21 Hugo, 2015, loc. 3052–63.
22 Hugo, 2015, loc. 3070–76.
23 Innis, 1950, Preface.
24 Innis, 1950, p. 215.
25 Innis, 1950, p. 7.
26 Patterson, Graeme H., 1990, *History and Communications: Harold Innis, Marshall McLuhan, the Interpretation of History*, Toronto: University of Toronto Press, p. 8.
27 Patterson, 1990, p. 8.
28 Innis, 1950, p. 209.
29 Innis, 1950, p. 140.
30 Patterson, 1990, p. 17.
31 Innis, 1950, p. 20.
32 Innis, 1950, p. 46.
33 Spread, 2016a, pp. 294–6, 300.
34 See Spread, 2013, pp. 171–4.
35 Spread, 2013, pp. 174–6.
36 See Spread, 2016a, pp. 294–8.
37 Poe, 2011, p. 98.
38 Poe, 2011, p. 149.
39 Poe, 2011, pp. 199, 249.
40 Poe, 2011, p. 150.
41 Poe, 2011, pp. 115–51.

42 Poe, 2011, p. 150, Table 4, and text pp. 116–49.
43 Poe, 2011, pp. 105–14.
44 Poe, 2011, p. 109.
45 Poe, 2011, p. 106.
46 Poe, 2011, p. 109.
47 Poe, 2011, p. 110.
48 Poe, 2011, pp. 103–5
49 Poe, 2011, p. 105.
50 Finkelstein, Sidney, 1968, *Sense and Nonsense of McLuhan*, New York: International Publishers, p. 47.
51 Patterson, 1990, p. 38.
52 Poe, 2011, p. 3.
53 McLuhan, Marshall, 1964, *Understanding Media: The Extensions of Man*, Abingdon: Routledge, p. 7.
54 McLuhan, 1964, p. 9.
55 McLuhan, 1964, pp. 13–14.
56 McLuhan, 1964, p. 57.
57 McLuhan, 1964, pp. 8–9.
58 McLuhan, 1964, p. 57.
59 McLuhan, 1964, p. 19.
60 Poe, 2011, p. 3.
61 McLuhan, 1964, p. 337.
62 McLuhan, 1964, p. 337.
63 Poe, 2011, p. 26.
64 Innis, 1950, p. 68.
65 Innis, 1950, p. 11.
66 Innis, 1950, p. 70.
67 McLuhan, 1964, pp. 12–13.
68 Poe, 2011, pp. 114–15.
69 McLuhan, 1964, pp. 7–8, 12–13.
70 Spread, 2013, p. 245.
71 Spread, 2016a, p. 286.
72 McLuhan, 1964, p. 227.
73 McLuhan, 1964, p. 20.
74 See Spread, 2016, pp. 296–8.
75 See in particular McLuhan, 1964, pp. 59–60.
76 Poe, 2011, p. 3.
77 Finkelstein, 1968, pp. 13–14. On McLuhan's historical distortions, see Finkelstein, 1968, Chapter 2, 'McLuhanese history vs. real history'.
78 Finkelstein, 1968, p. 24.
79 Finkelstein, 1968, p. 14.
80 McLuhan, 1964, pp. 73–4.
81 McLuhan, 1964, pp. 24–35.
82 McLuhan, 1964, p. 19.
83 Mills, C. Wright, 1956, *The Power Elite*, Oxford: Oxford University Press. For comment on this, see Spread, 2013, pp. 74–9.
84 McLuhan, 1964, p. 93.

8 Media, governance and the information interface

It was suggested in Chapter 2 that rather than constructing 'reality' societies construct an information interface in which to conduct their processes of support-bargaining and money-bargaining. Subsequent chapters were concerned with ideas of reality, truth, economic exchange, governance, psychology, science and so on that go to form the information interface. The ideas were largely those emerging at some intellectual distance from the process of government. They were concerned mainly with intellectual support-bargaining in an academic context. Academic institutions are established by societies in the expectation that they will produce useful theories regarding the workings of society, untrammelled by the interests that prejudice the thinking of people in the ordinary course of life. Such institutions have been prime contributors to the information interface, concerned particularly with the establishment of those theoretical frames of reference which are so central to the understanding of people and societies, and hence central to their governance.

This chapter is concerned with processes of government and a different context of intellectual support-bargaining. A 'reality' is created as an information interface through which the processes of government can be carried on. Under a support convention violence is largely eliminated and people engage in a 'battle of ideas'. They seek to assemble support for their ideas and interests, rather than assembling soldiers to fight for their causes. It is intellectual support-bargaining for the establishment of policies and programmes that will assemble support. It is not theory-making, but something with direct relevance to the situations that face governments. Government 'policies' constitute the reactions of governments to the situations that confront them. They summarise what a government regards as essential courses of action. Policies create the focus necessary to the assembly of support and the formulation of government programmes and action to rectify the defects in the current situation. Adoption of policies oriented towards the alleviation of poverty, for example, will result in all situations and potential actions being evaluated by reference to this prime focus. 'Facts' of varying status will be established about the extent of poverty and its nature, and these will constrain bargaining positions, rule out certain courses of action, and suggest others. In the political sphere an information interface is constructed which influences the assembly of support in the society at large and creates the context in which the narrower administrative processes of government can be carried on.

One basic claim of support-bargaining is that it gives a far superior account of the functioning of countries that are recognised as 'democracies' than is possible with the idea of democracy. The idea of democracy has helped ensure that people are engaged in national government through elections and representation in legislatures. Majorities in a representative legislature are entitled to govern. But it gives little further account of the mechanisms by which government is to be effected. Political parties and pressure groups do not have an obvious part to play under democratic principles – it might even be said that they are inimical to democratic principles. It is evident that people 'rule' only in a very limited sense.

When it comes to questions about the role of information, democracy is yet more vague. There should be 'free speech', but only up to a point. People exercising their freedom of speech may still suffer for it, even if they are not actually arrested. Democratic theory makes no demands for evidence; sets no criteria for what can be regarded as truth; has no view on what will be taken as 'reality'. It is assumed that people will be sufficiently honest with their fellow citizens as to permit the recognition of a common good for the advancement of their society. Social 'truth' will emerge from democratic debate. 'Information' in a democratic system is assumed to be available. Democratic principles assume that people will be informed in some way that is sufficient for them to govern.

The theory of democracy is no more than a set of principles setting out how government might or should be conducted, without providing a workable account of how it can be and is conducted. It was noted in the previous chapter that the very limited accounts of the media provided by such writers as Harold Innis and Marshall McLuhan are only possible when there are no more substantial accounts of the role of information. The idea of an information interface in a support-bargaining system makes plain the role of information as a major factor in the assembly of support. Support-bargaining is conducted in an information interface. Citizens disseminate information to the interface in accordance with their interests, and must determine what other information they will take into account in identifying their best courses of action.

The weakness of the democratic account of information is apparent from Alvin Goldman's treatment of 'Democracy and the press'.[1] Goldman conceives the function of the press as providing the truth about political processes, or responding to a popular requirement for 'core voter knowledge' about policies and programmes. The press is seen as comprising expert intermediaries who can put the complexity of government into forms comprehensible to voters. He writes, 'Ideally, I suggest, the press should comprise a set of experts who would report, interpret, and explain political events in a way that serves the veritistic interests of voters, especially their interest in core voter knowledge'.[2] Goldman sees the obstacles to the performance of this role as the profit motive which drives media organisations and the lack of appropriate training of journalists – they lack systematic training in the liberal arts, natural sciences, or sociological or economic analysis. Complications arise with Goldman's concept of 'core voter knowledge'. This depends on each voter's assessment of outcomes from his or her point of view.[3] 'By full core knowledge I mean a situation in which every voter knows the true answer to his or her core question. "Knowledge" of truth means either categorical belief in it or a DB [Degree of Belief] greater than .50'.[4] Whatever the complications of voter knowledge, the role of the press is straightforward: to meet the veritistic interests of voters, particularly with regard to core voter knowledge. This is the simple 'democratic' faith in a good, self-denying, public-spirited and honest press that pursues no interests other than the good of its society, subject only to the constraints inherent in its limitations of training and the pursuit of profit. Goldman recommends extension of public broadcasting, free from considerations of profit, as most likely to deliver the qualities he sees as desirable in a press.[5] True 'knowledge' or true 'information' is necessary to the democratic process. Its delivery potentially clouds the decision making of democracies. Democratic principles are compromised by the profit motive of media organisations but to what extent is left open to question. It can certainly be said that some practical compromises are necessary, but that only confirms that democratic principles provide no comprehensive theory of governance and, even in so far as they go, they are not practical. In the understanding of support-bargaining and money-bargaining, information and the manipulation of information, the creation and use of an information interface, are fundamental to the group formation and group rivalry that constitute the central dynamic of the support-bargaining and money-bargaining process. Goldman's account makes clear the inadequacy of the democratic account of information; it also makes apparent the lack of any adequate academic media theory.

A support-bargaining system runs on information, so that the process of government might be said to run on information. Governments run on information. Whole societies run on information. Earlier societies might be regarded as run by violence, or the threat of violence, but even such societies used information to assemble support for the exercise of violence. The move from societies of violence to a support convention puts a premium on ideas, making information a matter of central importance. Most of the information used is testimonial information, since any individual politician has direct perceptual knowledge only of a very limited range of government activity and interest. The scope of government requires acting for the most part on testimonial information; the availability of such information dictates the scope of government. Politicians in Britain can respond to events in the South China Sea or in Cornwall on the basis of testimonial information received from those areas. Information in the form of reports and statistics, and conclusions drawn therefrom, floods their desks from the hands of civil servants whose every hour is spent acquiring, absorbing and interpreting information and deriving from it appropriate courses of action. People in general also depend for their participation in politics, in anything other than a crude material or tribal way, on access to information. Television provides testimonial information in the form of perceptual information. All this escapes the understanding of those whose frame of reference is confined to the principles of 'democracy'. The 'pens' have largely driven the 'swords' from the field and vie for ascendancy through the accumulation of support for their ideas.

Companies also run on information, though here the dependence is perhaps not so abundantly apparent. The owners and managers of small companies have direct perceptual knowledge of a large part of the arena in which they work, and being perceptual information, it seems not so much information as the direct knowledge of reality. But it is nevertheless information – the sort of thing our minds can accommodate. At the same time, the owners and managers of small companies must deal with large volumes of testimonial information. In large companies, the prominence of testimonial information means that dependence on information is fully apparent. The controllers of a large company know its operations, and make their decisions, on the basis of copious reports and accounts from across the company regarding its situation and concerns. Their concerns, and consequently the information they assemble, is more limited in its scope than that of governments. The controllers of companies are concerned with sustained accommodation of a monetary viability condition. Their assembly and evaluation of information is related to the monetary imperative of ensuring that revenues exceed costs. Governments, however, are concerned with the assembly and retention of support. The retention of support involves accommodation of a much more diverse range of interests, and hence attention to a much wider range of information.

This importance of information to the assembly of support, and hence to governance, implies the importance of those who principally create the information interface accessible to ordinary people – that is, the media. How the media manipulate the information that goes into the information interface has a crucial bearing on the distribution of support in a society, and hence on the way a society is governed. The media are then major players in the process of government. The media theory of the Toronto School was queried in the previous chapter. This chapter seeks to provide a better explanation of the role, functioning and significance of the media.

A government, as was seen in Chapter 4, has an important role in an economy as regulator and provider of services. It is also administrator of any national currency. The role of the media in governance consequently means also that the media have a role in the conduct of an economy. Support assembled for different economic interests through the media causes governments to adjust their economic policies and interventions. This includes such momentous decisions as the withdrawal from the European Union, involving withdrawal from the communal arrangements on trade, investment and the movement of people.

The importance of the media to the distribution of support attracts the attention of other agencies concerned to assemble support. 'Pressure groups' or 'interest groups' of all kinds, keen to assemble support for their causes, and keen to have government acknowledge their support and act in accordance with it, use the media to assemble support. Media reports derived from agencies promoting child welfare, overseas aid, environmental protection, business regulation and a host of other causes will influence support for the causes. Such agencies can, on occasions, or over time, through the media, bring about significant erosion of support for a government. They can also help governments in the assembly of support. Put crudely, the understanding is that favourable government response will be rewarded with favourable reports in the media, but unfavourable response will result in condemnation in the media. The media act as arbiters of what goes into the information interface, and in what form.

Intellectual support-bargaining and government

The intellectual support-bargaining of the academic arena is inclined to more or less timeless issues regarding the nature of society and the nature of the world. The intellectual support-bargaining that is part of the process of government is concerned with matters having immediate relevance to the assembly of support and the conduct of a nation's affairs. To achieve the volumes of support necessary to political action it is necessary to focus support. Organisation – most notably the establishment of political parties – is an essential part of the achievement of focus.[6] But intellectual support-bargaining is also involved in the focusing of attention and interest on particular issues. There is constant competition to gain prominence for issues and causes in the information interface. This involves the development of policies by political parties and governments to perform the functions previously described as pertaining to 'frames of reference'. As noted above, policies focus attention on a particular approach to an issue, in the expectation of focusing support on that approach, to the advantage of the policy maker. Governments develop policies for an economy, education, health services, the environment, etc. in the expectation of assembling support for the courses of action implied by the policies.

The policies themselves are often derived from prominent theoretical frames of reference, such as economic theory or socialist theory. The selections and interpretations to which such theoretical frames of reference give rise determine the concepts of situation that are formed in government. Policies are responses to these concepts of situation. The frames of reference are identifiably reflective of the basic division in support-bargaining processes between those who favour an individualist approach and those favouring the dominance of group interests. This division is likely to be reflected also in policies. It is expected that some of the support attaching to the broad frames of reference will readily attach also to policies based on them.

The policies provide a focus for the research of those professionally engaged in the intellectual support-bargaining of the political process, including civil servants. It is testament to the importance of the information interface that the great majority of those involved in politics, at least at national level in Britain, have distinctive skills in the codification and transmission of information. Politicians are almost of necessity highly articulate. Those who climb to the top of government hierarchies, whether political hierarchies or civil service hierarchies, commonly have educational qualifications that imply high skill in the use and evaluation of information. Civil services with entry based on demonstrated capacity for the evaluation of information emerged in Europe as the importance of ideas and information in the conduct of politics grew with increasing acceptance of the support convention. Civil services constitute agencies specifically established for the purpose of collection and interpretation of information relevant to government. There is a parallel with the establishment of universities to evaluate information relating to society and the world in general.

The role of the British civil service was described in *A Theory of Support and Money Bargaining* in terms of the identification of facts and the constraints that facts impose on politicians.[7] This distinguishes their role, at least conceptually, from that of politicians, whose concern must be with the assembly of support. Defining 'situations' means to a large degree defining 'facts' on which effective policies can be based. This inevitably involves the manipulation of information. Civil servants select and shape information for relevance to the policies of governments. The shaping is generally done in an unobtrusive process of intellectual support-bargaining, whereby changes are proposed, accepted, rejected, or modified to an acceptable form. Politicians could not possibly deal with the range of issues that is nominally their responsibility without the evaluations and recommendations provided by civil servants. Civil servants, however, like those engaged in other spheres of activity, are inclined to determine for themselves what they will regard as 'truth' or 'fact'. They do not necessarily assess by reference to the same policies or frames of reference as those of the politicians to whom they are in principle responsible.[8] Their determinations do not always accord with those of politicians. Richard Crossman, when Minister for Housing in Britain in the 1960s, objected to the influence wielded by civil servants through their control of information, when in democratic theory they were designated 'neutral'.[9] The civil servants could 'pre-cook' a whole issue; could arrange the facts in such a way that the politicians could only come to the same conclusions as the civil servants had previously reached. Tony Benn, when Secretary of State for Energy from 1975 to 1979, first with Harold Wilson as prime minister and then with James Callaghan, had sharp differences with his civil servants over options for nuclear power and the drafting of energy policy.[10] The civil servants were effectively shutting down options that the minister wanted to keep open.

The difficulties of establishing dependable assessments of situations, or facts of high status, are in large measure the difficulties of acquiring evidence. Requirements for evidence constitute an important constraint on the tendency for the manipulation of information by interested agencies to tip over into deception and outright falsehood. It was seen in the discussion of natural scientific method in Chapter 6 that when evidence that meets natural scientific standards for the establishment of theories or facts is not available, the scientific community resorts to intellectual support-bargaining. The more facts are available, the less scope there is for support-bargaining. In the sphere of political support-bargaining it is much more difficult to establish facts on the basis of evidence comparable in status to that of natural scientific requirements. The issues confronting governments, commonly involving human behaviour and human volition, do not lend themselves to identification of the sort of evidence that can be established about the nature of materially based interactions. Furthermore, the exigencies of political support-bargaining often mean that there is little time for time-consuming procedures to establish comprehensive evidence for what are to be regarded as facts. There are plenty of facts that are very solid and readily agreed that have to be taken into account in the formulation of political action. The work of ten people cannot be done by one in the same time. A car park with 100 spaces cannot take 200 cars. 'Facts' of minimal quality, based on evidence of a rudimentary kind, are nevertheless sometimes adopted as a basis for decision making. Something less than refined evidence often has to suffice in the helter-skelter of government. Sometimes the truth, or facts of higher status, emerge later to the embarrassment of those concerned, if they are still around.

External reports commissioned by governments constitute a response to requirements for evidence, for 'facts' of high status. The expectation is that outside agencies will have the time and specialist expertise to assemble evidence that is as near to the natural scientific ideal as the nature of the material permits. Specialists from universities are commonly involved with such reports, thus establishing a link between the immediate intellectual support-bargaining sphere of the political system and the less-time-constrained intellectual support-bargaining of the university environment.[11]

While a civil service will shape or manipulate information to give it relevance to the interests of politicians or other civil servants, the media manipulate information to give it relevance to the interests of potential buyers of their products or services. They may use the opportunities presented by a largely committed readership to advance their own agendas for government action. While in 'democratic' understanding, such as that described by Goldman, the media exist to report dispassionately on the ideas and activities of government, they are, in a support-bargaining system, active participants in the assembly of support for different interests. They are the immediate creators of the publicly accessible information interface in which political decisions are made. Their behaviour is more that of pressure groups than reporters.

This partisan engagement of the media was much in evidence in the referendum over United Kingdom membership of the European Union in June 2016. 'Leave' and 'remain' campaigns had distinctly different collections of 'facts' on which to base their case. Some newspapers took highly partisan positions. Agreed facts, or facts of the highest status, that might have constrained the levels of manipulation were found to be in short supply. There are too many facts about the European Union for there to be a comprehensive assessment of facts. 'Leave' and 'remain' factions freely selected their 'relevant' facts, which were inevitably facts convenient to their cause. Group commitment to causes elevated opinions to the status of facts. The campaigns were, moreover, largely about future prospects. There are no facts about the future, only probabilities and possibilities, and the two are easily confused, particularly where ardent interests are involved. Many of the 'facts' in dispute concerned the economic benefits and disadvantages of withdrawal from the trade arrangements and arrangements for movement of people that are integral to membership of the European Union. When 'facts' are so confused and confusing, people tend to make decisions on the basis of a simple sense of group affiliation. A sense of European group affiliation has never taken strong hold in Britain.

Partisan engagement of the media and the extremes of manipulation are apparent in the information disseminated by the *Sun* newspaper when it switched its allegiance from the Labour Party and the prime minister Gordon Brown to the Conservative Party in the run-up to the general election in Britain of 2010. Nick Davies, a journalist for the *Guardian*, describes the treatment as 'a sustained campaign of distortion' and provides a page of specific examples: when Brown advocated change for a global age, it was reported as a 'tacit admission that New Labour has failed'; when Brown spoke of the bravery of British troops in Afghanistan, it was reported that he had spent only 35 seconds paying tribute to them; when Brown emphasised the importance of costing of government policies, it was reported as a failure to admit the government was broke and had no money for its policies; a programme of free child care was reported as unravelling immediately as middle-class parents reacted with fury.[12] Even in the context of political campaigns, the reporting seems awkwardly contrived.

These partisan positions of the media are in part dictated by the preferences of their proprietors and editors, but they reflect also the preferences of readers. Media organisations, like other companies, format for provision of material that people will pay for. Other opportunities for viable format arise in relation to the promotion of political causes. Public relations companies perform a function in support-bargaining networks similar to that of advertising agencies in money-bargaining. Some companies offer services to both support-bargaining and money-bargaining organisations. Public relations companies codify and transmit information in a form that is calculated to assemble support for the interests of their clients in an intellectual support-bargaining process. Information is shaped for relevance to the interests of intended recipients. Representations to government will, for example, present a client's interests as consistent with the government's stated policies, or relevant to some prominent current issue. The information is shaped, in effect, to gain a place in the defined bargaining sets of the intended recipients. It is transmitted in appropriate codification – speech, writing, print, photographic, video, digital, etc. – to those whose support is assessed to be important and potentially forthcoming.

Intellectual support-bargaining in the political sphere is dominated by organisations such as political parties and media groups. Their dominance of the information interface gives these organisations the strong bargaining positions they use to influence the course of government. It is within these organisations that the critical decisions are made over policies and, in the case of political parties, the manifestos on which they will campaign for support in elections. While collectively these organisations dominate the information interface, the strength of their bargaining positions is diminished by competition between them for ascendancy. Political parties compete for political ascendancy, which depends on the competitive assembly of support; media groups compete for readers, listeners and viewers, and more fundamentally for revenues.

There is, nevertheless, a personal dimension to the intellectual support-bargaining immediately attendant on the assembly of political support. Certain individuals exercise a significant degree of influence over the information interface, as leaders of major organisations. The 'big fish' are those who wield the bargaining strength of major organisations. Those close to them may also be influential. In the old days the 'groom of the stool' was the man to go to for special favours from the king. The various aides and advisors surrounding prime ministers today have considerable influence in the inner circles of government. There are also the thousands of personal exchanges, in meetings, offices, bars, coffee houses, restaurants and over dinners that distil certain issues and attitudes as dominant out of the multitude of possibilities amongst those involved on a day-to-day basis with political issues. Politicians marry journalists, civil servants or researchers. Heirs and heiresses are still in demand. Introductions are made and alliances are formed. Aversions and hatreds emerge. Bullies from the playground find new outlets for their talents, both within hierarchies and in informal relationships. At the grand end in Britain Tony Blair, the prime minister, socialises with Rebecca Brookes, the influential editor of the *News of the World*, a tabloid newspaper.[13] The exchanges of those engaged around the 'Westminster village' and the centres of political power in general have most influence on the emergence of political opinion. Spoken information is easily communicated and largely ephemeral, and consequently well-suited to intimate support-bargaining. These personal relationships are built also on face-to-face contact, in which facial expressions, dress, deportment, gestures, physical contact, the giving of time, social generosity and other factors all convey information that is understood psychologically as indicative of support or opposition. It is perhaps too much to describe these exchanges as a form of 'intellectual' support-bargaining; much of it is more like 'gossip'. But gossip moves support.

There is also a 'churn' of employment that influences intellectual support-bargaining in the political sphere. People do not necessarily stay with one point of view, one frame of reference, one policy commitment. Politicians become journalists and journalists become politicians. George Osborne, formerly Chancellor of the Exchequer, raised eyebrows in March 2017 when he was appointed editor of the *Evening Standard*, in addition to his work with a large financial institution, without resigning his position as Member of Parliament for Totton. People move from the finance houses of the City of London into politics or the civil service. Lawyers become politicians or take up with pressure groups. The moves mean that the people concerned take on different responsibilities and adopt different situational references. They manipulate information in different ways. The prosecutor becomes the defence. A 'lefty' journalist joins a right-wing newspaper and modifies his or her position. Yet the movers may not dispense entirely with their old outlook. They will understand better the different positions, and will thereby become more tolerant of alternatives. This is conducive to the fluidity of support that is necessary to the operation of a support-bargaining system. It can nevertheless impede the performance of certain functions. The teeth of a 'watchdog' institution may be blunted by sympathy for old colleagues in the organisations it is supposed to watch.

Certain harmonies of thought may also arise not from the churn of employment but from common earlier educational experience. Most leading politicians, civil servants and journalists have in their youth been to universities and absorbed some of the same ostensibly timeless theories about their societies, and will apply them, wittingly or otherwise, in the evaluation of information related to their new concerns.

Money-bargaining and the information interface

The woolly ideas on information associated with democratic principles give little guidance on how information is to be disseminated in a democratic society. Awareness of the importance of information in political processes is nevertheless apparent in the debates over provision. The importance of information to the functioning of a support-bargaining society, and the cost of providing information, suggest that it might be appropriate to make information available as a communal service. But communal services are normally provided by governments. In the case of government provision of information there arises the prospect of government preponderance in the supply of information, and even the establishment of a monopoly position, implying government control of the information interface. Information is the one communal benefit that cannot be provided with communal benefit through the agency established for the provision of communally identified benefits. Democratic principle requires 'free speech' and that can only be exercised through private provision of information.

In Britain the option of government provision of information has not been entirely dismissed. The BBC was established in the 1920s as a statutory authority for the provision of information, education and entertainment. As far as control of content is concerned, it has been placed at 'arm's length' from government by the establishment of a trust to run it. As far as finance is concerned, it has been placed at 'arm's length' from government as direct paymaster by the requirement that all who use televisions pay a licence fee to the BBC. The arrangements are heavily criticised by private organisations providing information services, on the grounds that BBC competition is unfair and damaging to them. It provides a service to an audience effectively obliged to pay a government-determined price in competition with those who can provide a service only to those who choose to receive it at prices governed by the viability condition. But the BBC has managed to establish so strong a reputation for good service, with standards of impartiality that are widely admired, even if not universally acknowledged, that communal support for retention of the BBC has outweighed support for proposals to alter radically its constitution. Even so, a state-controlled organisation like the BBC would not be tolerable if it had not proved possible for a large variety of other sources of information to operate alongside it.

The extensive requirements for dissemination of information and the major disadvantages of provision by public authorities means there are extensive opportunities for private companies to provide information. Private provision necessarily takes the form of private money-bargaining agencies. A major part of the provision of information in Britain to ordinary people lies with private money-bargaining organisations – companies that must pursue as a priority the viability condition. Newspapers in Britain are entirely provided by companies. Television services are extensively provided by companies. This means that the provision of information in Britain, on which the functioning of the support-bargaining system depends, is heavily conditioned by monetary considerations. Information may be distorted not so much for the assembly of support as for the acquisition of money. Specialist money-bargaining agencies have a central role in the dissemination of information that determines the distribution of support in society.

The information received by the general populace, on which its informed participation in political support-bargaining depends, is thus primarily a matter of what it will pay for. Media organisations have not generally found it easy to meet the viability condition. Meeting the condition 'sales × price > unit cost × production' has involved two broad solutions, the solutions apparent in almost all industries: there can be high volumes of production and sales at low unit cost and low prices; or there can be low volumes of production and sales at high unit cost and high prices. The former involves content attractive to large numbers of relatively unthoughtful people and the latter involves content appealing to a more thoughtful section of the community, many of them professionally thoughtful. Table 8.1 below shows the circulations and prices of selected newspapers in the United Kingdom.

The *News of the World* had a Sunday circulation of around 2.9 million at its closure in 2011. The *Sun on Sunday* was introduced to replace it, but has not achieved comparable circulation. The *Independent*, with a circulation of about 56,000 at the end of 2015, ceased print publication in March 2016.

Newspapers categorised as 'high circulation at low price' are mostly what are referred to in Britain as 'tabloids', while those categorised as 'low circulation at high price' are mainly 'broadsheets'. However, since some more expensive newspapers are published in tabloid form, newspapers are also classified as 'popular' or 'quality'. Some newspapers operate on the borders of the two format categories. As can be seen from the above table, the *Daily Telegraph* and *The Times* have circulations close to those of the low-cost newspapers

Table 8.1 Circulation and prices of selected United Kingdom newspapers, 2016

	Average circ. (May 2016)	*Price (pence) (June 2016)*	*Share of total (per cent)*
Daily newspapers			
The *Sun*	1,716,768	30	26.2
Daily Mail	1,544,084	55	23.6
Daily Mirror	778,650	45	11.9
Daily Star	508,838	30	7.8
The *Daily Telegraph*	490,800	120	7.5
The Times	438,159	120	6.7
Daily Express	415,023	45	6.3
i	285,734	20	4.4
Financial Times	198,396	220	3.0
The *Guardian*	165,702	180	2.5
Total above daily papers	6,542,154		100.0
Sunday newspapers			
The *Sun on Sunday*	1,450,523	100	25.0
The *Mail on Sunday*	1,351,128	150	23.3
The Sunday Times	777,834	250	13.4
Sunday Mirror	707,914	100	12.2
The *Sunday Telegraph*	370,926	200	6.4
Sunday Express	362,295	135	6.2
Daily Star – Sunday	320,833	100	5.5
Sunday People	270,170	100	4.7
The *Observer*	189,091	220	3.3
Total above Sunday papers	5,800,714		100.0

Sources: circulation: *Press Gazette*, www.pressgazette.co.uk. Price: Insley Stores, www.insleymedia.co.uk/prices.html. Both accessed 21 June 2016.

with the smallest circulations, though they sell at substantially higher price. Neither, however, comes close to the largest circulation tabloids. *The Sunday Times* achieves a circulation substantially above rivals selling at a much lower price. The technology of printing presses lends itself to high print runs with low unit costs. The 'high volume at low price', or tabloid, format has generally been more profitable than the 'low circulation at high price', or broadsheet, format. Media organisations commonly produce both tabloid and broadsheet newspapers, with the former in some cases permitting the latter to remain in publication when falling short of the viability condition on their own. Shared use of printing presses and other assets gives some discretion over the allocation of costs across titles. Newspapers, particularly those using a high circulation format, have found that people do not spend heavily on the purer forms of information and analysis related to political issues. They pay for sensation, drama, scandal, entertainment. Political information has to be punchy, relevant and brief. The different content options lie behind the alternative classification of newspapers as 'popular' and 'quality'. The quality of the content of the former is often referred to in highly pejorative terms.

Revenues from sales in both the 'high circulation' and 'low circulation' format options are commonly supplemented by revenues from those who wish to disseminate information about products and services. This form of funding is also used as an independent format option – some newspapers are provided free of charge to readers, with revenues for the publisher entirely derived from advertising. Circulation is important to both the 'high circulation' format and the 'low circulation' format, since advertisers buy access to numbers. However, they pay also for access to people with large budgets, so that the 'low circulation' format newspapers have a feature denied to the 'high circulation' format option. Their readers mostly have greater spending power than newspapers using the high circulation format.

Newspaper proprietors in the United States have generally, from an early date, been more inclined to cultivate advertising as a source of revenue than British proprietors, apparently because of concerns in Britain that high advertising revenues might excessively influence content.[14] The concern over mixing advertising with news was nevertheless apparent in the United States with the start of radio broadcasting in the 1920s when Herbert Hoover, then Secretary for Commerce, declared it, 'inconceivable that we should allow so great a prospect for service and for news and for entertainment and education to be drowned in advertising chatter'.[15]

The requirement for 'stand-alone' viable formats for media organisations is in some cases obviated by receipt of revenues from other sources. Some proprietors have financed newspapers from funds acquired in other industries. The *Guardian* is supported by a trust fund.

The information interface is created by the dissemination of information that will enhance the bargaining positions of the disseminators. Hence many agents are attracted by the large circulations of newspapers as channels for the dissemination of information. Companies use the media to disseminate information about their products and services. Advertising revenues have been of major importance to media organisations as part of the revenues that enable them to meet the viability condition. Competition for circulation and subscribers is competition also for advertising revenues. The loss of advertising revenue to the *News of the World* following the revelations of the hacking of Milly Dowler's phone was a factor in the closure of the newspaper.[16]

New technologies are now profoundly affecting the dissemination of news. The internet provides numerous free sources of news, with the suppliers deriving revenues from advertising. Newspapers in the traditional formats in Britain, both tabloid and broadsheet, deriving revenues mainly from sales, are experiencing declining sales. Most now provide online services, but find it difficult to raise viable revenues with this mode of transmission.

Increased circulation means lower unit costs and the capacity to remain profitable at a low selling price. Media companies strive to expand circulation by cutting costs and prices. Circulations can also be raised and bargaining positions strengthened by takeovers of other media operations. Takeovers also offer diversification and hence some protection against the weakening of any particular format. The threat from digital technologies has made newspaper owners yet more inclined to diversify into other forms of information provision. Provision of entertainment has long been an important form of diversification. News Corp, Rupert Murdoch's American media conglomerate, had over 800 subsidiaries in 2009, including a film studio, a book publisher and a social networking site, in addition to newspapers and TV channels.[17]

The increased security arising from large circulations and extensive diversification has meant that media organisations have become large and diverse. Some have become highly profitable, so that the pressures to meet the viability condition are diminished. With that comes greater freedom to disseminate information that a proprietor wishes to disseminate – that is, freedom to pursue political interests. Rather than being confined to traditional concerns over government control of the information interface, the concerns of Western nations now extend to the control of the information interface by particular media groups. Legislation restricts the market shares of media organisations in provision of information. In the United States, AT&T, a media company concerned with the transmission of information, bid $85 billion in October 2016 for Time Warner, a company making programmes. Time Warner shareholders approved the takeover in February 2017, but President Trump expressed opposition to it. On the face of it, such an acquisition significantly strengthens the bargaining position of AT&T in provision of information and entertainment by reducing the content options available to rivals. The acquisition nevertheless received judicial approval and was completed in 2018.

Information provided by the media has primarily to be shaped so as to bring in the necessary revenues, whether from buyers or advertisers. In general, information has to be of a kind that fits the bargaining sets of the potential buyers. In a manufacturing company products are moulded to the tastes of potential customers – giving furniture, say, the modish curves and colours that potential buyers will see as fitting into their living rooms or bedrooms. Information has similarly to be moulded to the tastes of buyers. In the case of the tabloids, this can be a matter of snappy headlines and stories that impart political information through their impact on specific people. They employ staff skilled in the presentation of psychologically compelling information, with comparatively small analytical content. In the case of the broadsheets, information tends to be presented in a less dramatic and more analytical style – there is stimulus for the brain rather than instinctive reaction. They employ staff with skills in the analysis of information. The use of 'shock' headlines is consistent with the identification of the amygdala as a part of the brain dealing as a matter of priority with urgent threats, overriding other perceptions, as described in Chapter 5. In some cases newspapers mould their information to the inherent divisions of support-bargaining. In Britain the *Guardian* and *Daily Mirror* provide information that is readily acceptable to those with left-wing preconceptions, those who favour the group and group sentiment, while the *Daily Telegraph* and the *Daily Mail* are more likely to shape information to the taste of the right wing, with sympathy for individualism and enterprise. Diversity of presentation is important to the flexibility of support that is essential to the functioning of a full support-bargaining system. Most individuals, however, stick with just a few sources of information that roughly share their outlook on life.

Money is conceived in the idea of support-bargaining and money-bargaining as an alternative bargaining counter to support, functioning most effectively in those areas where precision and divisibility are useful characteristics. Support has implications of violence, so that as a bargaining counter it is effective in contexts involving group formation and security. While money is more individualistic, it still has implications for security. It implies capacity for assembly of people to give protection. An army can be formed from those who support a cause, but an army can also be formed by paying for soldiers. Even an army assembled in support of a cause has to be paid. People may work from devotion to a good cause, or for payment, but mostly they work for a good enough cause so long as they are paid. The changes in outlook arising from the churn of employment are responses to changes in sources of income. People pursue the interests of the organisations that pay them.

Money and support are interchangeable for some purposes, but they are also frequently used to complement each other. People give money to causes they support. Paying money for something implies a liking for it; in the case of a newspaper or television services, it implies a liking for the services provided. It may imply a liking primarily for the entertainment and diversion provided, but it may be a liking also, or support, for the sort of information provided. People assimilate most easily information that accords with their assessment of the political and social situation, or with a frame of reference they have already assimilated, such as socialism or a 'free market' philosophy, so that buying a newspaper has an implication of support for the understanding of circumstances displayed by the newspaper. People buy information that fits their preconceptions of situation, just as they buy clothes that fit their size and fit their preconceptions of personal identity and status.

Hence newspapers find it profitable in many cases to associate themselves with particular political factions. A newspaper, in the persons of its proprietor, editors and journalists, forms a kind of group sharing a common understanding with its readers. High circulation of a newspaper is consequently taken as indicative of support for the sort of commitments made by the paper. Monetary payments for newspapers, magazines, television services, internet access and so on are linked to the way they manipulate information. High circulation then suggests also a degree of trust in and receptiveness to the information conveyed. If information pertaining to a certain political persuasion cannot be sold there is an implication that the information does not accord with the understanding of any distinct group of readers. A political faction formed on the basis of such information is unlikely to assemble the support necessary to advance of its interests.

The different character of the intellectual support-bargaining around government from that around institutions of higher education is partly a consequence of these monetary considerations. The latter are at least to some degree insulated from the strong monetary considerations that preoccupy media organisations.

One perhaps surprising feature of the support-bargaining and money-bargaining system is that the companies which have such a prominent role in the dissemination of information do not wholeheartedly support a prominent role for a money-bargaining system, at least through the information they purvey. The explanation seems to be that they know their readers. Companies are not held in high regard.[18] Many readers favour greater allocation of benefits of all kinds on a communal basis over the allocations of a money-bargaining system dominated by companies. Meeting the viability condition requires that media organisations dissemble over the commitment to companies implicit in their own operations. Operating as a company would presumably be seen by the more left wing and radical media organisations as the only way of advancing the ideas that will change the existing order of society. Media companies are the arch-exponents of the companies' purpose of providing what people will pay for, except that once they have met and exceeded the viability condition they have the latitude to purvey what they themselves want people to think.

The daily dissemination of information to millions of people goes far in determining the distribution of support in a society. Since every individual has a vote, the high-circulation popular tabloids are potentially more important in their impact on support than the thoughtful broadsheets. Elections and referendums are more likely to be decided by the rather crude dissemination of information through the tabloid press, rather than by the more thoughtful assessments of the quality press. Serious people can debate serious policy issues as much as they like, but the decisions are based on tabloid representations designed to appeal to relatively unthoughtful people. But such people suffer or prosper in accordance with the decisions, which is some reason for according them the responsibility for taking them. They may not like the outcomes which their decisions lead to, but they cannot blame others for bringing them about. Dislike of outcomes brought about by the decisions of others is potentially more disruptive of a society. Besides, the maintenance of a support convention depends on acceptance of conclusions reached through its observance. The consolation for the thoughtful, such as it is, is that the information presented in the tabloids is for the most part distilled and simplified from conclusions reached through more thoughtful analysis, so that the thoughtful are not entirely without influence on the information which goes into mass circulation.

No political leader can ignore the influence either of the mass circulation media reaching relatively unthoughtful people or the quality media that reach people prominent in the intellectual support-bargaining of the political sphere. The work of the media has profound implications for the fortunes of political agencies, giving the media bargaining positions in relation to political agencies.

The large media groups in particular can steer substantial volumes of support to or away from governments and political parties. When their financial positions are reasonably secure as a result of high circulations and diversification, they have some scope to please themselves in the shaping of the information they disseminate. The attractions of being the proprietor of a major media group are not only money, but the influence it brings over government policies. Historically, wealthy men have tolerated considerable financial losses as media proprietors for the opportunities to meet with leading politicians and shape government policies that go with their influence over public support.

The impact of the media is very publicly apparent in the way governments formulate their annual budgets. Knowing that what is said and done will be a focus of media attention, British chancellors of the exchequer use their budgets to assemble support for the government. Precedent to elections, chancellors are inclined to 'give away' large sums of money by reducing taxes to favoured groups and increasing expenditures in areas of popular concern. In December 2014 George Osborne announced high-interest savings opportunities for those over 65 through the NS&I, a government savings organisation, presented as a means of helping pensioners in the face of low commercial interest rates. Pensioners have high rates of turn-out in elections. Both Gordon Brown and George Osborne liked to include in their budgets incidental sops to particular interest groups, knowing that the media would amplify their importance. Chancellors face the risk that their more serious economic measures will be traduced to their political disadvantage by their treatment in the media. Osborne's attempt to impose VAT on hot foods for takeaway in the 2012 budget was ridiculed in the media as a 'pasty tax'. In 2017 Philip Hammond's increase in national insurance contributions for the self-employed was castigated in the media as an assault on 'White Van Man'. Reaction to such reporting, whether it is enjoyed or condemned, probably depends mainly on party affiliations.

Government and media

It was seen above that the desire of companies to disseminate information advantageous to their interests to the information interface gives media organisations an important source of revenues. Governments also need to disseminate information to the information interface for advance of their interests. They amass large volumes of information. Governments want large volumes of information disseminated to raise support, but they will wish to withhold information that is likely to erode their support. Their people will have an interest in a large volume of information from government, including information that governments would prefer was withheld.

The desire of governments for the dissemination of information is an important factor in the viability of the formats of national media organisations. Many leading media organisations depend quite heavily on receipt of information from governments which they can sell on, suitably reconditioned, to their customers. There is scope for the mutual accommodation of interest that is the driving dynamic of bargaining systems. For the most part, exchanges are carried on smoothly. Government press offices issue press releases to the media, and the contents are presented, in a manner more or less acceptable to the government, to the people who read newspapers, watch television or access the internet. In Britain, a 'lobby' of journalists is briefed regularly on government activities and policies, and the media report what is said in a form more or less acceptable to government. Each keeps its side of the bargain. The government generally provides information to all, so that no particular media organisation gains commercial advantage from exclusive access.

Information is apparently delivered through the system to the media much as goods are delivered through supply chains to supermarkets. Lance Price remarks, in the context of the appointment of the first government press officer in 1930, 'So the Downing Street press office was born, and with it the habit of spoon-feeding political journalists at their own request'.[19] Most of the material is good saleable stuff. The government accumulates support through propagation of information largely conducive to its interests. The media appear to be providing well-sourced information to their customers, and gain revenues from its provision. A substantial part of the information interface relevant to the formal support-bargaining process is negotiated on a more or less routine basis between governments and the media.

There is often a broader confluence of interests. The political agendas of media proprietors and their editors sometimes accord closely with the policies of governments, enabling them to make substantially common cause. This can relate to broad ideological commitments, such as the commitments of the *Daily Mirror* and the *Guardian* to the left and the *Daily Telegraph* and *Daily Mail* to the right, with consequent tendencies to support Labour or Conservative governments. There is a long history of temporary and something like permanent alliances between political parties and the media. In 1922 the Trades Union Congress bought into the *Daily Herald*, aligning it with the labour movement. George Lansbury, a former editor of the *Daily Herald*, became leader of the Labour Party in 1931.

There can arise also links of a more personal nature, a general sympathy of outlook between a political leader and a newspaper proprietor. Nick Davies catalogues the relationships between News International and Labour and Conservative governments, starting with the Conservative government of Margaret Thatcher elected in 1979. Rupert Murdoch, the proprietor of News International, and Margaret Thatcher held similar views on principles of good government: business, including media business, should operate in a free market, with minimal regulation. They also shared similar views on the reform of trade unions in Britain in the 1980s. Thatcher's disapproval of the European Community was also shared by Murdoch.[20] The support of Murdoch's media for Thatcher's government was apparently worth a few favours. Thatcher contributed to the growth of the Murdoch conglomerate by letting the establishment of BSkyB go ahead in advance of legislation that might have held up or blocked the merger that created BSkyB.[21]

While there is considerable complementarity of interest between governments and media, there is also friction. Governments tend to present their position in terms of democratic principles: they are the representatives of the people and entitled to have their views conveyed to the people in the form in which they are provided. The media should act as a conduit by which a government can inform its people. It is unacceptable on democratic principles that media should change the information provided by governments, and potentially thwart the intentions of the people's representatives, in pursuit of money revenues. The media, however, claim to be guardians of the people's right to know the truth, and know it all. They regard themselves as entitled to interpret in their own way the information provided, and present it accordingly to their readers. They regard it as their duty to root out the information that governments do not want disseminated and provide it to their readers. In terms of the present theory, both governments and media have interests in disseminating information to the information interface that will influence the distribution of support in their societies.

A notable source of friction between governments and the media is naturally the secrecy of governments. Governments' understanding of their democratic status does not make them frank providers of information to the people. Ian Waller refers to, 'a traditional lack of openness in British politics; the feeling that politics and government are a matter for the insiders and nothing to do with either the press or public'.[22] The 'tradition' seems to derive from earlier more authoritarian governments. But even in modern democratic times the reluctance to release information is wholly understandable. The information interface is the basis on which support-bargaining is conducted, so any agency naturally prefers that information that potentially weakens its support-bargaining position remains secret. Governments do not want publicity for their internal dissensions, misjudgements, manipulations, omissions, cover-ups, deceptions and mistakes. They do not want evidence released suggesting that their policies are failing. Any suggestion that the quality of their provision to people is deficient weakens their bargaining position and erodes their support. Governments know well that any information they release will be interpreted and presented by the media in accordance with the interests of the media. Secrecy is as valuable to governments as it is to private companies. If it is revealed that a manufacturer's motor vehicles are emitting much higher levels of carbon than claimed by the company, as happened to Volkswagen, the product is seen as of lesser quality and sales are more difficult. Governments keep secrets to prevent similar downgrading. Government secrecy also weakens the bargaining positions of others, since they are unable to form accurate ideas of the situations on which their interests depend, or the quality of what is on offer from government. For the media, much of the information that governments wish to keep secret is very saleable. The commitment of the press to rooting out information that governments do not want disseminated is an important antidote to the instinct for secrecy. The Freedom of Information Act passed in 2000 reduced the scope of governments to withhold information.

Amongst its consequences, however, must be a tendency by all those involved in the process of government to exercise more caution over what they codify in accessible form.

The strength of the bargaining positions of major media organisations in relation to governments became starkly apparent in revelations arising from the Leveson inquiry into the conduct of News International, in particular the conduct of the tabloid *News of the World*, over the hacking of phones of various prominent people and the phone of a teenage murder victim, Milly Dowler.[23] Scrutiny of press practices in the course of the inquiry revealed that leading politicians had made great efforts to gain favourable coverage for their policies and electoral campaigns in the 'Murdoch Press'. Tony Blair in particular, apparently mindful of the damage the Murdoch newspapers had done to Neil Kinnock's chances of winning the 1992 general election, made strenuous efforts to gain the support of Rupert Murdoch and his British editors. The Conservative Prime Minister after the 2010 election also cultivated the support of Murdoch. David Cameron appointed Andy Coulsen, a former editor of the *News of the World*, as his director of communications, even though Coulsen's reputation was already clouded by allegations concerning illegal phone-hacking. The neighbourly socialising of Cameron with Rebecca Brookes, the editor of the *News of the World*, takes on different significance in the context of the efforts of leading politicians to ingratiate themselves with the Murdoch press.

Murdoch's British media outlets, *The Times*, *The Sunday Times*, the *Sun* and the *News of the World*, and *Sky* television, constituted a formidable force in the dissemination of information conducive to the support of causes favoured by the proprietor. Such capacity for shaping the information interface on which people would be making their decisions necessarily drew the attention of the leading contenders for government. Yet the contrast with the role of information as understood in democratic terms was shocking. The nation seemed to have had a different system of government forced upon it by a modern 'media baron'. Academic theories of government seemed unaware of such a system. Media theory, at least as represented by the Toronto School, had nothing to offer by way of explanation. In that school, the information conveyed by Murdoch's newspapers and television channels was no more than distraction.

The understanding of government in democratic terms suggests that there should be no commercial element in the communication of governments with the people. Nor should the owners of channels of communication be using the channels to advance their own particular interests. But understood in terms of a bargaining society, and particularly with the understanding of the role of information in a bargaining society, the media assume a role that is indispensable for people's participation in the support-bargaining process. The media largely create the information interface that is essential to people's understanding and participation in a national support-bargaining process. The media are an integral part of a political support-bargaining system. They enable people to participate in political affairs with something more than quasi-tribal affiliations to parties, social class, religious faith, local loyalties or similar groups based on an instinctive sense of shared interest. There cannot be the semblance of 'democracy' without propagation of diverse information by the media, though the system cannot be understood in a democratic frame of reference.

In such a context, the media constitute part of the process of government. There is conflict between government and the media, but conflict is part of the process, like conflict between government and opposition. Lance Price's title, *Where Power Lies: Prime Ministers v The Media*, presents the relationship in terms of conflict. Price worked in the press office of Prime Minister Tony Blair, giving him 'front line' experience of the role of information in government. Price presents the situation as a matter of conflict between governments that want their views and actions presented in the best possible light to the electorate, and the press, which wants news which it can sell, which means news that can be presented in dramatic or sensational form, or news it can propagate in support of the views of its proprietors. Price emphasises conflict, but he also recognises the media as part of the process of government: 'The media . . . don't merely observe the political system; they are part of it. They don't just scrutinise the exercise of power . . . they are elements of the machinery through which it is exercised'.[24] The media directly establish much of the information interface which governs movements of support in a country. They cannot be other than major players in the process of government. They are not part of the formal or constitutional processes of government. If they were, they would not be able to perform the function ascribed to them. But they are nevertheless a key part of the governance of a support-bargaining society.

The media are apt to present themselves as in conflict with governments, as 'watchdogs' over the probity and good sense of government action. But to ordinary citizens they may appear as 'insiders' to the political process; part of the process that evaluates and approves certain measures and rejects others. In the understanding of support-bargaining, people define groups relative to their interests. Someone's own group is conceived as legitimately in pursuit of certain benefits to which it is surely entitled. Other groups may be identified as opposed to such interests, and will be labelled in a way that registers disapproval. Some groups will be identified as being so ardently opposed as to constitute an 'enemy'. 'Enemy' status imputes to another group aspirations to ascendancy. An 'enemy' group has the valuable function of posing a threat to a home group, and consequently increasing the cohesion of the home group.[25] The media find it expedient to identify themselves as in conflict with governments, though outsiders may be more inclined to see the media as part of the process of government.

Ordinary citizens may see themselves as ruled by an 'establishment' of insiders, including media organisations that work with governments of right and left to sustain the rule of an intellectual and privileged elite. The 'establishment' may be impugned as 'out of touch' with the predicaments and thoughts of common people. People's 'champions' emerge from time to time to challenge the establishment. Nigel Farage, the leader of the United Kingdom Independence Party, successfully challenged the elites of both the United Kingdom and Europe to take Britain out of the European Union, though with the qualification that a substantial part of the ruling Conservative Party favoured withdrawal, and a substantial part of the media also promoted 'Brexit'. It is announced this morning, Wednesday 9 November 2016, that Donald Trump has been elected President of the United States. Trump challenged the 'Washington establishment', albeit nominated by the Republican Party as their candidate for the presidency. Whatever else, he has a talent for the manipulation of information.

Yet what is to an outsider an impenetrable ruling 'establishment' is to those inside a perpetual competition between factions for ascendancy. To many insiders of Westminster government, 'the establishment' is something different to that of outsiders. 'Insiders' may identify an 'establishment' as the modern successors to a traditional 'right' of monarchs and their retinues, with characteristics such as right-wing political affiliation, family wealth, private education, at least nominal membership of the Church of England and connections with the financial services industry in the City of London. 'Insiders' on the left tend to designate such an 'establishment' as 'the ruling class', providing an 'enemy' that enhances the cohesion of the supposedly insurgent 'left'. 'The establishment' is such a popular 'enemy' that everyone on the left rallies support by boldly fronting up to it. The designations follow the right–left, or individualist–group, dichotomy that forms the psychological foundation of support-bargaining. Davies sees his work on phone-hacking as that of an 'outsider' exposing the criminal behaviour of 'insiders', though to an outsider it can be seen as an ethically meritorious instance of one insider media organisation exposing the criminal behaviour of other insider organisations.[26]

The reluctance of the media to take up the issue of illegal phone hacking arose in part from the perception that the accusations were based on little more than the prejudice of a left-wing newspaper, the *Guardian*, against the right wing Murdoch group.[27] The allegations only received extensive treatment in the media after it was suggested in the *Guardian* that the *News of the World* had deleted messages on the mobile phone of Milly Dowler after she had been murdered.

With the media as a prominent part of the 'democratic' form of government, concerns over 'control' of the information interface take on a different character. There is no question of a government imposing the historic form of control over information, involving threats of violence; rather the greatest potential for control over information lies in a government's alliances with the media. With very large media organisations, with circulations accounting for a significant part of the electorate, something like control can potentially be exercised if a government negotiates an advantageous arrangement with its media. News International gained its political influence through the reach of its four leading titles, including the *News of the World*, to 37 per cent of United Kingdom newspaper readers.[28] This, along with the pugnacious manipulation of newspapers such as the *Sun* and the *News of the World*, was enough to exert strong influence, but significantly short of a position that would, even in alliance with a government, amount to control. Silvio

Berlusconi, four times Prime Minister of Italy, had wide-ranging media interests which enabled him to exercise a degree of control over the information disseminated about his governments.

While the media collectively appear to have a very strong bargaining position in relation to governments, it is dissipated by the diversity of information disseminated by different media organisations. Alternative sources of a benefit diminish the bargaining positions of each source. Each media organisation, or media group, exercises a degree of influence related to the extent of its sales. Media organisations have capacity to move support for or against a government, but support moved one way by one media organisation is often counterbalanced by support moved another way by a different organisation.

The bargaining positions of 'old' media – newspapers, television, radio – have been affected also by the growth of social media. Companies have been formatted to provide opportunities over the internet for ordinary people to communicate with each other and express their views. 'Old' media companies supplement revenues from sales with revenues from advertising, or even depend wholly on advertising for their revenues. Social media companies similarly derive their revenues from advertisers, so that the use of social media is without cost to the users. As noted above, the use of the internet in general has led to declining sales of newspapers. Those using the social media are able to participate in the creation of the information interface through which political decisions are made. Politicians increasingly use social media to communicate directly with their people. Donald Trump, a media star before becoming President of the United States, uses social media for communication of his ideas without the 'old' media as intermediaries. The latter he has accused of purveying 'fake news'. The social media make ordinary people something like the 'insiders' of established political processes, in the sense that they form a community debating issues on a personal basis. It is not, however, exclusive. Nor is it 'face to face', as are many of the personal exchanges of the political 'insiders' described above. Nor in many cases does it have the characteristics of 'gossip' in the amiable 'over the fence' sense. The anonymity of much online debate means that people can comment without regard to the potential loss of support arising from their comments. People are frequently abusive and even threatening. Debates on social media can nevertheless assemble substantial support for or against certain policies or actions, which cannot be ignored by politicians.

The strength of the bargaining positions of media organisations in Britain lies not solely in their capacity for disseminating favourable or unfavourable information concerning government policies and actions, but also in their capacity for vilification of individuals with abuse and revelations about their private lives. This capacity is something that cannot be reckoned with in democratic principle, nor in communal ideas of 'common decency'. The lack of any applicable theory and the general disgust at such practices makes it easy to overlook their existence in a theoretical context. It is nevertheless clear from Davies' investigations that they are a significant deterrent to the dissemination of certain information. Editors of tabloid newspapers find that readers will pay to read sensationalised revelations about the private lives of prominent people. Politicians, celebrities and others in the public eye tread with care in the treatment of newspapers and their staff for fear of what is called 'monstering' in their pages. The *Daily Mail* exposed the sex life of the QC who had subjected its editor to particularly sharp questioning at a Leveson hearing.[29] Aside from the personal offence, the attacks alienate support from their subjects and from organisations. As mentioned above, Blair's efforts to gain support from the Murdoch media group in the run up to the 1998 election was in part prompted by recognition of the damage done to Neil Kinnock and the Labour Party in the 1992 general election by 'monstering' in the *Sun*. Davies notes that it is as much the fear of what might be done as what is actually done that keeps politicians attentive to the sensibilities of media companies and their operatives.[30]

Truth and free speech

In the British system of government a civil service is concerned as a matter of structure to produce 'facts' of high status to steer government in dependable directions. They are supposed to be impartial and without interest. The media, by contrast, are money-bargaining agencies and have to concern themselves first with the sale of their product in the face of competition with other providers. They sell information, but they also sell entertainment, so that it is easy for the two to become confused. The media act also in what is commonly a context even more time constrained than that of a civil service, so time does not permit elaborate processes for the assembly and testing of evidence relating to the variety of information that a media organisation retails. The media are likely to have a much lesser commitment to 'truth' and 'facts' than a civil service.

The media nevertheless, like other groups, develop their own criteria regarding what will be regarded as true, factual or realistic. Davies' account of his investigation into phone hacking suggests in passing a media version of what can be taken as 'true' or 'realistic'. Journalists need two independent sources of information before they accept information as 'true' to a standard adequate for publication.[31] There are echoes here of the 'multiple observations' test of scientific method, or more proximately the requirements for corroborative evidence in a court of law.

Courts of law attach considerable importance to the credibility of witnesses. That people lie to defend their interests is largely taken for granted, so that a legal process involves assessment of which witnesses are likely to be lying and which are not. Lawyers try to discredit witnesses whose evidence is contrary to the interests of their client. Journalists, by contrast, are not required even to reveal their sources; on the contrary, they are required not to reveal their sources. The reliability of the source is a matter of the judgement of the journalist receiving the information, who will normally have an interest in accepting a source and its information as reliable. The circumstances in which journalists operate impose constraints on their standards of veracity. If required to reveal their sources, there would be many fewer sources open to them. News gathering would be diminished. Less information would reach the information interface. Newspaper circulations would fall. High standards for truth have been compromised in favour of a greater volume of likely-to-be-true information. The result has inescapably been high levels of misinformation.

Journalistic 'approved practice' is not necessarily followed across the media. Davies notes that tabloid journals accept far lower standards than those of the quality broadsheet newspapers in Britain, even to the extent of publishing what they know to be false in order to gain sales. To expand circulation and revenues, tabloid newspapers will publish information that is unlikely to be true, if it makes a good story. Davies describes an editor of the *Sun* as 'uninterested even in the most fundamental rule of all, to try to tell the truth'.[32]

Even Davies came unstuck over the deletion of information on the voicemail system of Milly Dowler, the murdered teenager. The deletion suggested that Milly might still be alive. The *Guardian* published a story suggesting that the phone hackers at the *News of the World* had made the deletion. The report triggered public outrage and a more intense focus of attention on the issue of phone hacking. Later evidence indicated that it was most unlikely that the *News of the World* had deleted Milly's voicemail.[33] The evidence accepted by Davies perhaps fitted too closely to the patterns of behaviour he had identified at the *News of the World* to be properly queried.

The campaigns for 'remain' and 'leave' in the referendum over British membership of the European Union of June 2016 dramatically displayed the difficulties of establishing 'facts' or 'truth' with consensual agreement and the scope that arises from such difficulties for the exercise of free speech in manipulation, deception and falsehood. But such misinformation regarding the European Union is nothing new. Price remarks on the treatment in the media of Britain's relationship with the European Union during the period when Margaret Thatcher was Prime Minister: 'No set of institutions has ever suffered such a sustained barrage of misinformation and distortion as those of the European Community at the hands of the Conservative Party and its friends in the British press'.[34] Another 'but' has to be added: the 'but' that copious misinformation in general is nothing new. Price remarks of the press during the Thatcher period: 'The level of distortion and deliberate misinformation by the press was arguably greater and certainly more sustained than in the late 1930s'. When a Minister commented on her good press, Thatcher replied, 'That's because I've been so kind to them'.[35]

The media are able to cite in defence of their undemanding approach to truth the democratic principle of 'free speech'. Rather than striving for an unobtainable truth, it is held better that the media, and everyone else, should say what they want to say. 'Better' means that the health of society, of a political system, or a support-bargaining system, will be better maintained in that way; that a variety of interests will be able to seek support and hence stand a chance of gaining accommodation. An open and diverse information interface is a better foundation for the functioning of a support-bargaining system than a system constrained by high standards of evidence. The creation of the information interface is itself a matter of support-bargaining and money-bargaining. Information will be established in the interface in accordance with the interests and bargaining positions of the agents involved. The standards adopted for the formation of the information interface will be those engineered through support-bargaining and money-bargaining. There is no superior means of establishing truth and falsehood than the support-bargaining system that gives rise to the problems.

Few would defend the deliberate dissemination of false information for the advance of interests within a society. But information manipulated so as to be misleading is not so readily condemned. There is tolerance of the dissemination of information in pursuit of interest that may not be entirely truthful – information that is selective, uses a loaded vocabulary, omits important points, imputes motivations, imputes psychological causation, or otherwise misleads. The convention of 'free speech' is generally understood as requiring toleration of such manipulation. It stems partly from the recognition that much of what appears to be manipulation can be the result of a different frame of reference. People with different frames of reference will identify different phenomena and give phenomena different interpretations. The treatment of Gordon Brown by the *Sun*, referred to above, might be regarded as a legitimate alternative point of view, were it not that the comments seem so plainly motivated by the desire to discredit Brown. The nearest possible approaches to truth derive from the agreement of multiple observers on what is significant and the evidence that supports the interpretation. When observers have come to different situational preconceptions and are pursuing different outcomes in a political system, agreement is unlikely. They do not necessarily deceive others, but the fervent pursuit of desired outcomes easily gives rise to deception, wilful or not. In the strictest terms we cannot know what is beyond the information interface; what is beyond our minds. In the context of human relations, it is often difficult to assemble evidence to confirm what is true even in a loose sense. The unexpressed thoughts of others, their motivations and psychological drives, seem inaccessible, whatever multiple observers may agree on. Support-bargaining societies as a whole, and within sub-groups, establish their own notions of truth; what they can best support; a truth that has to suffice for their purposes. In certain sub-groups, including tabloid media in Britain, what suffices is probably not sufficient in the estimation of the society at large.

It is not necessarily the case that societies will be 'better' in the above sense if there is complete freedom of speech. A society in which the information interface was wholly untrustworthy, because of the exercise of rights to free speech, might cause people to lose confidence in the support-bargaining system. Informal social support-bargaining goes some way in deterring mendacious behaviour. Most people retain a sense of shame when caught telling lies, and the influence extends to organisational behaviour. The press in Britain at least acknowledges collectively an obligation to fair dealing by establishing 'self-policing' arrangements whereby a body established by the media makes judgements on particular appeals against media reports. Evidence of some kind is needed to support statements; evidence to the contrary has to be taken into account. Nevertheless, constraints on mendacity seemed conspicuously ineffective in the campaigns over the United Kingdom referendum on European Union membership. In money-bargaining, voluminous contract law provides significant protection against misinformation and deception for those involved.

The British state has intervened most prominently to protect individuals against the dissemination of false information about them. Libel laws impose perhaps the most severe constraints on what media can publish in Britain. Their content can effectively impose restrictions on free speech that go beyond the protection of personal reputations alone. Heavy fines and in some cases imprisonment can result from libellous comment. In Britain publication of information that might otherwise be regarded as libellous is permissible if it can be shown that publication of the information is in the public interest.

Libel laws seem to provide extensive protection for individuals, but their effect is limited by financial considerations. Law firms operate as money-bargaining agencies, primarily concerned to meet the viability condition. Most aspire to exceed handsomely the modest requirements of the viability condition. The fees involved in litigation mean that the protection of libel laws is for the most part confined to the wealthy. The budgets of media organisations publishing sensational personal revelations – mostly the tabloid newspapers – permit them to probe the limits of the legislation. They can employ for themselves the best legal expertise in the field. Those bringing libel cases against them risk serious damage to their budgets, to the point of bankruptcy. Some of the individuals whose phones were hacked by the *News of the World* were wealthy. It was, however, only when Max Mosley, the head of Formula 1 motor racing, guaranteed them against loss if legal costs were awarded against them by the courts that legal action was taken against the newspaper. Mosley himself had been the victim of 'monstering' by the *News of the World*.[36]

It is not only ordinary citizens that struggle with the costs of litigation, nor is it only a problem encountered solely in connection with libel laws. The Crown Prosecution found itself heavily outspent by News International and struggling to substantiate its cases in court against the journalists accused of responsibility for hacking of phones.[37]

In a democratic context 'free speech' is understood as desirable as a means of attaining truth, recognising that truth is not always abundantly apparent. It is a further instance of the recognition that the consistency of multiple sources is the best possible approach to the attainment of truth. In the context of a support-bargaining system, however, 'free speech' is necessary to the pursuit of interest. That may include the pursuit of truth, but it is a markedly different quest. The support-bargaining context makes clear the impulses involved in the contention over 'free speech'. Language is the most common form of codification for the transmission of information. Individuals, groups and organisations use linguistic communication for the dissemination of information to advance their interests. Individuals, groups or organisations of one interest will prefer that those of an opposing interest do not disseminate information conducive to that opposing interest. They will 'rubbish' such information as is disseminated in opposition to their interests. If a member of a particular group 'speaks out' in defiance of the group, he or she is effectively 'betraying' the group interest. Outspoken behaviour can usually be related to the interests of some other group. 'Whistle-blowers' commonly expose the misbehaviour of organisations by reference to the ethical interests of society as a whole. A speaker may be approved and rewarded by those whose interests are advanced by his or her statements, but the 'betrayed' group or organisation will try to ensure that the speaker is discredited. 'Free speech' is a matter of freedom to disseminate information for the assembly of support. It is an essential element in a support-bargaining society, but inevitably subject to the gains and losses of support that are the lifeblood of a support-bargaining society. 'Free speech' is paid for or rewarded by support or the withdrawal of support. That can take many forms, including, on the one hand, praise, promotion and increase in income and, on the other hand, abuse, loss of income and loss of employment. Organisations, whether companies, religious organisations or charitable organisations, preserve their support by suppressing adverse information about themselves. They often react oppressively to those who 'betray' them. The informal constraints on mendacity referred to above function through the application or withdrawal of support. In the democratic political context, the principle of 'free speech' is the principle that there should be no laws that would permit the silencing of critics of government by incarcerating them. In a broader social context, it is a requirement amongst citizens for tolerance for the expression of opinion with which they may not agree. It is perhaps the most fundamental of the group attitudes and behaviour that are essential to the functioning of a support-bargaining society.

Government, media and money-bargaining

It was seen in Chapter 4 that governments are prominently engaged in money-bargaining as well as in the support-bargaining that is their first concern. What governments do, the economic actions they take, is dictated by support-bargaining, but the impact is economic. Since much support depends on economic performance – particularly the availability and security of employment – much of the intellectual support-bargaining around government is concerned with the state of money-bargaining.

By virtue of their role in intellectual support-bargaining over issues related to government and their dissemination of information beyond 'insiders' the media play a central role in government. This means they are also necessarily prominent in the conduct of money-bargaining. The media engage at all levels, from 'pasty taxes' in the tabloids to sophisticated analysis in the broadsheets. The central contention of support-bargaining between the individual and the group is reflected in ideological debate over economic policies. The right extols the expansionary effects of the 'invisible hand' of 'free markets' while the left deprecates the inequalities that arise from their operation. Markets with moderate regulation may produce jobs and incomes but, as Thomas Piketty records, they tend to generate inequalities.[38] The media employ economic journalists with expertise in economic issues, as well as a variety of 'pundits' with forthright opinions. They engage in the intellectual support-bargaining surrounding the conduct of money-bargaining in the same way as they engage in the intellectual support-bargaining over other issues. Their first concern has to be that they assist their employing organisation to meet the viability condition, which means concern for the attraction and retention of readers. But with that achieved, and subject to the policy preferences of proprietors and editors, there is scope for commentators to express their own preferences.

While the ideological content of neoclassical economics is prominent in the media, media coverage is concerned also with analysis based on macroeconomic theory which is, as was seen in Chapter 4, more realistic than neoclassical theory. The media follow the many statistics issued by government and other agencies. They review the many reports on economic issues emanating from the treasury and other government departments, from various 'think tanks' and pressure groups concerned with money-bargaining, and from international economic agencies. They monitor the changing situation of the national economy and the world economy of which it is part, identifying potential improvements that lie within the capacities of government. Regulations, taxation and expenditures are widely debated in the media. The media transmit also economic information deriving from government and other sources to companies and other agencies engaged in money-bargaining. The role of government in money-bargaining and the importance of information give the media their prominent role in economic affairs.

Notes

1 Goldman, Alvin J., 2003, *Knowledge in a Social World*, Oxford, Clarendon Press, pp. 340–2.
2 Goldman, 2003, p. 340.
3 Goldman, 2003, pp. 323, 326.
4 Goldman, 2003, p. 326.
5 Goldman, 2003, p. 342.
6 See Spread, Patrick, 2008, *Support-Bargaining: The Mechanics of Democracy Revealed*, Sussex: Book Guild, pp. 39–41, Chapter 5: Organisations: function and format.
7 Spread, Patrick, 1984a, *A Theory of Support and Money Bargaining*, London: Macmillan, paras 7.70–77.
8 Cf. Sedgemoor, Brian, 1980, *The Secret Constitution*, London: Hodder & Stoughton, pp. 32–3, 148.
9 Crossman, Richard, 1975, *The Diaries of a Cabinet Minister: Volume 1: Minister of Housing 1964–66*, London: Book Club Associates, pp. 168–9, 198. See also Spread, 1984a, paras 7.71, 73, 76, 99.
10 Sedgemoor, 1980, pp. 108–25, 130. See also Spread, 1984a, paras 7.74, 79, 95, 101–2.
11 See Spread, 2008, Chapter 10: Intellectual support-bargaining.
12 Davies, Nick, 2015, *Hack Attack: How the Truth Caught Up with Rupert Murdoch*, London: Vintage Books, pp. 233–4.

13 Davies, 2015, pp. 182–3.
14 Briggs, Asa and Burke, Peter, 2009, *A Social History of the Media: From Gutenberg to the Internet*, Third Edition, Cambridge: Polity Press, p. 190.
15 Briggs and Burke, 2009, p. 155. For an account of the 'veritistic' impact of modern advertising on the media in the United States see Goldman, 2003, pp. 182–5.
16 Davies, 2015, pp. 338, 340.
17 Davies, 2015, pp. 167–8.
18 Cf. Spread, 2008, pp. 140–3.
19 Price, Lance, 2010, *Where Power Lies: Prime Ministers v The Media*, New York: Simon and Schuster, p. 78.
20 Price, 2010, p. 274.
21 Price, 2010, p. 277.
22 Waller, Ian, 1969, 'The press and politicians' in Rose, Richard (ed.), 1969, *Studies in British Politics*, London: Macmillan.
23 Leveson, Lord Justice Brian, 2012, *An Inquiry into the Culture, Practices and Ethics of the Press*, Volumes 1–4, London: Department of Culture, Media and Sport, Leveson Inquiry, November.
24 Price, 2010, p. 7.
25 On group formation, see Spread, 2008; see also Spread, Patrick, 2015c, 'The political significance of certain types of group', in 2015b, *Aspects of Support-Bargaining and Money-Bargaining*, E-Book, World Economics Association.
26 Davies, 2015, p. 405.
27 Cf. Davies, 2015, pp. 346, 405–8.
28 Davies, 2015, p. 168.
29 Davies, 2015, p. 391.
30 Davies, 2015, pp. 173, 177–8.
31 Davies, 2015, p. 337.
32 Davies, 2015, p. 83.
33 Davies, 2015, pp. 375–8.
34 Price, 2010, p. 274.
35 Price, 2010, p. 245.
36 Davies, 2015, pp. 260–5.
37 Davies, 2015, p. 397.
38 Piketty, Thomas, 2014, *Capital in the 21st Century*, tr. Arthur Goldhammer, Cambridge MA: Belknap Press, p. 47.

Conclusion

Economics for an information age

It was suggested in the Introduction that neoclassical economic theory was developed in response to a question regarding the relationship of individual interest to communal interest and the allocation of resources, rather than in response to the question, 'How does economic exchange work?' The question regarding resource allocation coincided with a further aspiration of neoclassical economists: the desire to formulate a theory that would have status comparable to that of physics. The question of resource allocation required the use of mathematics, and mathematics was seen as the definitive tool of physicists. Neoclassical economists perhaps picked their question by reference to the particular tool they could wield. The mathematical tool was expected to provide a more precise and less ambiguous account of economic exchange than was possible with linguistic codification. The neoclassical model defined 'reality' and 'truth' as working propositions for the neoclassical theory group, just as civil servants, lawyers, scientists and ordinary people establish their own ideas of what they will regard as reality, in accordance with their purpose.[1]

The phenomena of economic interest were not, however, the material phenomena of the physical world, untrammelled by the unpredictable volition of humans, but creations of human interest and aspiration. To establish mathematical codification, it was necessary to give them a form that was amenable to mathematical codification. The phenomena had to be distorted from the way they were ordinarily understood so as to make mathematical codification workable. They had to be simple, discrete, unitary, uniform, quantifiable. The 'humans' were reduced to rational automatons who would choose what was quantifiably 'the best'. The process involved elimination of vast amounts of information relating to the phenomena at issue that could not be given mathematical codification. This was accomplished by adopting an assumption that all information necessary to a transaction as conceived in the model was available, while all other information was irrelevant. The resultant model was more limited and less realistic that the linguistically codified information it was supposed to replace.[2]

The efforts made to extend the model, or qualify it, with an 'economics of information' fail to reconcile the information issues with the model. A model that assumes perfect information for transactions designed to accommodate the exercise of reason cannot be reconciled with large volumes of information relating to the highly diverse transactions of actual humans. It is not possible to graft information issues onto a model that is designed to exclude them. The effect is more to discredit the basic model; to make plain its inadequacy for the purpose it is supposed to fulfil.[3] The requirement is for a theory that takes account in its foundations of the role of information, including the manipulation of information.

The idea of money-bargaining provides such a theory. In money-bargaining suppliers have to establish their products prominently in the minds of potential buyers and convince them that they are the best available. They build into their products mind-catching features. They disseminate information that conveys to potential buyers the functions and qualities that will accommodate their interests or fit their situations. Information detrimental to their purpose is withheld, however much it may bear on the transactions they seek to conclude. They use linguistic and other codifications to impart to potential buyers functions and qualities that will cause the potential buyers to covet them, but which are not intrinsic to the products and may not even be honestly attributable to them. The information disseminated is so potentially misleading with regard to the capacity of a product to meet the interests of its buyers as to make monetary exchange a matter of high risk. In recognition of this, money-bargaining is extensively regulated through support-bargaining systems to reduce risk. Low risk encourages participation in money-bargaining and makes possible its rapid expansion. The dissemination of misleading information is made possible by the disparities in access to information between different agents of bargaining systems.[4] A company inevitably knows much more about its products than a potential buyer, and is in a position to control the flow of information to potential buyers. Disparities of information between agents are an intrinsic feature of money-bargaining.

This dissemination of information by suppliers gives rise to counterpart responses from potential buyers. They need to assemble information by which they can determine which amongst the products available will best fit their circumstances. They need to sift the information available by checking different sources of information for consistency. Information from a supplier regarding the availability of 'juicy peaches fresh from the tree' needs to be checked against information from observation and perhaps tactile experience regarding the state of the available peaches. They may just be 'overripe'. The checks are effectively application of the 'multiple source' criterion that is used in the natural sciences. More complex transactions will involve more systematic use of the criterion, including research to identify and evaluate different sources. Information about material products may be substantially a matter of perceptual information, and adequate checks may be easily conducted. A transaction will nevertheless involve non-material considerations, such as place and time of sale, terms of sale and arrangements for payment, which involve testimonial information. Services will be provided very largely on the basis of testimonial information. Constraints on suppliers arising from regulation do much to reduce risk for buyers, but they do not eliminate it. Information remains a crucial part of rivalry in a money-bargaining system; a critical element in the dynamic of exchange.

The tolerance of neoclassical economic theory for the omission of any consideration of the complexity of information in its basic model, and the further tolerance of extensions to the theory that deal so inadequately with the issue, has been possible because the model deals essentially with a material concept of economic exchange.[5] Suppliers supply and consumers consume clear material things like shoes and bread. These things are recognised perceptually, with a consequent impression of direct acquaintance with them, rather than reception of information about them. Mainstream theory is thus consistent with common understanding of material things. It is only when the variations of features and qualities of things have to be considered that the importance of information becomes apparent.[6] Shoe types and styles, and different kinds of bread, are matters of information. What is provided as services is frequently known almost entirely by information, so that the role of information is readily apparent.

The idea of money-bargaining is built on these conceptions of choice dictated by situation and companies as bargaining agencies formatted to meet a viability condition.[7] The link between what buyers want and what companies offer is a matter of conceptual 'fit' rather than rational necessity. People form a sense of situation, influenced by family and group identity as well as by individual assessment, and judge their requirements by reference to that identified situation. Companies design their products and services so as to fit with the requirements of potential buyers. The assessments of 'fit' are made in the minds of buyers on the basis of information available to them through the information interface. It involves the human sense of symmetry. Selection by 'fit' means that consumers can very often make on-the-spot choices, rather than going through a laborious process of rational analysis. They may even choose subconsciously before applying checks involving more systematic thought. Someone may see a carpet and conclude half-consciously that it is 'just the thing' for the living room, before considering questions about size, material, costs and other features.

The use of a situation reference in decision-making is instinctive and pervasive. In the context of natural selection, it would plainly have been important to be able to assess a situation on the instant and identify necessary actions for self-preservation. Decision-making based on situation seems to extend also to the multifarious requirements of advancement in a cultural setting. Human culture evolves from situation to situation. Money-bargaining evolves from situation to situation.[8] The instinct is so strong that when asked to respond to questions posed in terms of probabilities people respond in accordance with their assessments of situation.

Psychologists have provided poor material for the adaptation of mainstream economic theory to a more realistic foundation in human psychology. They have failed to identify either the link between security and support-seeking or the general use of situation as a reference for selection. If people feel insecure, they seek support from their associates and groups are formed, bound together by support. Since people are always insecure – an inheritance of the psychology by which the human species survived – the pursuit of support and the bargaining for support is eternal and ubiquitous, a permanent and fundamental feature of human society. The link of support to violence gives it a distinctive power of holding people together and 'fixing' concepts and beliefs in groups as if they were absolutely true.

The neglect in psychology of situation as reference is the stranger in that common understanding relates interests to circumstances. People wait to 'see what the situation is' before they determine appropriate choices or actions.[9] Behavioural theorists applying psychology to economic activities have drawn on a very limited theoretical resource. Daniel Kahneman recognises the human use of 'anchors', 'primes' and 'framing', but on a micro-psychological scale. Such references are not elevated to the full and extensive role they have in the conception of situation-related selection in support-bargaining and money-bargaining. As a consequence, behavioural theory has largely conceded to neo-classical theory the primacy of 'rationality' as the essential human characteristic, only modifying that characteristic to 'bounded rationality', which is being as rational as possible in circumstances of information overload. Behavioural theory has accordingly been assimilated into neoclassical theory as a minor appendage, without threatening the essentials of neoclassical theory.[10]

The assimilation has been made easier by the methodological similarity of behavioural theory to that of neoclassical theory. Behavioural theorists expect people to respond to questions based on probabilities in accordance with mathematical probability theory, just as neoclassical economists expect people to respond rationally to product and price information. For behavioural theorists, as with neoclassical theorists, mathematical modelling has been given preference over conceptual realism.[11]

Both behavioural theorists and neoclassical economists take mathematical formulations as their truth. The reference to mathematics to assert the oddity, or 'bias', of human behaviour suggests a further failure of psychologists to recognise that human psychology has evolved to protect human interests, rather than pursue truth.[12] Where humans do pursue truth, it is only consequent on the recognition that human interest frequently depends on identification of the truth.

Situation-related selection and the format of companies give rise to money-bargaining systems rather than the 'markets' of neoclassical theory. Rather than the establishment of 'market prices' by the interaction of 'supply', deriving from many autonomous small firms making the same product, and 'demand', deriving from the preferences of many buyers, companies take the initiative by shaping products and services in ways that they anticipate will fit the situation-related requirements of buyers. They set prices by reference to the unit costs of production, adjusted by reference to their assessed or experienced bargaining-position, which is broadly a matter of the appeal of their product and the appeal of similar offerings from rival companies in the same location at the same time.[13] A neoclassical 'market' offers in its simplest conception the 'optimal allocation of resources'. The attractions of an 'optimal' allocation are self-evident, but the intrusion of even a little realism, such as economies of scale, or imperfect information, discounts it even as a possibility. A money-bargaining system offers the prospect of products and services that closely meet situation-related requirements and a range of prices for any product group that will meet the capacities of a range of budgets. The close connection between scale of production and unit cost of production is important to the successful format of companies. The connection is very often determined by the technology used.

There is no claim to support for a money-bargaining system on the basis of any 'optimal' allocation. But rewards will go for the most part to those who best meet the requirements of others. Well-formatted companies will meet the requirements of buyers and are likely to survive, while those that are not well-formatted will not meet the viability condition and will fail. The chief claim to support for the system rests on its effectiveness in providing people with what they want, the innovations that are made in doing so, the opportunities for remunerative employment provided by successful companies, and the offtakes of money that can be made from successful private money-bargaining for provision of communally defined services.

While neoclassical markets tend towards equilibrium, money-bargaining systems evolve. Situations change and requirements change in accordance with the changing situations. Business people and technologists change their products and services to fit the new requirements. Decisions can cause an economy to evolve in a way that is adverse to many interests.[14] Much of the evolutionary momentum of money-bargaining is provided by the introduction of new technology to produce new products and reduce unit costs of production. That innovation is itself generated through education and training of the individuals involved in money-bargaining and extensive engagement in research.

While meeting the viability condition is the condition for survival, companies can develop such strong bargaining positions that revenues far exceed costs. Some people achieve everyone's dream – they become rich. One major focus of the individual-versus-group or right-versus-left contention in bargaining societies is the disparities between rich and poor, arising mostly as a consequence of the operations of companies. In the West the activities of companies have eliminated the direst forms of poverty but the personal and political sympathies attaching to the notion of 'poverty' are retained in the idea of 'poverty' as a relative state. Rising ratios of personal incomes of the highest paid to those of the lowest paid generate resentment in societies. Those in charge of companies with strong bargaining positions can, through internal support-bargaining, apportion to themselves personal incomes that are exorbitant in the common reckoning.

The information interface is an essential concept since it is only information that can be processed by human minds. Whether perceptual information, the information derived from sight, sound, smell, taste and touch, or testimonial information, the information derived from reports, all contact with any possible external reality has to be in the form of information, because that is the only form in which it will register in human minds.[15] For the communication of information, humans have invented many means of codification and transmission. The forms of codification incorporate means of imparting or withholding support. Successive innovations have had major impacts on human societies.[16] The present 'information age' features major innovations in the digital codification, transmission and analysis of information. A second wave of innovation may be upon us involving quantum codification, transmission and analysis.[17]

The sense of direct acquaintance with the material things that dominates the mainstream concept of economic exchange has helped to sustain tolerance of the assumptions on information of mainstream theory. The importance of information becomes apparent in consideration of the features and qualities attaching to products, and yet more apparent in relation to services. The link of money-bargaining with support-bargaining makes the importance of information yet further apparent. Politics, social intercourse and intellectual debate all centre on abstract ideas codified and communicated as information. Manipulation and deception are commonplace. The pursuit of interest in support-bargaining, and the associated use of information, contrasting with the 'democratic' understanding of information, makes possible the identification of information and the information interface as crucial aspects of the conduct of society. From this, the corresponding role of information in money-bargaining is apparent. While the integrity of information in a money-bargaining system can be effectively protected by regulations derived from support-bargaining, protection of a support-bargaining system is dependent on the system itself.

The use of information in economic exchange follows the same dynamic as the use of information in support-bargaining. This affinity can be attributed to the origin of money-bargaining in support-bargaining. 'Money', and hence money-bargaining, are creations of support-bargaining. The fixing power of support makes it possible for people to sustain the significance of their adopted money through group support. The lack of ambiguity in money, its material precision and its divisibility make money well suited to exchanges between individuals, so that the adoption of money and money-bargaining advances the individual interest in a society, as opposed to the group interest. Support-bargaining gives rise also to abstract ideas such as 'sovereignty', 'divine right', 'government', 'fairness', 'human rights' and 'duty'. Through both support-bargaining and money-bargaining an information interface is created in which the political, social, intellectual and economic affairs of societies are conducted. Support functions formally in politics and psychologically as a proxy for violence.

While the 'situation' reference in money-bargaining is closely bound up with ideas of material situation, in the more abstract context of political and intellectual support-bargaining reference is provided by 'frames of reference'. Groups develop theoretical concepts to provide references by which the attention and understanding of others can be focussed on phenomena in accordance with the interests of the creators of the frame. Theory making is a matter of group support-bargaining for the advance of interests. Individualist economic interests and freedom both of economic enterprise and political endeavour are advanced through the neoclassical economic model. The functioning of a money-bargaining system is conditioned by the theories applied in the regulation of it, since the violent associations of support normally give support ascendancy over money. People engaged in money-bargaining will normally concede the right of those engaged in support-bargaining to regulate their activity. Frames of reference strongly established in an information interface influence the assembly of support and the conduct of societies.

The theory of support-bargaining and money-bargaining establishes a frame of reference by which other frames of reference can be identified and explained. It is, in this sense, a 'frame of frames' or a 'master-frame'.[18] It provides a capacious frame of reference which identifies and explains not just the limited phenomena that are the fields of understanding of other theoretical frames of reference, but also the phenomena that are the theories themselves, along with the intellectual support-bargaining that goes into the making of them. They make the information interface an intricate and contested creation.

Situation-related selection and frames of reference imply a human capacity for identifying how phenomena of all kinds, abstract and material, 'fit' together. This seems to be a fundamental cognitive capacity, essential to survival as well as the subsequent development of human society. It is more important than 'rationality' in the understanding of human behaviour. Psychologists have again failed to establish an important foundation. As with the 'anchors' and 'primes', psychologists have identified the importance of 'patterns' at the 'micro-psychological' level, the laboratory context, but have done little to enlarge the idea to the everyday use of the sense of symmetry in all spheres of human activity. Along with recognition of the importance of support, recognition of the importance of symmetry, or 'fit', would have provided a psychological door to the theory of support-bargaining. The idea of fitting together and its reverse, not fitting together, is the idea of consistency. The requirement for consistency and an absence of inconsistency forms the basis of the multiple source and replicative testing that is scientific method and the most used approach to the establishment of truth. The ubiquity of symmetry gives strong credence also to the notion that what is conceived as 'reality', independent of our minds, is exactly that.[19]

Governments established through formal support-bargaining not only regulate money-bargaining but play an active part in it. The regulation itself confines money-bargaining to certain channels and imposes certain constraints. It also actively encourages engagement in money-bargaining systems, since it reduces the risks of swindling and disappointments. The internet raises many new opportunities for 'scams' and requires a degree of government regulation to ensure that the risks are kept to tolerable levels. A money-bargaining system also requires extensive physical infrastructure, including transport infrastructure, which is most effectively provided on a communal basis. A major feature of a money-bargaining system, unknown to the neoclassical economic model, is that it can generate such levels of monetary exchange as to permit large offtakes of finance to government for the provision of infrastructure and other services. This capacity of private money-bargaining to provide tax revenues to governments gives governments a direct incentive to promote the expansion of private money-bargaining.

With the large money-budgets established with these revenues governments can play a central role in money-bargaining systems. Their budgets enable governments of developed money-bargaining systems to expend large sums on services, including education, health and housing services. These expenditures respond to ideas of group interest, offsetting to a considerable extent the individual interest that is most fundamentally advanced through money-bargaining. Governments assemble and retain support through judicious allocations of expenditure.

This 'socialisation' of money-bargaining has been an important factor in improving the capacities of people in their societies. People effectively receive substantial 'income in kind' in the form of education, health, housing and other services. This has the effect of reducing overall income disparities, since public provision 'in kind' constitutes a larger proportion of the total income of those in the lower strata of an income distribution than of those in the upper strata. The building of human capacities, or 'human capital', is important to the overall distribution of income in a society.

Education in particular provides people with the essential capacity in a support-bargaining and money-bargaining system for the reception and evaluation of information. Illiterate people are dependent on the educated, and inevitably come off second-best in social bargaining. Unchecked, the educated use their advantage to subordinate the uneducated. Education also enhances human capacities for rewarding participation in a great variety of activities, individual and communal.[20] Public provision of education is then of particular importance to those in the lower strata of an income distribution, since without public provision they are deprived of the advantages of education, whilst those at the upper end of the distribution can make private provision. The same applies in some degree to public provision of health services.

Support-bargaining controls money-bargaining, but the money-bargaining system has a major role in the conduct of support-bargaining – much more than is apparent from 'democratic' theory. Support-bargaining runs on information. In the variety in which it is required, such information must be provided mainly by private organisations. Government provision alone would merely advance the interests of government. The only incentive that will cause private organisations to make such provision on the scale required is that of monetary reward. Media companies are primarily money-bargaining agencies, formatted to meet and surpass the viability condition. But they provide the information which forms the basis of political decisions. They thus play, as money-bargaining agencies, a central role in the conduct of government.

They then play a central role in what is commonly understood as the 'democratic' ordering of a society. While elections with a universal adult franchise make it possible for large numbers of people to express their support for particular political organisations or individuals, and hence give an appearance of popular government, the capacity of the people to choose between the different programmes and policies of the candidates depends on their access to information and debate about them. They are heavily dependent on information and opinion deriving from media organisations. Incumbent governments that control their media can easily ensure their re-election. Governments that control the conduct of elections can easily determine their outcome. Elections are wholly insufficient as expressions of popular opinion unless there is copious provision of relevant information through media organisations. While homage is paid to 'democracy' and great efforts have been made to establish 'democracy' around the world, the essential part played in support-bargaining by companies makes the practice of democracy markedly inconsistent with the ideal. 'Democracy', in the sense of an open support-bargaining system, is defined by an open information interface formed in large part by the activities of media organisations. Money-bargaining organisations, whether 'old' or new media, are the foundations of popular involvement in governance.[21]

Besides overtaking the democratic ideal in this way, the importance of information gives prominent importance to those adept in the handling of information. People with skills in the codification and analysis of information necessarily play a more prominent role in determining the directions taken by a society than those who lack linguistic facility and skills in analysis. An 'educated elite' has much greater influence on the course of government than the great majority that lacks comparable facility in the handling of information.[22] 'Democracy' is a contest for the assembly of support through dissemination of ideas and consequently a form of government advantageous to those with the appropriate intellectual capacities.

This means that, while 'democracy' means in literal terms 'the rule of the people' it is in practice different from 'populist' rule. The 'populist' approach tends to reject complex theory and the 'experts' that formulate it in favour of forceful leadership with clear and simple purpose. Forceful leadership implies impatience with opposition, including opposition in the form of unsupportive information. Loyalty to the leader overrides considerations of 'truth', in the sense of facts regarding performance. A populist movement accepts as its truth whatever the leader says is true. Any alleged shortcomings are typically attributed to malicious propaganda and interference of 'enemies'. The 'enemies' may be foreigners or internal, such as immigrants, ethnic minorities, the 'unpatriotic', or 'the elite'. Populist policies tend to be hard on malefactors – capital punishment gets wide support. Complicated 'rights' of citizens may be suppressed in favour of uncomplicated assertion of vengeful notions of justice. Civil rights may be abridged or ignored in furtherance of autocratic control. Extra-judicial application of popular notions of 'justice' by police and security services may be tolerated. Populist themes are natural reservoirs of support and consequently attractive to politicians and media organisations pursuing circulation. All democracies are infused with undemocratic but populist notions. They emerge from time to time with strong prominence, as now in the United States under the presidency of Donald Trump. Autocrats such as Vladimir Putin in Russia derive support from populist measures. In the United Kingdom themes of 'taking back control' and defiance of experts assembled majority support for leaving the European Union, whose structures ensure that it makes few concessions to populism. 'Democracy' can be seen through the idea of support-bargaining as a very sophisticated and complex form of government, rather than a 'popular' form of government, requiring a grasp of ideas and qualities of empathy and tolerance in its peoples before it can be sustainably established. Societies with a preponderance of rigid groups will have particular difficulties in the establishment of democratic arrangements. Democracy is the 'five star' form of government.[23] It takes time to develop, but can be lost quickly.

The internet provides much more scope for the expression of opinion, with perhaps fewer of the constraints that are imposed on the dissemination of information through other media. Dissemination of information on the internet is cheap and can be anonymous. Information and opinion circulating through the old media are largely filtered through people with an understanding of what will sell in the necessary volume. They are also responsible for the information they disseminate. The scope for dissemination of individual opinion without regard to cost is clearly a major advantage of the internet, giving a platform for people who would otherwise not be heard as far as the conduct of national affairs is concerned. But it facilitates the assembly of support for populist ideas which are not entirely consistent with democratic principles or the idea of an open support-bargaining society. Anonymity facilitates dissemination of information designed to assemble support against certain communities and for actions that are incompatible with a support-bargaining society. It makes possible dissemination of false information without the constraints operative on a named provider. Anonymous postings on the internet cannot be subject to formal or informal sanctions of support-bargaining. There is evidence suggesting that false information (in the form of 'tweets') spreads faster than true information.[24] A support-bargaining society has to come to terms with the characteristics, attractive and unattractive, of this new means of transmission of information.

Whatever the implications of the internet for support-bargaining and democracy, the increased scope for the dissemination of information greatly facilitates the conduct of money-bargaining. The development of roads and railways expands the vendor sets of suppliers, enabling companies to sell their products over much wider areas, and hence giving much greater opportunities for meeting the viability condition. The internet opens up many similar new opportunities for vendor sets and the format of companies in general. It is an indicator of the importance of the information interface that the internet has given rise to company formats heavily dependent on the opportunities arising from internet communications. All company formats have been affected by the internet. The remarkable size of leading internet companies confirms the importance of the dissemination of information for engagement in monetary transactions, and the significance of low unit costs associated with technological innovation in the meeting and exceeding of the viability condition. Such phenomena confirm also the necessity of an economic theory that explains the way economic exchange is conducted in an information age.

Notes

1 Chapter 6: Groups and their reality.
2 Chapter 4: Codification and the neoclassical model.
3 Chapter 1: Economics of information.
4 Chapter 4: Communal interest and government.
5 Chapter 4: Money bargaining and the information interface; cf. Chapter 1: Knowledge and institutions, quotation from Mark Casson, at note 62.
6 Cf. Chapter 1: Knowledge and institutions, reference to Kelvin Lancaster at note 54.
7 Chapter 4: Money-bargaining and the information interface; see also Spread, Patrick, 2011, 'Situation as determinant of selection and valuation', *Cambridge Journal of Economics*, Vol. 35, No. 2, March, pp. 335–56; Spread, Patrick, 2016b, 'Companies and markets: economic theories of the firm and a conception of companies as bargaining agencies', *Cambridge Journal of Economics,* Vol. 40, No. 3, May, pp. 727–53. These articles reproduced in Spread, Patrick, 2015b, *Aspects of Support-Bargaining and Money-Bargaining,* E-Book, World Economics Association.
8 Spread, Patrick, 2013, *Support-Bargaining, Economics and Society: A Social Species,* Abingdon: Routledge, pp. 31–4, 40–51, 210–28.
9 Chapter 2: Support-bargaining and the information interface; see also Spread, Patrick, 2016a, *The Evolution of Economies: Money-Bargaining, Economic Change and Industrial Revolution,* Abingdon: Routledge, pp. 3–6.
10 Chapter 5: Behavioural psychology and the psychology of support-bargaining.
11 Chapter 5: Prospect theory and situation reference.
12 Chapter 5: Fusion of instinct and analysis.
13 On bargaining position, see Spread, Patrick, 2008, *Support-Bargaining: The Mechanics of Democracy Revealed,* Sussex: Book Guild, pp. 93–7.
14 Chapter 4: Neoclassical economic theory as a frame of reference; see also Spread, 2016a, pp 29–33, 44–55, 316–19.
15 Introduction; Chapter 1: Individual knowledge and social construction; Chapter 6: The information interface and reality.
16 Chapter 8: Intellectual support-bargaining and government; see also Spread, 2016a, Chapter 9: Information and the evolution of communications.
17 See, for example, *The Economist*, 2017, Technology Quarterly: 'Quantum devices: here, there and everywhere', 11 March.
18 Chapter 3: Creation and manipulation of the information interface; see also Spread, 2008, pp. 341–3, 362.

19 Chapter 6: The symmetry connection.
20 Chapter 4: Communal interest and government.
21 Chapter 8: Governance and media.
22 Chapter 8: Governance and media.
23 Spread, 2013, Conclusion: Support-bargaining as ideology.
24 *The Economist*, 2018, 'Falsehood flies', 10 March, p. 80. Article based on: Vosoughi, Soroush; Roy, Deb and Ara, Sinan, 2018, 'The spread of true and false news online', *Science*, Vol. 359, No. 6380 (9 March), pp. 1146–51.

References

Akerlof, George, 1970, 'The market for lemons: quality, uncertainty and the market mechanism', *Quarterly Journal of Economics*, Vol. 84, No. 3, pp. 488–500.

Akerlof, George and Shiller, Robert, 2015, *Phishing for Phools*, Princeton: Princeton University Press, p. 164.

Alchian, Armen A. and Demsetz, Harold, 1972, 'Production, information costs, and economic organization', *The American Economic Review*, Vol. 62, No. 5, pp. 777–95.

Allais, Maurice, 1992, 'The economic science of today and global disequilibrium', in Baldassarri, Mario, McCallum, John and Mundell, Robert (eds), *Global Disequilibrium in the World Economy*, Basingstoke: Macmillan.

Backhouse, Roger E., 1993, *Economists and the Economy: The Evolution of Economic Ideas*, London: Transaction, p. 196.

Backhouse, Roger E., 2002, *The Penguin History of Economics*, London: Penguin Books.

Baldassarri, Mario, McCallum, John and Mundell, Robert (eds), *Global Disequilibrium in the World Economy*, Basingstoke: Macmillan.

Baranzini, Mauro and Scazzieri, Roberto (eds), 1986, *Foundations of Economics: Structures of Enquiry and Economic Theory*, Oxford: Blackwell.

Benicourt, Emmanuelle, 2004, 'Five pieces of advice for students studying microeconomics', in Fullbrook, Edward, 2004, *A Guide to What's Wrong with Economics*, London: Anthem Press.

Berger, Peter and Luckman, Thomas, 1991, *The Social Construction of Reality*, London: Penguin. First published 1966.

Beveridge, William, 1937, 'The place of the social sciences in human knowledge', *Politica*, Vol. 2, No. 9, September, pp. 459–79; farewell address as Director of the London School of Economics and Political Science, 24 June 1937.

Blau, Peter, 1964, *Exchange and Power in Social Life*, New York: Wiley.

Briggs, Asa and Burke, Peter, 2009, *A Social History of the Media: From Gutenberg to the Internet*, Third Edition, Cambridge: Polity Press.

Brotton, Jerry, 2013, *A History of the World in Twelve Maps*, London: Penguin.

Bruni, Luigino and Sugden, Robert, 2007, 'The road not taken: how psychology was removed from economics, and how it might be brought back', *The Economic Journal*, Vol. 117, No. 516, January, pp. 146–73.

Casson, Mark, 2000, 'An entrepreneurial theory of the firm', in Foss, Nicolai and Mahuke, Volker, 2000, *Competence, Governance and Entrepreneurship*, Oxford: Oxford University Press, pp. 116–45.

Chaiken, Shelly and Trope, Yaacov, 1999, *Dual Process Theories in Social Psychology*, New York: Guilford Press.

Chater, Nick (ed.), 2012, *Judgement and Decision Making*, Los Angeles and London: Sage.

Coase, Ronald H., 1937, 'The nature of the firm', *Economica*, New Series, Vol. 4, No. 16, pp. 386–405.

Crossman, Richard, 1975, *The Diaries of a Cabinet Minister: Volume 1: Minister of Housing 1964–66*, London: Book Club Associates.

Darwin, Charles, 2004, *The Descent of Man, and Selection in Relation to Sex*, London: Penguin.

Daston, Lorraine 1980, 'Probabilistic expectation and rationality in classical probability theory', *Historia Mathematica*, Vol. 7, No. 3, pp. 234–60.

Davies, Nick, 2015, *Hack Attack: How the Truth Caught Up with Rupert Murdoch*, London: Vintage Books.

Derrida, Jacques, 1976, *Of Grammatology*, trans. G. Spivak, Baltimore: Johns Hopkins University Press.

Dow, Sheila, 2017, 'How far are economists purveyors of fake news?', Annual Conference of the Institute for New Economic Thinking, October, available at: www.ineteconomics.org/research/research-papers/how-far-are-economists-purveyors-of-fake-news. Accessed 12 January 2018.

Downing, Lisa, 2016, 'George Berkeley', in Zalta, Edward N. (ed.), *The Stanford Encyclopedia of Philosophy*, Summer 2016 Edition, available at: http://plato.stanford.edu/archives/sum2016/entries/berkeley.

Earl, Peter, 1988, *Behavioural Economics*, Cheltenham: Edward Elgar.

Earl, Peter, 1995, *Microeconomics for Business and Marketing*, Cheltenham: Edward Elgar.

Earl, Peter (ed.), 2002, *Information, Opportunism and Economic Coordination*, Cheltenham: Edward Elgar.

Evans, Jonathan St B. I., 2008, 'Dual-processing accounts of reasoning, judgment and social cognition', *Annual Review of Psychology*, Vol. 59, pp. 255–78.

Finkelstein, Sidney, 1968, *Sense and Nonsense of McLuhan*, New York: International Publishers.

Foss, Nicolai and Loasby, Brian (eds), 2013, *Economic Organization, Capabilities and Coordination: Essays in Honour of G. B. Richardson*, Abingdon: Routledge; electronic resource, Bodleian Library, Oxford.

Foss, Nicolai and Mahuke, Volker (eds), 2000, *Competence, Governance and Entrepreneurship*, Oxford: Oxford University Press.

Foucault, Michel, 1977, *Discipline and Punish: The Birth of the Prison*, London: Allen Lane.

Fransman, Martin 1994, 'Information, knowledge, vision and theories of the firm', *Industrial and Corporate Change*, Vol. 3, No. 3, pp. 713–57.

Freese, Jeremy, 2009, 'Preferences', in Hedström, Peter and Bearman, Peter (eds), 2009, *The Oxford Handbook of Analytical Sociology*, Oxford: Oxford University Press, pp. 94–114.

Friedman, Milton, 1953, 'The methodology of positive economics', in Friedman, Milton, 1953, *Essays in Positive Economics*, Chicago: University of Chicago Press.

Friedman, Milton, 1953, *Essays in Positive Economics*, Chicago: University of Chicago Press.

Fullbrook, Edward, 2004, *A Guide to What's Wrong with Economics*, London: Anthem Press.

Galatin, Malcolm and Leiter, Robert D., 1981, *The Economics of Information*, The Hague: Martinus Nijhoff Publishing.

Geanakoplos, John, 2004, 'The Arrow-Debreu Model of General Equilibrium', *Cowles Foundation Paper No. 1090*, Cowles Foundation for Research in Economics at Yale University.

Gigerenzer, Gerd; Swijtink, Zeno; Porter, Theodore; Daston, Lorraine; Beatty, John and Kruger, Lorenz, 1989, *The Empire of Chance: How Probability Changed Science and Everyday Life*, Cambridge: Cambridge University Press.

Gigerenzer, Gerd, 1991, 'How to make cognitive illusions disappear: beyond "heuristics and biases"', *European Review of Social Psychology*, Vol. 2, No. 1, pp. 83–115.

Gigerenzer, Gerd, 2008, *Rationality for Mortals: How People Cope with Uncertainty*, Oxford: Oxford University Press.

Gilbert, Margaret, 1989, *On Social Facts*, Abingdon: Routledge.

Gilovich, Thomas, Griffin, Dale W. and Kahneman, Daniel (eds), 2002, *Heuristics and Biases: The Psychology of Intuitive Judgement*, Cambridge: Cambridge University Press.

Goffman, Irving, 1974, *Frame Analysis: An Essay on the Organisation of Experience*, Cambridge MA: Harvard University Press.

Goldman, Alvin and Blanchard, Thomas, 2016, 'Social epistemology', in Zalta, Edward N. (ed.), *The Stanford Encyclopedia of Philosophy*, Summer Edition, available at: http://plato.stanford.edu/archives/sum2016/entries/epistemology-social.

Goldman, Alvin, 2003, *Knowledge in a Social World*, Oxford: Clarendon Press.

Goldman, Alvin, 2010, 'Social epistemology', in Zalta, Edward N. (ed.), *The Stanford Encyclopedia of Philosophy*, Summer Edition, available at: http://plato.stanford.edu/archives/sum2010/entries/epistemology-social.

Gregory, Richard L. (ed.), 2004, *The Oxford Companion to the Mind*, Second Edition, Oxford: Oxford University Press.

Hammond, Kenneth R., 1996, *Human Judgment and Social Policy: Irreducible Uncertainty, Inevitable Error, Unavoidable Injustice*, Oxford: Oxford University Press.

Harford, Tim, 2014, 'Behavioural economics and public policy', *Financial Times*, 21 March.

Harvey, Paul D. A., 2002, *Mappa Mundi: The Hereford World Map*, Hereford: Hereford Cathedral.

Hayek, Friedrich A., 1952, *The Sensory Order, An Enquiry into the Foundations of Theoretical Psychology*, Chicago: University of Chicago Press.

Hedström, Peter and Bearman, Peter (eds), 2009, *The Oxford Handbook of Analytical Sociology*, Oxford: Oxford University Press.

Heilbroner, Robert L., 1917, 'Adam Smith', *Encyclopaedia Britannica*, London: Encyclopædia Britannica.

Heilbroner, Robert, 2000, *The Worldly Philosophers: The Lives, Theories and Ideas of the Great Economic Thinkers*, London: Penguin. First published 1953.

Hennings, Klaus H., 1986, 'The exchange paradigm and the theory of production and distribution', in Baranzini, Mauro and Scazzieri, Roberto (eds), 1986, *Foundations of Economics: Structures of Enquiry and Economic Theory*, Oxford: Blackwell.

Hore, Peter, n.d., 'The Quantum Robin', *Navigation News*, available at: http://hore.chem.ox.ac.uk/PDFs/The_Quantum_Robin.pdf. Accessed 12 August 2015.

Hugo, Victor, 2015, *The Hunchback of Notre Dame*, Waxkeep Publishing, Kindle Edition. First published 1831.

Huyssen, Andreas, 1986, *After the Great Divide: Modernism, Mass Culture, and Postmodernism*, Bloomington: Indiana University Press.

Ietto-Gillies, Grazia, 2008, 'A XXI-century alternative to XX-century peer review', *Real-World Economics Review*, Issue 45, pp. 10–22.

Innis, Harold, 1950, *Empire and Communications*, Oxford: Oxford University Press.

Jain, Anil and Duin, Robert, 2004, 'Pattern recognition', in Gregory, Richard L. (ed.), 2004, *The Oxford Companion to the Mind*, Second Edition, Oxford: Oxford University Press.

Jensen, Michael and Meckling, William, 1976, 'Theory of the firm: managerial behaviour, agency costs, and ownership structure', *The Journal of Financial Economics*, Vol. 3, No. 4, pp. 305–60.

Kahneman, Daniel and Frederick, Shane, 2002, 'Representativeness revisited: attribution substitution in intuitive judgement', in Gilovich, Thomas, Griffin, Dale W. and Kahneman, Daniel (eds), 2002, *Heuristics and Biases: The Psychology of Intuitive Judgement*, Cambridge: Cambridge University Press, pp. 49–81.

Kahneman, Daniel and Tversky, Amos, 1979, 'Prospect theory: an analysis of decision under risk', *Econometrica*, Vol. 47, No. 2, pp. 263–91.

Kahneman, Daniel, 2003, 'Maps of bounded rationality: psychology for behavioural economics', *American Economic Review*, Vol. 93, No. 5. pp. 1449–75.

Kahneman, Daniel, 2012, *Thinking, Fast and Slow*, London: Penguin.

Kaye, Howard, 1986, *The Social Meaning of Modern Biology*, New Haven: Yale University Press.

Keynes, John Maynard, 1961, *The General Theory of Employment, Interest and Money*, London: Macmillan; New York: St. Martin's Press. First published 1936.

Krugman, Paul, 1996, 'What economists can learn from evolutionary theorists', talk given to the European Association for Evolutionary Political Economy, available at: http://web.mit.edu/krugman/www/evolute.html. Accessed 16 May 2017.

Krugman, Paul, 2009, 'How did economists get it so wrong?', *New York Times*, 2 September.

Kuhn, Thomas S., 1970, *The Structure of Scientific Revolutions*, Chicago: Chicago University Press. First published 1962.

Lamberton, Don M. (ed.), 1971, *Economics of Information and Knowledge*, London: Penguin.

Lamberton, Don M. (ed.), 1996, *The Economics of Communication and Information*, Cheltenham: Edward Elgar.

Lancaster, Kelvin J., 1981, 'Information and product differentiation', in Galatin, Malcolm and Leiter, Robert D., 1981, *The Economics of Information*, The Hague: Martinus Nijhoff Publishing.

Langbein, John H., 1996, 'Historical foundations of the law of evidence: a view from the Ryder Sources', *Columbia Law Review*, Vol. 96, No. 5, pp. 1168–202.

Latour, Bruno, 1987, *Science in Action*, Cambridge: Harvard University Press.

Latour, Bruno and Woolgar, Steve, 1986, *Laboratory Life: The Construction of Scientific Facts*, Princeton: Princeton University Press. First published 1979, Sage Publications.

Latsis, Spiros J. (ed.), 1976a, *Method and Appraisal in Economics*, Cambridge: Cambridge University Press.

Latsis, Spiros J., 1976b, 'A research programme in economics', in Latsis, S. J. (ed.), 1976, *Method and Appraisal in Economics*, Cambridge: Cambridge University Press.

Leveson, Lord Justice Brian, 2012, *An Inquiry into the Culture, Practices and Ethics of the Press*, Volumes 1–4, London: Department of Culture, Media and Sport, Leveson Inquiry, November.

Levine, David K., 2012, *Is Behavioral Economics Doomed? The Ordinary Versus the Extraordinary*, Cambridge: Open Book Publishers (electronic resource).

Lewis, Paul (ed.), 2004, *Transforming Economics: Perspectives on the Critical Realist Project*, Abingdon: Routledge.

Loasby, Brian, 1999, *Knowledge, Institutions and Evolution in Economics*, Abingdon: Routledge.

Mankiw, Greg, 2006, 'The macroeconomist as scientist and engineer', *Journal of Economic Perspectives*, Vol. 20, No. 4, pp. 42–3.

Mannheim, Karl, 1936, *Ideology and Utopia: An Introduction to the Sociology of Knowledge*, trans. Louis Worth and Edward Shils, London: Harcourt.

March, James and Simon, Herbert, 1993, *Organisations*, Oxford: Blackwell Business. First published 1958, New York: Wiley.

Markovitz, Harry 1952, 'The utility of wealth', *Journal of Political Economy*, Vol. 60, No. 2, pp. 151–58.

Marshall, Alfred, 1920, *Principles of Economics*, Eighth Edition, London: Macmillan. First published 1890.

Maslow, Abraham H., 1970, *Motivation and Personality*, Third Edition, London: Harper & Row. First published 1954.

McLuhan, Marshall, 1964, *Understanding Media: The Extensions of Man*, Abingdon: Routledge.

Mills, C. Wright, 1956, *The Power Elite*, Oxford: Oxford University Press.

Mitroff, Ian I., 1974, *The Subjective Side of Science: A Philosophical Inquiry into the Psychology of the Apollo Moon Scientists*, New York: Elsevier.

Mohseni, Masoud; Omar, Yasser; Engel, Gregory and Plenio, Martin (eds), 2014, *Quantum Effects in Biology*, Cambridge: Cambridge University Press.

Molho, Ian, 2001, *The Economics of Information: Lying and Cheating in Markets and Organisations*, Oxford: Blackwell.

Morgenson, Gretchen and Rosner, Joshua, 2012, *Reckless Endangerment*, New York: St Martin's Griffin.

Nelson, Richard R. and Winter, Sidney G., 1982, *An Evolutionary Theory of Economic Change*, Cambridge, MA: The Belknap Press.

Patterson, Graeme H., 1990, *History and Communications: Harold Innis, Marshall McLuhan, the Interpretation of History*, Toronto: University of Toronto Press.

Phlips, Louis, 1988, *The Economics of Imperfect Information*, Cambridge: Cambridge University Press.

Piketty, Thomas, 2014, *Capital in the 21st Century*, trans. Arthur Goldhammer, Cambridge MA: Belknap Press.

Poe, Marshall T., 2011, *A History of Communications: Media and Society from the Evolution of Speech to the Internet*, Cambridge: Cambridge University Press.

Popper, Karl, 1963, *Conjectures and Refutations*, London: Routledge and Kegan Paul.

Price, Lance, 2010, *Where Power Lies: Prime Ministers v The Media*, New York: Simon and Schuster.

Rader, Trout, 1970, 'Resource allocation with increasing returns to scale', *The American Economic Review*, Vol. 60, No. 5, pp. 814–25.

Richardson, George B., 1990, *Information and Investment: A Study in the Working of the Competitive Economy*, Second Edition, Oxford: Oxford University Press. First published 1960.

Richardson, George B., 1998, *The Economics of Imperfect Knowledge: Collected Papers of G. B. Richardson*, Cheltenham: Edward Elgar.

Robbins, Lionel, 1932, *An Essay on the Nature and Significance of Economic Science*, London: Macmillan.

Rohlf, Michael, 2016, 'Immanuel Kant', in Zalta, Edward N. (ed.), *The Stanford Encyclopedia of Philosophy*, Spring Edition, available at: <http://plato.stanford.edu/archives/spr2016/entries/kant.

Romer, Paul, 2016, 'The trouble with macroeconomics', lecture, delivered 5 January, as the Commons Memorial Lecture of the Omicron Delta Epsilon Society, available at: https://paulromer.net/wp-content/uploads/2016/09/WP-Trouble.pdf. Accessed 27 April 2017.

Rose, Richard (ed.), 1969, *Studies in British Politics*, London: Macmillan.

Searle, John R. 1996, *The Construction of Social Reality*, London: Penguin Books.

Sedgemoor, Brian, 1980, *The Secret Constitution*, London: Hodder & Stoughton.

Shakespeare, William, 1994, 'Hamlet, Prince of Denmark' in *The Complete Works of William Shakespeare*, London: HarperCollins.

Shapin, Steven, 1994, *A Social History of Truth*, Chicago: University of Chicago Press.

Sherif, Muzafer, 1935, 'A study of some social factors in perception', *Archives of Psychology*, Vol. 27, No. 187, pp. 1–60.

Sherif, Muzafer, 1936, *The Psychology of Social Norms*, New York: Harper & Brothers.

Simon, Herbert A., 1956, 'Rational choice and the structure of the environment', *Psychological Review*, Vol. 63, No. 2, pp. 129–38.

Simon, Herbert A., 1957, *Models of Man: Social and Rational: Mathematical Essays on Rational Human Behaviour in a Social Setting*, New York: Wiley.

Simon, Herbert A., 1983, *Reason in Human Affairs*, Stanford: Stanford University Press, p. 106.

Simon, Herbert A., 1997, *Administrative Behaviour: A Study of Decision-Making Processes in Administrative Organizations*, Fourth Edition, New York: Free Press. First published 1947, New York: Macmillan.

Sloman, Steven A., 2002, 'Two systems of reasoning', in Gilovich, Thomas, Griffin, Dale W. and Kahneman, Daniel (eds), 2002, *Heuristics and Biases: The Psychology of Intuitive Judgement*, Cambridge: Cambridge University Press.

Sloman, Steven A., 1996, 'The empirical case for two systems of reasoning', *Psychological Bulletin*, Vol. 119, pp. 3–22.

Smith, Adam, 1986, *The Wealth of Nations*, Books I–III, London: Penguin Classics. First published 1776.

Smith, Adam, 2008, *An Inquiry into the Nature and Causes of the Wealth of Nations*, A Selected Edition, Oxford: Oxford World's Classics. First published 1776.

Smith, Adam, 2009, *An Inquiry into the Nature and Causes of the Wealth of Nations*, Project Gutenberg E-book, Adobe Digital Editions. First published 1776.

Solov'yov, Ilia A.; Ritz, Thorsten; Schulten, Klaus and Hore, Peter J., 2014, 'A chemical compass for bird navigation', in Mohseni, Masoud, Omar, Yasser, Engel, Gregory and Plenio, Martin (eds), 2014, *Quantum Effects in Biology*, Cambridge: Cambridge University Press.

Spence, Michael, 1973, 'Job market signalling', *Quarterly Journal of Economics*, Vol. 87, No. 3, pp. 355–74.

Spread, Patrick, 1984a, *A Theory of Support and Money Bargaining*, London: Macmillan.

Spread, Patrick, 1984b, 'Blau's exchange theory, support and the macrostructure', *British Journal of Sociology*, Vol. 35, No. 2, pp. 157–73.

Spread, Patrick, 2004, *Getting It Right: Economics and the Security of Support*, Sussex: Book Guild.

Spread, Patrick, 2008, *Support-Bargaining: The Mechanics of Democracy Revealed*, Sussex: Book Guild.

Spread, Patrick, 2011, 'Situation as determinant of selection and valuation', *Cambridge Journal of Economics*, Vol. 35, No. 2, pp. 335–56. Reprinted in Spread, Patrick, 2015b, *Aspects of Support-Bargaining and Money-Bargaining*, E-Book, World Economics Association.

Spread, Patrick, 2012, 'Science and support: the struggle for mastery in economics', *Real-World Economics Review*, Issue 59, 12 March, pp. 39–57. Reprinted in Spread, Patrick, 2015b, *Aspects of Support-Bargaining and Money-Bargaining*, E-Book, World Economics Association.

Spread, Patrick, 2013, *Support-Bargaining, Economics and Society: A Social Species*, Abingdon: Routledge.

Spread, Patrick, 2015a, 'Asymmetric information, critical information and the information interface', *Real World Economics Review*, Issue 70. Reprinted in Spread, Patrick, 2015b, *Aspects of Support-Bargaining and Money-Bargaining*, E-Book, World Economics Association.

Spread, Patrick, 2015b, *Aspects of Support-Bargaining and Money-Bargaining*, E-Book, World Economics Association.

Spread, Patrick, 2015c, 'The political significance of certain types of group', in Spread, Patrick, 2015b, *Aspects of Support-Bargaining and Money-Bargaining*, E-Book, World Economics Association.

Spread, Patrick, 2015d, 'Intellectual support-bargaining and Mannheim's conjectures on a science of politics', in Spread, Patrick, 2015b, *Aspects of Support-Bargaining and Money-Bargaining*, E-Book, World Economics Association.

Spread, Patrick, 2016a, *The Evolution of Economies: Money-Bargaining, Economic Change and Industrial Revolution*, Abingdon: Routledge.

Spread, Patrick, 2016b, 'Companies and markets: economic theories of the firm and a concept of companies as bargaining agencies', *Cambridge Journal of Economics*, Vol. 40, No. 3, pp. 727–53, doi (2015): 10.1093/cje/bev029. Reprinted in Spread, Patrick, 2015b, *Aspects of Support-Bargaining and Money-Bargaining*, E-Book, World Economics Association.

Stanovich, Keith E. and West, Richard F., 2002, 'Individual differences in reasoning: implications for the rationality debate?', in Gilovich, Thomas, Griffin, Dale W. and Kahneman, Daniel (eds), 2002, *Heuristics and Biases: The Psychology of Intuitive Judgement*, Cambridge: Cambridge University Press.

Steup, Matthias, 2014, 'Epistemology', in Zalta, Edward N. (ed.), *The Stanford Encyclopedia of Philosophy*, Spring Edition, available at: http://plato.stanford.edu/archives/spr2014/entries/epistemology.

Stewart, Ian and Golubitsky, Martin, 1992, *Fearful Symmetry: Is God a Geometer?* London: Penguin.

Stigler, George J., 1971, 'The economics of information', in Lamberton, Don M. (ed.), 1971, *Economics of Information and Knowledge*, London: Penguin, p. 61. Original emphasis. First published 1961, *Journal of Political Economy*, Vol. 69, No. 3, pp. 213–25.

Stiglitz, Joseph E., 1985, 'Information and economic analysis: a perspective', *The Economic Journal*, Vol. 95, Supplement, pp. 21–41.

Stiglitz, Joseph E., 2000, 'The contributions of the economics of information to twentieth century economics,' *The Quarterly Journal of Economics*, Vol. 115, No. 4, pp. 1441–78.

Stiglitz, Joseph E., 2002, 'Information and the change in the paradigm in economics', *American Economic Review*, Vol. 92, No. 3, pp. 460–501.

Syll, Lars Pålsson, 2016, 'Paul Romer's assault on "post-real" macroeconomics', *Real-World Economics Review*, Issue 76, September, pp. 43–54.

Taleb, Nassim Nicholas, 2010, *The Black Swan: The Impact of the Highly Improbable*, New York: Random House.

The Economist, 2015, 'The Paris agreement marks an unprecedented political recognition of the risks of climate change', 12 December, available at: www.economist.com/news/international/21683990-paris-agreement-climate-change-talks. Accessed 2 February 2017.

The Economist, 2016a, 'The scientific method: let's just try that again', 6 February, p. 78.

The Economist, 2016b, 'The shadow economy: unregulated, untaxed, unloved', 15 October, p. 57.

The Economist, 2016c, '"Inside the bear", special report on Russia', 22 October, after p. 44.

The Economist, 2017, Technology Quarterly: 'Quantum devices: here, there and everywhere', 11 March.

The Economist, 2018, 'Falsehood flies', 10 March, p. 80.

Tuomela, Raimo and Miller, Kaarlo, 1988, 'We-intentions', *Philosophical Studies*, Vol. 53, No. 3, pp. 367–89.

Tuomela, Raimo, 2013, *Social Ontology: Collective Intentionality and Group Agents*, Oxford: Oxford University Press.

Vosoughi, Soroush, Roy, Deb and Ara, Sinan, 2018, 'The spread of true and false news online', *Science*, Vol. 359, No. 6380 (9 March), pp. 1146–51.

Waller, Ian, 1969, 'The press and politicians' in Rose, Richard (ed.), 1969, *Studies in British Politics*, London: Macmillan.

Walras, Léon, 1954, *Elements of Pure Economics: or, The Theory of Social Wealth*, Translated by William Jaffé, London: Allen and Unwin. First published 1874.

Watson, James and Jones, Steve, 1999, *The Double Helix: A Personal Account of the Discovery of the Structure of DNA*, Second Revised Edition, London: Penguin.

Wikipedia, 2015, 'Martin Luther'. Accessed 11 September 2015.

Williamson, Oliver E., 1987, *The Economic Institutions of Capitalism*, New York: Free Press.

World Bank, 2014, E-mail communication on *World Development Report 2015*, 4 December.

World Bank, 2015, *World Development Report 2015: Mind, Society and Behaviour*, Washington DC: World Bank, doi: 10.1596/978-1-4648-0342-0.

Zalta, Edward N. (ed.), *The Stanford Encyclopedia of Philosophy*, Editions: Spring 2010; Summer 2010; Spring 2014; Spring 2016; Summer 2016.

Index

For Product Safety Concerns and Information please contact our EU representative GPSR@taylorandfrancis.com Taylor & Francis Verlag GmbH, Kaufingerstraße 24, 80331 München, Germany